Data Mining

Data Mining
Multimedia, Soft Computing, and Bioinformatics

SUSHMITA MITRA
Associate Professor
Machine Intelligence Unit
Indian Statistical Institute
Kolkata, India

TINKU ACHARYA
Senior Executive Vice President
Chief Science Officer
Avisere Inc.
Tucson, Arizona
and
Adjunct Professor
Department of Electrical Engineering
Arizona State University
Tempe, Arizona

A JOHN WILEY & SONS, INC., PUBLICATION

Library of Congress Cataloging-in-Publication Data:

Mitra, Sushmita
    Data mining : multimedia, soft computing, and bioinformatics /
Sushmita Mitra and Tinku Acharya.
       p. cm.
    Includes bibliographical references and index.
    ISBN 0-471-46054-0 (cloth)
    1. Data mining.   I. Acharya, Tinku.   II.Title.
  QA76.9.D343M8 2003
  006.3—dc21   2003011394

Printed in the United States of America.

10 9 8 7 6 5 4 3 2 1

To Ma, who made me what I am,
and to Somosmita, who let me feel like a supermom.
—Sushmita

To Lisa, Arita, and Arani
—Tinku Acharya

Contents

Preface

The success of the digital revolution and the growth of the Internet have ensured that huge volumes of high-dimensional multimedia data are available all around us. This information is often mixed, involving different datatypes such as text, image, audio, speech, hypertext, graphics, and video components interspersed with each other. The World Wide Web has played an important role in making the data, even from geographically distant locations, easily accessible to users all over the world. However, often most of this data are not of much interest to most of the users. The problem is to *mine* useful information or patterns from the huge datasets. Data mining refers to this process of extracting knowledge that is of interest to the user.

Data mining is an evolving and growing area of research and development, both in academia as well as in industry. It involves interdisciplinary research and development encompassing diverse domains. In our view, this area is far from being saturated, with newer techniques and directions being proposed in the literature everyday. In this age of multimedia data exploration, data mining should no longer be restricted to the mining of knowledge from large volumes of high-dimensional datasets in traditional databases only. Researchers need to pay attention to the mining of different datatypes, including numeric and alphanumeric formats, text, images, video, voice, speech, graphics, and also their mixed representations. Efficient management of such high-dimensional very large databases also influence the performance of data mining systems. Data Compression technologies can play a significant role.

It is also important that special multimedia data compression techniques are explored especially suitable for data mining applications.

With the completion of the Human Genome Project, we have access to large databases of biological information. Proper analysis of such huge data, involving decoding of genes in the DNA and the three-dimensional protein structures, holds immense promise in Bioinformatics. The applicability of data mining in this domain cannot be denied, given the lifesaving prospects of effective drug design. This is also of practical interest to the pharmaceutical industry.

Different forms of ambiguity or uncertainty inherent in real-life data need to be handled appropriately using soft computing. The goal is to arrive at a low-cost, reasonably good solution, instead of a high-cost, best solution. Fuzzy sets provide the uncertainty handling capability, inherent in human reasoning, while artificial neural networks help incorporate learning to minimize error. Genetic algorithms introduce effective parallel searching in the high-dimensional problem space.

Since all these aspects are not covered in that elaborate form in current books available in the market, we wanted to emphasize them in this book. Along with the traditional concepts and functions of data mining, like classification, clustering, and rule mining, we wish to highlight the current and burning issues related to mining in multimedia applications and Bioinformatics. Storage of such huge datasets being more feasible in the compressed domain, we also devote a reasonable portion of the text to data mining in the compressed domain. Topics like text mining, image mining, and Web mining are covered specifically.

Current trends show that the advances in data mining need not be constrained to stochastic, combinatorial, and/or classical so-called hard optimization-based techniques. We dwell, in greater detail, on the state of the art of soft computing approaches, advanced signal processing techniques such as Wavelet Transformation, data compression principles for both lossless and lossy techniques, access of data using matching pursuits in both raw and compressed data domains, fundamentals and principles of classical string matching algorithms, and how all these areas possibly influence data mining and its future growth. We cover aspects of advanced image compression, string matching, content based image retrieval, etc., which can influence future developments in data mining, particularly for multimedia data mining.

There are 10 chapters in the book. The first chapter provides an introduction to the basics of data mining and outlines its major functions and applications. This is followed in the second chapter by a discussion on soft computing and its different tools, including fuzzy sets, artificial neural networks, genetic algorithms, wavelet transforms, rough sets, and their hybridizations, along with their roles in data mining.

We then present some advanced topics and new aspects of data mining related to the processing and retrieval of multimedia data. These have direct applications to information retrieval, Web mining, image mining, and text mining. The huge volumes of data required to be retrieved, processed, and stored make compression techniques a promising area to explore, in the context of both images and texts. Chapter 3 introduces the readers to the fundamentals of multimedia data compression and some popular algorithms for data compression. We discuss the principles of string matching and some classical algorithms in Chapter 4. Results of string matching hold ample promise both in multimedia applications and in Bioinformatics.

Chapters 5 to 8 concentrate on classification, clustering, and rule mining. In each of these topics, in addition to the classical discussions that are usually available in the books currently in the market, we strive to incorporate new algorithms and results based on soft computing and advanced signal processing techniques with recent developments.

We deal with multimedia data mining in Chapter 9. In this chapter we have discussed text mining, image mining, and Web mining issues. Next we introduce the readers to issues from Bioinformatics, in Chapter 10. In each case we discuss the related algorithms, showing how these can be a growing area of study in the light of data mining in the near future.

Finally, we pose some research problems, issues, and new direction of thoughts for researchers and developers. We have kept the presentation concise and included an exhaustive bibliography at the end of each chapter. Because reported research articles in relevant domains are scarce and scattered, we have tried to make them collectively accessible from the unified framework of this book. Some portion of the material in this book also covers our published work, which has been presented and discussed in different seminars, conferences, and workshops.

The book may be used in a graduate-level course as a part of the subject of data mining, machine learning, information retrieval, and artificial intelligence, or it may be used as a reference book for professionals and researchers. It is assumed that the readers have adequate background in college-level mathematics and introductory knowledge of statistics and probability theory.

For the major part of this project we worked from the two ends of this world, often communicating via the Internet. We have collected a great deal of rich information from the Internet. Thereby, we were the true beneficiaries of today's information technology. Progress in data mining will further pave the way for usage of information technology in every walk of life in near future. We are glad that we could complete this project in a short time within the schedule.

We take this opportunity to thank Dr. Val Moliere of John Wiley & Sons, Inc., for her initiative and encouragement throughout this project. She was very helpful in every stage of compilation of this book. We are grateful to Mr. B. Uma Shankar, Mr. Sudip Chakraborty, and Ms. Maya Dey for their valuable assistance while preparing the camera-ready manuscript. We sincerely thank Dr. Ping-Sing Tsai, who assisted by reviewing a number of chapters of the book and who provided valuable suggestions to further enrich the content. We extend our gratitude to Dr. Amit K. Das of Bengal Engineering College in India, who supplied some material on content-based image retrieval in a very short notice. Prof. Malay K. Kundu, Prof. Chaitali Chakraborti, Dr. Andrew J. Griffis, Dr. Dragos Arotaritei, Dr. Rajat K. De, Dr. Pabitra Mitra, Mr. Roger Undhagen, and Mr. Jose M. Rodriguez deserve special thanks for their continuous encouragement and support towards the compilation of this treatise. We would also like to thank the anonymous reviewers of our book proposal for their very constructive review and suggestions.

Finally, sincere gratitude goes to each member of our families for bearing with us, especially by putting up with our erratic schedules during the final phase of this project. We are truly indebted to them for their love, encouragement, dedication, and support.

Sushmita Mitra

Tinku Acharya

April 2003

1

Introduction to Data Mining

1.1 INTRODUCTION

The digital revolution has made digitized information easy to capture, process, store, distribute, and transmit [1]–[3]. With significant progress in computing and related technologies and their ever-expanding usage in different walks of life, huge amount of data of diverse characteristics continue to be collected and stored in databases. The rate at which such data are stored is growing phenomenally. We can draw an analogy between the popular Moore's law and the way data are increasing with the growth of information in this world of data processing applications. The advancement of data processing and the emergence of newer applications were possible, partially because of the growth of the semiconductor and subsequently the computer industry. According to Moore's law, the number of transistors in a single microchip is doubled every 18 months, and the growth of the semiconductor industry has so far followed the prediction. We can correlate this with a similar observation from the data and information domain. If the amount of information in the world doubles every 20 months, the size and number of databases probably increases at a similar pace. Discovery of knowledge from this huge volume of data is a challenge indeed. Data mining is an attempt to make sense of the information explosion embedded in this huge volume of data [4].

Today, data are no longer restricted to tuples of numeric or character representations only. The advanced database management technology of today is enabled to integrate different types of data, such as image, video, text, and other numeric as well as non-numeric data, in a provably single database in order to facilitate multimedia processing. As a result, traditional *ad hoc* mixtures of statistical techniques and data management tools are no longer adequate for analyzing this vast collection of mixed data.

The current Internet technology and its growing demand necessitates the development of more advanced data mining technologies to interpret the information and knowledge from the data distributed all over the world. In the 21st century this demand will continue to grow, and the access of large volumes of multimedia data will become a major transforming theme in the global society. As an example, a report on the United States Administrations initiative in the "Information Technology for 21st Century" [5] indicated improved Internet and multimedia applications in World Wide Web encompassing information visualization, interpretation, processing, analysis, etc. Hence development of advanced data mining technology will continue to be an important area of study, and it is accordingly expected that lots of energy will be spent in this area of development in the coming years.

There exist several domains where large volumes of data are stored in centralized or distributed databases. Some of the examples include the following.

- Digital library: This is an organized collection of digital information stored in large databases in the form of text (encoded or raw) and possibly as a large collection of document imagery [6].

- Image archive: This consists of large database of images, in either compressed or raw form. Often the image data are interspersed with text and numeric data for proper indexing, retrieval, and storage management.

- Bioinformatics: The machinery of each human body is built and run with 50,000 to 100,000 different kinds of genes or protein molecules, and we have five and half billion population in this diverse world. Bioinformatics involves analyzing and interpreting this vast amount of data stored in these large genomic databases [7].

- Medical imagery: Large volumes of medical data are generated everyday in the form of digital images such as digital radiographs, EKG, MRI, CAT, SCAN, etc. They are stored in large centralized or distributed databases in medical management systems. Automatic mining of these data is important to the medical community.

- Health care: In addition of the above medical image data, other non-image datatypes are also generated everyday. This may include health insurance information, patient's personal care physician's information, specialist information, patient's medical history, etc. In addition to these, several diagnostic information are stored by hospital management systems [8] for ready reference or research.

- Finance and investment: Finance and investment is a big data domain of interest for data mining. It includes, but is not limited to, stock indices, stock prices, historical performance of each stock, information about the bonds, notes, treasury and other security investments, banking information, interest rates, loan information, credit card data, debit card data, ATM card information, credit history of an individual, and fraud detection [9].

- Manufacturing and production: A huge volume of manufacturing and production data is generated in different forms in factories. Efficient storage and access of these data and their analysis for process optimization and trouble shooting is very important in the manufacturing industry [10].

- Business and marketing: Data need to be analyzed for sales forecast, business planning, marketing trend, etc.

- Telecommunication network: There are different types of data generated and stored in this application domain. They may be used to analyze calling patterns, call tracing, network management, congestion control, error control, fault management, etc.

- Scientific domain: This consists of astronomical observations [11], genomic data, biological data, etc. There has been an exponential growth in the collection and storage of biological databases over the last couple of years, the human genome database being one such example.

- The World Wide Web (WWW) [12]: A huge volume of multimedia data of different types is distributed everywhere in the Internet. The World Wide Web can be considered as the largest distributed database that ever existed. It consists of data that are heterogeneous in nature, and it happens to be the most unorganized database management system known today.

- Biometrics: Because of the need of extraordinary security of human lives today, biometric applications will continue to grow for positive identification of persons. A huge volume of biometric data such as fingerprint, face imagery, etc., need to be stored and used, for access and search toward this end.

Raw data are rarely of direct benefit. Its true value is predicated on (a) the ability to extract information useful for decision support or exploration and (b) understanding the phenomenon governing the data source. In most domains, data analysis was traditionally a manual process. One or more analyst(s) would become intimately familiar with the data and, with the help of statistical techniques, provide summaries and generate reports. In effect, the analyst acted as a sophisticated query processor. However, such an approach rapidly broke down as the size of data grew and the number of dimensions increased. Databases containing number of data on the order of 10^9 or above and dimension on the order of 10^3 are becoming increasingly common. When the scale of data manipulation, exploration and inferencing goes beyond human capacities, people need the aid of computing technologies for automating the process.

All these have prompted the need for intelligent data analysis methodologies, which could discover useful knowledge from data. The term KDD refers to the overall process of *knowledge discovery in databases*. While some people treat *data mining* as a synonym for KDD, some others view it as a particular step in this process involving the application of specific algorithms for extracting patterns (models) from data. The additional steps in the KDD process, such as data preparation, data selection, data cleaning, incorporation of appropriate prior knowledge, and proper interpretation of the results of mining, ensures that useful knowledge is derived from the data.

Data mining tasks can be descriptive, (i.e., discovering interesting patterns or relationships describing the data), and predictive (i.e., predicting or classifying the behavior of the model based on available data). In other words, it is an interdisciplinary field with a general goal of predicting outcomes and uncovering relationships in data [13]–[16]. It uses automated tools that (a) employ sophisticated algorithms to discover mainly hidden patterns, associations, anomalies, and/or structure from large amounts of data stored in *data warehouses* or other information repositories and (b) filter necessary information from this big dataset.

The subject of Knowledge Discovery in Databases (KDD) has evolved, and continues to evolve, from the intersection of research from such fields as databases, machine learning, pattern recognition, statistics, information theory, artificial intelligence, reasoning with uncertainties, knowledge acquisition for expert systems, data visualization, machine discovery, and high-performance computing. KDD systems incorporate theories, algorithms, and methods from all these fields. Many successful applications have been reported from varied sectors such as marketing, finance, banking, manufacturing, security, medicine, multimedia, telecommunications, etc. Database theories and tools provide the necessary infrastructure to store, access and manipulate data. A good overview of KDD can be found in Refs. [17] and [18].

Data warehousing [2] refers to the current business trends in collecting and cleaning transactional data and making them available for analysis and decision support. Data mining works hand in hand with warehouse data. Data warehousing is analogous to a mechanism that provides an enterprize with a memory, while its mining provides the enterprize with intelligence.

KDD focuses on the overall process of knowledge discovery from large volumes of data, including the storage and accessing of such data, scaling of algorithms to massive datasets, interpretation and visualization of results, and the modeling and support of the overall human machine interaction. Efficient storage of the data, and hence its structure, is very important for its

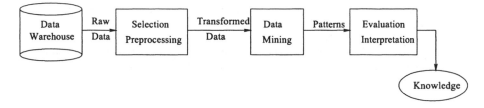

Fig. 1.1 The KDD process.

representation and access. Knowledge from modern data compression technologies should be utilized to explore how this storage mechanism can further be improved.

Data mining also overlaps with machine learning, statistics, artificial intelligence, databases, and visualization. However, the stress is more on the

- scalability of the number of features and instances,

- algorithms and architectures (while the foundations of methods and formulations are provided by statistics and machine learning), and

- automation for handling large volumes of heterogeneous data.

In the remaining part of this chapter we consider data mining from the perspective of machine learning, pattern recognition, image processing, and artificial intelligence. We begin by providing the basics of knowledge discovery and data mining in Section 1.2. Sections 1.3–1.7 deal with brief introductions to data compression, information retrieval, text mining, Web mining, and image mining. Their applicability to multimedia data are also highlighted. This is followed, in Sections 1.8–1.10, by a treatise on some of the major functions of data mining like classification, clustering, and rule mining. String matching, another important aspect of data mining with promising applications to Bioinformatics, is described in Section 1.11. An introduction to the research issues in Bioinformatics is provided in Section 1.12. The details on all these topics are provided in subsequent chapters of this book. In Section 1.13 we briefly present the concept of data warehousing. Section 1.14 highlights the applications of data mining and some existing challenges to future research. Finally, Section 1.15 concludes the chapter.

1.2 KNOWLEDGE DISCOVERY AND DATA MINING

Knowledge discovery in databases (KDD) is defined as *the nontrivial process of identifying valid, novel, potentially useful, and ultimately understandable patterns in data* [17, 19]. The overall process consists of turning low-level data into high-level knowledge. The KDD process is outlined in Fig. 1.1. It is interactive and iterative involving, more or less, the following steps [20]:

1. *Understanding the application domain*: This includes relevant prior knowledge and goals of the application.

2. *Extracting the target dataset*: This is nothing but selecting a dataset or focusing on a subset of variables, using feature ranking and selection techniques.

3. *Data preprocessing*: This is required to improve the quality of the actual data for mining. This also increases the mining efficiency by reducing the time required for mining the preprocessed data. Data preprocessing involves data cleaning, data transformation, data integration, data reduction or data compression for compact representation, etc.

   (a) *Data cleaning*: It consists of some basic operations, such as normalization, noise removal and handling of missing data, reduction of redundancy, etc. Data from real-world sources are often erroneous, incomplete, and inconsistent, perhaps due to operational error or system implementation flaws. Such low-quality data needs to be cleaned prior to data mining.

   (b) *Data integration*: Integration plays an important role in KDD. This operation includes integrating multiple, heterogeneous datasets generated from different sources.

   (c) *Data reduction and projection*: This includes finding useful features to represent the data (depending on the goal of the task) and using dimensionality reduction, feature discretization, and feature extraction (or transformation) methods. Application of the principles of data compression can play an important role in data reduction and is a possible area of future development, particularly in the area of knowledge discovery from multimedia dataset.

4. *Data mining*: Data mining constitutes one or more of the following functions, namely, classification, regression, clustering, summarization, image retrieval, discovering association rules and functional dependencies, rule extraction, etc.

5. *Interpretation*: This includes interpreting the discovered patterns, as well as the possible (low-dimensional) visualization of the extracted patterns. Visualization is an important aid that increases understandability from the perspective of humans. One can evaluate the mined patterns automatically or semiautomatically to identify the truly interesting or useful patterns for the user.

6. *Using discovered knowledge*: It includes incorporating this knowledge into the performance system and taking actions based on the knowledge.

In other words, given huge volumes of heterogeneous data, the objective is to efficiently extract meaningful patterns that can be of interest and hence useful to the user. The role of interestingness is to threshold or filter the large number of discovered patterns, and report only those which may be of some use. There are two approaches to designing a measure of interestingness of a pattern, namely, objective and subjective. The former uses the structure of the pattern and is generally quantitative. Often it fails to capture all the complexities of the pattern discovery process. The *subjective* approach, on the other hand, depends additionally on the *user* who examines the pattern. Two major reasons why a pattern is interesting from the subjective (user-oriented) point of view are as follows [21].

- *Unexpectedness*: When it is "surprising" to the user, and this potentially delivers new information to the user.

- *Actionability*: When the user can act on it to her/his advantage to fulfill the goal.

Though both these concepts are important, it has often been observed that actionability and unexpectedness are correlated. In literature, unexpectedness is often defined in terms of the dissimilarity of a discovered pattern from a predefined vocabulary provided by the user.

As an example, let us consider a database of student evaluations of different courses offered at some university. This can be defined as EVALUATE (TERM, YEAR, COURSE, SECTION, INSTRUCTOR, INSTRUCT_RATING, COURSE_RATING). We describe two patterns that are interesting in terms of actionability and unexpectedness respectively. The pattern that Professor X is consistently getting the overall INSTRUCT_RATING below overall COURSE_RATING can be of interest to the chairperson, because this shows that Professor X has room for improvement. If, on the other hand, in most of the course evaluations the overall INSTRUCT_RATING is higher than COURSE_RATING and it turns out that in most of Professor X's rating the overall INSTRUCT_RATING is lower than COURSE_RATING, then such a pattern is unexpected and hence interesting.

Data mining is a step in the KDD process consisting of a particular enumeration of patterns over the data, subject to some computational limitations. The term *pattern* goes beyond its traditional sense to include models or structures in the data. *Historical* data are used to discover regularities and improve future decisions [22]. The data can consist of (say) a collection of time series descriptions that can be learned to predict later events in the series.

Data mining involves fitting models to or determining patterns from observed data. The fitted models play the role of inferred knowledge. Deciding whether the model reflects useful knowledge or not is a part of the overall KDD process for which subjective human judgment is usually required. Typically, a data mining algorithm constitutes some combination of the following three components.

- *The model*: The function of the model (e.g., classification, clustering) and its representational form (e.g., linear discriminants, decision trees).

A model contains parameters that are to be determined from data for the chosen function using the particular representational form or tool.

- *The preference criterion*: A basis for preference of one model or set of parameters over another, depending on the given data. The criterion is usually some form of goodness-of-fit function of the model to the data, perhaps tempered by a smoothing term to avoid over-fitting, or generating a model with too many degrees of freedom to be constrained by the given data.

- *The search algorithm*: The specification of an algorithm for finding particular models or patterns and parameters, given the data, model(s), and a preference criterion.

A particular data mining algorithm is usually an instantiation of the model-preference-search components. Some of the common model functions in current data mining practice include [13, 14]:

1. Classification: This model function classifies a data item into one of several predefined categorical classes.

2. Regression: The purpose of this model function is to map a data item to a real-valued prediction variable.

3. Clustering: This function maps a data item into one of several clusters, where clusters are natural groupings of data items based on similarity metrics or probability density models.

4. Rule generation: Here one mines or generates rules from the data. Association rule mining refers to discovering association relationships among different attributes. Dependency modeling corresponds to extracting significant dependencies among variables.

5. Summarization or condensation: This function provides a compact description for a subset of data. Data compression may play a significant role here, particularly for multimedia data, because of the advantage it offers to compactly represent the data with a reduced number of bits, thereby increasing the database storage bandwidth.

6. Sequence analysis: It models sequential patterns, like time-series analysis, gene sequences, etc. The goal is to model the states of the process generating the sequence, or to extract and report deviation and trends over time.

The rapid growth of interest in data mining [22] is due to the (i) advancement of the Internet technology and wide interest in multimedia applications in this domain, (ii) falling cost of large storage devices and increasing ease of collecting data over networks, (iii) sharing and distribution of data over the network, along with adding of new data in existing data repository, (iv) development of robust and efficient machine learning algorithms to process this data, (v) advancement of computer architecture and falling cost of computational power, enabling use of computationally intensive methods for data analysis, (vi) inadequate scaling of conventional querying or analysis methods, prompting the need for new ways of interaction, (vii) strong competitive pressures from available commercial products, etc.

The notion of scalability relates to the efficient processing of large datasets, while generating from them the best possible models. The most commonly cited reason for scaling up is that increasing the size of the training set often increases the accuracy of learned classification models. In many cases, the degradation in accuracy when learning from smaller samples stems from overfitting, presence of noise, and existence of large number of features. Again, scaling up to very large datasets implies that fast learning algorithms must be developed. Finally, the goal of the learning (say, classification accuracy) must not be substantially sacrificed by a scaling algorithm. The three main approaches to scaling up include [23]

- designing a fast algorithm: improving computational complexity, optimizing the search and representation, finding approximate solutions to the computationally complex (NP complete or NP hard) problems, or taking advantage of the task's inherent parallelism;

- partitioning the data: dividing the data into subsets (based on instances or features), learning from one or more of the selected subsets, and possibly combining the results; and

- using a relational representation: addresses data that cannot feasibly be treated as a single flat file.

Some examples of mined or discovered patterns include

1. Classification:

   (a) People with age less than 25 and salary $> 40K$ drive sports cars.

   (b) Set of images that contain a car as an object.

2. Association rules:

   (a) 80% of the images containing a car as an object also contain a blue sky.

   (b) 98% of people who purchase diapers also buy baby food.

3. Similar time sequences:

   (a) Stocks of companies A and B perform similarly.

   (b) Sale of furniture increases with the improvement of real estate business.

4. Outlier detection:

    (a) Residential customers for a telecom company, with businesses at home.

    (b) Digital radiographs of lungs, with suspicious spots.

1.3 DATA COMPRESSION

With growing demands of various applications, storage requirements of digital data are growing explosively. Some examples, demonstrating this, are given below.

- A high-quality audio signal requires approximately 1.5 megabits per second for digital representation and storage.

- A digitized 14×17 square-inch radiograph, scanned at 70 μm, occupies nearly 45 megabytes of storage.

- A television-quality low-resolution color video of 30 frames per second, with each frame containing 640×480 pixels (24 bits per color pixel), needs more than 210 megabits per second of storage. As a result, a digitized one hour color movie would require approximately 95 gigabytes of storage.

- The storage requirement for the upcoming High-Definition-Television (HDTV)-quality video of resolution 1280×720 at 60 frames per second is many-fold. A digitized one-hour color movie of HDTV-quality video will require approximately 560 gigabytes of storage.

- A small document collection in electronic form in a digital library system may easily require to store several billion characters.

- The total amount of data spread over Internet sites is mind-boggling.

Although the cost of storage has decreased drastically over the past decade due to significant advancement in the microelectronics and storage technology, the requirement of data storage and data processing applications is growing explosively to outpace this achievement. Hence data compression continues to be a challenging area of research and development in both academia and industry, particularly in the context of large databases.

Interestingly enough, most of the datatypes for practical applications such as still image, video, voice, and text generally contain a significant amount of superfluous and redundant information in their canonical representation. Data redundancy may appear in different forms in the digital representation of different categories of datatypes. A few examples are as follows.

1. In English text files, common words (e.g., *"is"*, "are", *"the"*) or similar patterns of character strings (e.g., *'ze'*, *'th'*, *'ing'*) are usually used repeatedly. It is also observed that the characters in an English text occur in a well-documented distribution, with letter *"e"* and "space" being the most popular.

2. In numeric data files, often we observe runs of similar numbers or predictable interdependency amongst the numbers.

3. The neighboring pixels in a typical image are highly correlated to each other, with the pixels in a smooth region of an image having similar values.

4. Two consecutive frames in a video are often mostly identical when motion in the scene is slow.

5. Some audio data beyond the human audible frequency range are useless for all practical purposes.

Data compression is the technique to reduce the redundancies in data representation in order to decrease data storage requirements and, hence, communication costs when transmitted through a communication network [24, 25]. Reducing the storage requirement is equivalent to increasing the capacity of the storage medium. If the compressed data are properly indexed, it may improve the performance of mining data in the compressed large database as well. This is particularly useful when interactivity is involved with a data mining system. Thus the development of efficient compression techniques, particularly suitable for data mining, will continue to be a design challenge for advanced database management systems and interactive multimedia applications.

Depending upon the application criteria, data compression techniques can be classified as *lossless* and *lossy*. In lossless methods we compress the data in such a way that the decompressed data can be an exact replica of the original data. Lossless compression techniques are applied to compress text, numeric, or character strings in a database – typically, medical data, etc. On the other hand, there are application areas where we can compromise with the accuracy of the decompressed data and can, therefore, afford to lose some information. For example, typical image, video, and audio compression techniques are lossy, since the approximation of the original data during reconstruction is good enough for human perception.

In our view, data compression is a field that has so far been neglected by the data mining community. The basic principle of data compression is to reduce the redundancies in data representation, in order to generate a shorter representation for the data to conserve data storage. In earlier discussions, we emphasized that *data reduction* is an important preprocessing task in data mining. Need for reduced representation of data is crucial for the success of very large multimedia database applications and the associated economical usage of data storage. Multimedia databases are typically much larger than, say, business or financial data, simply because an attribute itself in a multimedia database could be a high-resolution digital image. Hence storage and subsequent access of thousands of high-resolution images, which are possibly interspersed with other datatypes as attributes, is a challenge. Data compression offers advantages in the storage management of such huge data. Although data compression has been recognized as a potential area for data reduction in literature [13], not much work has been reported so far on how the data compression techniques can be integrated in a data mining system.

Data compression can also play an important role in data condensation. An approach for dealing with the intractable problem of learning from huge databases is to select a small subset of data as representatives for learning. Large data can be viewed at varying degrees of detail in different regions of the feature space, thereby providing adequate importance depending on the underlying probability density [26]. However, these condensation techniques are useful only when the structure of data is well-organized. Multimedia data, being not so well-structured in its raw form, leads to a big bottleneck in the application of existing data mining principles. In order to avoid this problem, one approach could be to store some predetermined feature set of the multimedia data as an index at the header of the compressed file, and subsequently use this condensed information for the discovery of information or data mining.

We believe that integration of data compression principles and techniques in data mining systems will yield promising results, particularly in the age of multimedia information and their growing usage in the Internet. Soon there will arise the need to automatically discover or access information from such multimedia data domains, in place of well-organized business and financial data only. Keeping this goal in mind, we intended to devote significant discussions on data compression techniques and their principles in multimedia data domain involving text, numeric and non-numeric data, images, etc.

We have elaborated on the fundamentals of data compression and image compression principles and some popular algorithms in Chapter 3. Then we have described, in Chapter 9, how some data compression principles can improve the efficiency of information retrieval particularly suitable for multimedia data mining.

1.4   INFORMATION RETRIEVAL

Users approach large information spaces like the Web with different motives, namely, to (i) search for a specific piece of information or topic, (ii) gain familiarity with, or an overview of, some general topic or domain, and (iii) locate something that might be of interest, without a clear prior notion of what "interesting" should look like. The field of information retrieval develops methods that focus on the first situation, whereas the latter motives are mainly addressed in approaches dealing with exploration and visualization of the data.

Information retrieval [28] uses the Web (and digital libraries) to access multimedia information repositories consisting of mixed media data. The information retrieved can be text as well as image document, or a mixture of both. Hence it encompasses both text and image mining. Information retrieval automatically entails some amount of summarization or compression, along with retrieval based on content. Given a user query, the information system has to retrieve the documents which are related to that query. The potentially large size of the document collection implies that specialized indexing techniques must be used if efficient retrieval is to be achieved. This calls for proper indexing and searching, involving *pattern* or *string matching*.

With the explosive growth of the amount of information over the Web and the associated proliferation of the number of users around the world, the difficulty in assisting users in finding the best and most recent information has increased exponentially. The existing problems can be categorized as the absence of

- filtering: a user looking for some topic on the Internet receives too much information,

- ranking of retrieved documents: the system provides no qualitative distinction between the documents,

- support of relevance feedback: the user cannot report her/his subjective evaluation of the relevance of the document,

- personalization: there is a need of personal systems that serve the specific interests of the user and build user profile,

- adaptation: the system should notice when the user changes her/his interests.

Retrieval can be efficient in terms of both (a) a high recall from the Internet and (b) a fast response time at the expense of a poor precision. Recall is the percentage of relevant documents that are retrieved, while precision refers to the percentage of documents retrieved that are considered as relevant [29]. These are some of the factors that are considered when evaluating the relevance feedback provided by a user, which can again be explicit or implicit. An implicit feedback entails features such as the time spent in browsing a Web page, the number of mouse-clicks made therein, whether the page is printed or bookmarked, etc. Some of the recent generations of search engines involve Meta-search engines (like Harvester, MetaCrawler) and intelligent Software Agent technologies. The intelligent agent approach [30, 31] is recently gaining attention in the area of building an appropriate user interface for the Web.

Therefore, four main constituents can be identified in the process of information retrieval from the Internet. They are

1. Indexing: generation of document representation.

2. Querying: expression of user preferences through natural language or terms connected by logical operators.

3. Evaluation: performance of matching between user query and document representation.

4. User profile construction: storage of terms representing user preferences, especially to enhance the system retrieval during future accesses by the user.

1.5   TEXT MINING

Text is practically one of the most commonly used multimedia datatypes in day-to-day use. Text is the natural choice for formal exchange of information by common people through electronic mail, Internet chat, World Wide Web, digital libraries, electronic publications, and technical reports, to name a few. Moreover, huge volumes of text data and information exist in the so-called "gray literature" and they are not easily available to common users outside the normal book-selling channels. The gray literature includes technical reports, research reports, theses and dissertations, trade and business literature, conference and journal papers, government reports, and so on [32]. Gray literature is typically stored in text (or document) databases. The wealth of information embedded in the huge volumes of text (or document) databases distributed all over is enormous, and such databases are growing exponentially with the revolution of current Internet and information technology. The popular data mining algorithms have been developed to extract information mainly from well-structured classical databases, such as relational, transactional, processed warehouse data, etc. Multimedia data are not so structured and often less formal. Most of the textual data spread all over the world are not very formally structured either. The structure of textual data formation and the underlying syntax vary from one language to another language (both machine and human), one culture to another, and possibly user to user. Text mining can be classified as the special data mining techniques particularly suitable for knowledge and information discovery from textual data.

Automatic understanding of the content of textual data, and hence the extraction of knowledge from it, is a long-standing challenge in artificial intelligence. There were efforts to develop models and retrieval techniques for semistructured data from the database community. The information retrieval community developed techniques for indexing and searching unstructured text documents. However, these traditional techniques are not sufficient for knowledge discovery and mining of the ever-increasing volume of textual databases.

Although retrieval of text-based information was traditionally considered to be a branch of study in information retrieval only, text mining is currently emerging as an area of interest of its own. This became very prominent with the development of search engines used in the *World Wide Web*, to search and retrieve information from the Internet. In order to develop efficient text mining techniques for search and access of textual information, it is important to take advantage of the principles behind classical string matching techniques for pattern search in text or string of characters, in addition to traditional data mining principles. We describe some of the classical string matching algorithms and their applications in Chapter 4.

In today's data processing environment, most of the text data is stored in compressed form. Hence access of text information in the compressed domain will become a challenge in the near future. There is practically no remarkable effort in this direction in the research community. In order to make progress in such efforts, we need to understand the principles behind the text compression methods and develop underlying text mining techniques exploiting these. Usually, classical text compression algorithms, such as the Lempel–Ziv family of algorithms, are used to compress text databases. We deal with some of these algorithms and their working principles in greater detail in Chapter 3.

Other established mathematical principles for data reduction have also been applied in text mining to improve the efficiency of these systems. One such technique is the application of *principal component analysis* based on the matrix theory of *singular value decomposition*. Use of *latent semantic analysis* based on the *principal component analysis* and some other text analysis schemes for text mining have been discussed in great detail in Section 9.2.

1.6 WEB MINING

Presently an enormous wealth of information is available on the Web. The objective is to mine interesting nuggets of information, like which airline has the cheapest flights in December, or search for an old friend, etc. Internet is definitely the largest multimedia data depository or library that ever existed. It is the most disorganized library as well. Hence mining the Web is a challenge.

The Web is a huge collection of documents that comprises (i) semistructured (HTML, XML) information, (ii) hyper-link information, and (iii) access and usage information and is (iv) dynamic; that is, new pages are constantly being generated. The Web has made cheaper the accessibility of a wider audience to various sources of information. The advances in all kinds of digital communication has provided greater access to networks. It has also created free access to a large publishing medium. These factors have allowed people to use the Web and modern digital libraries as a highly interactive medium. However, present-day search engines are plagued by several problems like the

- *abundance* problem, as 99% of the information is of no interest to 99% of the people,

- *limited coverage* of the Web, as Internet sources are hidden behind search interfaces,

- *limited query interface*, based on keyword-oriented search, and

- *limited customization* to individual users.

Web mining [27] refers to the use of data mining techniques to automatically retrieve, extract, and evaluate (generalize or analyze) information for knowledge discovery from Web documents and services. Considering the Web as a huge repository of distributed hypertext, the results from text mining have great influence in Web mining and information retrieval. Web data are typically unlabeled, distributed, heterogeneous, semistructured, time-varying, and high-dimensional. Hence some sort of human interface is needed to handle context-sensitive and imprecise queries and provide for summarization, deduction, personalization, and learning.

The major components of Web mining include

- information retrieval,

- information extraction,

- generalization, and

- analysis.

Information retrieval, as mentioned in Section 1.4, refers to the automatic retrieval of relevant documents, using document indexing and search engines. Information extraction helps identify document fragments that constitute the semantic core of the Web. Generalization relates to aspects from pattern recognition or machine learning, and it utilizes clustering and association rule mining. Analysis corresponds to the extraction, interpretation, validation, and visualization of the knowledge obtained from the Web.

Different aspects of Web mining have been discussed in Section 9.5.

1.7   IMAGE MINING

Image is another important class of multimedia datatypes. The World Wide Web is presently regarded as the largest global multimedia data repository, encompassing different types of images in addition to other multimedia datatypes. As a matter of fact, much of the information communicated in the real-world is in the form of images; accordingly, digital pictures play a pervasive role in the World Wide Web for visual communication. Image databases are typically very large in size. We have witnessed an exponential growth in the generation and storage of digital images in different forms, because of the advent of electronic sensors (like CMOS or CCD) and image capture devices such as digital cameras, camcorders, scanners, etc.

There has been a lot of progress in the development of text-based search engines for the World Wide Web. However, search engines based on other multimedia datatypes do not exist. To make the data mining technology successful, it is very important to develop search engines in other multimedia datatypes, especially for image datatypes. Mining of data in the imagery domain is a challenge. Image mining [33] deals with the extraction of implicit knowledge, image data relationship, or other patterns not explicitly stored in the images. It is more than just an extension of data mining to the image domain. Image mining is an interdisciplinary endeavor that draws upon expertise in computer vision, pattern recognition, image processing, image retrieval, data mining, machine learning, database, artificial intelligence, and possibly compression.

Unlike low-level computer vision and image processing, the focus of image mining is in the extraction of patterns from a large collection of images. It, however, includes content-based retrieval as one of its functions. While current content-based image retrieval systems can handle queries about image contents based on one or more related image features such as color, shape, and other spatial information, the ultimate technology remains an important challenge. While data mining can involve absolute numeric values in relational databases, the images are better represented by relative values of pixels. Moreover, image mining inherently deals with spatial information and often involves multiple interpretations for the same visual pattern. Hence the mining algorithms here need to be subtly different than in traditional data mining.

A discovered image pattern also needs to be suitably represented to the user, often involving feature selection to improve visualization. The information representation framework for an image can be at different levels, namely, pixel, object, semantic concept, and pattern or knowledge levels. Conventional image mining techniques include object recognition, image retrieval, image indexing, image classification and clustering, and association rule mining. Intelligently classifying an image by its content is an important way to mine valuable information from a large image collection [34].

Since the storage and communication bandwidth required for image data is pervasive, there has been a great deal of activity in the international standard committees to develop standards for image compression. It is not practical to store the digital images in uncompressed or raw data form. Image compression standards aid in the seamless distribution and retrieval of compressed images from an image repository. Searching images and discovering knowledge directly from compressed image databases has not been explored enough. However, it is obvious that image mining in compressed domain will become a challenge in the near future, with the explosive growth of the image data depository distributed all over in the World Wide Web. Hence it is crucial to understand the principles behind image compression and its standards, in order to make significant progress to achieve this goal.

We discuss the principles of multimedia data compression, including that for image datatypes, in Chapter 3. Different aspects of image mining are described in Section 9.3.

1.8   CLASSIFICATION

Classification is also described as supervised learning [35]. Let there be a database of tuples, each assigned a class label. The objective is to develop a model or profile for each class. An example of a profile with good credit is $25 \leq age \leq 40$ and $income > 40$K or $married = $ "yes". Sample applications for classification include

- Signature identification in banking or sensitive document handling (match, no match).

- Digital fingerprint identification in security applications (match, no match).

- Credit card approval depending on customer background and financial credibility (good, bad).

- Bank location considering customer quality and business possibilities (good, fair, poor).

- Identification of tanks from a set of images (friendly, enemy).

- Treatment effectiveness of a drug in the presence of a set of disease symptoms (good, fair, poor).

- Detection of suspicious cells in a digital image of blood samples (yes, no).

The goal is to predict the class $C_i = f(x_1, \ldots, x_n)$, where $x_1, \ldots, x_n$ are the input attributes. The input to the classification algorithm is, typically, a dataset of training records with several attributes. There is one distinguished attribute called the dependent attribute. The remaining predictor attributes can be numerical or categorical in nature. A numerical attribute has continuous, quantitative values. A categorical attribute, on the other hand, takes up discrete, symbolic values that can also be class labels or categories. If the dependent attribute is categorical, the problem is called classification with this attribute being termed the class label. However, if the dependent attribute is numerical, the problem is termed regression. The goal of classification and regression is to build a concise model of the distribution of the dependent attribute in terms of the predictor attributes. The resulting model is used to assign values to a database of testing records, where the values of the predictor attributes are known but the dependent attribute is to be determined. Classification methods can be categorized as follows.

1. Decision trees [36], which divide a decision space into piecewise constant regions. Typically, an information theoretic measure is used for assessing the discriminatory power of the attributes at each level of the tree.

2. Probabilistic or generative models, which calculate probabilities for hypotheses based on Bayes' theorem [35].

3. Nearest-neighbor classifiers, which compute minimum distance from instances or prototypes [35].

4. Regression, which can be linear or polynomial, of the form $ax_1+bx_2+c = C_i$ [37].

5. Neural networks [38], which partition by nonlinear boundaries. These incorporate learning, in a *data-rich* environment, such that all information is encoded in a distributed fashion among the connection weights.

Neural networks are introduced in Section 2.2.3, as a major soft computing tool. We have devoted the whole of Chapter 5 to the principles and techniques for classification.

1.9 CLUSTERING

A cluster is a collection of data objects which are similar to one another within the same cluster but dissimilar to the objects in other clusters. Cluster analysis refers to the grouping of a set of data objects into clusters. Clustering is also called unsupervised classification, where no predefined classes are assigned [35].

Some general applications of clustering include

- Pattern recognition.

- Spatial data analysis: creating thematic maps in geographic information systems (GIS) by clustering feature spaces, and detecting spatial clusters and explaining them in spatial data mining.

- Image processing: segmenting for object-background identification.

- Multimedia computing: finding the cluster of images containing flowers of similar color and shape from a multimedia database.

- Medical analysis: detecting abnormal growth from MRI.

- Bioinformatics: determining clusters of signatures from a gene database.

- Biometrics: creating clusters of facial images with similar fiduciary points.

- Economic science: undertaking market research.

- WWW: clustering Weblog data to discover groups of similar access patterns.

A good clustering method will produce high-quality clusters with high *intraclass* similarity and low *interclass* similarity. The quality of a clustering result depends on both (a) the similarity measure used by the method and (b) its implementation. It is measured by the ability of the system to discover some or all of the hidden patterns.

Clustering approaches can be broadly categorized as

1. Partitional: Create an initial partition and then use an iterative control strategy to optimize an objective.

2. Hierarchical: Create a hierarchical decomposition (dendogram) of the set of data (or objects) using some termination criterion.

3. Density-based: Use connectivity and density functions.

4. Grid-based: Create multiple-level granular structure, by quantizing the feature space in terms of finite cells.

Clustering, when used for data mining, is required to be (i) scalable, (ii) able to deal with different types of attributes, (iii) able to discover clusters with arbitrary shape, (iv) having minimal requirements for domain knowledge to determine input parameters, (v) able to deal with noise and outliers, (vi) insensitive to order of input records, (vii) of high dimensionality, and (viii) interpretable and usable. Further details on clustering are provided in Chapter 6.

1.10   RULE MINING

Rule mining refers to the discovery of the relationship(s) between the attributes of a dataset, say, a set of *transactions*. Market basket data consist of a set of items bought together by customers, one such set of items being called a transaction. A lot of work has been done in recent years to find associations among items in large groups of transactions [39, 40].

A rule is normally expressed in the form $X \Rightarrow Y$, where X and Y are sets of attributes of the dataset. This implies that transactions which contain X also contain Y. A rule is normally expressed as IF $< some\_conditions\_satisfied >$ THEN $< predict\_values\_for\_some\_other\_attributes >$. So the association $X \Rightarrow Y$ is expressed as IF X THEN Y. A sample rule could be of the form

IF $(salary \geq 12000)$ AND $(unpaid\_loan = "no")$
THEN $(select\_for\_loan = "yes")$.

Rule mining can be categorized as

1. Association rule mining: An expression of the form $X \Rightarrow Y$, where X and Y are subsets of all attributes, and the implication holds with a confidence $\geq c$, where c is a user-defined threshold. This implies IF X THEN Y, with at least c confidence.

2. Classification rule mining: A supervised process uses a training dataset to generate the rules. The objective is to predict a predefined class or goal attribute, which can never appear in the antecedent part of a rule. The generated rules are used to predict the class attribute of an unknown test dataset.

3. Dependency rule modeling: This is also a supervised process, with the goal attribute being chosen from a predefined set of attributes. While non-goal attributes can occur only in the antecedent part of a rule, the goal attributes can appear in either its consequent or antecedent parts.

Let us consider an example from medical decision-making. Often data may be missing for various reasons; for example, some examinations can be risky for the patient or contraindications can exist, an urgent diagnostic decision may need to be made and some very informative but prolonged test results may have to be excluded from the feature set, or appropriate technical equipment may not be available. In such cases, the system can *query* the user for additional information only when it is particularly necessary to infer a decision. Again, one realizes that the final responsibility for any diagnostic decision always has to be accepted by the medical practitioner. So the physician may want to verify the justification behind the decision reached, based on personal expertise. This requires the system to be able to explain its mode of reasoning for any inferred decision or recommendation, preferably in classification rule form, to convince the user that its reasoning is correct.

Important association rule mining techniques have been considered in detail in Chapter 7. Generation of classification rules, in a modular framework, have been described in Chapter 8.

1.11 STRING MATCHING

String matching is a very important area of research for successful development of data mining systems, particularly for text databases and in mining of data through the Internet by a text-based search engine. In this section, we briefly introduce the string matching problem [24].

Let $P = a_1 a_2 \ldots a_m$ and $T = b_1 b_2 \ldots b_n$ denote finite strings (or sequences) of characters (or symbols) over a finite alphabet Σ, where m, n are positive integers greater than 0. In its simplest form, the *pattern* or *string match-ing* problem consists of searching the text T to find the occurrence(s) of the pattern P in T $(m \leq n)$.

Several variants of the basic problem can be considered. The pattern may consist of a finite set of sequences $P = \{P^1, P^2, \ldots, P^k\}$, where each P^i is a pattern from the same alphabet and the problem is to search for occurrence(s) of any one of the members of the set in the text. The patterns may be *fully* or *partially specified*.

- Let \$ denote a *"don't care"* or *"wild card"* character; then the pattern $A\$B$ denotes a set of patterns AAB, ABB, ACB, etc. – that is, any pattern that begins with A, ends with B, and has a single unspecified character in the middle. The character \$ is called a *"fixed length don't care"* (*FLDC*) character and may appear at any place in the pattern.

- A special character ϕ is used to denote the infinite set of patterns $\phi = \{\$, \$\$, \$\$\$, \ldots\}$ and is called a *"variable length don't care"* (*VLDC*) character.

Patterns containing special characters \$ or ϕ are called partially specified; otherwise, they are termed fully specified.

The string matching problem has been extensively studied in the litera-ture. Several linear time algorithms for the *exact* pattern matching problem (involving fully specified patterns) have been developed by researchers [41]–[43].

No linear time algorithm is yet known for the string matching problem with a partially specified pattern. The best known result for pattern matching us-ing a pattern consisting of wild card characters is by Fischer and Patterson [44] with complexity $O(n \log^2 m \log \log m \log c)$, where c is the size of the alpha-bet. Several two-dimensional exact pattern matching algorithms have been proposed in Refs. [45]–[47].

There are other variation of the string matching when the pattern is not fully specified. For example, finding the occurrences of similar patterns with small differences in the text. Let us consider trying to find the occurrences of patterns similar to (say) "birth," with maximum difference in two character positions in the text. Here the patterns "birth," "broth," "booth," "worth," "dirty," etc., will be considered to be valid occurrence in the text. All these above variations of the string matching problem is usually known as *Approx-imate String Matching* in the literature.

The string (or pattern) matching problem becomes even more interest-ing when one attempts to directly match a pattern in a compressed text or database. String matching finds widespread applications in diverse areas such as text editing, text search, information retrieval, text mining, Web mining, Bioinformatics, etc. String matching is a very essential component in text analysis and retrieval in order to automatically extract the words, keywords, and set of terms in a document, and also in query processing when used in text mining.

We have devoted Chapter 4 to string matching, encompassing a detailed description of the classical algorithms along with a number of examples for each of them.

1.12   BIOINFORMATICS

A gene is a fundamental constituent of any living organism. Sequence of genes in a human body represent the signature(s) of the person. The genes are portions of the deoxyribonucleic acid, or DNA for short. J. D. Watson and F. H. Crick proposed a structure of DNA in 1953, consisting of two strands or chains. Each of these chains is composed of *phosphate* and *deoxyribose sugar* molecules joined together by covalent bonds. A *nitrogenous* base is attached to each sugar molecule. There are four bases: *adenine* [A], *cytosine* [C], *guanine* [G], and *thymine* [T]. From information theoretic perspective, the DNA can be considered as a string or sequence of symbols. Each symbol is one of the four above bases A, C, G, or T.

In the human body there are approximately 3 billion such base pairs. The whole stretch of the DNA is called the *genome* of an organism. Obviously, such a long stretch of DNA cannot be sequenced all at once. Mapping, search, and analysis of patterns in such long sequences can be combinatorially explosive and can be impractical to process even in today's powerful digital computers.

Typically, a DNA sequence may be 40,000–100,000 base pairs long. In practice, such a long stretch of DNA is first broken up into 400–2000 small fragments. Each such small fragment typically consists of approximately 1000 base pairs. These fragments are sequenced experimentally, and then reassembled together to reconstruct the original DNA sequence. Genes are encoded in these fragments of DNA. Understanding what parts of the genome encode which genes is a main area of study in computational molecular biology or Bioinformatics [7, 48]. The results of string matching algorithms and their derivatives have been applied in search, analysis and sequencing of DNA, and other developments in Bioinformatics.

Microarray experiments are done to produce gene expression patterns, that provide dynamic information about cell function. The huge volume of such data, and their high dimensions, make gene expression data to be suitable candidates for the application of data mining functions like clustering, visualization, and string matching. Visualization is used to transform these high-dimensional data to lower-dimensional, human understandable form. This aids subsequent useful analysis, leading to efficient knowledge discovery. Microarray technologies are utilized to evaluate the level of expression of thousands of genes, with applications in colon, breast, and blood cancer treatment [48].

Proteins are made up of polypeptide chains of amino acids, which consist of the DNA as the building block. General principles of protein structure, stability, and folding kinetics are being explored in Bioinformatics, using lattice models. These models represent protein chains involving some parameters, and they allow complete explorations of conformational and sequence spaces. Interactions among spatially neighboring amino acids, during folding, are controlled by such factors as bond length, bond angle, electrostatic forces, hydrogen bonding, hydrophobicity, entropy, etc. [49]. The determination of an optimal conformation of a three-dimensional protein structure constitutes protein folding. This has wide-ranging applications in *pharmacogenomics*, and more specifically to drug design.

The different aspects of the applicability of data mining to Bioinformatics are described in detail in Chapter 10.

1.13   DATA WAREHOUSING

A data warehouse is a decision support database that is maintained separately from the organizations operational database. It supports information processing by providing a solid platform of consolidated, historical data for analysis. A data warehouse [13] is a subject-oriented, integrated, time-variant, and nonvolatile collection of data in support of managements decision-making process. Data warehousing deals with the process of constructing and using data warehouses.

Database systems are of two types, namely, on-line transaction processing systems, like OLTP; and decision support systems, like warehouses, on-line analytical processing (OLAP), and mining. Historical data from OLTP systems form decision support systems, the goal being to learn from past experiences. While OLTP involves many short, update-intensive commands, a decision support system requires fewer but complex queries. OLTP is a major task of traditional relational database management systems. It involves day-to-day operations like purchasing, inventory, banking, manufacturing, payroll, registration, accounting, etc. OLAP, on the other hand, is a primary task of a data warehouse system. It concentrates on data analysis and decision making, based on the content of the data warehouse.

A data warehouse is subject-oriented, being organized around major subjects such as customer, product, and sales. It is constructed by integrating multiple, heterogeneous data sources, like relational databases, flat files, and on-line transaction records, in a uniform format. Data cleaning and data integration techniques are applied to ensure consistency in naming conventions, encoding structures, attribute measures, etc., among different data sources.

While an operational database is concerned with current value data, the data warehouse provides information from a historical perspective (e.g., past 5–10 years). Every key structure in the data warehouse contains an element of time, explicitly or implicitly, although the key of operational data may or may not contain the time element. Data warehouse constitutes a physically separate store of data, transformed from the operational environment. Operational update of data does not occur in the data warehouse environment.

It does not require transaction processing, recovery, and concurrency control mechanisms. It requires only two operations, namely, initial loading of data and its access.

Traditional heterogeneous databases build wrappers or mediators on top of the databases and adopt a query-driven approach. When a query is posed to a client site, a meta-dictionary is used to translate the query into a form appropriate for individual heterogeneous sites involved, and the results are integrated into a global answer set. This involves complex information filtering and a competition for resources. Data warehouses, on the other hand, are high-performance systems providing a multidimensional view for complex OLAP queries. Information from heterogeneous sources is integrated in advance, and it is stored in warehouses for direct query and analysis.

OLAP helps provide fast, interactive answers to large aggregate queries at multiple levels of abstraction. A *data cube* allows such multidimensional data to be effectively modeled and viewed in the n dimensions. Typical OLAP operations include

1. Roll up (drill-up): Summarize data by climbing up hierarchy or by dimension reduction.

2. Drill down (roll down): Reverse of roll-up from higher level summary to lower level summary or detailed data, or introducing new dimensions.

3. Slice and dice: Project and select.

4. Pivot (rotate): Reorient the cube, transform from $3D$ to a series of $2D$ planes, and provide better visualization.

5. Drill across: Involving more than one fact table.

6. Drill through: From the bottom level of the cube to its back-end relational tables (using structured query languages SQL).

1.14 APPLICATIONS AND CHALLENGES

Some of the important issues in data mining include the identification of applications for existing techniques, and developing new techniques for traditional as well as new application domains, like the Web, E-commerce, and Bioinformatics. Some of the existing practical uses of data mining exist in (i) tracking fraud, (ii) tracking game strategy, (iii) target marketing, (iv) holding on to good customers, and (v) weeding out bad customers, to name a few. There are many other areas we can envisage, where data mining can be applied. Some of these areas are as follows.

- Medicine: Determine disease outcome and effectiveness of treatments, by analyzing patient disease history to find some relationship between diseases.

- Molecular or pharmaceutical: Identify new drugs.

- Security: Face recognition, identification, biometrics, etc.

- Judiciary: Search and access of historical data on judgement of similar cases.

- Biometrics: Positive identification of a person from a large image, fingerprint or voice database.

- Multimedia retrieval: Search and identification of image, video, voice, and text from multimedia database, which may be compressed.

- Scientific data analysis: Identify new galaxies by searching for subclusters.

- Web site or Web store design, and promotion: Find affinity of visitors to Web pages, followed by subsequent layout modification.

- Marketing: Help marketers discover distinct groups in their customer bases, and then use this knowledge to develop targeted marketing programs.

- Land use: Identify areas of similar land use in an earth observation database.

- Insurance: Identify groups of motor insurance policy holders with a high average claim cost.

- City-planning: Identify groups of houses according to their house type, value, and geographical location.

- Geological studies: Infer that observed earthquake epicenters are likely to be clustered along continental faults.

The first generation of data mining algorithms has been demonstrated to be of significant value across a variety of real-world applications. But these work best for problems involving a large set of data collected into a single database, where the data are described by numeric or symbolic features. Here the data invariably do not contain text and image features interleaved with these features, and they are carefully and cleanly collected with a particular decision-making task in mind.

Development of new generation algorithms is expected to encompass more diverse sources and types of data that will support mixed-initiative data mining, where human experts collaborate with the computer to form hypotheses and test them. The main challenges to the data mining procedure, to be considered for future research, involve the following.

1. *Massive datasets and high dimensionality.* Huge datasets create combinatorially explosive search space for model induction, and they increase

the chances that a data mining algorithm will find spurious patterns that are not generally valid. Possible solutions include robust and efficient algorithms, sampling approximation methods, and parallel processing. Scaling up of existing techniques is needed – for example, in the cases of classification, clustering, and rule mining.

2. *User interaction and prior knowledge.* Data mining is inherently an interactive and iterative process. Users may interact at various stages, and domain knowledge may be used either in the form of a high-level specification of the model or at a more detailed level. Visualization of the extracted model is also desirable for better user interaction at different levels.

3. *Over-fitting and assessing the statistical significance.* Datasets used for mining are usually huge and available from distributed sources. As a result, often the presence of spurious data points leads to over-fitting of the models. Regularization and re-sampling methodologies need to be emphasized for model design.

4. *Understandability of patterns.* It is necessary to make the discoveries more understandable to humans. Possible solutions include rule structuring, natural language representation, and the visualization of data and knowledge.

5. *Nonstandard and incomplete data.* The data can be missing and/or noisy. These need to be handled appropriately.

6. *Mixed media data.* Learning from data that are represented by a combination of various media, like (say) numeric, symbolic, images, and text.

7. *Management of changing data and knowledge.* Rapidly changing data, in a database that is modified or deleted or augmented, may make previously discovered patterns invalid. Possible solutions include incremental methods for updating the patterns.

8. *Integration.* Data mining tools are often only a part of the entire decision-making system. It is desirable that they integrate smoothly, both with the database and the final decision-making procedure.

9. *Compression.* Storage of large multimedia databases is often required to be in compressed form. Hence the development of compression technology, particularly suitable for data mining, is required. It would be even more beneficial if data can be accessed in the compressed domain [24].

10. *Human Perceptual aspects for data mining.* Many multimedia data mining systems are intended to be used by humans. So it is a pragmatic

approach to design multimedia systems and underlying data mining techniques based on the needs and capabilities of the human perceptual system. The ultimate consumer of most perceptual information is the '*Human Perceptual System*'. Primarily, the *Human Perceptual System* consists of the '*Human Visual System*' and the '*Human Auditory System*'. How these systems work synergistically is still not completely understood and is a subject of ongoing research. We also need to focus some attention in this direction so that their underlying principles can be adopted while developing data mining techniques, in order to make these more amenable and natural to the human customer.

11. *Distributed database.* Interest in the development of data mining systems in a distributed environment will continue to grow. In today's networked society, data are not stored or archived in a single storage system unit. Problems arise while handling extremely large heterogeneous databases spread over multiple files, possibly in different disks or across the Web in different geographical locations. Often combining such data in a single very large file may be infeasible. Development of algorithms for mining data from distributed databases will open up newer areas of applications in the near future.

1.15 CONCLUSIONS AND DISCUSSION

Data mining is a good area of scientific study, holding ample promise for the research community. Recently a lot of progress has been reported for large databases, specifically involving association rules, classification, clustering, similar time sequences, similar text document retrieval, similar image retrieval, outlier discovery, etc. Many papers have been published in major conferences and leading journals. However, it still remains a promising and rich field with many challenging research issues.

In this chapter we have provided an introduction to knowledge discovery from databases and data mining. The major functions of data mining have been described from the perspectives of machine learning, pattern recognition, and artificial intelligence. Handling of multimedia data, their compression, matching, and their implications to text and image mining have been discussed. We have also stated principles of string matching, explaining how they can be applied in text retrieval and in Bioinformatics for DNA search type of operations. Different application domains and research challenges have also been highlighted.

Since the databases to be mined are often very large, parallel algorithms are desirable [50]. However, one has to explore a trade-off between computation, communication, memory usage, synchronization, and the use of problem-specific information, in order to select a suitable parallel algorithm for data mining. One can also partition the data appropriately and distribute the subsets to multiple processors, learning concept descriptions in parallel and then combining them. This corresponds to loosely coupled collections of otherwise independent algorithms and is termed *distributed data mining* [51]. Traditional data mining algorithms require all data to be mined in a single, centralized data warehouse. A fundamental challenge is to develop distributed versions of data mining algorithms, so that data mining can be done while leaving some of the data in different places. In addition, appropriate protocols, languages, and network services are required for mining distributed data, handling the meta-data and the mappings required for mining the distributed data.

Spatial database systems involve spatial data – that is, point objects or spatially extended objects in a 2D/3D or some high-dimensional feature space. Knowledge discovery is becoming more and more important in these databases, as increasingly large amounts of data obtained from satellite images, X-ray crystallography, or other automatic equipment are being stored in the spatial framework. Image mining holds promise in handling such databases. Moreover, Bioinformatics offers applications in modeling or analyzing protein structures that are represented as spatial data.

There exist plenty of scope for the use of soft computing in data mining, because of the imprecise nature of data in many application domains. For example, neural nets can help in the learning, the fuzzy sets for natural language representation and imprecision handling, and the genetic algorithms for search and optimization. However, not much work has been reported in the use of soft computing tools in data mining. The relevance of soft computing lies in its ability to (i) handle subjectivity, imprecision, and uncertainty in queries, (ii) model document relevance as a *gradual* instead of a *crisp* property, (iii) provide deduction capability to the search engines, (iv) provide personalization and learning capability, and (v) deal with the dynamism, scale, and heterogeneity of Web documents.

We take this opportunity to compile in this book the existing literature on the various aspects of data mining, highlighting its application to multimedia information and Bioinformatics. Soft computing, an emergent technology, has also demonstrated ample promise in data mining. Chapter 2 focuses on an introduction to soft computing, its tools, and finally its role in the different functions of data mining. The fundamentals of multimedia data compression, particularly text and image compression, are dealt with in Chapter 3. Chapter 4 deals in-depth with various issues in string matching. Here we provide examples to show how patterns are matched in general text, as well as how they can be applied in DNA matching in Bioinformatics. The different tasks of data mining like classification, clustering and association rules are covered in Chapters 5, 6, and 7, respectively. The issue of rule generation and modular hybridization, in the soft computing framework, is described in Chapter 8. Multimedia data mining, including text mining, image mining, and Web mining, is dealt with in Chapter 9. Finally, certain aspects of Bioinformatics, as an application of data mining, are discussed in Chapter 10.

REFERENCES

1. U. Fayyad and R. Uthurusamy, "Data mining and knowledge discovery in databases," *Communications of the ACM*, vol. 39, pp. 24–27, 1996.

2. W. H. Inmon, "The data warehouse and data mining," *Communications of the ACM*, vol. 39, pp. 49–50, 1996.

3. T. Acharya and W. Metz, "Multimedia applications: Issues and challenges," in *Proceedings of the International Conference on Communications, Computers and Devices* (Indian Institute of Technology, Kharagpur, India), pp. 27–34, December 2000.

4. P. Piatetsky-Shapiro and W. J. Frawley, eds., *Knowledge Discovery in Databases.* Menlo Park, CA: AAAI/MIT Press, 1991.

5. President's Information Technology Advisory Committee's report, Washington, *http://www.ccic.gov/ac/interim/*, 1998.

6. M. Lesk, *Practical Digital Libraries: Books, Bytes, and Bucks.* San Francisco: Morgan Kaufmann, 1997.

7. S. L. Salzberg, D. B. Searls, and S. Kasif, eds., *Computational Methods in Molecular Biology.* Amsterdam: Elsevier Sciences B. V., 1998.

8. R. L. Blum, *Discovery and Representation of Causal Relationships from a Large Time-Oriented Clinical Database: The RX Project*, vol. 19 of *Lecture Notes in Medical Informatics.* New York: Spinger-Verlag, 1982.

9. J. A. Major and D. R. Riedinger, "EFD–a hybrid knowledge statistical-based system for the detection of fraud," *International Journal of Intelligent Systems*, vol. 7, pp. 687–703, 1992.

10. R. Heider, "Troubleshooting CFM 56-3 engines for the Boeing 737–using CBR and data-mining," *Lecture Notes in Computer Science*, vol. 1168, pp. 512–523, 1996.

11. U. Fayyad, D. Haussler, and P. Stolorz, "Mining scientific data," *Communications of the ACM*, vol. 39, pp. 51–57, 1996.

12. O. Etzioni, "The World-Wide Web: Quagmire or goldmine?," *Communications of the ACM*, vol. 39, pp. 65–68, 1996.

13. J. Han and M. Kamber, *Data Mining: Concepts and Techniques.* San Diego: Academic Press, 2001.

14. S. Mitra, S. K. Pal, and P. Mitra, "Data mining in soft computing framework: A survey," *IEEE Transactions on Neural Networks*, vol. 13, pp. 3–14, 2002.

15. D. Hand, H. Mannila, and P. Smyth, *Principles of Data Mining*. London: MIT Press, 2001.

16. M. Kantardzic, *Data Mining: Concepts, Models, Methods, and Algorithms*. Hoboken, NJ: Wiley Interscience, IEEE Press, 2002.

17. U. M. Fayyad, G. Piatetsky-Shapiro, P. Smyth, and R. Uthurusamy, eds., *Advances in Knowledge Discovery and Data Mining*. Menlo Park, CA: AAAI/MIT Press, 1996.

18. "Special issue on knowledge discovery in data- and knowledge bases," *International Journal of Intelligent Systems*, vol. 7, no. 7, 1992.

19. K. J. Cios, W. Pedrycz, and R. Swiniarski, *Data Mining Methods for Knowledge Discovery*. Dordrecht: Kluwer, 1998.

20. U. Fayyad, G. P. Shapiro, and P. Smyth, "The KDD process for extracting useful knowledge from volumes of data," *Communications of the ACM*, vol. 39, pp. 27–34, 1996.

21. A. Silberschatz and A. Tuzhilin, "What makes patterns interesting in knowledge discovery systems," *IEEE Transactions on Knowledge and Data Engineering*, vol. 8, pp. 970–974, 1996.

22. T. M. Mitchell, "Machine learning and data mining," *Communications of the ACM*, vol. 42, pp. 30–36, 1999.

23. F. Provost and V. Kolluri, "A survey of methods for scaling up inductive algorithms," *Data Mining and Knowledge Discovery*, vol. 2, pp. 131–169, 1999.

24. T. Acharya, *VLSI Algorithms and Architectures for Data Compression*. Ph.D. thesis, Department of Computer Science, University of Central Florida, Orlando, FL, August 1994.

25. K. Sayood, *Introduction to Data Compression*. San Francisco: Morgan Kaufmann, 2000.

26. P. Mitra, C. A. Murthy, and S. K. Pal, "Density based multiscale data condensation," *IEEE Transactions on Pattern Analysis and Machine Intelligence*, vol. 24, pp. 734–747, 2002.

27. R. Kohavi, B. Masand, M. Spilipoulou, and J. Srivastava, "Web mining," *Data Mining and Knowledge Discovery*, vol. 6, pp. 5–8, 2002.

28. R. Baeza-Yates and B. Ribeiro-Neto, *Modern Information Retrieval*. Reading, MA: Addison-Wesley, 1999.

29. G. Salton and M. J. McGill, *Introduction to Modern Information Retrieval*. New York: McGraw-Hill, 1983.

30. O. Etzioni and D. S. Weld, "Intelligent agents on the Internet: Facts, fiction, and forecast," *IEEE Expert*, vol. 10, pp. 44–49, August 1995.

31. P. Maes, "Agents that reduce work and information overload," *Communications of the ACM*, vol. 37, pp. 30–40, 1994.

32. I. H. Witten, A. Moffat, and T. C. Bell, *Managing Gigabytes: Compressing and Indexing Documents and Images*. San Francisco: Morgan Kaufmann, 1999.

33. J. Zhang, W. Hsu, and M. L. Lee, "Image mining: Issues, frameworks and techniques," in *Proceedings of the 2nd International Workshop on Multimedia Data Mining and the ACM SIGKDD Conference (MDM/KDD '01)* (San Francisco), pp. 13–20, August 2001.

34. A. Vailaya, A. T. Figueiredo, A. K. Jain, and H. J. Zhang, "Image classification for content-based indexing," *IEEE Transactions on Image Processing*, vol. 10, pp. 117–130, 2001.

35. J. T. Tou and R. C. Gonzalez, *Pattern Recognition Principles*. London: Addison-Wesley, 1974.

36. J. R. Quinlan, "Induction on decision trees," *Machine Learning*, vol. 1, pp. 81–106, 1986.

37. L. Breiman, J. H. Friedman, R. A. Olshen, and C. J. Stone, *Classification and Regression Trees*. Monterey, CA: Wadsworth and Brooks/Cole, 1984.

38. S. Haykin, *Neural Networks: A Comprehensive Foundation*. New York: Macmillan College Publishing Co., 1994.

39. R. Agrawal, T. Imielinski, and A. Swami, "Mining association rules between sets of items in large databases," in *Proceedings of 1993 ACM SIGMOD International Conference on Management of Data* (Washington, D.C.), pp. 207–216, May 1993.

40. R. Agrawal and R. Srikant, "Fast algorithms for mining association rules in large databases," in *Proceedings of 20th International Conference on Very Large Databases*, pp. 478–499, September 1994.

41. D. Knuth, J. Morris, and V. Pratt, "Fast pattern matching in strings," *SIAM Journal of Computing*, vol. 6, pp. 323–350, 1977.

42. R. Boyer and J. A. Moore, "A fast string searching algorithm," *Communications of the ACM*, vol. 20, pp. 762–772, 1977.

43. G. A. Stephen, *String Searching Algorithms*. Singapore: World Scientific, 2001.

44. M. J. Fischer and M. S. Paterson, "String matching and other products," in *Complexity of Computation, SIAM-AMS Proceedings* (R. M. Karp, ed.), vol. 7, pp. 113–125, 1974.

45. T. P. Baker, "A technique for extending rapid exact-match string matching to arrays of more than one dimension," *SIAM Journal of Computing*, vol. 7, pp. 533–541, 1978.

46. R. S. Bird, "Two dimensional pattern matching," *Information Processing Letters*, vol. 6, pp. 168–170, 1977.

47. A. Amir, G. M. Landau, and U. Vishkin, "Efficient pattern matching with scaling," *Journal of Algorithms*, vol. 13, pp. 2–32, 1992.

48. "Special Issue on Bioinformatics, Part I: Advances and Challenges," *Proceedings of the IEEE*, vol. 90, November 2002.

49. K. A. Dill, S. Bromberg, K. Yue, K. M. Fiebig, D. P. Yee, P. D. Thomas, and H. S. Chan, "Principles of protein folding–A perspective from simple exact models," *Protein Science*, vol. 4, pp. 561–602, 1995.

50. R. Agrawal and J. C. Shafer, "Parallel mining of association rules," *IEEE Transactions on Knowledge and Data Engineering*, vol. 8, pp. 962–969, 1996.

51. H. Kargupta and P. Chan, eds., *Advances in Distributed and Parallel Knowledge Discovery*. Cambridge, MA: MIT Press, 2000.

2

Soft Computing

2.1 INTRODUCTION

Data mining is a form of knowledge discovery essential for solving problems in domains involving large volumes of data. The individual datasets may be gathered and studied collectively for purposes other than those for which they were originally created. New knowledge may also be obtained in the process, while eliminating the cost of additional data collection. Besides, data often exist in vast quantities over the Internet in an unstructured format. The application of data mining facilitates systematic analysis in such cases and helps the user in extracting relevant information. Sometimes different kinds of data can be interspersed for better semantic representation, and often data may be erroneous.

As an example, in medical data, numeric and textual information may be interspersed, different symbols can be used with the same meaning, redundancy often exists, and erroneous or misspelled medical terms are common. Hence a robust preprocessing system is required in order to extract any kind of knowledge from even medium-sized datasets.

Typically, real-life data must not only be cleaned of errors and redundancy, but must also be organized in a fashion that makes sense to the problem. There can exist imperfections in raw input data needed for knowledge acquisition, mainly due to uncertainty, vagueness, and incompleteness. While incompleteness arises due to missing or unknown data, uncertainty (or vagueness) can be caused by errors in physical measurements due to incorrect measuring devices or by a mixture of noisy and pure signals.

Soft computing is a consortium of methodologies that works synergistically and provides, in one form or another, flexible information processing capability for handling real-life ambiguous situations [1]. Its aim is to exploit the tolerance for imprecision, uncertainty, approximate reasoning, and partial truth in order to achieve tractability, robustness, and low-cost solutions. The guiding principle is to devise methods of computation that lead to an *acceptable* solution at *low* cost, by seeking for an approximate solution to an imprecisely or precisely formulated problem [2].

Recently, various soft computing methodologies have been applied to handle the different challenges posed by data mining [3]. The main constituents of soft computing, at this juncture, include fuzzy logic, neural networks, genetic algorithms, rough sets, and signal processing tools such as wavelets. Each of them contribute a distinct methodology for addressing problems in its domain. This is done in a cooperative, rather than a competitive, manner. The result is a more intelligent and robust system providing a human-interpretable, low-cost, approximate solution, as compared to traditional techniques.

This chapter provides an overview of the available literature on data mining, which is scarce, in the soft computing framework [3]. An introduction to soft computing and its constituent tools are provided in Section 2.2. Sections 2.3–2.8 explain the role of the different soft computing tools and their hybridizations, categorized on the basis of different data mining functions implemented. The utility and applicability of different soft computing methodologies is highlighted. It may be mentioned that there is no universally best data mining method; choosing particular soft computing tool(s) or some combination with traditional methods is entirely dependent on the particular application, and it requires human interaction to decide on the suitability of an approach.

Fuzzy sets provide a natural framework for the process in dealing with uncertainty or imprecise data. Generally, they are suitable for handling the issues related to understandability of patterns, incomplete and noisy data, and mixed media information and human interaction and can provide approximate solutions faster. Neural networks are nonparametric and robust and exhibit good learning and generalization capabilities in data-rich environments. Genetic algorithms (GAs) provide efficient search algorithms to optimally select a model, from mixed media data, based on some preference criterion or objective function. Rough sets are suitable for handling different types of uncertainty in data. Neural networks and rough sets are widely used for classification and rule generation. Application of wavelet-based signal processing techniques is new in the area of soft computing. Wavelet transformation of a signal results in decomposition of the original signal in different multiresolution subbands [4, 5]. This is useful in dealing with compression and retrieval of data, particularly images. Other approaches like case-based reasoning [6] and decision trees [7, 8] are also widely used to solve data mining problems.

Section 2.9 concludes the chapter. Some challenges to data mining and the possible application of soft computing methodologies are indicated.

2.2 WHAT IS SOFT COMPUTING?

Usually the primary considerations of traditional computing are precision, certainty, and rigor. We distinguish this as "hard" computing. In contrast, the principal notion in soft computing is that precision and certainty carry a cost; and that computation, reasoning, and decision-making should exploit (wherever possible) the tolerance for imprecision, uncertainty, approximate reasoning, and partial truth for obtaining low-cost solutions. This leads to the remarkable human ability of understanding distorted speech, deciphering sloppy handwriting, comprehending the nuances of natural language, summarizing text, recognizing and classifying images, driving a vehicle in dense traffic, and, more generally, making rational decisions in an environment of uncertainty and imprecision. The challenge, then, is to exploit the tolerance for imprecision by devising methods of computation that lead to *an acceptable solution at low cost*. This, in essence, is the guiding principle of soft computing [1].

There are ongoing efforts to integrate artificial neural networks (ANNs), fuzzy set theory, genetic algorithms (GAs), rough set theory and other methodologies in the *soft computing* paradigm. Hybridization [2, 9] exploiting the characteristics of these theories include *neuro-fuzzy, rough-fuzzy, neuro-genetic, fuzzy-genetic, neuro-rough, rough-neuro-fuzzy* approaches. However, among these, *neuro-fuzzy* computing is the most visible. Let us now begin our discussion by pointing out the relevance of soft computing.

2.2.1 Relevance

The traditional hard computing paradigm is seldom suitable for many real-life problems. Let us illustrate it with an example. Suppose that X is driving a car and X watches a "red light" (traffic signal). X has to stop. So X has to decide when to press the brake and how strongly. In a "precise framework," the steps followed by X may be to find the distance of the car from the "light," and then, depending on the current speed of the car, press the brake. To realize this, the car should be provided with a laser-gun-type arrangement so that the distance can be obtained. X should also know a set of rules of the form
"If the car is at a distance of d ft and moving at a speed of s ft/s, then press the brake with p poundal for t seconds right now."
This is a precise rule governed by the laws of physics. Hence, if the brake is applied according to such rules, the car will stop where X wants it to.

Theoretically, such concepts are fine, but impractical because of the following reasons:

- The addition of a laser gun to a car increases its cost.

- The number of precise rules required will be too great to realize in a practical system.

- For the sake of argument, even if we assume that we know the rules to be followed, application of the brakes following the rule will be a very difficult task.

Precise solutions are not always feasible. In fact, we do not need a precise solution to such a problem. The exact position where the car stops is not important, but it should stop before the "red light" and should not hit any other car standing ahead of it. Hence an approximate idea about the distance of the car from the car or traffic signal ahead and the speed of the car should be enough. Under this situation X can control the car using rules of the form "If the car is moving *very fast* and the 'red light' is *close,* then press the brake *pretty hard.*" We can easily say that the action is purely guided by the intuition of an individual, the resultant decision being taken in *imprecise* terms.

Note that the rule has three vague clauses "very fast," "close," and "pretty hard." These make the rule an imprecise one, and it will generate an approximate solution to the problem. The solution is less expensive and fast (real-time) also. This is one facet of what the soft computing paradigm for emulating the human-like decision making (also, a real-world computing system) attempts to achieve. Thus, to achieve higher machine IQ, the system should have the capability of modeling vagueness and making approximate decisions on that basis. Fuzzy sets are good for handling this aspect of soft computing. In fact, this distinguished characteristic of fuzzy sets led to the emergence of soft computing.

Let us now make the driving problem a bit more complex. Suppose that X is driving on a very crowded road and has to reach the destination D. From the present coordinate of X, there are a couple of alternative paths to reach D. Depending on the traffic conditions, X should try to pick up an optimal path. Note that the traffic conditions (traffic flows in either direction, number of traffic signals that will appear on a path, raining or clear, etc.) change with time, and hence what X thinks as the optimal path now may not remain optimal after some time. Consequently, X has to dynamically (adaptively) change the route. Human beings make approximate decisions for such problems on the basis of their experience (learning from previous driving experiences). If we want an intelligent system to achieve this capability, it should have the ability to learn from experience and examples. Artificial neural networks are adaptive systems and can deal with this aspect of the problem.

Any artificial neural network (ANN) that can be used for handling the problem just mentioned must be fed with relevant information. In other words, the ANN system has to be trained with adequate number of examples. The popular gradient descent (say, backpropagation)-type learning algorithms are usually very slow in learning and may get stuck at some local minimum. *Genetic algorithms* (GAs), in such situations, may be very effectively used for learning. If the number of free parameters of the network is large, GAs may also become slow, but for GA-based learning, the chance of getting stuck to a local minimum would be low. Consequently, we can expect a better generalization ability of the network.

In the remaining part of this section we present the basics of the different soft computing tools.

2.2.2 Fuzzy sets

We are continuously having to recognize people, objects, handwriting, voice, images, and other patterns, using distorted or unfamiliar, incomplete, occluded, fuzzy, and inconclusive data, where a pattern should be allowed to have membership or belongingness to more than one class. This is also very significant in (say) medical diagnosis, where a patient afflicted with a certain set of symptoms can be simultaneously suffering from more than one disease. Again, the symptoms need not necessarily be strictly numerical. It would be in *natural* terms, defined as linguistic and/or set variables such as *very high, more or less low, between* $50^{\circ}C$ *and* $55^{\circ}C$. This is how the concept of *fuzziness* comes into the picture.

Let us explain the concept of membership with an example. You ask a friend to meet you at 10 a.m. tomorrow. It is highly likely that your friend will arrive *any* time *around* 10 a.m., say, from 9.55 a.m. to 10.05 a.m. This defines the concept of a membership function along the time axis, with a peak (membership of 1) at 10 a.m. sharp having a bandwidth of 10 min. As you move away either side from the peak, the membership approaches the value 0. The bandwidth, again, is problem- and context-dependent. Hence if the person is serious, the bandwidth would be less, whereas otherwise the bandwidth would usually be more. Thus we see that although 10 a.m. is a *crisp* concept with $\{0, 1\}$ *hard* characterizing function, in reality it becomes fuzzy with $[0, 1]$ graded membership function. One may note that the membership value reflects the degree of compatibility or similarity of an event with an imprecise concept representing a fuzzy set, whereas the probability of an event is related to the number of times it occurs (i.e., its frequency).

Fuzzy sets were introduced in 1965 by Zadeh [10] as a new way of representing vagueness in everyday life. This theory provides an approximate and yet effective means for describing the characteristics of a system that is too complex or ill-defined to admit precise mathematical analysis [11, 12]. The fuzzy approach is based on the premise that the key elements in human thinking are not just numbers but can be approximated to tables of fuzzy sets, or, in other words, classes of objects in which the transition from membership to nonmembership is gradual rather than abrupt. Much of the logic behind human reasoning is not the traditional two-valued or even multivalued logic, but logic with fuzzy truths, fuzzy connectives, and fuzzy rules of inference.

Fuzzy set theory is reputed to handle, to a reasonable extent, uncertainties (arising from deficiencies of information) in various applications particularly in decision-making models under different kinds of risks, subjective judgment, vagueness, and ambiguity. The deficiencies may result from various reasons, namely, incomplete, imprecise, not fully reliable, vague, or contradictory information depending on the problem. Since this theory is a generalization of the classical set theory, it has greater flexibility to capture various aspects of incompleteness or imperfection in information about a situation.

The use of linguistic variables may be viewed as a form of data compression, which can be termed *granulation* [1]. The same effect can also be achieved by conventional quantization. However, in the case of quantization the values are intervals, whereas in the case of granulation the values are overlapping fuzzy sets. The advantages of granulation over quantization are that

- It is more general.

- It mimics the way in which humans interpret linguistic values.

- The transition from one linguistic value to a contiguous linguistic value is gradual rather than abrupt, resulting in continuity and robustness.

Again, the uncertainty in classification or clustering of patterns may arise from the overlapping nature of the various classes. This overlapping may result from fuzziness or randomness. In the conventional classification technique, it is usually assumed that a pattern belongs to only one class. This is not necessarily realistic physically, and certainly not mathematically. A pattern can and should be allowed to have degrees of membership in more than one class. It is therefore necessary to convey this information while classifying a pattern or clustering a dataset.

Let us now consider the problem of processing and recognizing a gray tone image pattern. In a conventional vision system, each operation in low level, middle level, and high level involves crisp decisions to make regions, features, primitives, relations, and interpretations crisp. Since the regions in an image are not always crisply defined, uncertainty can arise at every phase of recognition tasks. Therefore it becomes convenient and natural and may be appropriate to avoid committing ourselves to specific (hard) decision by allowing the segments or contours to be fuzzy subsets of the image; the subsets are characterized by the possibility (degree) of a pixel belonging to them.

A fuzzy set A in a space of points $R = \{r\}$ is a class of events with a continuum of grades of membership, and it is characterized by a membership function $\mu_A(r)$ that associates with each element in R a real number in the interval $[0, 1]$ with the value of $\mu_A(r)$ at r representing the grade of membership of r in A. Formally, a fuzzy set A with its finite number of supports

$r_1, r_2, \ldots, r_n$ is defined as a collection of ordered pairs

$$\begin{aligned} A &= \{(\mu_A(r_i), r_i), i = 1, 2, \ldots, n\} \\ &= \{(\tfrac{\mu_A(r_i)}{r_i}), i = 1, 2, \ldots, n\}, \end{aligned}$$

where the support of A is an ordinary subset of R and is defined as

$$S(A) = \{r | r \in R \text{ and } \mu_A(r) > 0\}.$$

Here μ_i, the grade of membership of r_i in A, denotes the degree to which an event r_i may be a member of A or belong to A. Note that $\mu_i = 1$ indicates the strict containment of the event r_i in A. If, on the other hand, r_i does not belong to A, then $\mu_i = 0$.

If the support of a fuzzy set is only a single point $r_1 \in R$, then

$$A = \frac{\mu_1}{r_1}$$

is called a *fuzzy singleton*. Thus $A = (1/r_1)$, for $\mu_1 = 1$, would obviously denote a nonfuzzy singleton.

In terms of the constituent singletons the fuzzy set A with its finite number of supports $r_1, r_2, \ldots, r_n$ can also be expressed in union form as

$$\begin{aligned} A &= \frac{\mu_1}{r_1} + \frac{\mu_2}{r_2} + \cdots + \frac{\mu_n}{r_n} \\ &= \sum_i \frac{\mu_i}{r_i}, \ i = 1, 2, \ldots, n \\ &= \bigcup_i \frac{\mu_i}{r_i}, \ i = 1, 2, \ldots, n, \end{aligned} \qquad (2.1)$$

where the $+$ sign denotes the union.

Fuzzy logic is based on the theory of fuzzy sets and, unlike classical logic, aims at modeling the imprecise (or inexact) modes of reasoning and thought processes (with linguistic variables) that play an essential role in the remarkable human ability to make rational decisions in an environment of uncertainty and imprecision. This ability depends, in turn, on our ability to infer an approximate answer to a question based on a store of knowledge that is inexact, incomplete, or not totally reliable. In fuzzy logic, everything, including truth, is a matter of degree [13]. Zadeh has developed a theory of approximate reasoning based on fuzzy set theory. By approximate reasoning we refer to a type of reasoning that is neither very exact nor very inexact. This theory aims at modeling the human reasoning and thinking process with linguistic variables [11] in order to handle both soft and hard data, as well as various types of uncertainty. Many aspects of the underlying concept have been incorporated in designing decision-making systems [14, 15].

Assignment of membership functions of a fuzzy subset is subjective in nature and reflects the context in which the problem is viewed. It cannot be assigned arbitrarily. In many cases, it is convenient to express the membership function of a fuzzy subset in terms of standard S and π functions. Note that fuzzy membership function and probability density function are conceptually different.

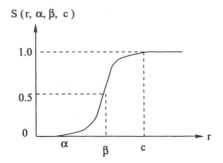

Fig. 2.1   Standard S function.

2.2.2.1 Membership functions   It is frequently convenient to employ standardized functions with adjustable parameters (e.g., the S and π functions) which are defined in the following equations (see also Fig. 2.1):

$$
\begin{aligned}
S(r;\ \alpha,\beta,c) &= 0 && \text{for } r \le \alpha \\
&= 2(\tfrac{r-\alpha}{c-\alpha})^2 && \text{for } \alpha \le r \le \beta \\
&= 1 - 2(\tfrac{r-c}{c-\alpha})^2 && \text{for } \beta \le r \le c \\
&= 1 && \text{for } r \ge c.
\end{aligned} \tag{2.2}
$$

$$
\begin{aligned}
\pi(r;\ c,\lambda) &= S(r; c-\lambda, c-\tfrac{\lambda}{2}, c) && \text{for } r \le c \\
&= 1 - S(r; c, c+\tfrac{\lambda}{2}, c+\lambda) && \text{for } r \ge c.
\end{aligned} \tag{2.3}
$$

In $S(r;\ \alpha,\beta,c)$, the parameter $\beta,\beta = (\alpha+c)/2$, is the *crossover point*, that is, the value of r at which S takes the value 0.5. In $\pi(r; c,\lambda)$, λ is the *bandwidth*, that is, the distance between the crossover points of π, while c is the central point at which π is unity.

Let us consider the linguistic variable age (x). Here the linguistic values *young* and *old* play the role of primary fuzzy sets which have a specified meaning, for example,

$$
\mu_{young} = 1 - S(20, 30, 40), \tag{2.4}
$$

$$
\mu_{old} = S(50, 60, 70), \tag{2.5}
$$

where the S and π functions are defined by Eqs. (2.2) and (2.3), and μ_{young} and μ_{old} denote the membership functions of *young* and *old*, respectively.

In pattern recognition problems we often need to represent a class with fuzzy boundary in terms of a π function. A representation for such a π function, with range [0,1] and $r \in I\!\!R^n$, may be given as [2]

$$
\pi(r; c, \lambda) = \begin{cases}
2\left(1 - \frac{\|r-c\|}{\lambda}\right)^2, & \text{for } \frac{\lambda}{2} \le \|r-c\| \le \lambda \\
1 - 2\left(\frac{\|r-c\|}{\lambda}\right)^2, & \text{for } 0 \le \|r-c\| \le \frac{\lambda}{2} \\
0, & \text{otherwise,}
\end{cases} \tag{2.6}
$$

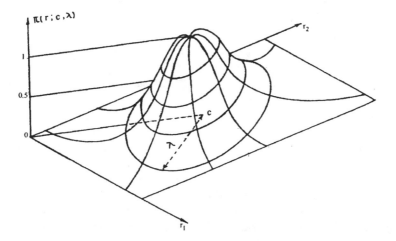

Fig. 2.2 π function when $r \in R^2$.

where $\lambda > 0$ is the radius of the π function with c as the central point and $\|.\|$ denotes the Euclidean norm. This is shown in Fig. 2.2 for $r \in I\!\!R^2$. Note that when the pattern r lies at the central point c of a class, then $\|r - c\| = 0$ and its membership value is maximum, that is, $\pi(c; c, \lambda) = 1$. The membership value of a point decreases as its distance from the central point c (i.e., $\|r-c\|$) increases. When $\|r - c\| = \lambda/2$, the membership value of r is 0.5, and this is called a *crossover* point.

2.2.2.2 *Basic operations*
Basic operations related to fuzzy subsets A and B of R having membership values $\mu_A(r)$ and $\mu_B(r)$, $r \in R$ respectively, are summarized here [15].

- A is equal to B (i.e., $A = B$) $\Rightarrow \mu_A(r) = \mu_B(r)$, for all $r \in R$.

- A is a complement of B (i.e., $A = \overline{B}$) $\Rightarrow \mu_A(r) = \mu_{\overline{B}}(r) = 1 - \mu_B(r)$ for all $r \in R$.

- A is contained in B ($A \subseteq B$) $\Rightarrow \mu_A(r) \leq \mu_B(r)$ for all $r \in R$.

- The union of A and B ($A \cup B$) $\Rightarrow \mu_{A \cup B}(r) = \vee(\mu_A(r), \mu_B(r))$ for all $r \in R$, where $\vee$ denotes maximum.

- The intersection of A and B ($A \cap B$) $\Rightarrow \mu_{A \cap B}(r) = \wedge(\mu_A(r), \mu_B(r))$ for all $r \in R$, where $\wedge$ denotes minimum.

We also have the modifiers *not, very,* and *more or less*. These are explained, in terms of the linguistic value *young*, as follows:

$$\mu_{not\ young} = 1 - \mu_{young}, \tag{2.7}$$

$$\mu_{very\ young} = (\mu_{young})^2, \tag{2.8}$$

$$\mu_{not\ very\ young} = 1 - (\mu_{young})^2, \tag{2.9}$$

$$\mu_{more\ or\ less\ young} = (\mu_{young})^{0.5}. \tag{2.10}$$

2.2.3 Neural networks

There are millions of very simple processing elements or *neurons* in the brain, linked together in a massively parallel manner. This is believed to be responsible for the human intelligence and discriminating power. All information is stored in a distributed fashion among the connection weights. There is also a large amount of redundancy inherent among the connections, leading to a *graceful degradation* of performance in case of any damage. Artificial neural networks (ANNs) or connectionist models implement important aspects of a pattern recognition system like robustness, adaptivity, speed, and learning. An ANN learns through examples the discriminating characteristics among various pattern classes, by reducing the error and automatically discovering inherent relationships in a data-rich environment. No rules or programmed information sequences need to be specified beforehand. This procedure bears an analogy to how a baby learns to recognize objects, or perhaps learns to speak.

Artificial neural networks (ANNs) [16]–[21] are signal processing systems that try to emulate the behavior of biological nervous systems by providing a mathematical model of combination of numerous neurons connected in a network. These can be formally defined as *massively parallel interconnections of simple (usually adaptive) processing elements that interact with objects of the real world in a manner similar to biological systems*. ANNs attempt to replicate the *computational* power (low-level arithmetic processing ability) of biological neural networks and, thereby, hopefully endow machines with some of the (higher-level) *cognitive abilities* that biological organisms possess (due in part, perhaps, to their low-level computational prowess).

The origin of ANNs can be traced to the work of Hebb [22], where a local learning rule was proposed. This rule assumed that correlations between the states of two neurons determined the strength of the coupling between them. Subsequently, a synaptic connection that was very active grew in strength and vice versa.

The various models are designated by the network topology, node characteristics, and the status updating rules. Network topology refers to the structure of interconnections among the various nodes (neurons) in terms of layers and/or feedback or feedforward links. Node characteristics mainly specify the operations it can perform, such as summing the weighted inputs incident on it and then amplifying or applying some aggregation operators on it. The updating rules may be for weights and/or states of the processing elements (neurons). Normally, an objective function, representing the status of the network, is defined such that its set of minima correspond to the set of stable states of the network.

Tasks that neural networks can perform include pattern classification, clustering or categorization, function approximation, prediction or forecasting, optimization, retrieval by content, and control. ANNs can be viewed as weighted directed graphs in which artificial neurons are nodes and directed edges (with weights) are connections between neuron outputs and neuron inputs. On the basis of the connection pattern (architecture), ANNs can be grouped into two categories:

- *Feedforward* networks, in which graphs have no loops – for example, single-layer perceptron, multilayer perceptron, radial basis function networks, Kohonen network

- *Recurrent* (or *feedback*) networks, in which loops occur because of feedback connections – for example, Hopfield network, adaptive resonance theory (ART) models

The computational neuron model proposed by McCulloch and Pitts [23] is a simple binary threshold unit.

$$\begin{aligned} \text{Thus} \quad x_j\,(t+1) \;&=\; f(\textstyle\sum_i w_{ij}\,x_i(t) \;-\; \theta_j), \\ \text{where} \quad f(x) \;&=\; 1 \quad \text{if} \quad x \;\geq\; 0 \\ &=\; 0 \quad \text{otherwise,} \end{aligned}$$

and x_j is the input of the jth neuron with threshold θ_j. If the synaptic weight $w_{ij} > 0$, then it is called an *excitatory* connection; if $w_{ij} < 0$, it is viewed as an *inhibitory* connection. A synchronous assembly of McCulloch–Pitts neurons is capable, in principle, of universal computation for suitably chosen weights [17]. Such an assembly can perform any computation that an ordinary digital computer can.

The adaptability of a neural network comes from its capability of learning from "environments." Broadly, there are three paradigms of learning: supervised, unsupervised (or self-organized), and reinforcement. Sometimes, reinforcement is viewed as a special case of supervised learning. Under each category there are many algorithms. In supervised learning (learning with a teacher), adaptation is done on the basis of direct comparison of the network output with known correct or desired answer. Unsupervised learning does not learn any specific input–output relation. Here the network is tuned to the statistical regularities of the input data to form categories (or partitions) by optimizing, with respect to the free parameters of the network, some task-independent measure of quality of the representation. The reinforcement learning, on the other hand, attempts to learn the input–output mapping through trial and error with a view to maximizing a performance index called *reinforcement signal*. Here the system only knows whether the output is correct, but not what the correct output is.

ANNs are natural classifiers having resistance to noise, tolerance to distorted images or patterns (ability to generalize), superior ability to recognize partially occluded or degraded images or overlapping pattern classes or classes with highly nonlinear boundaries, and potential for parallel processing. They use nonparametric adaptive learning procedures, learn from examples, and discover important underlying regularities in the task domain.

For example, consider the case of supervised classification. Here a pattern is characterized by a number of features, each taking up different weights in characterizing the classes. A multilayer perceptron in which the input layer has neurons equal to the number of features and the output layer has neurons equal to the number of classes can be used to tackle this classification problem. Here the importance of different features will automatically be encoded in the connection links during training. The nonlinear decision boundaries are modeled, and class labels are assigned by taking collective decisions.

There has been widespread activity aimed at extracting the embedded knowledge in trained ANNs in the form of symbolic rules [2, 24, 25]. This serves to identify the attributes that, either individually or in a combination, are the most significant determinants of the decision or classification. Since all information is stored in a distributed manner among the neurons and their associated connectivity, any individual unit cannot essentially be associated with a single concept or feature of the problem domain.

Generally ANNs consider a fixed topology of neurons connected by links in a predefined manner. These connection weights are usually initialized by small random values. *Knowledge-based networks* [26, 27] constitute a special class of ANNs that consider crude domain knowledge to generate the initial network architecture, which is later refined in the presence of training data. The use of knowledge-based nets helps in reducing the searching space and time while the network traces the optimal solution. Typically, one extracts causal factors and functional dependencies from the data domain for initial encoding of the ANN [25, 28] and later generates refined rules from the trained network.

2.2.3.1 Single-layer perceptron The concept of *perceptron* [29, 30] was one of the most exciting developments during the early days of pattern recognition. The classical (single-layer) perceptron, given two classes of patterns, attempts to find a linear decision boundary separating the two classes.

A perceptron consists of a single neuron with adjustable weights, $w_j, j = 1, 2, \ldots, n$, and threshold θ. Given an input vector $x = [x_1, x_2, \ldots, x_n]^T$, the net input to the neuron is

$$v = \sum_{j=1}^{n} w_j x_j - \theta. \tag{2.11}$$

The output y of the perceptron is $+1$ if $v > 0$ and is 0 otherwise. In a two-class classification problem, the perceptron assigns an input pattern to one class if $y = 1$ and to the other class if $y = 0$. The linear equation $\sum_{j=1}^{n} w_j x_j - \theta = 0$ defines the decision boundary (a hyperplane in the n-dimensional input space) that halves the space. Rosenblatt [30] developed a learning procedure to determine the weights and threshold in a perceptron, given a set of training patterns. This algorithm is outlined as follows:

1. Initialize the weights and threshold to small random numbers.

2. Present a pattern vector $[x_1, x_2, \ldots, x_n]^T$ and evaluate the output of the neuron.

3. Update the weights according to

$$w_j(t+1) = w_j(t) + \varepsilon(d - y)x_j, \qquad (2.12)$$

where d is the desired output, t is the iteration number, and ε ($0.0 < \varepsilon < 1.0$) is the learning rate (step size).

Note that learning occurs only when the perceptron makes an error. This has an interesting explanation from the information theoretic perspective. Usually we expect new information when there is occurrence of an error, and hence it provides an opportunity for new learning.

Rosenblatt proved that when training patterns are drawn from two linearly separable classes, the perceptron learning procedure converges after a finite number of iterations. If the pattern space is not linearly separable, the perceptron fails [31]. A single-layer perceptron is inadequate for situations with multiple classes and nonlinear separating boundaries. Hence the invention of the multilayer perceptron network.

2.2.3.2 Multilayer perceptron (MLP) using backpropagation of error The multilayer perceptron (MLP) [18] consists of multiple layers of simple, two-state, sigmoid processing elements (nodes) or neurons that interact using weighted connections. After a lowermost input layer there are one or more intermediate *hidden* layers, followed by an output layer at the top. There exist no interconnections within a layer, while all neurons in a layer are fully connected to neurons in adjacent layers.

An external input vector is supplied to the network by clamping it at the nodes in the input layer. For conventional classification problems, during training, the appropriate output node is clamped to state 1 while the others are clamped to state 0. This is the desired output supplied by the *teacher*. The number of units in the output layer H corresponds to the number of output classes.

Consider the network given in Fig. 2.3. The total input x_j^{h+1} received by neuron j in layer $h+1$ is defined as

$$x_j^{h+1} = \sum_i y_i^h w_{ji}^h - \theta_j^{h+1}, \qquad (2.13)$$

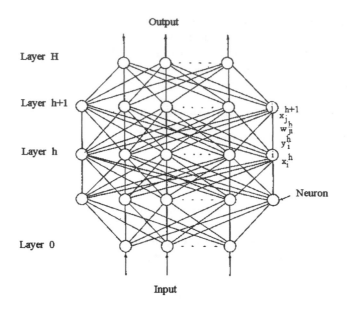

Fig. 2.3 MLP with three hidden layers.

where y_i^h is the state of the ith neuron in the preceding hth layer, w_{ji}^h is the weight of the connection from the ith neuron in layer h to the jth neuron in layer $h + 1$ and θ_j^{h+1} is the threshold of the jth neuron in layer $h + 1$. Threshold θ_j^{h+1} may be eliminated by giving the unit j in layer $h + 1$ an extra input line with a fixed activity level of 1 and a weight of $-\theta_j^{h+1}$.

The output of a neuron in any layer other than the input layer ($h > 0$) is a monotonic nonlinear function of its total input and is expressed as

$$y_j^h = \frac{1}{1 + e^{-x_j^h}}. \tag{2.14}$$

For nodes in the input layer

$$y_j^0 = x_j^0, \tag{2.15}$$

where x_j^0 is the jth component of the input vector clamped at the input layer. Learning consists of minimizing the error by updating the weights. It involves searching a very large parameter space and therefore is usually rather slow.

The least mean square (LMS) error in output vectors, for a given network weight vector w, is defined as

$$E(w) = \frac{1}{2} \sum_{j,p} (y_{j,p}^H(w) - d_{j,p})^2, \tag{2.16}$$

where $y_{j,p}^H(\boldsymbol{w})$ is the state obtained for output node j in layer H for input–output pattern p and $d_{j,p}$ is its desired state specified by the teacher. One method for minimization of $E(\boldsymbol{w})$ is to apply the method of gradient descent by starting with any set of weights and repeatedly updating each weight by an amount

$$\triangle w_{ji}^h(t) = -\varepsilon \frac{\partial E}{\partial w_{ji}} + \alpha \triangle w_{ji}^h(t-1), \qquad (2.17)$$

where the positive constant ε controls the descent, $0 \le \alpha \le 1$ is the damping coefficient or momentum, and t denotes the number of the iteration currently in progress. Generally ε and α are set at constant values, but there exist approaches that vary these parameters. Initially the connection weights w_{ji}^h between each pair of neurons i in layer h and j in layer $h+1$ are set to small random values lying in the range $[-0.5, 0.5]$.

From Eqs. (2.13)–(2.14) and (2.16), we have

$$\frac{\partial E}{\partial w_{ji}} = \frac{\partial E}{\partial y_j} \frac{dy_j}{dx_j} \frac{\partial x_j}{\partial w_{ji}} = \frac{\partial E}{\partial y_j} y_j^h (1 - y_j^h) y_i^{h-1}. \qquad (2.18)$$

For the output layer ($h = H$), we substitute in Eq. (2.18)

$$\frac{\partial E}{\partial y_j} = y_j^H - d_j. \qquad (2.19)$$

For the other layers, using Eq. (2.13), we substitute in Eq. (2.18)

$$\frac{\partial E}{\partial y_j} = \sum_k \frac{\partial E}{\partial y_k} \frac{dy_k}{dx_k} \frac{\partial x_k}{\partial y_j} = \sum_k \frac{\partial E}{\partial y_k} \frac{dy_k}{dx_k} w_{kj}^h, \qquad (2.20)$$

where units j and k lie in layers h and $h+1$, respectively.

During training, each pattern of the training set is used in succession to clamp the input and output layers of the network. A sequence of forward and backward passes using Eqs. (2.13)–(2.20) constitute a *cycle*, and such a cycle through the entire training set is termed a *sweep*. After a number of sweeps through the training data, the error $E(\boldsymbol{w})$ in Eq. (2.16) may be minimized. At this stage the network is supposed to have discovered (learned) the relationship between the input and output vectors in the training samples.

In the testing phase the neural net is expected to be able to utilize the information encoded in its connection weights to assign the correct output labels for the test vectors that are now clamped only at the input layer. It should be noted that the optimal number of hidden layers and the number of units in each such layer are generally determined empirically, although growing, pruning, and other optimization techniques are also in vogue.

2.2.3.3 *Kohonen network* The essential constituents of Kohonen neural network model are as follows [19]:

- An array of neurons receiving coherent inputs, simultaneously, and computing a simple output function.

- A mechanism for comparing the neuronal outputs to select the neuron producing maximum output.

- A local interaction between the selected neuron and its neighbors.

- An adaptive mechanism that updates the interconnection weights.

The self-organizing feature map (SOFM) is an unsupervised learning network [19], which transforms p-dimensional input patterns to a q-dimensional (usually $q = 1$ or 2) discrete map in a topologically ordered fashion. Input points that are close in p-dimension are also mapped closely on the q-dimensional lattice. Each lattice cell is represented by a neuron that has a p-dimensional adaptable weight vector associated with it. With every input the match with each weight vector is computed. Then the best matching weight vector and some of its topological neighbors are adjusted to match the input points a little better. Initially, the process starts with a large neighborhood; with passage of time (iteration), the neighborhood size is reduced gradually. At a given time instant, within the neighborhood, the weight vector associated with each neuron is not updated equally. The strength of interaction between the winner and a neighboring node is inversely related to the distance (on the lattice) between them.

Consider the self-organizing network given in Fig. 2.4. Let M input signals be simultaneously incident on each of an $N \times N$ array of neurons. The output of the ith neuron is defined as

$$\eta_i(t) = \sigma \left[[\boldsymbol{m}_i(t)]^T \, \boldsymbol{x}(t) + \sum_{k \in S_i} w_{ki} \, \eta_k(t - \Delta t) \right], \qquad (2.21)$$

where $\boldsymbol{x}$ is the M-dimensional input vector incident on it along the connection weight vector $\boldsymbol{m}_i$, k belongs to the subset S_i of neurons having interconnections with the ith neuron, w_{ki} denotes the fixed feedback coupling between the kth and ith neurons, $\sigma[.]$ is a suitable sigmoidal output function, t denotes a discrete time index, and T stands for the transpose.

Initially the components of the $\boldsymbol{m}_i$ values are set to small random values lying in the range $[0, 0.5]$. If the best match between vectors $\boldsymbol{m}_i$ and $\boldsymbol{x}$ occurs at neuron c, then we have

$$\|\boldsymbol{x} - \boldsymbol{m}_c\| = \min_i \, \|\boldsymbol{x} - \boldsymbol{m}_i\|, \quad i = 1, 2, \ldots, N^2, \qquad (2.22)$$

where $\|.\|$ indicates the Euclidean norm.

The weight updating is given as [19]

$$\boldsymbol{m}_i(t+1) = \begin{cases} \boldsymbol{m}_i(t) + \alpha(t) \, (\boldsymbol{x}(t) - \boldsymbol{m}_i(t)) & \text{for } i \in N_c \\ \boldsymbol{m}_i(t) & \text{otherwise,} \end{cases} \qquad (2.23)$$

where $\alpha(t)$ is a positive constant that decays with time and N_c defines a topological neighborhood around the maximally responding neuron c, such that

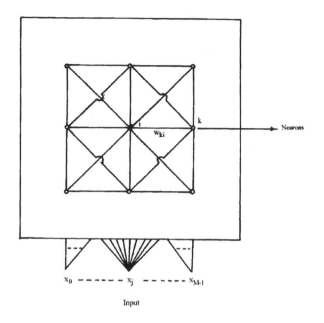

Fig. 2.4 Kohonen neural network.

it also decreases with time. Different parts of the network become selectively sensitized to different inputs in an ordered fashion so as to form a continuous map of the signal space. After a number of sweeps through the training data, with weight updating at each iteration obeying Eq. (2.23), the asymptotic values of m_i cause the output space to attain proper topological ordering. This is basically a variation of *unsupervised* learning.

2.2.3.4 Learning vector quantization (LVQ) Vector quantization can be seen as a mapping from an n-dimensional Euclidean space into a finite set of prototypes. Based on this principle, Kohonen proposed an unsupervised learning algorithm, which is a special case of SOFM and is known as LVQ [19]. In LVQ, only the weight vector associated with the winner node is updated with every data point by Eq. (2.23). The topological neighborhood is not updated here. Such a learning scheme, where all nodes compete to become the winner, is termed *competitive learning*. It is essentially a clustering network that does not care about preserving the topological order. Its main uses are for clustering, classification, and image data compression [32].

There exists a family of LVQs, termed LVQ1 and LVQ2 [19]. These algorithms are supervised learning schemes, essentially used as classifiers. The basic idea behind LVQ1 is as follows. If the winner prototype m_i has the same class label as that of the data point x, then bring m_i closer to x; otherwise, move m_i away from x. Nonwinner nodes are not updated. LVQ2, a modified

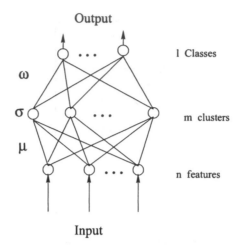

Output

ω

σ

μ

l Classes

m clusters

n features

Input

Fig. 2.5   Radial basis function network.

form of LVQ1, is designed to make the learning scheme comply better with Bayes' decision-making philosophy (described in Section 5.3). This algorithm considers the winner along with the runner-up (second winner).

2.2.3.5   Radial basis function network   A radial basis function (RBF) network [33, 34] consists of two layers as shown in Fig. 2.5. The connection weight vectors of the input and output layers are denoted as μ and w, respectively. The basis (or kernel) functions in the hidden layer produce a localized response to the input stimulus. The output nodes form a weighted linear combination of the basis functions computed by the hidden nodes.

The input and output nodes correspond to the input features and output classes, while the hidden nodes represent the number of clusters (specified by the user) that partition the input space. Let $x = (x_1, \ldots, x_i, \ldots, x_n) \in R^n$ and $y = (y_1, \ldots, y_i, \ldots, y_l) \in R^l$ be the input and output, respectively, and let m be the number of hidden nodes.

The output u_j of the jth hidden node, using the *Gaussian kernel* function as a basis, is given by

$$u_j = \exp\left[-\frac{(x - \mu_j)^T(x - \mu_j)}{2\sigma_j^2}\right], \quad j = 1, 2, \ldots, m, \qquad (2.24)$$

where x is the input pattern, μ_j is its input weight vector (*i.e.*, the center of the Gaussian for node j), and σ_j^2 is the normalization parameter, such that $0 \le u_j \le 1$ (the closer the input is to the center of the Gaussian, the larger the response of the node).

The output y_j of the jth output node is

$$y_j = w_j^T u, \quad j = 1, 2, \ldots, l, \qquad (2.25)$$

where w_j is the weight vector for this node, and u is the vector of outputs from the hidden layer. The network performs a linear combination of the nonlinear basis functions of Eq. (2.24).

The problem is to minimize the error

$$E = \frac{1}{2} \sum_{p=1}^{N} \sum_{j=1}^{l} (y_{j,p} - d_{j,p})^2, \qquad (2.26)$$

where $d_{j,p}$ and $y_{j,p}$ are desired and computed output at the jth node for the pth pattern, N is the size of the data set, and l is the number of output nodes.

Learning in the hidden layer, typically, uses the c-means clustering algorithm (described in Section 6.3.1.1). Let the cluster centers, so determined, be denoted as μ_j, $j = 1, \ldots, m$. The normalization parameter σ_j represents a measure of the spread of data associated with each node.

Learning in the output layer is performed after the parameters of the basis functions have been determined. The weights are typically trained using the LMS algorithm given by

$$\triangle w_j = -\varepsilon (y_j - d_j) u, \qquad (2.27)$$

where ε is the learning rate.

2.2.4 Neuro-fuzzy computing

The concept of ANNs was inspired by *biological neural networks*, which are inherently nonlinear, adaptive, highly parallel, robust, and fault tolerant. Fuzzy logic, on the other hand, is capable of modeling vagueness, handling uncertainty, and supporting human-type reasoning. One may therefore naturally think of judiciously integrating them by augmenting each other in order to build a more intelligent information system, in *neuro-fuzzy computing* paradigm [2, 35, 36], with recognition performance better than those obtained by the individual technologies. It incorporates both the generic and application-specific merits of ANNs and fuzzy logic into the hybridization.

Both fuzzy systems and ANNs are soft computing approaches to modeling expert behavior. The goal is to mimic the actions of an expert who solves complex problems. A learning process can be part of knowledge acquisition. In the absence of an expert, or sufficient time or data, one can resort to reinforcement learning instead of supervised learning. If one has knowledge expressed as linguistic rules, one can build a fuzzy system. On the other hand, if one has data, or can learn from a simulation or the real task, ANNs are more appropriate. The integration of neural and fuzzy systems leads to a symbiotic relationship, in which fuzzy systems provide a powerful framework for expert knowledge representation, while neural networks provide learning capabilities and suitability for computationally efficient hardware implementations.

It has been proved [37] that (i) any rule-based fuzzy system may be approximated by a neural net, and (ii) any neural net (feedforward, multilayered) may be approximated by a rule-based fuzzy system. Jang and Sun [38] have shown that fuzzy systems are functionally equivalent to a class of radial basis function (RBF) networks, based on the similarity between the local receptive fields of the network and the membership functions of the fuzzy system.

Fuzzy systems can be broadly categorized into two families. The first includes linguistic models based on collections of IF–THEN rules, whose antecedents and consequents utilize fuzzy values. It uses fuzzy reasoning, and the system behavior can be described in *natural* terms. The *Mamdani* model [39] falls in this group. The knowledge is represented as

$$R^i: \quad \text{IF} \quad x_1 \text{ is } A_1^i \text{ AND } x_2 \text{ is } A_2^i \ldots \text{ AND } x_n \text{ is } A_m^i$$
$$\text{THEN} \quad y^i \text{ is } B^i, \tag{2.28}$$

where $R^i (i = 1, 2, \ldots, l)$ denotes the ith fuzzy rule, $x_j (j = 1, 2, \ldots, n)$ is the input, y^i is the output of the fuzzy rule R^i, and $A_i^1, A_i^2, \ldots, A_m^i, B^i (i = 1, 2, \ldots, l)$ are fuzzy membership functions usually associated with linguistic terms.

The second category, based on *Sugeno*-type systems [40], uses a rule structure that has fuzzy antecedent and *functional* consequent parts. This can be viewed as the expansion of piecewise linear partition represented as

$$R^i: \quad \text{IF} \quad x_1 \text{ is } A_1^i \text{ AND } x_2 \text{ is } A_2^i \ldots \text{ AND } x_n \text{ is } A_m^i$$
$$\text{THEN} \quad y^i = a_0^i + a_1^i x_1 + \ldots + a_n^i x_n. \tag{2.29}$$

The approach approximates a nonlinear system with a combination of several linear systems, by decomposing the whole input space into several partial fuzzy spaces and representing each output space with a linear equation. Such models are capable of representing both qualitative and quantitative information and allow relatively easier application of powerful learning techniques for their identification from data. They are capable of approximating any continuous real-valued function on a compact set to any degree of accuracy [41].

There is always a trade-off between readability and precision. If one is interested in a more precise solution, then one is usually not so bothered about its linguistic interpretability. Sugeno-type systems are more suitable in such cases. Otherwise, the choice is for Mamdani-type systems.

Extraction of rules from neural nets enables humans to understand their prediction process in a better manner. This is because rules are a form of knowledge that human experts can easily verify, transmit, and expand. Representing rules in *natural* form aids in enhancing their comprehensibility for humans. This aspect is suitably handled using fuzzy set-based representations.

Neuro-fuzzy hybridization [2] is done broadly in two ways: a neural network equipped with the capability of handling fuzzy information [termed *fuzzy–neural network* (FNN)], and a fuzzy system augmented by neural networks to enhance some of its characteristics like flexibility, speed, and adaptability [termed *neural–fuzzy system* (NFS)].

In an FNN either the input signals and/or connection weights and/or the outputs are fuzzy subsets or a set of membership values to fuzzy sets (e.g., Refs. [42]–[44]). Usually, linguistic values (such as *low, medium*, and *high*) or fuzzy numbers or intervals are used to model these. Neural networks with fuzzy neurons are also termed FNNs because they are capable of processing fuzzy information.

A neural–fuzzy system (NFS), on the other hand, is designed to realize the process of fuzzy reasoning, where the connection weights of the network correspond to the parameters of fuzzy reasoning (e.g., Refs. [45] and [46]. Using the backpropagation-type learning algorithms, the NFS can identify fuzzy rules and learn membership functions of the fuzzy reasoning. Typically, the NFS architecture has distinct nodes for antecedent clauses, conjunction operators, and consequent clauses.

The state of the art for the different techniques of judiciously combining neuro-fuzzy concepts involves synthesis at various levels. In general, these methodologies can be broadly categorized as follows. Note that categories 1 and 3–5 relate to FNNs while category 2 refers to NFS.

1. Incorporating fuzziness into the neural net framework: fuzzifying the input data, assigning fuzzy labels to the training samples, possibly fuzzifying the learning procedure, and obtaining neural network outputs in terms of fuzzy sets [44, 47, 43].

2. Designing neural networks guided by fuzzy logic formalism: designing neural networks to implement fuzzy logic and fuzzy decision-making, and to realize membership functions representing fuzzy sets [48]–[46].

3. Changing the basic characteristics of the neurons: neurons are designed to perform various operations used in fuzzy set theory (like fuzzy union, intersection, aggregation) instead of the standard multiplication and addition operations [49, 50, 51].

4. Using measures of fuzziness as the error or instability of a network: the fuzziness or uncertainty measures of a fuzzy set are used to model the error or instability or energy function of the neural network-based system [52].

5. Making the individual neurons fuzzy: the input and output of the neurons are fuzzy sets and the activity of the networks, involving the fuzzy neurons, is also a fuzzy process [42].

2.2.5 Genetic algorithms

Genetic algorithms (GAs) [53, 54] are adaptive and robust computational search procedures, modeled on the mechanics of natural genetic systems. They act as a biological metaphor and try to emulate some of the processes observed in natural evolution. While evolution operates on encodings of biological entities in the form of a collection of genes called a chromosome, GAs operate on string representation of possible solutions in terms of individuals or chromosomes containing the features. The feature value, the string structure and the string structure's decoded value in case of a GA correspond to the allele, genotype, and phenotype in natural evolution.

The components of a GA consist of

- Population of individuals

- Encoding or decoding mechanism of the individuals

- Objective function and an associated fitness evaluation criterion

- Selection procedure

- Genetic operators like recombination or crossover, mutation

- Probabilities to perform the genetic operations

- Replacement technique

- Termination conditions

Let us consider, as an example, the optimization of a function

$$y = f(x_1, x_2, \ldots, x_p).$$

A binary vector is used as a chromosome to represent real values of the variables x_i, with the length of the vector depending on the required precision. A population is a set of individuals (chromosomes) representing the concatenated parameter set $x_1, x_2, \ldots, x_p$, where each member refers to a coded *possible* solution. For example, a sample chromosome

$$0000|0100|\ldots|1100$$

could correspond to $x_1 = 0000$, $x_2 = 0100$, and $x_p = 1100$. The chromosomes can be of fixed or variable size. Selection obeys the Darwinian survival of the fittest strategy, with the objective function playing the role of Nature (environment). Variation is introduced in the population through the genetic operations like recombination (crossover) and mutation. Normally the initial population is chosen randomly.

Encoding is used to convert parameter values into chromosomal representation. In case of continuous-valued parameters, a decimal-to-binary conversion is used. For example, using a 5-bit representation, 13 is encoded as 01101. In case of parameters having categorical values, a particular bit position in the chromosomal representation is set to 1 if it comes from a certain category. For example, the gender of a person can have values from {male, female}, such that male/female is represented by the string 10/01. These strings (representing the parameters of a problem) are concatenated to form a chromosome.

Decoding is the reverse of encoding. For a continuous-valued parameter the binary representation is converted to a continuous value by the expression

$$lower\_bound + \frac{\sum_{i=0}^{bits\_used-1} bit_i * 2^i}{2^{bits\_used} - 1} * (upper\_bound - lower\_bound).$$

Hence 01101 in five bits ($bits\_used$) is decoded back to 13, using $lower\_bound = 0$ and $upper\_bound = 31$. In case of categorical parameters, the value is found by consulting the original mapping.

The fitness function provides a measure of a chromosome's performance. Selection gives more chance to better-fitted individuals, thereby mimicking the natural selection procedure. Some of the popular selection techniques include roulette wheel selection, stochastic universal sampling, linear normalization selection, and tournament selection. The roulette wheel selection procedure initially sums the fitness values (f_is) of all the N chromosomes in the population, and it stores them in slots sized accordingly. Let this sum be given by $total\_fitness$. The probability of selection p_i for the ith chromosome is expressed as

$$p_i = \frac{f_i}{total\_fitness}, \tag{2.30}$$

while the cumulative probability q_i after inclusion of the ith chromosome is given by

$$q_i = \sum_{j=1}^{i} p_j. \tag{2.31}$$

Selection is made by spinning the roulette wheel N times, on each occasion generating a random number n_r in $[0, total\_fitness]$. This returns the first chromosome whose fitness, when added to the fitness of the preceding population members, is greater than or equal to n_r. In rule form, we have

IF $n_r < q_1$ THEN select the first chromosome,
ELSE select the ith chromosome such that $q_{i-1} < n_r \leq q_i$.

For example, let there be five chromosomes with fitness values 40, 30, 18, 10, 2, having $total\_fitness = 100$. These constitute slots sized 40%, 30%, 18%, 10%, and 2% of the area of the wheel. Each time one requires to select a chromosome, for applying crossover or mutation, a simple spin of the roulette wheel is made with n_r. Here, with $n_r = 45$, the algorithm selects the second chromosome, since $40 + 30 > 45$.

Recombination or crossover is modeled by choosing mating pairs from the selected chromosomes. Crossover probability p_c is used to determine whether a pair should be crossed over, and then the corresponding chromosome segments are interchanged. A random number n_{rc} is generated in the range $[0, 1]$. If

$n_{rc} < p_c$, the corresponding chromosome pair is selected for crossover. Again, crossover can be one point, two point, multipoint, or uniform. Let us consider, as an example, two parent chromosomes $xyxyxyxy$ and $abababab$ where x, y, a, b are binary. In one-point crossover at the 6th bit involving the parent chromosomes

$$xyxyx|yxy$$

$$ababa|bab,$$

one generates the children

$$xyxyx|bab$$

$$ababa|yxy.$$

Here the segment involving bits 6 to 8 is interchanged between the parents. In case of two-point crossover at the 3rd and 6th bits, involving parent chromosomes

$$xy|xyx|yxy$$

$$ab|aba|bab,$$

we obtain the children chromosomes

$$xy|aba|yxy$$

$$ab|xyx|bab.$$

Here the segment constituting bits 3 to 5 is swapped between the parents to generate the pair of offsprings.

Mutation is used to introduce diversity in the population. Mutation probability p_m determines whether a bit should be mutated, and then the corresponding location is flipped. For example, a mutation at the 3rd bit would transform the chromosome $00|1|000$ to $00|0|000$. Probabilities p_c and p_m can be fixed or variable, and they typically have values ranging between 0.6 to 0.9, and 0.001 to 0.01, respectively.

Let us consider a simple example related to minimizing the surface area A of a solid cylinder, given radius r and height h, to illustrate the working principle of GAs. Here the fitness function can be expressed as

$$A = 2\pi * r * h + 2\pi * r^2 = 2\pi * r(h + r).$$

We need to encode the parameters r and h in a chromosome. Using a 3-bit representation, we demonstrate encoding, crossover, and mutation. For $r_1 = 3$, $h_1 = 4$ and $r_2 = 4$, $h_2 = 3$, we generate parent chromosomes $011|100$ and $100|011$ with $A_1 = 132$, $A_2 = 176$, respectively. Let there be one-point crossover at bit 4, producing the children chromosomes $011|011$ and $100|100$. This is decoded as $r_{1c} = 3$, $h_{1c} = 3$ and $r_{2c} = 4$, $h_{2c} = 4$, with $A_{1c} = 16.16$ and $A_{2c} = 28.72$, respectively. Now, let there be mutation at bit 5 of the first child. This generates the chromosome $0110|0|1$, for $r_{1cm} = 3$ and $h_{1cm} = 1$, with $A_{1cm} = 10.77$. This is the minimum value of fitness obtained thus far. Consecutive applications of the genetic operations of selection, crossover, and mutation, up to termination, enable the minimization (optimization) of the chosen fitness function.

The replacement techniques can be

1. Generational, where all the n individuals are replaced at a time by the n children created by reproduction. *Elitism* is often introduced to retain the best solution obtained so far.

2. Steady state, where $m < n$ members are replaced at a time by the m children reproduced.

The terminating criterion for the algorithm can be on the basis of

- execution for a fixed number of generations or iterations,

- a bound on the fitness value of the generated solution, or

- acquiring of a certain degree of homogeneity by the population.

GAs have been applied in diverse problems involving optimization, scheduling, graph coloring, genetic programming, pattern recognition, image processing, data mining, artificial immune systems, and financial prediction or bidding strategies.

2.2.6   Rough sets

The theory of *rough sets* [55] has recently emerged as another major mathematical tool for managing uncertainty that arises from granularity in the domain of discourse – that is, from the indiscernibility between objects in a set. The intention is to approximate a *rough* (imprecise) concept in the domain of discourse by a pair of *exact* concepts, called the lower and upper approximations. These exact concepts are determined by an *indiscernibility* relation on the domain, which, in turn, may be induced by a given set of *attributes* ascribed to the objects of the domain. The lower approximation is the set of objects definitely belonging to the vague concept, whereas the upper approximation is the set of objects possibly belonging to the same. These approximations are used to define the notions of *discernibility matrices*, *discernibility functions*, *reducts*, and *dependency factors*, all of which play a fundamental role in the reduction of knowledge. Figure 2.6 provides a schematic diagram of a rough set. Let us now present some requisite preliminaries of rough set theory.

An *information system* is a pair $S = < U, A >$, where U is a nonempty finite set called the *universe* and A is a nonempty finite set of *attributes* $\{a\}$. An attribute a in A can be regarded as a function from the domain U to some value set V_a.

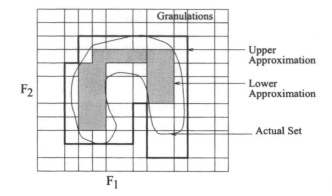

Fig. 2.6 Lower and upper approximations in a rough set.

With every subset of attributes $B \subseteq A$, one can easily associate an equivalence relation I_B on U:
$$I_B = \{(x, y) \in U : \text{ for every } a \in B, \ a(x) = a(y)\}.$$
Then $I_B = \bigcap_{a \in B} I_a$.

If $X \subseteq U$, the sets $\{x \in U : [x]_B \subseteq X\}$ and $\{x \in U : [x]_B \cap X \neq \emptyset\}$, where $[x]_B$ denotes the equivalence class of the object $x \in U$ relative to I_B, are called the *B-lower* and *B-upper approximations* of X in S and denoted by $\underline{B}X$ and $\overline{B}X$, respectively.

$X(\subseteq U)$ is *B-exact* or *B-definable* in S if $\underline{B}X = \overline{B}X$. It may be observed that $\underline{B}X$ is the greatest B-definable set contained in X, and $\overline{B}X$ is the smallest B-definable set containing X.

Let us consider, for example, an *information system* $< U, \{a\} >$ where the domain U consists of the students of a school, and there is a single attribute a – that of "belonging to a class." Then U is partitioned by the classes of the school.

Now consider the situation when an infectious disease has spread in the school, and the authorities take the two following steps.

1. If at least one student of a class is infected, all the students of that class are vaccinated. Let $\overline{B}$ denote the union of such classes.

2. If every student of a class is infected, the class is temporarily suspended. Let $\underline{B}$ denote the union of such classes.

Then $\underline{B} \subseteq \overline{B}$. Given this information, let the following problem be posed:
• *Identify the collection of infected students.* Clearly, there cannot be a unique answer. But any set I that is given as an answer must contain $\underline{B}$ *and* at least one student from each class comprising $\overline{B}$. In other words, it must have $\underline{B}$ as its *lower approximation* and $\overline{B}$ as its *upper approximation*.
• I is then a *rough* concept or set in the information system $< U, \{a\} >$. Further, it may be observed that any set I' given as another answer is *roughly*

equal to I, in the sense that both are represented (characterized) by $\overline{B}$ and $\underline{B}$.

The effectiveness of the theory of rough sets has been investigated in the domains of artificial intelligence and cognitive sciences, especially for representation of and reasoning with vague and/or imprecise knowledge, data classification and analysis, machine learning, and knowledge discovery [56]. Their role in data mining is elucidated in Section 2.6, with particular reference to rough clustering in Section 6.5.4.

2.2.7 Wavelets

Application of wavelets have had a growing impact in signal and image processing over the last two decades. But *wavelet* is by no means a new theory, and it existed in mathematics since 1909 when Haar discovered the Haar transform. Since then, mathematicians have been working on wavelets, and "wavelet analysis" used to be called "atomic decomposition" for a long time [57]. The *wave* in physics is defined as a disturbance propagated in media, typically as an oscillating function of time or space such as a sinusoid. The *wavelet* can be considered a snapshot of a wave oscillating within a short window of time or space. As a result, mathematically, the wavelet can be considered as a function which is both oscillating and localized.

Representation of a signal using sinusoids is very effective for *stationary signals*, which are statistically predictable and are time-invariant in nature. *Wavelet* representation is found to be very effective for *nonstationary* signals, which are not statistically predictable and time-varying in nature.

Variation of intensity to form edges is a very important visual characteristic of an image. From signal theoretic perspective, discontinuities of intensities occur at the edges in any image and hence it can be prominently visualized by the human eye. The time and frequency localization property of wavelets makes it attractive for analysis of images because of discontinuities at the edges.

Wavelets are functions generated from one single function called the *mother wavelet* by dilations (scalings) and translations (shifts) in time (frequency) domain. If the mother wavelet is denoted by $\psi(t)$, the other wavelets $\psi^{a,b}(t)$ for $a > 0$ and a real number b can be represented as

$$\psi^{a,b}(t) = \frac{1}{\sqrt{a}}\psi\left(\frac{t-b}{a}\right), \tag{2.32}$$

where a and b represent the parameters for dilations and translations in the time domain. The parameter a causes contraction in time domain when $a < 1$ and expansion when $a > 1$. In Fig. 2.7, we illustrate a mother wavelet and its contraction and dilation.

We discuss further details of wavelet transformation and its properties in Section 3.8.3, and we describe how it can be applied for efficient image compression. Its application to data clustering is provided in Section 6.5.3.

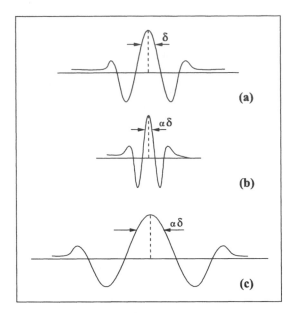

Fig. 2.7 (a) Mother wavelet $\psi(t)$. (b) $\psi(t/\alpha)$: $0 < \alpha < 1$. (c) $\psi(t/\alpha)$: $\alpha > 1$.

2.3   ROLE OF FUZZY SETS IN DATA MINING

Fuzzy sets constitute the earliest and most widely reported constituent of soft computing. As mentioned in Section 2.2.2, the modeling of imprecise and qualitative knowledge as well as the transmission and handling of uncertainty at various stages are possible through the use of fuzzy sets. In this section we provide a glimpse of the available literature pertaining to the use of fuzzy sets in data mining [3].

Knowledge discovery in databases is mainly concerned with identifying interesting patterns and describing them in a concise and meaningful manner [58]. Despite a growing versatility of knowledge discovery systems, there is an important component of human interaction that is inherent to any process of knowledge representation, manipulation, and processing. Fuzzy sets are naturally inclined towards coping with linguistic domain knowledge and producing more interpretable solutions.

The notion of *interestingness*, which encompasses several features such as validity, novelty, usefulness, and simplicity, can be quantified through fuzzy sets. Fuzzy dissimilarity of a discovered pattern with a user-defined vocabulary has been used as a measure of this interestingness [59]. As an extension to the above methodology, *unexpectedness* can also be defined in terms of a *belief system*, where if a belief b is based on previous evidence ξ, then $d(b|\xi)$ denotes the degree of belief b. In soft belief systems, a weight w_i is attached to each belief b_i. The degree of a belief may be measured with conditional probability, Dempster–Shafer belief function, or frequency of the raw data. Here, the interestingness of a pattern X relative to a belief system B and evidence ξ may be formally defined as

$$I(X, B, \xi) = \sum_{b_i \in B} w_i \left| d(b_i | X, \xi) - d(b_i | \xi) \right|. \tag{2.33}$$

This definition of interestingness measures the amount by which the degrees of belief change as a result of a new pattern X.

There is a growing indisputable role of fuzzy set technology in the realm of data mining [60]. Various data browsers have been implemented using fuzzy set theory [61]. Analysis of real-world data in data mining often necessitates simultaneous dealing with different types of variables, namely, categorical, symbolic, and numerical data. Pedrycz [62] discusses some constructive and fuzzy set-driven computational vehicles of knowledge discovery and establishes the relationship between data mining and fuzzy modeling. The role of fuzzy sets is categorized below based on the different functions of data mining that are modeled.

2.3.1 Clustering

Data mining aims at sifting through large volumes of data in order to reveal useful information in the form of new relationships, patterns, or clusters, for decision-making by a user [63]. Fuzzy sets support a focused search, specified in linguistic terms, through data. They also help discover dependencies between the data in qualitative or semiqualitative format. In data mining, one is typically interested in a focused discovery of structure and an eventual quantification of functional dependencies existing therein. This helps prevent searching for meaningless or trivial patterns in a database. Researchers have developed fuzzy clustering algorithms for this purpose [64]. Russell and Lodwick [65] have explored fuzzy clustering methods for mining telecommunications customer and prospect databases to gain residential and business customer market share.

Pedrycz has designed fuzzy clustering algorithms [66] using (a) contextual information and (b) induced linguistic space, for better focusing of the search procedure in KDD. Krishnapuram et al. [67] have developed a robust fuzzy c-medoids algorithm for clustering Web data. Further details on these algorithms are provided in Section 6.5.1.

2.3.2 Granular computing

Achieving focus is important in data mining because there are too many attributes and values to be considered, which can result in combinatorial explosion. Most unsupervised data mining approaches try to achieve attribute focus by first recognizing the most interesting features. Mazlack [68] suggests a converse approach of progressively reducing the dataset by partitioning and eliminating the least important attributes to reduce intra-item dissonance within the partitions. A *soft* focus is used to handle both crisp and imprecise data. It works by progressive reduction of cognitive dissonance, leading to an increase in useful information. The objective is to generate cohesive and comprehensible information *nuggets* by sifting out uninteresting attributes. A combined distance metric takes care of different types of attributes simultaneously, thus avoiding any taxonomic structure. Non-crisp values are handled by granularization followed by partitioning.

Granular computing [69] is useful in finding meaningful patterns in data by expressing and processing chunks of information (granules). These are regarded as essential entities in all cognitive pursuits geared toward establishing meaningful patterns in data. Soft granules can be defined in terms of membership functions. Increased granularity reduces attribute distinctiveness, resulting in loss of useful information, while finer grains lead to partitioning difficulty. The concept of granular computing allows one to concentrate all computational effort on some specific and problem-oriented subsets of a complete database. It also helps split an overall computing effort into several subtasks, leading to a *modularization* effect.

We deal with the classification aspect of granular computing in Section 5.4.6. Modularization in soft computing, for data mining, is described in Section 8.3.

2.3.3 Association rules

An important area of data mining research deals with the discovery of *association rules* [70], which describe interesting association relationship among different attributes. A boolean association involves binary attributes, a generalized association involves attributes that are hierarchically related, and a quantitative association involves attributes that can take on quantitative or categorical values. The use of fuzzy techniques has been considered to be one of the key components of data mining systems because of their affinity with human knowledge representation [71].

Wei and Chen [72] have mined generalized association rules with fuzzy taxonomic structures. A crisp taxonomy assumes that a child belongs to its ancestor with degree one. A fuzzy taxonomy is represented as a directed acyclic graph, each of whose edges represents a fuzzy *IS-A* relationship with degree μ ($0 \leq \mu \leq 1$). The partial belonging of an item in a taxonomy is taken into account while computing the degrees of support and confidence.

Au and Chan [73] utilize an *adjusted difference* between observed and expected frequency counts of attributes for discovering fuzzy association rules in relational databases. Instead of dividing quantitative attributes into fixed intervals, they employ linguistic terms to represent the revealed regularities and exceptions. Here no user-supplied thresholds are required, and quantitative values can be directly inferred from the rules. The linguistic representation leads to the discovery of *natural* and more understandable rules. The algorithm allows one to discover both *positive* and *negative* rules, and can deal with fuzzy class boundaries as well as missing values in databases. The use of fuzzy techniques buries the boundaries of adjacent intervals of numeric quantities, resulting in resilience to noises such as inaccuracies in physical measurements of real life entities. The effectiveness of the algorithm was demonstrated on a transactional database of a PBX system and a database concerning industrial enterprises in mainland China.

We describe fuzzy association rules in greater detail in Section 7.10.

2.3.4 Functional dependencies

Fuzzy logic has been used for analyzing inference based on functional dependencies (FDs), between variables, in database relations. Fuzzy inference generalizes both imprecise (set-valued) and precise inference. Similarly, fuzzy relational databases generalize their classical and imprecise counterparts by supporting fuzzy information storage and retrieval [74]. FDs are interesting from knowledge discovery standpoint since they allow one to express, in a condensed form, some properties of the real world which are valid on a given database. These properties can then be used in various applications such as reverse engineering or query optimization. Bosc et al. [75] use a data mining algorithm to extract or discover extended FDs, represented by gradual rules composed of linguistic variables.

2.3.5 Data summarization

Summary discovery is one of the major components of knowledge discovery in databases. This provides the user with comprehensive information for grasping the essence from a large amount of information in a database. Fuzzy set theory is also used for data summarization [76]. Typically, fuzzy sets are used for an interactive top-down summary discovery process which utilizes fuzzy *IS-A* hierarchies as domain knowledge.

Linguistic summaries of large sets of data are derived as linguistically quantified propositions with a degree of validity [77]. This corresponds to the preference criterion involved in the mining task. The system consists of a summarizer (like *young*), a quantity in agreement (like *most*), and the truth or validity (say, 0.7).

It is found that often the most interesting linguistic summaries are nontrivial and human-consistent concepts, involving complicated combinations of attributes. In practice, this cannot be generated automatically and *human assistance or interaction* is required. Kacprzyk and Zadrozny [78] have developed *FQUERY* for an interactive linguistic summarization, using *natural* terms and *comprehensible* quantifiers. It supports various fuzzy elements in queries, including interval attributes with membership for matching in a fuzzy relation and importance coefficients. First the user has to formulate a set of linguistic summaries of interest. The system then retrieves records from the database and calculates the validity of each summary. Finally, the most appropriate linguistic summary is selected. The scheme has also been used for fuzzy querying over the Internet, using browsers like Microsoft Explorer or Netscape Navigator. The definition of fuzzy values, fuzzy relations, and linguistic quantifiers is via Java applets.

Chiang et al. [79] have used fuzzy linguistic summary for mining time series data. The system provides human interaction, in the form of a graphic display tool, to help users premine a database and determine what knowledge could be discovered. The model is used to predict the on-line utilization ranks of different resources, including CPU and real storage.

2.3.6   Image mining

Recent increase in the size of *multimedia* information repositories, consisting of mixed media data, has made content-based image retrieval (CBIR) an active research area. Unlike traditional database techniques which retrieve images based on exact matching of keywords, CBIR systems represent the information content of an image by visual features such as color, texture, and shape, and they retrieve images based on similarity of features. Frigui [80] has developed an *interactive* and *iterative* image retrieval system that takes into account the *subjectivity* of human perception of visual content. The feature relevance weights are learned from the user's positive and negative feedback, and the Choquet integral is used as a dissimilarity measure. The smooth transition in the user's feedback is modeled by continuous fuzzy membership functions. Medasani and Krishnapuram [81] have designed a fuzzy approach to handle complex linguistic queries consisting of multiple attributes. Such queries are usually more *natural, user-friendly*, and *interpretable* for image retrieval. The degree to which an image satisfies an attribute is given by the membership value of the feature vector, corresponding to the image, in the membership function for the attribute. Fuzzy connectives are used to combine the degrees of satisfaction of multiple attributes in a complex query, to arrive at an overall degree of satisfaction while ranking images for retrieval.

Video as the format of computer-related material is becoming more and more common these days, and many Web pages involve small pieces of movies or video-clips or animation. Fuzzy time related queries are used in Ref. [82] to retrieve information inside a video. The queries are handled using Zadeh's principle of *computing with words*, which allows a human-friendly interface. The system is implemented on a Java Search Engine.

Querying for a target image and retrieving it from Web and image databases, based on image similarity, is presented in Ref. [83]. A fuzzy c-means algorithm is used to cluster intrinsic image characteristics extracted from subregions of the image. A measure of similarity between pairs of images is determined in terms of the rotation-invariant attributes like color, texture, and shape. Color is defined [84] in terms of the hue, saturation, and value representation of the average color of the pixel in the region. Texture is represented in terms of the co-occurrence matrices in four directions involving Haralick's parameters [85]. For each database image, the system calculates its attribute matrix and does a whitening transformation before fuzzy clustering to store the representative centroids. When a target image is supplied, the system adopts a similar procedure in order to retrieve the most similar image (in terms of the stored centroid) from the database in response to a query.

In this section we have briefly summarized some research on soft computing-based image mining. The traditional image mining techniques, based on context-based image retrieval systems, have been covered in Section 9.3.

2.4 ROLE OF NEURAL NETWORKS IN DATA MINING

Neural networks were earlier thought to be unsuitable for data mining because of their inherent *black-box* nature. No information was available from them in symbolic form, suitable for verification or interpretation by humans. However, recent investigations have concentrated on extracting the embedded knowledge in trained networks in the form of symbolic rules [25]. Unlike fuzzy sets, the main contribution of neural nets towards data mining stems from rule extraction and clustering [3].

2.4.1 Rule extraction

In general, the primary input to a connectionist rule extraction algorithm is a representation of a trained (layered) neural network, in terms of its nodes, links, and sometimes the dataset. One or more hidden and output units are used to automatically derive the rules, which may later be combined and simplified to arrive at a more comprehensible rule set. These rules can also provide new insights into the application domain. The use of neural nets helps in (i) incorporating parallelism and (ii) tackling optimization problems in the data domain. The models are usually suitable in *data-rich* environments.

Typically, a network is first trained to achieve the required accuracy rate. Redundant connections of the network are then removed using a pruning algorithm. The link weights and activation values of the hidden units in the network are analyzed, and classification rules are generated [25, 86]. Further details on rule generation can be obtained in Section 8.2.

2.4.2 Rule evaluation

Here we provide some quantitative measures to evaluate the performance of the generated rules [87]. This relates to the *goodness of fit* chosen for the rules. Let the (i, j)th element of an $l \times l$ matrix, n_{ij}, indicate the number of objects (patterns) actually belonging to class i, but classified as class j.

- *Accuracy*: It is the correct classification percentage, provided by the rules on a test set defined as

$$\frac{n_{ic}}{n_i} * 100,$$

where n_i is equal to the number of objects in class i such that n_{ic} of these are correctly classified.

- *User's accuracy*: It gives a measure of the confidence that a classifier attributes to a region as belonging to a class. If n_i' objects are found to be classified into class i, then the user's accuracy (U) is defined as

$$U = \frac{n_{ic}}{n_i'} * 100.$$

In other words, it denotes the level of purity associated with a region.

- *Kappa*: The coefficient of agreement, kappa, measures the relationship of beyond chance agreement to expected disagreement. It uses all the cells in the confusion matrix, not just the diagonal elements. The kappa value for class i (K_i) is defined as

$$K_i = \frac{N.n_{ic} - n_i.n_i'}{N.n_i' - n_i.n_i'}, \tag{2.34}$$

where N indicates the total number of data samples. The estimate of kappa is the proportion of agreement, after chance agreement is removed from consideration. The numerator and denominator of overall kappa are obtained by summing the respective numerators and denominators of K_i separately over all classes.

- *Fidelity*: It is measured as the percentage of the test set for which network and the rulebase output agree [87].

- *Confusion*: This measure quantifies the goal that the "*confusion should be restricted within minimum number of classes.*" Let $\hat{n}_{ij}$ be the mean of all n_{ij} for $i \neq j$. Then [87]

$$Conf = \frac{Card\{n_{ij} : n_{ij} \geq \hat{n}_{ij}, i \neq j\}}{l} \tag{2.35}$$

for an l class problem. The lower the value of confusion, the smaller the number of classes between which confusion occurs.

- *Coverage*: The percentage of examples from a test set for which *no rules are fired* is used as a measure of the uncovered region. A rulebase having a smaller uncovered region is superior.

- *Rulebase size*: This is measured in terms of the number of rules. The lower its value, the more compact the rulebase. This leads to better understandability.

- *Computational complexity*: This is measured in terms of the CPU time required.

- *Confidence*: The confidence of the rules is defined by a confidence factor cf. We use [87]

$$cf_j = \inf_{j: \; all \; nodes \; in \; the \; path} \frac{(\Sigma_i w_{ji} - \theta_j)}{\Sigma_i w_{ji}}, \qquad (2.36)$$

where w_{ji} is the ith incoming link weight to node j and θ_j is its threshold.

2.4.3 Clustering and self-organization

One of the big challenges to data mining is the organization and retrieval of documents from archives. Kohonen et al. [88] have demonstrated the utility of a huge self-organizing map (SOM) with more than one million nodes to partition a little less than seven million patent abstracts, where the documents are represented by 500-dimensional feature vectors. Very large text collections have been automatically organized into *document maps* that are suitable for visualization and intuitive exploration of the information space. Vesanto et al. [89] employ a stepwise strategy by partitioning the data with a SOM, followed by its clustering. Alahakoon et al. [90] perform hierarchical clustering of SOMs, based on a spread factor which is independent of the dimensionality of the data. Further details of these algorithms are provided in Section 6.5.2.

Shalvi and De Claris [91] have designed a data mining technique, combining Kohonen's self-organizing neural network with data visualization, for clustering a set of pathological data containing information regarding the patients' drugs, topographies (body locations) and morphologies (physiological abnormalities). Koenig [92] has combined SOM and Sammon's nonlinear mapping for reducing the dimension of data representation for visualization purposes.

2.4.4 Regression

Neural networks have also been used for a variety of classification and regression tasks [93]. Time series prediction has been attempted by Lee and Liu [94]. They have employed a neural oscillatory elastic graph matching model, with hybrid radial basis functions, for tropical cyclone identification and tracking.

2.4.5 Information retrieval

The SOM has been used for information retrieval [95]. A map of text documents arranged using the SOM is organized in a meaningful manner, so that items with similar content appear at nearby locations of the two-dimensional map display, such that the data is clustered. This results in an approximate model of the data distribution in the high-dimensional document space. A document map is automatically organized for browsing and visualization, and it is successfully utilized in speeding up document retrieval while maintaining high perceived quality. The objective of the search is to locate a small number N' of best documents in the order of goodness corresponding to a query. The strategy is outlined below.

- Indexing phase: Apply the SOM to partition a document collection of D documents into K subsets or clusters, representing each subset by its centroid.

- Search phase: For a given query,

  - Pre-select: select the best subsets, based on comparison with the centroids, and collect the documents in these subsets until K' documents ($K' \geq N'$) are obtained.

  - Refine: perform an exhaustive search among the K' prospective documents and return the N' best ones in the order of goodness.

A collection of 1460 document vectors was organized on a 10×15 SOM, using the WEBSOM principles, so that each map unit could contain an average of 10 documents.

2.5   ROLE OF GENETIC ALGORITHMS IN DATA MINING

GAs are adaptive, robust, efficient and global search methods, suitable in situations where the search space is large. They optimize a *fitness function*, corresponding to the preference criterion of data mining, to arrive at an optimal solution using certain genetic operators. Knowledge discovery systems have been developed using genetic programming concepts [96, 97]. The *MASSON* system [98], where intentional information is extracted for a given set of objects, is popular. The problem addressed is to find common characteristics of a set of objects in an object-oriented database. Genetic programming is used to automatically generate, evaluate, and select object-oriented queries. GAs are also used for several other purposes like fusion of multiple datatypes in multimedia databases, as well as automated program generation for mining multimedia data [99].

However, the literature in the domain of GA-based data mining is not as rich as that of fuzzy sets. We provide below a categorization of few such interesting systems based on the functions modeled [3].

2.5.1   Regression

Besides discovering human-interpretable patterns, data mining also encompasses prediction [58], where some variables or attributes in the database are used to determine unknown or future values of other variables of interest. The traditional weighted average or linear multiregression models for prediction require a basic assumption that there is no interaction among the attributes. GAs, on the other hand, are able to handle attribute interaction in a better manner. Xu et al. [100] have designed a multi-input single-output system using a nonlinear integral. An adaptive GA is used for learning the nonlinear multiregression from a set of training data.

Noda et al. [101] use GAs to discover *interesting* rules in a dependence modeling task, where different rules can predict different goal attributes. Generally, attributes with high information gain are good predictors of a class when considered individually. However attributes with low information gain could become more relevant when attribute interactions are taken into account. This phenomenon is associated with rule interestingness. The degree of interestingness of the consequent is computed based on the relative frequency of the value being predicted by it. In other words, the rarer the value of a goal attribute, the more interesting a rule it predicts. The authors attempt to discover (or mine) a few interesting rules (knowledge nuggets) instead of a large set of accurate (but not necessarily interesting) rules. The concept of interestingness has been represented using Eq. (2.33). It is also discussed in Section 7.4, with reference to association rule mining.

2.5.2   Association rules

Multiobjective GAs deal with finding the optimal solutions to problems having multiple objective functions or constraints. The solution to this is a *Pareto optimal* set of solutions, such that there exists no solution in the search space which dominates any member of this set. These are used for rule mining, which often involves a large search space with huge number of attributes and records. A global search is performed with multiple objectives, involving a combination of factors like predictive accuracy, comprehensibility, and interestingness.

Rules are typically encoded in two ways, namely, the Michigan approach (each individual encoding a single rule) and the Pittsburgh approach (each individual encoding a set of rules). The antecedent and consequent parts are encoded separately. To avoid generation of invalid chromosomes during crossover, some alignment is necessary in the position of the different attribute values. While a categorical attribute is represented by its value, a continuous-valued attribute is encoded by its binary representation. Selection and mutation operators are the same as in standard GAs. Although conventional crossover may be used, one can also resort to generalized or specialized crossover operators that involve logical OR/AND operations over the appropriate segment of the parent chromosomes.

Lopes et al. [102] evolve association rules of IF C THEN P type, which provide a high degree of accuracy and coverage. While the *accuracy* of a rule measures its degree of confidence, its *coverage* is interpreted as the comprehensive inclusion of all the records that satisfy the rule. Hence

$$Accuracy = \frac{|C \bigcap P|}{|C \bigcap P| + |C \bigcap \overline{P}|} \tag{2.37}$$

and

$$Coverage = \frac{|C \bigcap P|}{|C \bigcap P| + |\overline{C} \bigcap P|} \tag{2.38}$$

are defined. Note that other quantitative measures for rule evaluation have been discussed in Section 2.4.2, with reference to neural networks.

2.6   ROLE OF ROUGH SETS IN DATA MINING

The theory of rough sets [55] has proved to be useful in a variety of KDD processes. It offers mathematical tools to discover hidden patterns in data; therefore its importance, as far as data mining is concerned, can in no way be overlooked [3]. A fundamental principle of a rough set-based learning system is to discover redundancies and dependencies between the given features of a problem to be classified. It approximates a given concept from below and from above, using *lower* and *upper approximations.*

A rough set learning algorithm can be used to obtain a set of rules in IF–THEN form from a *decision table*. Every decision rule has two conditional probabilities associated with it, namely, certainty and coverage factors. These are closely related to the fundamental concepts of lower and upper approximations [103]. The rough set method provides an effective tool for extracting knowledge from databases. Here one first creates a knowledge base, classifying objects and attributes within the created decision tables. Then a knowledge discovery process is initiated to remove some undesirable attributes. Finally the data dependency is analyzed, in the reduced database, to find the minimal subset of attributes called *reduct*.

Rough set applications to data mining generally proceed along the following directions.

1. *Decision rule induction from attribute value table* [104]–[106]. Most of these methods are based on generation of discernibility matrices and reducts.

2. *Data filtration by template generation* [107]. This mainly involves extracting elementary blocks from data based on equivalence relation. Genetic algorithms are also sometimes used in this stage for searching, so that the methodologies can be used for large datasets.

Besides these, reduction of memory and computational requirements for rule generation, and working on dynamic databases [106] are also considered.

Some of the rough set-based systems developed for data mining include (i) the KDD-R system based on the VPRS (Variable Precision Rough Set) model [108] and (ii) the rule induction system based on LERS (Learning from Examples based on Rough Set Theory) [109]. LERS has been extended in Ref. [110] to handle *missing* attributes using the closest fit.

Document clustering has been recognized as a means for improving the efficiency and effectiveness of information retrieval and text mining. A non-hierarchical document clustering algorithm [111], based on a tolerance rough set model, has been applied to large document databases characterized by a few index terms or keywords. Unlike hierarchical algorithms, requiring time and space complexities of $O(N^3)$ and $O(N^2)$ respectively (with N being the total number of terms in a textual database), this approach requires complexities of $O(N \log N)$ and $O(N)$. The concept of upper approximation in rough sets makes it possible to exploit the semantic relationship between a few index terms in a large text document.

2.7   ROLE OF WAVELETS IN DATA MINING

Role of wavelets in different aspects of data mining is gaining significant importance. Today it has become a very powerful signal processing tool in different application areas such as image processing, compression, image indexing and retrieval, digital libraries, image clustering, and databases [112]–[116].

Spatial data mining aims to handle the huge amounts of spatial data obtained from satellite images, medical equipments, Geographic Information Systems (GIS), image database exploration, etc. The objective is to automate the process of understanding spatial data by concise representation and reorganization, to accommodate data semantics. Clustering is often required at hierarchical levels of coarseness, grouping the spatial objects at different levels of accuracy. This gives rise to the concept of multiresolution representation of an image. Wavelets [5] are found to be very useful in appropriately modeling such situations because of the nonstationary property of the image signals formed around the edges and correlation amongst the image pixels.

Wavelet transform is a signal processing technique that decomposes a signal or image into different frequency subbands at number of levels and multiple resolutions. In every level of decomposition, the high-frequency subband captures the discontinuities in the signals – for example, the edge information in an image. The low-frequency subband is nothing but a subsampled version of the original image, with similar statistical and spatial properties as the original signal. As a result, the low-frequency subband can be further decomposed into higher levels of resolution, and it helps in representing spatial objects in different coarser levels of accuracy in multiresolution subbands. This property led to the application of wavelet transforms in edge detection, object isolation, object detection, medical image fusion, and others [117].

One has to apply the wavelet transform on the feature space to find dense regions or clusters. Wavelet transform is not a single uniquely defined mathematical function like the Discrete Cosine Transform. There are many wavelet basis functions available in the literature. The wavelet transform is usually represented as a pair of Finite Impulse Response (FIR) filters, namely, the high-pass filter and the low-pass filter. A one-dimensional signal s can be filtered by convolving the filter coefficients c_k of such a filter with the signal values

$$\hat{s}_i = \sum_{k=1}^{M} c_k s_{i+k} - \frac{M}{2}, \qquad (2.39)$$

as an example, where M is the number of coefficients in the filter and $\hat{s}$ is the result of the convolution. The *Cohen–Daubechies–Feauveau* (2,2) biorthogonal wavelet is one of the most commonly used wavelet transform in data clustering applications. It is a hat-shaped filter that emphasizes regions where points cluster, while suppressing the weaker information along their boundary. This makes it easier to find the connected components in the transformed space.

Wavelets have been used for efficiently clustering large datasets [116]. This is discussed in Section 6.5.3. We provide further details on wavelet transformation and its application to image compression in Section 3.8.3.

2.8   ROLE OF HYBRIDIZATIONS IN DATA MINING

Let us first consider neuro-fuzzy hybridization in the context of data mining [3]. The rule generation aspect of neural networks is utilized to extract more *natural* rules from fuzzy neural networks [118], incorporating the better interpretability and understandability of fuzzy sets. The fuzzy MLP [119] and fuzzy Kohonen network [120] have been used for linguistic rule generation and inferencing. Here the input, besides being in quantitative, linguistic, or set forms, or a combination of these, can also be incomplete. Output decision is provided in terms of class membership values. The models are capable of

- Inferencing based on complete and/or partial information

- Querying the user for unknown input variables that are key to reaching a decision

- Producing justification for inferences in the form of IF–THEN rules.

The connection weights and node activation values of the trained network are used in the process. A *certainty factor* determines the confidence in an output decision. Figure 2.8 gives an overall view of the various stages involved in the process of inferencing and rule generation.

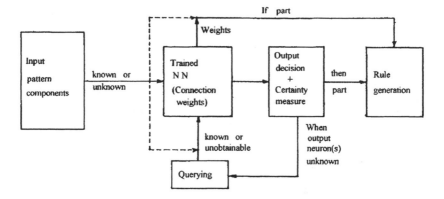

Fig. 2.8 Block diagram of inferencing and rule generation phases.

Zhang et al. [121] have designed a granular neural network to deal with numerical-linguistic data fusion and granular knowledge discovery in databases. The network is capable of learning internal granular relations between input and output and predicting new relations. Low-level granular data can be compressed to generate high-level granular knowledge in the form of rules.

A neuro-fuzzy knowledge-based network by Mitra et al. [122] is capable of generating both *positive* and *negative* rules in linguistic form to justify any decision reached. In the absence of positive information regarding the belonging of a pattern to class C_k, the complementary information is used for generating negative rules. The network topology is automatically determined, in terms of the *a priori* class information and distribution of pattern points in the feature space, followed by refinement using growing and/or pruning of links and nodes.

Banerjee et al. [28] have used a *rough–neuro-fuzzy* integration to design a knowledge-based system, where the theory of rough sets is utilized for extracting domain knowledge. The extracted crude domain knowledge is encoded among the connection weights. Rules are generated from a decision table by computing relative reducts. The network topology is automatically determined and the dependency factors of these rules are encoded as the initial connection weights. The hidden nodes model the conjuncts in the antecedent part of a rule, while the output nodes model the disjuncts.

A promising direction in mining a huge dataset is to (a) partition it, (b) develop classifiers for each module, and (c) combine the results. A modular approach has been pursued [87, 123, 124] to combine the knowledge-based rough–fuzzy MLP subnetworks or modules generated for each class, using GAs. An l-class classification problem is split into l two-class problems. Figure 2.9 depicts the knowledge flow for the entire process for $l = 2$. Dependency rules, shown on the top left corner of the figure, are extracted directly from real-valued attribute table consisting of fuzzy membership values by adap-

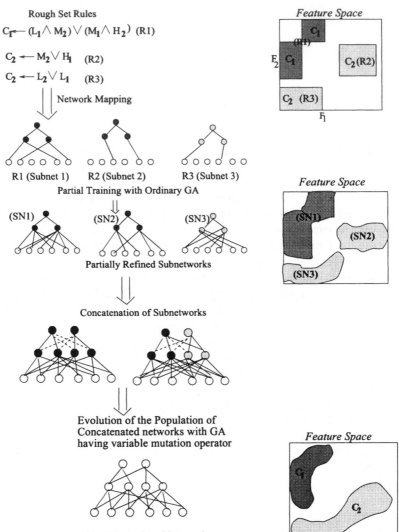

Rough Set Rules

$C_1 \leftarrow (L_1 \wedge M_2) \vee (M_1 \wedge H_2)$ (R1)

$C_2 \leftarrow M_2 \vee H_1$ (R2)

$C_2 \leftarrow L_2 \vee L_1$ (R3)

Network Mapping

R1 (Subnet 1)   R2 (Subnet 2)   R3 (Subnet 3)

Partial Training with Ordinary GA

(SN1)   (SN2)   (SN3)

Partially Refined Subnetworks

Concatenation of Subnetworks

Evolution of the Population of
Concatenated networks with GA
having variable mutation operator

Final Solution Network

Feature Space

Feature Space

Feature Space

Fig. 2.9 Knowledge flow in a modular rough–neuro–fuzzy–genetic system.

tively applying a threshold. The nature of the decision boundaries, at each stage, are depicted on the right side of the figure. The topology of the subnetworks are initially mapped using the dependency rules. Evolution using GA leads to partial refinement. The final network (represented as a concatenation of the subnetworks) is evolved using a GA with restricted mutation operator, in a novel *rough–neuro–fuzzy–genetic* framework. The *divide-and-conquer* strategy, followed by evolutionary optimization, is found to enhance the performance of the network. The method is described in further detail in Section 8.3.

George and Srikanth [125] have used a *fuzzy–genetic* integration, where GAs are applied to determine the most appropriate data summary. Kiem and Phuc [126] have developed a *rough–neuro–genetic* hybridization for discovering conceptual clusters from a large database.

2.9   CONCLUSIONS AND DISCUSSION

Current research in data mining mainly focuses on the discovery algorithm and visualization techniques. There is a growing awareness that, in practice, it is easy to discover a huge number of patterns in a database where most of these patterns are actually obvious, redundant, and useless or uninteresting to the user. To prevent the user from being overwhelmed by a large number of uninteresting patterns, techniques are needed to identify only the useful or interesting patterns and present them to the user.

Soft computing methodologies, involving fuzzy sets, neural networks, genetic algorithms, rough sets, wavelets, and their hybridizations, have recently been used to solve data mining problems. They strive to provide approximate solutions at low cost, thereby speeding up the process. A categorization has been provided based on the different soft computing tools and their hybridizations used, the mining function implemented, and the preference criterion selected by the model.

Fuzzy sets, which constitute the oldest component of soft computing, are suitable for handling the issues related to understandability of patterns, incomplete or noisy data, mixed media information, and human interaction and can provide approximate solutions faster. They have been mainly used in clustering, discovering association rules and functional dependencies, summarization, time series analysis, Web applications, and image retrieval.

Neural networks are suitable in data-rich environments and are typically used for extracting embedded knowledge in the form of rules, quantitative evaluation of these rules, clustering or self-organization, classification, regression, Web mining, and information retrieval. They have an advantage over other types of machine learning algorithms for scaling [127].

Genetic algorithms provide efficient search algorithms to select a model, from mixed media data, based on some preference criterion or objective function. They have been employed in regression, discovering association rules and Web mining. Rough sets are suitable for handling different types of uncertainty in data, and they have been mainly utilized for extracting knowledge in the form of rules.

Hybridizations typically enjoy the generic and application-specific merits of the individual soft computing tools that they integrate. Data mining functions modeled by such systems include rule extraction, data summarization, clustering, incorporation of domain knowledge, and partitioning. It is to be noted that the notion of partitioning (i.e., the modular approach) provides an effective direction for scaling up algorithms and speeding up convergence.

An efficient integration of soft computing tools, according to Zadeh's Computational Theory of Perceptions [128], is needed. Feature evaluation and dimensionality reduction help improve prediction accuracy. Some recent work in this direction are available in Refs. [129]–[131]. Other issues, requiring attention, include (a) the choice of metrics and evaluation techniques to handle dynamic changes in data and (b) a quantitative evaluation of system performance.

Recently, several commercial data mining tools have been developed based on soft computing methodologies. These include

- Data Mining Suite, using fuzzy logic;

- Braincell, Cognos 4Thought and IBM Intelligent Miner for Data, using neural networks; and

- Nuggets, using GAs.

REFERENCES

1. L. A. Zadeh, "Fuzzy logic, neural networks, and soft computing," *Communications of the ACM*, vol. 37, pp. 77–84, 1994.

2. S. K. Pal and S. Mitra, *Neuro-fuzzy Pattern Recognition: Methods in Soft Computing*. New York: John Wiley & Sons, 1999.

3. S. Mitra, S. K. Pal, and P. Mitra, "Data mining in soft computing framework: A survey," *IEEE Transactions on Neural Networks*, vol. 13, pp. 3–14, 2002.

4. I. Daubechies, "The wavelet transform, time-frequency localization and signal analysis," *IEEE Transactions on Information Theory*, vol. 36, pp. 961–1005, 1990.

5. I. Daubechies, *Ten Lectures on Wavelets*. CBMS, Philadelphia: Society for Industrial and Applied Mathematics, 1992.

6. R. Heider, "Troubleshooting CFM 56-3 engines for the Boeing 737 - using CBR and data-mining," *Lecture Notes in Computer Science*, vol. 1168, pp. 512–523, 1996.

7. J. Furnkranz, J. Petrak, and R. Trappl, "Knowledge discovery in international conflict databases," *Applied Artificial Intelligence*, vol. 11, pp. 91–118, 1997.

8. J. R. Quinlan, *C4.5: Programs for Machine Learning*. San Mateo, CA: Morgan Kaufmann, 1993.

9. S. K. Pal and A. Skowron, eds., *Rough Fuzzy Hybridization: A New Trend in Decision Making*. Singapore: Springer-Verlag, 1999.

10. L. A. Zadeh, "Fuzzy sets," *Information and Control*, vol. 8, pp. 338–353, 1965.

11. L. A. Zadeh, "The concept of a linguistic variable and its application to approximate reasoning: Part 1, 2, and 3," *Information Sciences*, vol. 8, 8, 9, pp. 199–249, 301–357, 43–80, 1975.

12. L. A. Zadeh, "Fuzzy sets as a basis for a theory of possibility," *Fuzzy Sets and Systems*, vol. 1, pp. 3–28, 1978.

13. L. A. Zadeh, "The role of fuzzy logic in the management of uncertainty in expert systems," *Fuzzy Sets and Systems*, vol. 11, pp. 199–227, 1983.

14. H. J. Zimmermann, *Fuzzy Sets, Decision Making and Expert Systems*. Boston, MA: Kluwer Academic Publishers, 1987.

15. G. J. Klir and B. Yuan, *Fuzzy Sets and Fuzzy Logic: Theory and Applications*. Englewood Cliffs, NJ: Prentice-Hall, 1995.

16. S. Haykin, *Neural Networks: A Comprehensive Foundation*. New York: Macmillan College Publishing Co., 1994.

17. J. Hertz, A. Krogh, and R. G. Palmer, *Introduction to the Theory of Neural Computation*. Reading, MA: Addison-Wesley, 1994.

18. D. E. Rumelhart and J. L. McClelland, eds., *Parallel Distributed Processing: Explorations in the Microstructures of Cognition*, vol. 1. Cambridge, MA: MIT Press, 1986.

19. T. Kohonen, *Self-Organization and Associative Memory*. Berlin: Springer-Verlag, 1989.

20. J. M. Zurada, *Introduction to Artificial Neural Systems*. New York: West Publishing Company, 1992.

21. D. R. Hush and B. G. Horne, "Progress in supervised neural networks," *IEEE Signal Processing Magazine*, pp. 8–39, January 1993.

22. D. O. Hebb, *The Organization of Behaviour*. New York: John Wiley & Sons, 1949.

23. W. S. McCulloch and W. Pitts, "A logical calculus of the idea immanent in nervous activity," *Bulletin of Mathematical Biophysics*, vol. 5, pp. 115–133, 1943.

24. G. G. Towell and J. W. Shavlik, "Extracting refined rules from knowledge-based neural networks," *Machine Learning*, vol. 13, pp. 71–101, 1993.

25. A. B. Tickle, R. Andrews, M. Golea, and J. Diederich, "The truth will come to light: Directions and challenges in extracting the knowledge embedded within trained artificial neural networks," *IEEE Transactions on Neural Networks*, vol. 9, pp. 1057–1068, 1998.

26. L. M. Fu, "Knowledge-based connectionism for revising domain theories," *IEEE Transactions on Systems, Man, and Cybernetics*, vol. 23, pp. 173–182, 1993.

27. G. G. Towell and J. W. Shavlik, "Knowledge-based artificial neural networks," *Artificial Intelligence*, vol. 70, pp. 119–165, 1994.

28. M. Banerjee, S. Mitra, and S. K. Pal, "Rough fuzzy MLP: Knowledge encoding and classification," *IEEE Transactions on Neural Networks*, vol. 9, pp. 1203–1216, 1998.

29. F. Rosenblatt, "The perceptron: A probabilistic model for information storage and organization in the brain," *Psychological Review*, vol. 65, pp. 386–408, 1958.

30. F. Rosenblatt, *Principles of Neurodynamics, Perceptrons and the Theory of Brain Mechanisms*. Washington, D.C.: Spartan Books, 1961.

31. M. Minsky and S. Papert, *Perceptrons: An Introduction to Computational Geometry*. Cambridge, MA: MIT Press, 1969.

32. K. L. Oehler and R. M. Gray, "Combining image compression and classification using vector quantization," *IEEE Transactions on Pattern Analysis and Machine Intelligence*, vol. 17, pp. 461–473, 1995.

33. J. Moody and C. J. Darken, "Fast learning in networks of locally-tuned processing units," *Neural Computation*, vol. 1, pp. 281–294, 1989.

34. D. R. Hush, B. Horne, and J. M. Salas, "Error surfaces for multilayer perceptrons," *IEEE Transactions on Systems, Man, and Cybernetics*, vol. 22, pp. 1152–1161, 1993.

35. C. T. Lin and C. S. George Lee, *Neural Fuzzy Systems–A Neuro-Fuzzy Synergism to Intelligent Systems*. Englewood Cliffs, NJ: Prentice-Hall, 1996.

36. W. Pedrycz, *Computational Intelligence: An Introduction*. Boca Raton, NY: CRC Press, 1998.

37. Y. Hayashi and J. J. Buckley, "Approximations between fuzzy expert systems and neural networks," *International Journal of Approximate Reasoning*, vol. 10, pp. 63–73, 1994.

38. J. S. R. Jang and C. T. Sun, "Functional equivalence between radial basis function networks and fuzzy inference systems," *IEEE Transactions on Neural Networks*, vol. 4, pp. 156–159, 1993.

39. E. H. Mamdani and S. Assilian, "An experiment in linguistic synthesis with a fuzzy logic controller," *International Journal of Man Machine Studies*, vol. 7, pp. 1–13, 1975.

40. T. Takagi and M. Sugeno, "Fuzzy identification of systems and its application to modeling and control," *IEEE Transactions on Systems, Man, and Cybernetics*, vol. 15, pp. 116–132, 1985.

41. J. J. Buckley and T. Feuring, *Fuzzy and Neural: Interactions and Applications*. Studies in Fuzziness and Soft Computing, Heidelberg: Physica-Verlag, 1999.

42. S. C. Lee and E. T. Lee, "Fuzzy neural networks," *Mathematical Biosciences*, vol. 23, pp. 151–177, 1975.

43. S. K. Pal and S. Mitra, "Multi-layer perceptron, fuzzy sets and classification," *IEEE Transactions on Neural Networks*, vol. 3, pp. 683–697, 1992.

44. J. K. Keller and D. J. Hunt, "Incorporating fuzzy membership functions into the perceptron algorithm," *IEEE Transactions on Pattern Analysis and Machine Intelligence*, vol. 7, pp. 693–699, 1985.

45. J. M. Keller, R. R. Yager, and H. Tahani, "Neural network implementation of fuzzy logic," *Fuzzy Sets and Systems*, vol. 45, pp. 1–12, 1992.

46. J. R. Jang, "ANFIS: Adaptive-network-based fuzzy inference system," *IEEE Transactions on Systems, Man, and Cybernetics*, vol. 23, pp. 665–685, 1993.

47. S. Mitra, "Fuzzy MLP based expert system for medical diagnosis," *Fuzzy Sets and Systems*, vol. 65, pp. 285–296, 1994.

48. D. Nauck, F. Klawonn, and R. Kruse, *Foundations of Neuro-Fuzzy Systems*. Chichester, England: John Wiley & Sons, 1997.

49. J. M. Keller, R. Krishnapuram, and F. C. -H. Rhee, "Evidence aggregation networks for fuzzy logic inference," *IEEE Transactions on Neural Networks*, vol. 3, pp. 761–769, 1992.

50. S. Mitra and S. K. Pal, "Logical operation based fuzzy MLP for classification and rule generation," *Neural Networks*, vol. 7, pp. 353–373, 1994.

51. G. A. Carpenter, S. Grossberg, N. Markuzon, J. H. Reynolds, and D. B. Rosen, "Fuzzy ARTMAP: A neural network architecture for incremental supervised learning of analog multidimensional maps," *IEEE Transactions on Neural Networks*, vol. 3, pp. 698–713, 1992.

52. A. Ghosh, N. R. Pal, and S. K. Pal, "Self-organization for object extraction using multilayer neural network and fuzziness measures," *IEEE Transactions on Fuzzy Systems*, vol. 1, pp. 54–68, 1993.

53. D. E. Goldberg, *Genetic Algorithms in Search, Optimization and Machine Learning.* Reading, MA: Addison-Wesley, 1989.

54. Z. Michalewicz, *Genetic Algorithms + Data Structures = Evolutionary Programs.* Berlin: Springer-Verlag, 1994.

55. Z. Pawlak, *Rough Sets, Theoretical Aspects of Reasoning about Data.* Dordrecht: Kluwer Academic, 1991.

56. R. Slowiński, ed., *Intelligent Decision Support, Handbook of Applications and Advances of the Rough Sets Theory.* Dordrecht: Kluwer Academic, 1992.

57. Y. Meyer, *Wavelets: Algorithms and Applications.* Philadelphia: SIAM - Society for Industrial and Applied Mathematics, 1993.

58. U. M. Fayyad, G. Piatetsky-Shapiro, P. Smyth, and R. Uthurusamy, eds., *Advances in Knowledge Discovery and Data Mining.* Menlo Park, CA: AAAI/MIT Press, 1996.

59. B. Liu, W. Hsu, L. F. Mun, and H. Y. Lee, "Finding interesting patterns using user expectation," *IEEE Transactions on Knowledge and Data Engineering*, vol. 11, pp. 817–832, 1999.

60. R. R. Yager, "Database discovery using fuzzy sets," *International Journal of Intelligent Systems*, vol. 11, pp. 691–712, 1996.

61. J. F. Baldwin, "Knowledge from data using fuzzy methods," *Pattern Recognition Letters*, vol. 17, pp. 593–600, 1996.

62. W. Pedrycz, "Fuzzy set technology in knowledge discovery," *Fuzzy Sets and Systems*, vol. 98, pp. 279–290, 1998.

63. P. Piatetsky-Shapiro and W. J. Frawley, eds., *Knowledge Discovery in Databases.* Menlo Park, CA: AAAI/MIT Press, 1991.

64. I. B. Turksen, "Fuzzy data mining and expert system development," in *Proceedings of IEEE International Conference on Systems, Man, and Cybernetics* (San Diego, CA), pp. 2057–2061, October 1998.

65. S. Russell and W. Lodwick, "Fuzzy clustering in data mining for telco database marketing campaigns," in *Proceedings of NAFIPS 99* (New York), pp. 720–726, June 1999.

66. W. Pedrycz, "Conditional fuzzy c-means," *Pattern Recognition Letters*, vol. 17, pp. 625–632, 1996.

67. R. Krishnapuram, A. Joshi, O. Nasraoui, and L. Yi, "Low complexity fuzzy relational clustering algorithms for web mining," *IEEE Transactions on Fuzzy Systems*, vol. 9, pp. 595–607, 2001.

68. L. J. Mazlack, "Softly focusing on data," in *Proceedings of NAFIPS 99*, (New York), pp. 700–704, June 1999.

69. L. A. Zadeh, "Toward a theory of fuzzy information granulation and its centrality in human reasoning and fuzzy logic," *Fuzzy Sets and Systems*, vol. 19, pp. 111–127, 1997.

70. R. Agrawal, T. Imielinski, and A. Swami, "Mining association rules between sets of items in large databases," in *Proceedings of 1993 ACM SIG-MOD International Conference on Management of Data* (Washington, D.C.), pp. 207–216, May 1993.

71. A. Maeda, H. Ashida, Y. Taniguchi, and Y. Takahashi, "Data mining system using fuzzy rule induction," in *Proceedings of IEEE International Conference on Fuzzy Systems FUZZ IEEE 95* (Yokohama, Japan), pp. 45–46, March 1995.

72. Q. Wei and G. Chen, "Mining generalized association rules with fuzzy taxonomic structures," in *Proceedings of NAFIPS 99* (New York), pp. 477–481, June 1999.

73. W. H. Au and K. C. C. Chan, "An effective algorithm for discovering fuzzy rules in relational databases," in *Proceedings of IEEE International Conference on Fuzzy Systems FUZZ IEEE 98* (Alaska), pp. 1314–1319, May 1998.

74. J. Hale and S. Shenoi, "Analyzing FD inference in relational databases," *Data and Knowledge Engineering*, vol. 18, pp. 167–183, 1996.

75. P. Bosc, O. Pivert, and L. Ughetto, "Database mining for the discovery of extended functional dependencies," in *Proceedings of NAFIPS 99* (New York), pp. 580–584, June 1999.

76. D. H. Lee and M. H. Kim, "Database summarization using fuzzy ISA hierarchies," *IEEE Transactions on Systems Man and Cybernetics. Part B-Cybernetics*, vol. 27, pp. 68–78, 1997.

77. R. R. Yager, "On linguistic summaries of data," in *Knowledge Discovery in Databases* (W. Frawley and G. Piatetsky-Shapiro, eds.), pp. 347–363, Menlo Park, CA: AAAI/MIT Press, 1991.

78. J. Kacprzyk and S. Zadrozny, "Data mining via linguistic summaries of data: an interactive approach," in *Proceedings of IIZUKA 98* (Fukuoka, Japan), pp. 668–671, October 1998.

79. D. A. Chiang, L. R. Chow, and Y. F. Wang, "Mining time series data by a fuzzy linguistic summary system," *Fuzzy Sets and Systems*, vol. 112, pp. 419–432, 2000.

80. H. Frigui, "Adaptive image retrieval using the fuzzy integral," in *Proceedings of NAFIPS 99* (New York), pp. 575–579, June 1999.

81. S. Medasani and R. Krishnapuram, "A fuzzy approach to complex linguistic query based image retrieval," in *Proceedings of NAFIPS 99* (New York), pp. 590–594, June 1999.

82. M. Detyniecki, C. Seyrat, and R. Yager, "Interacting with web video objects," in *Proceedings of the 18th International Conference of the North American Fuzzy Information Processing Society (NAFIPS'99)*, pp. 914–917, 1999.

83. A. Filho, G. L. A. Mota, M. M. B. R. Vellasco, and M. A. C. Pacheco, "Query by image similarity using a fuzzy logic approach," in *Proceedings of Fourth International Conference on Computational Intelligence and Multimedia Applications (ICCIMA 2001)*, pp. 389–394, 2001.

84. R. C. Gonzalez and R. E. Woods, *Digital Image Processing*. Reading, MA: Addison-Wesley, 1992.

85. R. M. Haralick, K. Shanmugam, and I. Dinstein, "Textural features for image classification," *IEEE Transactions on Systems, Man, and Cybernetics*, vol. 3, pp. 610–621, 1973.

86. H. J. Lu, R. Setiono, and H. Liu, "Effective data mining using neural networks," *IEEE Transactions on Knowledge and Data Engineering*, vol. 8, pp. 957–961, 1996.

87. S. K. Pal, S. Mitra, and P. Mitra, "Rough Fuzzy MLP: Modular evolution, rule generation and evaluation," *IEEE Transactions on Knowledge and Data Engineering*, vol. 15, pp. 14–25, 2003.

88. T. Kohonen, S. Kaski, K. Lagus, J. Salojarvi, J. Honkela, V. Paatero, and A. Saarela, "Self organization of a massive document collection," *IEEE Transactions on Neural Networks*, vol. 11, pp. 574–585, 2000.

89. J. Vesanto and E. Alhoniemi, "Clustering of the self-organizing map," *IEEE Transactions on Neural Networks*, vol. 11, pp. 586–600, 2000.

90. D. Alahakoon, S. K. Halgamuge, and B. Srinivasan, "Dynamic self organizing maps with controlled growth for knowledge discovery," *IEEE Transactions on Neural Networks*, vol. 11, pp. 601–614, 2000.

91. D. Shalvi and N. De Claris, "Unsupervised neural network approach to medical data mining techniques," in *Proceedings of IEEE International Joint Conference on Neural Networks* (Alaska), pp. 171–176, May 1998.

92. A. Koenig, "Interactive visualization and analysis of hierarchical neural projections for data mining," *IEEE Transactions on Neural Networks*, vol. 11, pp. 615–624, 2000.

93. V. Ciesielski and G. Palstra, "Using a hybrid neural/expert system for database mining in market survey data," in *Proceedings Second International Conference on Knowledge Discovery and Data Mining (KDD-96)* (Portland, OR), p. 38, AAAI Press, August 2–4, 1996.

94. R. S. T. Lee and J. N. K. Liu, "Tropical cyclone identification and tracking system using integrated neural oscillatory elastic graph matching and hybrid RBF network track mining techniques," *IEEE Transactions on Neural Networks*, vol. 11, pp. 680–689, 2000.

95. K. Lagus, "Text retrieval using self-organized document maps," *Neural Processing Letters*, vol. 15, pp. 21–29, 2002.

96. I. W. Flockhart and N. J. Radcliffe, "A genetic algorithm-based approach to data mining," in *The Second International Conference on Knowledge Discovery and Data Mining (KDD-96)* (Portland, OR), p. 299, AAAI Press, August 2–4 1996.

97. M. L. Raymer, W. F. Punch, E. D. Goodman, and L. A. Kuhn, "Genetic programming for improved data mining: An application to the biochemistry of protein interactions," in *Genetic Programming 1996: Proceedings of the First Annual Conference* (Stanford University, CA), pp. 375–380, MIT Press, 28–31 July 1996.

98. T. Ryu and C. F. Eick, "MASSON: discovering commonalties in collection of objects using genetic programming," in *Genetic Programming 1996: Proceedings of First Annual Conference* (Stanford University, CA), pp. 200–208, MIT Press, July 28–31 1996.

99. A. Teller and M. Veloso, "Program evolution for data mining," *The International Journal of Expert Systems*, vol. 8, pp. 216–236, 1995.

100. K. Xu, Z. Wang, and K. S. Leung, "Using a new type of nonlinear integral for multi-regression: An application of evolutionary algorithms in data mining," in *Proceedings of IEEE International Conference on Systems, Man, and Cybernetics* (San Diego, CA), pp. 2326–2331, October 1998.

101. E. Noda, A. A. Freitas, and H. S. Lopes, "Discovering interesting prediction rules with a genetic algorithm," in *Proceedings of IEEE Congress on Evolutionary Computation CEC 99* (Washington, D.C.), pp. 1322–1329, July 1999.

102. C. Lopes, M. Pacheco, M. Vellasco, and E. Passos, "Rule-evolver: An evolutionary approach for data mining," in *Proceedings of RSFDGrC '99* (Yamaguchi, Japan), pp. 458–462, November 1999.

103. J. F. Peters and A. Skowron, "A rough set approach to knowledge discovery," *International Journal of Intelligent Systems*, vol. 17, pp. 109–112, 2002.

104. T. Mollestad and A. Skowron, "A rough set framework for data mining of propositional default rules," *Lecture Notes in Computer Science*, vol. 1079, pp. 448–457, 1996.

105. A. Skowron, "Extracting laws from decision tables–a rough set approach," *Computational Intelligence*, vol. 11, pp. 371–388, 1995.

106. N. Shan and W. Ziarko, "Data-based acquisition and incremental modification of classification rules," *Computational Intelligence*, vol. 11, pp. 357–370, 1995.

107. L. Polkowski and A. Skowron, *Rough Sets in Knowledge Discovery 1 and 2.* Heidelberg: Physica-Verlag, 1998.

108. W. Ziarko and N. Shan, "KDD-R: A comprehensive system for knowledge discovery in databases using rough sets," in *Proceedings of Third International Workshop on Rough Sets and Soft Computing RSSC '94*, pp. 164–173, 1994.

109. J. W. Grzymala-Busse, "LERS–A knowledge discovery system," in *Rough Sets in Knowledge Discovery 2, Applications, Case Studies and Software Systems* (L. Polkowski and A. Skowron, eds.), pp. 562–565, Heidelberg: Physica-Verlag, 1998.

110. J. W. Grzymala-Busse, W. J. Grzymala-Busse, and L. K. Goodwin, "A closest fit approach to missing attribute values in preterm birth data," in *Proceedings of RSFDGrC '99* (Yamaguchi, Japan), pp. 405–413, November 1999.

111. T. B. Ho and N. B. Nguyen, "Nonhierarchical document clustering based on a tolerance rough set model," *International Journal of Intelligent Systems*, vol. 17, pp. 199–212, 2002.

112. S. G. Mallat, "A theory for multiresolution signal decomposition: The wavelet representation," *IEEE Transactions on Pattern Analysis and Machine Intelligence*, vol. 11, pp. 674–693, 1989.

113. M. Antonini, M. Barlaud, P. Mathieu, and I. Daubechies, "Image coding using wavelet transform," *IEEE Transactions on Image Processing*, vol. 1, pp. 205–220, 1992.

114. F. Wang and Q. J. Zhang, "Incorporating functional knowledge into neural networks," in *Proceedings of IEEE International Conference on Neural Networks* (Houston, TX), pp. 266–269, 1997.

115. J. Z. Wang, G. Wiederhold, O. Firchein, and S. Wei, "Content-based image indexing and searching using Daubechies' wavelets," *International Journal of Digital Libraries*, vol. 1, pp. 311–328, 1998.

116. G. Sheikholeslami, S. Chatterjee, and A. Zhang, "WaveCluster: A multi-resolution clustering approach for very large spatial databases," in *Proceedings of 1998 International Conference on Very Large Data Bases (VLDB '98)* (New York), pp. 428–439, August 1998.

117. R. M. Rao and A. S. Bopardikar, *Wavelet Transforms: Introduction to Theory and Applications.* Massachusetts: Addison Wesley, 1998.

118. S. Mitra and Y. Hayashi, "Neuro-fuzzy rule generation: Survey in soft computing framework," *IEEE Transactions on Neural Networks*, vol. 11, pp. 748–768, 2000.

119. S. Mitra and S. K. Pal, "Fuzzy multi-layer perceptron, inferencing and rule generation," *IEEE Transactions on Neural Networks*, vol. 6, pp. 51–63, 1995.

120. S. Mitra and S. K. Pal, "Fuzzy self organization, inferencing and rule generation," *IEEE Transactions on Systems, Man and Cybernetics, Part A: Systems and Humans*, vol. 26, pp. 608–620, 1996.

121. Y. Q. Zhang, M. D. Fraser, R. A. Gagliano, and A. Kandel, "Granular neural networks for numerical-linguistic data fusion and knowldege discovery," *IEEE Transactions on Neural Networks*, vol. 11, pp. 658–667, 2000.

122. S. Mitra, R. K. De, and S. K. Pal, "Knowledge-based fuzzy MLP for classification and rule generation," *IEEE Transactions on Neural Networks*, vol. 8, pp. 1338–1350, 1997.

123. S. Mitra, P. Mitra, and S. K. Pal, "Evolutionary modular design of rough knowledge-based network using fuzzy attributes," *Neurocomputing*, vol. 36, pp. 45–66, 2001.

124. P. Mitra, S. Mitra, and S. K. Pal, "Staging of cervical cancer with soft computing," *IEEE Transactions on Biomedical Engineering*, vol. 47, pp. 934–940, 2000.

125. R. George and R. Srikanth, "Data summarization using genetic algorithms and fuzzy logic," in *Genetic Algorithms and Soft Computing* (F. Herrera and J. L. Verdegay, eds.), pp. 599–611, Heidelberg: Physica-Verlag, 1996.

126. H. Kiem and D. Phuc, "Using rough genetic and Kohonen's neural network for conceptual cluster discovery in data mining," in *Proceedings of RSFDGrC '99* (Yamaguchi, Japan), pp. 448–452, November 1999.

127. Y. Bengio, J. M. Buhmann, M. Embrechts, and J. M. Zurada, "Introduction to the special issue on neural networks for data mining and knowledge discovery," *IEEE Transactions on Neural Networks*, vol. 11, pp. 545–549, 2000.

128. L. A. Zadeh, "A new direction in AI: Towards a computational theory of perceptions," *AI Magazine*, vol. 22, pp. 73–84, 2001.

129. S. Bengio and Y. Bengio, "Taking on the curse of dimensionality in joint distribution using neural networks," *IEEE Transactions on Neural Networks*, vol. 11, pp. 550–557, 2000.

130. R. Kewley, M. Embrechta, and C. Breneman, "Data strip mining for the virtual design of pharmaceuticals with neural networks," *IEEE Transactions on Neural Networks*, vol. 11, pp. 668–679, 2000.

131. C. K. Shin, S. J. Yu, U. T. Yun, and H. K. Kim, "A hybrid approach of neural network and memory based learning to data mining," *IEEE Transactions on Neural Networks*, vol. 11, pp. 637–646, 2000.

3

Multimedia Data Compression

3.1 INTRODUCTION

Multimedia data mining is a growing area of interest, and its advancement will have impact on how we store, access, and process different datatypes for different application areas in the near future. Data mining usually deals with large datasets and involves the access of relevant information from them. Hence it becomes necessary to apply data compression in large datasets, in order to reduce storage requirements for practical data processing applications, particularly in the area of multimedia applications. The development of efficient compression techniques will continue to be a design challenge and an area of interest to researchers.

Although the basic premises of data compression offer promises to potentially improve the efficiency of data mining techniques, not much attention has been focused in this direction by researchers. In our view, data compression has been neglected by the data mining community. However, limited efforts have been made to reduce high-dimensional data to lower dimensions for its compact representation and better visualization. Classical data mining techniques deal with mining information from databases represented in the canonical form. Access of data in the compressed domain and development of data compression techniques particularly suitable for data mining, whereby it would be possible to efficiently index the compressed data for fast search and access from large databases, remains a challenge. This will immensely benefit Web mining as well since huge volumes of data are distributed worldwide, all over the Web, in compressed form.

In order to address the challenging problem of mining data in the compressed domain, it becomes essential to understand the principles behind current data compression techniques. Researchers can build on this knowledge to propose new data mining techniques in the compressed domain, thereby influencing future multimedia applications through mining.

The main advantage of compression is that it reduces the data storage requirements. It also offers an attractive approach to reduce the communication cost in transmitting high volumes of data over long-haul links via higher effective utilization of the available bandwidth in the data links. This significantly aids in reducing the cost of communication, due to the data rate reduction. Thereby, data compression also increases the quality of multimedia presentation through limited bandwidth communication channels. As a result, the audience can experience rich quality signals for audio-visual data representation.

For example, because of the application of sophisticated compression technologies applied in multimedia data, we can receive toll quality audio at the other side of the globe through the good old telecommunication channels at a much better price as compared to that of a decade ago. Because of the significant progress in image compression techniques, a single 6-MHz broadcast television channel can carry HDTV signals to provide better-quality audio and video at higher rates and enhanced resolution, without additional bandwidth requirements. Due to the reduced data rate offered by the compression techniques, the computer network and Internet usage is becoming more and more image and graphics friendly, rather than being just data and text centric phenomena. In short, high-performance compression has created new opportunities of creative applications such as digital library, digital archival, video teleconferencing, telemedicine, digital entertainment, to name a few. Researchers need to pay significant attention to develop techniques for mining of multimedia data in the compressed domains, in order to further excel in the usage of data mining technologies in multimedia applications.

The organization of this chapter is as follows. Section 3.2 introduces the basic concepts from information theory. Sections 3.3–3.5 provide details on the classification of compression algorithms, a data compression model, and the different measures of compression performance. Section 3.6 presents some source coding algorithms. This is followed by a treatise on Principal Component Analysis in Section 3.7. Principles of still image compression are described in Section 3.8. The JPEG image compression standard, JPEG lossless coding algorithm, and baseline JPEG compression are explained in Sections 3.9–3.11. Text compression is elaborated upon in Section 3.12. Finally, Section 3.13 concludes the chapter.

3.2 INFORMATION THEORY CONCEPTS

The *Mathematical Theory of Communication* [1]–[4], also called the *Information Theory*, was pioneered by Claude E. Shannon in 1948. It is considered to be the theoretical foundation of data compression research.

Representation of data is a combination of *information* and *redundancy* [1]. Information is the portion of data that must be preserved permanently in its original form in order to correctly interpret the meaning or purpose of the data. Redundancy, on the other hand, is that portion of data that can be removed when it is not needed or can be reinserted to interpret the data when needed. Data *compression* is essentially a redundancy reduction technique. The redundancy in data representation is reduced in such a way that it can be subsequently reinserted to recover the original data, through a process called *decompression* of this data. In literature, sometimes data compression is referred to as *coding*, while decompression is termed as *decoding*.

Usually development of a data compression scheme can be broadly divided into two phases, namely, *modeling* and *coding*. In the modeling phase, information about redundancy that exists in the data is extracted and described in a model. This enables us to determine how the actual data differs from the model, and it allows us to encode the difference in the *coding* phase. Obviously, a data compression algorithm becomes more effective if the model is closer to the characteristics of the data generating process which we often call the *source*. The model can be obtained by empirical observation of the statistics of the data generated by the source. In an empirical sense, any information-generating process can be described as a source that emits a sequence of symbols chosen from a finite set of all possible symbols generated by the source. This finite set of symbols is often called an *alphabet*. For example, we can think of this text as being generated by a source with an alphabet containing all the ASCII characters.

3.2.1 Discrete memoryless model and entropy

If the symbols produced by the information source are statistically independent to each other, the source is called a *discrete memoryless source*. This is described by its source alphabet $A = \{a_1, a_2, \ldots, a_N\}$ and the associated probabilities of occurrence $P = \{p(a_1), p(a_2), \ldots, p(a_N)\}$ of the symbols $a_1, a_2, \ldots, a_N$ in A.

The definition of *discrete memoryless source* model provides us a very powerful concept of quantification of *average information content per symbol* of the source and *entropy* of the data. The concept of "entropy" was first used by physicists as a thermodynamic parameter to measure the degree of "disorder" or "chaos" in a thermodynamic or molecular system. In statistical sense, we can view this as a measure of the degree of "surprise" or "uncertainty." In an intuitive sense, it is reasonable to assume that the appearance of a less probable event (symbol) gives us more surprise and hence we expect that it might carry more information. On the contrary, the more probable event (symbol) will carry less information because it was expected more. Note an analogy to the concept of surprising or interesting rules explained in Section 7.4.

With the above intuitive explanation, we can comprehend Shannon's definition of the relation between the source symbol probabilities and corresponding codes. The amount of *information* content, $I(a_i)$, in a source symbol a_i, in terms of its associated probability of occurrence $p(a_i)$ is

$$I(a_i) = \log_2 \frac{1}{p(a_i)} = -\log_2 p(a_i).$$

The base 2 in the logarithm indicates that the information is expressed in binary units or bits. In terms of binary representation of the codes, a symbol a_i that is expected to occur with probability $p(a_i)$ is best represented in approximately $-\log_2 p(a_i)$ bits. As a result, a symbol with higher probability of occurrence in a message is coded using a fewer number of bits.

If we average the amount of information content over all the possible symbols of the discrete memoryless source, we can find the average amount of information content per source symbol from the discrete memoryless source. This is expressed as

$$E = \sum_{i=1}^{N} p(a_i)I(a_i) = -\sum_{i=1}^{N} p(a_i) \log_2 p(a_i), \tag{3.1}$$

and is popularly known as "*entropy*" in information theory. Hence entropy is the expected length of a binary code over all possible symbols in a discrete memoryless source. Note the analogy of this definition with Eq. (5.1), expressing entropy in the context of pattern classification.

The concept of entropy is very powerful. In "stationary" systems, where the probabilities of occurrence of the source symbols are fixed, it provides a bound for the compression that can be achieved. This is a very convenient measure of the performance of a coding system.

3.2.2   Noiseless Source Coding Theorem

The *Noiseless Source Coding Theorem* by Shannon [1] establishes the minimum average code word length per source symbol that can be achieved, which in turn provides an upper bound on the achievable compression losslessly. The *Noiseless Source Coding Theorem* is also known as *Shannon's first theorem*. This is one of the major source coding results in information theory [1]–[3].

If the data generated from a discrete memoryless source A is considered to be grouped together in blocks of n symbols, to form an *n-extended source*, then the new source A^n has N^n possible symbols $\{a_i\}$, with probability $P(a_i) = P(a_{i_1})P(a_{i_2})\cdots P(a_{i_n}), i = 1, 2, \cdots, N^n$. By deriving the entropy of the new

n-extended source, it can be proven that

$$E(A^n) = nE(A),$$

where $E(A)$ is the entropy of the original source A. Let us now consider encoding the blocks of n source symbols, at a time, into binary codewords. For any $\epsilon > 0$, it is possible to construct a codeword for the block in such a way that the average number of bits per original source symbol, $\bar{L}$, satisfies

$$E(A) \leq \bar{L} < E(A) + \epsilon. \tag{3.2}$$

The left-hand inequality must be satisfied for any uniquely decodable code for the block of n source symbols.

The *Noiseless Source Coding Theorem* states that any infinitely long sequence of source symbols emanating from a discrete memoryless source can be losslessly encoded with a code whose average number of bits per source symbol is arbitrarily close to, but not less than, the source entropy E in bits. Hence this theorem provides us the intuitive (statistical) yardstick to measure the information emerging from a source.

3.2.2.1 Example 1:

Let us consider a *discrete memoryless source* with alphabet $A_1 = \{\alpha, \beta, \gamma, \delta\}$ having associated probabilities $p(\alpha) = 0.65$, $p(\beta) = 0.20$, $p(\gamma) = 0.10$, and $p(\delta) = 0.05$, respectively. The entropy of this source is $E = -(0.65 \log_2 0.65 + 0.20 \log_2 0.20 + 0.10 \log_2 0.10 + 0.05 \log_2 0.05)$, which is approximately 1.42 bits/symbol. As a result, a 2000-symbols-long datum can be represented using approximately 2820 bits.

Knowing something about the structure of the data sequence often helps in reducing the entropy estimation of the source. Let us consider that the numeric data sequence generated by a source of alphabet $A_2 = \{0, 1, 2, 3\}$ is $D = 0\ 1\ 1\ 2\ 3\ 3\ 3\ 3\ 3\ 3\ 3\ 3\ 3\ 2\ 2\ 2\ 3\ 3\ 3\ 3$, as an example. The probability of appearance of the symbols in alphabet A_2 are $p(0) = 0.05$, $p(1) = 0.10$, $p(2) = 0.20$, and $p(3) = 0.65$, respectively, as in alphabet A_1. Hence the estimated entropy of the sequence D is $E = 1.42$ bits per symbol. If we assume that correlation exists between two consecutive samples in this data sequence, we can reduce this correlation by simply subtracting a sample by its previous sample to generate the residual values $r_i = s_i - s_{i-1}$ for each sample s_i. Based on this assumption of the model, the sequence of residuals of the original data sequence is $\bar{D} = 0\ 1\ 0\ 1\ 1\ 0\ 0\ 0\ 0\ 0\ 0\ 0\ 0\ -1\ 0\ 0\ 1\ 0\ 0\ 0$, consisting of three symbols in a modified alphabet $\bar{A}_2 = \{-1, 1, 0\}$. The probability of occurrence of the symbols in the new alphabet $\bar{A}$ are $p(-1) = 0.05$, $p(1) = 0.2$, and $p(0) = 0.75$, respectively, as computed by the number of occurrences in the residual sequence. The estimated entropy of the transformed sequence is $\bar{E} = -(0.05 \log_2 0.05 + 0.2 \log_2 0.2 + 0.75 \log_2 0.75) = 0.992$, that is, 0.992 bits/symbol. Hence the data sequence can be represented with fewer number of bits, resulting in compression.

3.3   CLASSIFICATION OF COMPRESSION ALGORITHMS

In an abstract sense, we can describe *data compression* as a method that takes an input data D and generates a shorter representation of the data $c(D)$ with fewer number of bits compared to that of D. The reverse process is called *decompression*, and it takes the compressed data $c(D)$ and generates or reconstructs the data D' as shown in Fig. 3.1. Sometimes the *compression* (coding) and *decompression* (decoding) systems together are called a "CODEC," as marked by the broken box in Fig. 3.1. The reconstructed data D' could be identical to the original data D or it could be an approximation of the original data D, depending upon the reconstruction requirements. If the reconstructed data D' is an exact replica of the original data D, we call the algorithm applied to compress D and decompress $c(D)$ to be *lossless*. Otherwise, we call the algorithms to be *lossy*. Hence as far as the reversibility of the original data is concerned, the data compression algorithms can be broadly classified into two categories, namely, "*lossless*" and "*lossy*."

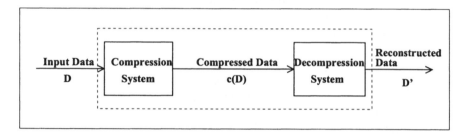

Fig. 3.1   Block diagram of CODEC.

Usually we need to apply lossless data compression techniques on text data or scientific data. For example, we cannot afford to compress the electronic copy of this textbook using a lossy compression technique. It is expected that we should be able to reconstruct the same text after the decompression process. A small error in the reconstructed text can have a completely different meaning. We do not expect the sentence "You should *not* delete this file" in a text to change to "You should *now* delete this file" as a result of some error introduced by a lossy compression or decompression algorithm. Similarly, if we compress a huge ASCII file containing a program written in "C" language, for example, we expect to get back the same "C" code after decompression because of obvious reasons.

The lossy compression techniques are usually applicable to data where high fidelity of reconstructed data is not required, for perception, by the human perceptual system. Examples of such types of data are image, video, graphics, speech, audio, etc. Some image compression applications may, however, require the compression scheme to be lossless; that is, each pixel of the decompressed image should be exactly identical to the original one. Medical imaging is an example of such an application, where compressing the digital radiographs with a lossy scheme could be a disaster if it has to compromise with the diagnostic accuracy. Similar observations are true for astronomical images of galaxies and stars.

3.4   A DATA COMPRESSION MODEL

A model of a typical data compression system can be described using the block diagram shown in Fig. 3.2. A data compression system mainly constitutes three major steps, namely, (i) removal or reduction in data redundancy, (ii) reduction in entropy, and (iii) entropy encoding.

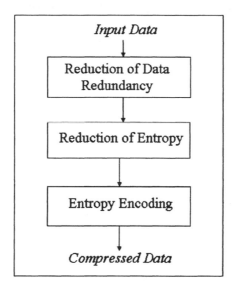

Fig. 3.2   A data compression model.

The redundancy in data may appear in different forms. For example, the neighboring pixels in a typical image are very much spatially correlated to each other. By correlation we mean that the pixel values are very similar in the non-edge smooth regions of the image [5, 6]. This correlation of the neighboring pixels is termed as spatial correlation. In case of moving pictures, the consecutive frames could be almost similar, with or without minor displacement, if the motion is slow. The composition of words or sentences in a natural text follows some context model, based on the grammar being used. Similarly, the records in a typical numeric database may have some sort of relationship amongst the atomic entities which comprise each record in the database. There are rhythms and pauses in regular intervals in any natural audio or speech data. All these redundancies in data representation can be reduced in order to achieve potential compression.

Removal or reduction in data redundancy is typically achieved by transforming the original data from one form of representation to another, in order to decorrelate the spatial information redundancies present in the data. The popular techniques used for spatial redundancy reduction are prediction of data samples using some model, transformation of the original data from spatial to frequency domain using methods such as Discrete Cosine Transform (DCT), decomposition of the original dataset into different subbands as in Discrete Wavelet Transformation (DWT), etc. In principle, this spatial redundancy reduction potentially yields more compact representation of the information in the original dataset, in terms of fewer transformed coefficients or equivalent, and hence makes it amenable to represent the data with fewer number of bits in order to achieve compression.

The next major step in a lossy data compression system is "quantization." Quantization techniques are applied on the decorrelated or transformed data, in order to further reduce the number of symbols or coefficients, by masking nonsignificant parts and preserving only the meaningful information in the data. This leads to reduction in entropy of the data, and hence makes it further amenable to compression by allocating less number of bits for transmission or storage. The reduction in entropy is achieved by dropping nonsignificant information in the transformed data and preserving fewer significant symbols only. For example, in case of an image transformed in frequency domain, the high-frequency transformed coefficients can be dropped because the human vision system is not sensitive to these. By preserving a smaller number of transformed coefficients in the meaningful low-frequency range, we can maintain the fidelity of the reconstructed image. The nature and amount of quantization dictate the quality of the reconstructed data. The quantized coefficients are then losslessly encoded, using some entropy encoding scheme to compactly represent the quantized data for storage or transmission. Since the entropy of the quantized data is less than that of the original one, it can be represented by a smaller number of bits compared to the original data set and hence we achieve compression.

The decompression system is just an inverse process to reconstruct the data.

3.5 MEASURES OF COMPRESSION PERFORMANCE

As in any other system, the metrics of performance of a data compression algorithm is an important criteria for its selection. The performance measures of data compression algorithms can be looked at from different perspectives depending upon the application requirements, namely, amount of compression achieved, objective and subjective quality of the reconstructed data, relative complexity of the algorithm, speed of execution, etc. We explain some of these below.

3.5.1 Compression ratio and bits per sample

The most popular performance measure of a data compression algorithm is the '*compression ratio*'. It is defined as the ratio of the number of bits in the original data to the number of bits in the compressed data. Consider a gray scale image of size 256 × 256. If each pixel is represented by a single byte, the image needs 65536 bytes of storage. If the compressed version of the image can be stored in 4096 bytes, the compression ratio achieved by the compression algorithm will be 16:1.

A variation of the *compression ratio* is '*bits per sample*'. This metric indicates the average number of bits to represent a single sample of the data – for example, *bits per pixel* for image coding. In case of an image, each pixel represents a sample. On the other hand, in case of a text file, each sample corresponds to a character in the text. If 65536 pixels of an image are compressed to 4096 bytes, we can say that the compression algorithm achieved 0.5 bits per pixel on the average. Hence the *bits per sample* can be measured by the ratio of the *number of bits* of a single uncompressed sample to the *compression ratio*.

3.5.2 Quality metric

The quality or fidelity metric is important for lossy compression algorithms used in video, image, voice, etc., because here the reconstructed data differs from the original one and the human perceptual system is the ultimate judge of the reconstructed quality. For example, if there is no perceivable difference between the reconstructed data and the original version, then the compression algorithm can be claimed to have achieved a very high quality or fidelity. The difference of the reconstructed data from the original one is called the *distortion*, and a lower distortion implies a higher quality of the reconstructed data. A quality measure can either be very subjective based on human perception, or be objectively defined using mathematical or statistical evaluation.

3.5.2.1 **Subjective quality metric:** There is no universally accepted measure for the subjective quality metrics. Often the subjective quality metric is defined as the *mean observer score* (MOS). Sometimes it is also called the *mean opinion score*. There are different statistical ways to compute MOS. In one of the simplest methods, a statistically significant number of observers are randomly chosen to evaluate the visual quality of the reconstructed images. All the images are compressed and decompressed by the same algorithm. Each observer assigns a numeric score to each reconstructed image based on his or her perception of quality of the image, say, within a range 1–5 to describe the quality of the image, with 5 and 1 being the best and worst quality, respectively. The average of the scores assigned by all the observers is the MOS, and it is considered as a viable subjective metric if all the observers are unbiased and evaluate the images under the same viewing or experimental conditions. There are different variations of this approach to calculate MOS, namely, absolute comparison, paired comparison, blind evaluation, etc.

The techniques of measurement of MOS could well be different for different perceptual data. For example, the methodology to evaluate the subjective quality of a still image could be entirely different from that for video or voice data.

3.5.2.2 Objective quality metric:

There is no universally accepted measure for the objective quality of data compression algorithms either. The most widely used objective quality metrics are root-mean-squared error ($RMSE$), signal-to-noise ratio (SNR), and peak signal-to-noise ratio ($PSNR$). If I is an $M \times N$ image and $\bar{I}$ is the corresponding reconstructed image after compression and decompression, $RMSE$ is calculated as

$$RMSE = \sqrt{\frac{1}{MN} \sum_{i=1}^{M} \sum_{j=1}^{N} [I(i,j) - \bar{I}(i,j)]^2}, \qquad (3.3)$$

where i, j refer to the pixel position in the image. The SNR in decibel unit (dB) is expressed as $SNR =$

$$20 \log_{10} \left(\frac{\sqrt{\frac{1}{MN} \sum_{i=1}^{M} \sum_{j=1}^{N} I^2(i,j)}}{RMSE} \right) = 10 \log_{10} \left(\frac{\sum_{i=1}^{M} \sum_{j=1}^{N} I^2(i,j)}{\sum_{i=1}^{M} \sum_{j=1}^{N} \left[I(i,j) - \bar{I}(i,j) \right]^2} \right).$$

$$(3.4)$$

In case of an 8-bit image, the corresponding $PSNR$ in dB is computed as

$$PSNR = 20 \log_{10} \left(\frac{255}{RMSE} \right), \qquad (3.5)$$

where 255 is the maximum possible pixel value in 8 bits.

It should be noted that a lower $RMSE$ (or equivalently, higher SNR or $PSNR$) does not necessarily always indicate a higher subjective quality. In fact these objective error metrics do not always correlate well with the subjective quality metrics. There are many cases where the PSNR of a reconstructed image can be reasonably high, but the subjective quality is really bad when visualized by human eyes. Hence the choice of the objective or subjective metrics, to evaluate a compression and decompression algorithm, often depends upon the application criteria.

Similar objective quality metrics are used for audio and speech signals as well.

3.5.3 Coding complexity

When the computational requirement to implement the CODEC in a particular computing platform is an important criterion, we often consider the coding complexity and computation time of a compression algorithm to be a performance measure. Implementation of a compression algorithm using special purpose digital signal processor (DSP) architectures is common in communication systems. In portable systems, the coding complexity is an important criterion from the perspective of low-power hardware implementation. The computational requirement is usually measured in terms of the number of arithmetic operations and the memory requirement. Usually, the number of arithmetic operations is described by MOPS (millions of operations per second). But in compression literature, the term MIPS (millions of instructions per second) is often used to measure the compression performance of a specific computing engine's architecture.

3.6 SOURCE CODING ALGORITHMS

From the information theoretic perspective, *source coding* can mean both lossless and lossy compression. However, researchers often use it to indicate lossless coding only. In the signal processing community, source coding is used to mean source model based coding. In this section, we describe some basic source coding algorithms such as Run-length coding and Huffman coding in greater detail.

3.6.1 Run-length coding

Run-length coding is a simple approach to source coding when there exists a long run of the same data, in a consecutive manner, in a dataset. As an example, the data d = '6 6 6 6 6 6 0 9 0 5 5 5 5 5 5 2 2 2 2 2 2 1 3 4 4 4 4 4 ...' contains long runs of 6's, 5's 2's 4's, etc. Rather than coding each sample in the run individually, the data can be represented compactly by simply indicating the value of the sample and the length of its run when it appears. For example, if a portion of an image is represented by "5 5 5 5 5 5 5 19 19 19 19 19 19 19 19 19 19 19 19 0 0 0 0 0 0 0 0 8 23 23 23 23 23 23," this can be run-length encoded as (5 7) (19 12) (0 8) (8 1) (23 6). For ease of understanding, we have shown a pair in each parenthesis. Here the first value represents the pixel, while the second indicates the length of its run.

In some cases, the appearance of runs of symbols may not be very apparent. But the data can possibly be preprocessed in order to aid run-length coding. Consider the data d = '26 29 32 35 38 41 44 50 56 62 68 78 88 98 108 118 116 114 112 110 108 106 104 102 100 98 96'. We can simply preprocess this data by taking the sample difference $e(i) = d(i) - d(i-1)$, to produce the processed data $\bar{e}$ = '26 3 3 3 3 3 3 6 6 6 6 10 10 10 10 10 -2 -2 -2 -2 -2

-2 -2 -2 -2 -2 -2'. This preprocessed data can now easily be run-length encoded as (26 1) (3 6) (6 4) (10 5) (-2 11). A variation of this technique is applied in the baseline JPEG standard for still picture compression [7]. The same technique can be applied to numeric databases as well.

On the other hand, binary (black and white) images, such as facsimile, usually consist of runs of 0's or 1's. As an example, if a segment of a binary image is represented as $d =$
"00000000011111111111100000000000000001110000000000000001001111111111,"
it can be compactly represented as $c(d) = (9, 11, 15, 3, 13, 1, 2, 10)$ by simply listing the lengths of alternate runs of 0's and 1's. While the original binary data d requires 65 bits for storage, its compact representation $c(d)$ requires 32 bits only under the assumption that each length of run is being represented by 4 bits. The early facsimile compression standard (CCITT Group 3, CCITT Group 4) algorithms have been developed based on this principle [8].

3.6.2 Huffman coding

In 1952, D. A. Huffman [9] invented a coding technique to produce the shortest possible average code length, given the source symbol set and the associated probability of occurrence of the symbols. The Huffman coding technique is based on the following two observations regarding optimum prefix codes.

- The more frequently occurring symbols can be allocated with shorter codewords than the less frequently occurring symbols.

- The two least frequently occurring symbols will have codewords of the same length, and they differ only in the least significant bit.

The average of the length of these codes is closed to the entropy of the source. Let us assume that there are m source symbols $\{s_1, s_2, \ldots, s_m\}$ with associated probabilities of occurrence $\{p_1, p_2, \ldots, p_m\}$. Using these probability values, we can generate a set of Huffman codes of the source symbols. The Huffman codes can be mapped into a binary tree, popularly known as the Huffman tree. We describe below the algorithm to generate the Huffman codes of the source symbols.

1. Produce a set $N = \{N_1, N_2, \ldots, N_m\}$ of m nodes as leaves of a binary tree. Assign a node N_i with the source symbol s_i, $i = 1, 2, \ldots, m$, and label the node with the associated probability p_i.
   (**Example:** As shown in Fig. 3.3, we start with eight nodes N_0, N_1, N_2, N_3, N_4, N_5, N_6, N_7 corresponding to the eight source symbols a, b, c, d, e, f, g, h, respectively. Probability of occurrence of each symbol is indicated in the associated parentheses.)

2. Find the two nodes with the two lowest probability symbols from the current node set, and produce a new node as a parent of these two nodes.

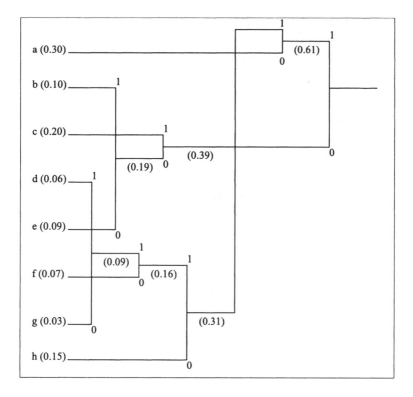

Fig. 3.3 Huffman tree construction for Example 2.

(**Example:** From Fig. 3.3 we find that the two lowest probability symbols g and d are associated with nodes N_6 and N_3, respectively. The new node N_8 becomes the parent of N_3 and N_6.)

3. Label the probability of this new parent node as the sum of the probabilities of its two child nodes.
   (**Example:** The new node N_8 is now labeled by probability 0.09, which is the sum of the probabilities 0.06 and 0.03 of the symbols d and g associated with the nodes N_3 and N_6, respectively.)

4. Label the branch of one child node of the new parent node as 1 and branch of the other child node as 0.
   (**Example:** The branch N_3 to N_8 is labeled by 1 and the branch N_6 to N_8 is labeled by 0.)

5. Update the node set by replacing the two child nodes with smallest probabilities by the newly generated parent node. If the number of nodes remaining in the node set is greater than 1, go to Step 2.
   (**Example:** The new node set now contains the nodes N_0, N_1, N_2, N_4, N_5, N_7, N_8 and the associated probabilities are 0.30, 0.10, 0.20, 0.09,

0.07, 0.15, 0.09, respectively. Since there are more than one node in
the node set, Steps 2 to 5 are repeated and the nodes N_9, N_{10}, N_{11},
N_{12}, N_{13}, N_{14} are generated in the next six iterations, until the node
set consists of N_{14} only.)

6. Traverse the generated binary tree from the root node to each leaf node
   N_i, $i = 1, 2, \ldots, m$, to produce the codeword of the corresponding
   symbol s_i, which is a concatenation of the binary labels (0 or 1) of the
   branches from the root to the leaf node.
   (**Example:** The Huffman code of symbol h is "110," formed by concatenating the binary labels of the branches N_{14} to N_{13}, N_{13} to N_{11} and
   N_{11} to N_7.)

Table 3.1   Huffman code table

Symbol	Probability	Huffman code
a	0.30	1 0
b	0.10	0 0 1
c	0.20	0 1
d	0.06	1 1 1 1 1
e	0.09	0 0 0
f	0.07	1 1 1 0
g	0.03	1 1 1 1 0
h	0.15	1 1 0

3.6.2.1 Example 2:   Assume an alphabet $S = \{a, b, c, d, e, f, g, h\}$ with
probabilities $p(a) = 0.30$, $p(b) = 0.10$, $p(c) = 0.20$, $p(d) = 0.06$, $p(e) = 0.09$,
$p(f) = 0.07$, $p(g) = 0.03$ and $p(h) = 0.15$, respectively. The Huffman tree
for this source is depicted in Fig. 3.3, while the Huffman code is shown in
Table 3.1.

Let us consider a string M of 200 symbols generated from the above source,
where the numbers of occurrences of a, b, c, d, e, f, g and h in M are 60,
20, 40, 12, 18, 14, 6, and 30, respectively. Size of the encoded message M
using the Huffman codes in Table 3.1 will be 550 bits. Here it requires 2.75
bits per symbol on the average. On the other hand, the length of the encoded
message M will be 600 bits if it is encoded by a fixed length code of length
3 for each of the symbols. This simple example demonstrates how we can
achieve compression using variable-length coding or source coding techniques.

3.7 PRINCIPAL COMPONENT ANALYSIS FOR DATA COMPRESSION

Principal Component Analysis has been a popular technique for data compression. It forms the basis of the Karhunen–Loeve (KL) transform for compact representation of data [5, 6, 10, 11]. The KL transform and the theory behind *principal component analysis* are of fundamental importance in signal and image processing. The principle has also found its place in data mining for reduction of large-dimensional datasets. It has been successfully applied to text analysis and retrieval for text mining as well [12]. The principal component analysis has been developed based on the matrix theory for *Singular Value Decomposition (SVD)*.

According to singular value decomposition (SVD) theory, for any arbitrary $M \times N$ matrix F of rank L there exists an $M \times M$ unitary matrix U and an $N \times N$ unitary matrix V so that

$$U^T F V = \Lambda^{\frac{1}{2}}, \tag{3.6}$$

where

$$\Lambda^{\frac{1}{2}} = \begin{bmatrix} \lambda^{\frac{1}{2}}(1) & & & & & & \\ & \lambda^{\frac{1}{2}}(2) & & & & & \\ & & \ddots & & & & \\ & & & \lambda^{\frac{1}{2}}(L) & & & \\ & & & & 0 & & \\ & & & & & \ddots & \\ & & & & & & 0 \end{bmatrix}$$

is an $M \times N$ diagonal matrix and the first L diagonal elements $\lambda^{\frac{1}{2}}(i)$, for $i = 1, 2, \ldots, L$, are called the *singular* values of input matrix F. Since U and V are unitary matrices, we have

$$UU^T = I_M,$$

$$VV^T = I_N,$$

where I_M and I_N are the identity matrices of dimension M and N, respectively. As a result, the input matrix F can be decomposed as

$$F = U \Lambda^{\frac{1}{2}} V^T. \tag{3.7}$$

The columns of U are chosen as the eigenvectors u_m of the symmetric matrix FF^T so that

$$U^T(FF^T)U = \begin{bmatrix} \lambda(1) & & & & & & \\ & \lambda(2) & & & & & \\ & & \ddots & & & & \\ & & & \lambda(L) & & & \\ & & & & 0 & & \\ & & & & & \ddots & \\ & & & & & & 0 \end{bmatrix}, \qquad (3.8)$$

where $\lambda(i)$, $i = 1, 2, \ldots, L$, are the nonzero eigenvalues of FF^T. Similarly, the columns of matrix V are eigenvectors v_n of the symmetric matrix F^TF as defined by

$$V^T(F^TF)V = \begin{bmatrix} \lambda(1) & & & & & & \\ & \lambda(2) & & & & & \\ & & \ddots & & & & \\ & & & \lambda(L) & & & \\ & & & & 0 & & \\ & & & & & \ddots & \\ & & & & & & 0 \end{bmatrix}, \qquad (3.9)$$

where $\lambda(i)$, $i = 1, 2, \ldots, L$ are the corresponding nonzero eigenvalues of F^TF. The input matrix can be represented in series form by these eigenvalues and eigenvectors as

$$F = \sum_{i=1}^{L} \lambda^{\frac{1}{2}}(i) u_i v_i^T. \qquad (3.10)$$

If the eigenvalues $\lambda(i)$, for $i = 1, 2, \ldots, L$ are sorted in decreasing order and only first K from the sorted list are significant ($K < L$), then we can approximate the input matrix F by a smaller-dimensional matrix $\bar{F}$ using these first K eigenvalues and corresponding eigenvectors only.

The eigenvector corresponding to the highest eigenvalue of F^TF is called the *first principal component*. Likewise, the *second principal component* is the eigenvector corresponding to the next highest eigenvalue of F^TF, and so on. Hence the kth *principal component* is the eigenvector corresponding to the kth largest eigenvalue of F^TF.

The principal component analysis-based data reduction technique has been very popular in data mining, particularly to reduce the high-order dimensionality of data to lower orders. This is also the foundation of Karhunen–Loeve Transform used in many multimedia processing applications [5, 6, 10, 11]. *Latent Semantic Analysis* (LSA) technique has been developed based on this theory of *SVD*, using a compact representation of the data in terms of a few

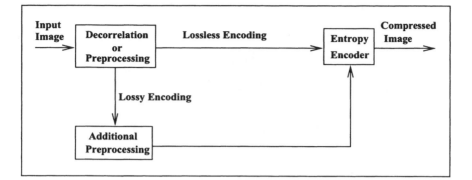

Fig. 3.4 A general image compression framework.

principal components only. LSA has been effectively applied in text analysis suitable for text mining [12], and has been described in detail in Section 9.2.5.

3.8 PRINCIPLES OF STILL IMAGE COMPRESSION

The statistical analysis of a typical image indicates that there is a strong correlation amongst neighboring pixels. This causes redundancy of information in the image. In general, still image compression techniques rely on two fundamental redundancy reduction principles, namely, *Spatial* and *Statistical*. Spatial redundancy is the similarity of neighboring pixels in an image and is reduced by decorrelating the pixels. The statistical redundancy reduction is referred to as *entropy encoding*, accomplished by a source coding algorithm.

The general model of a still image compression framework is shown as a block diagram in Fig. 3.4. The *decorrelation* or *preprocessing* block is the step for reducing the spatial redundancy of the image pixels. In lossless coding mode, this decorrelated image is directly processed by the entropy encoder. On the other hand, for lossy compression, the decorrelated image is further preprocessed as shown in Fig. 3.4 in order to mask irrelevant information depending upon the application criteria. This process is popularly called *Quantization*. The quantized pixels are then entropy-encoded using a source coding algorithm to compactly represent the image. We now discuss different image coding principles in the following sections.

3.8.1 Predictive coding

Since the adjacent pixels in a typical image are highly correlated, it is possible to extract a great deal of information about a pixel from its neighboring pixel values. In predictive coding, a pixel value is predicted by a set of previously encoded neighboring pixels. For an ideal prediction model, the predicted value

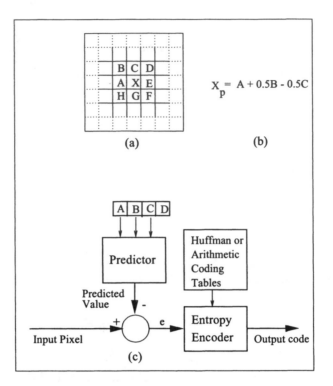

$$X_p = A + 0.5B - 0.5C$$

Fig. 3.5 DPCM showing (a) neighbors of pixel X to be encoded, (b) prediction function, and (c) block diagram.

of the pixel is similar to the actual value. But in reality, using an effective prediction model, we can predict a pixel value which is very close to its actual value. A practical approach to the prediction model is to take a linear combination of the previously encoded neighboring pixels. The reason for taking the previously encoded pixels is that the same pixels will be available to the decoder, when it decodes the pixels in the same order that they were encoded. The difference between the actual pixel value and the predicted value is called *differential* or *prediction error*. The error value e is then entropy-encoded using a variable-length encoding technique to generate the compressed image. This method is popularly known as *Differential Pulse Code Modulation* (DPCM). The block diagram is provided in Fig. 3.5(c).

In Fig. 3.5(a), let pixels A, B, C, D, E, F, G, and H be the immediate neighbors of pixel X to be encoded. If we follow the raster scan order convention to access the image from left-to-right and top-to-bottom, the previously encoded pixels available to the predictor will be A, B, C, D. We assume that the prediction function is $X_p = A + 0.5B - 0.5C$, using A, B, and C only, as shown in Fig. 3.5(b). The prediction error $e = X - X_p$ has less entropy as compared to X, because of the reduction in spatial redundancy. As

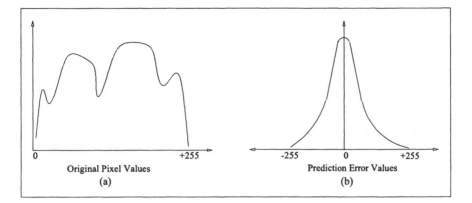

Fig. 3.6 Histogram of (a) a typical image and (b) its prediction error.

a result, the error value e can be encoded by less number of bits to achieve compression. Effectiveness of the error image for entropy encoding, as compared to direct encoding of the image, can be explained by the corresponding histograms shown in Fig. 3.6.

Statistical distribution of pixels in a typical image is uniform distribution in nature, as shown in Fig. 3.6(a). Because of uniform distribution, average number of bits per pixels in the range [0, 255] will be eight. In Fig. 3.6(b), we provide the statistical distribution of the prediction error values of the same image after applying the DPCM technique. The prediction error values belong to the range $[-255, +255]$. It is clear from Fig. 3.6(b) that the statistical distribution of the prediction errors of a typical image is Laplacian in nature, and most of the prediction errors are skewed around zero. As a result, we can apply a statistics-based entropy encoding technique to allocate smaller binary codes to the prediction error values close to zero and larger codes to bigger error values. Hence the average number of bits per pixel error will be less than eight, thereby resulting in compression.

3.8.2 Transform coding

In predictive coding, the coding process takes place pixel by pixel. *Transform coding* is an effective way of coding a group of spatially correlated pixels [10]. This technique takes advantage of the fact that the energy of most natural images is mainly concentrated in the low-frequency regions.

A suitable transformation technique produces fewer number of correlated transformed coefficients as compared to the original image, and a significant amount of image information is concentrated in these fewer correlated transformed coefficients. As a result, we can discard or mask the insignificant transformed coefficients, mainly consisting of the high-frequency components, using a suitable quantization technique without affecting the desired recon-

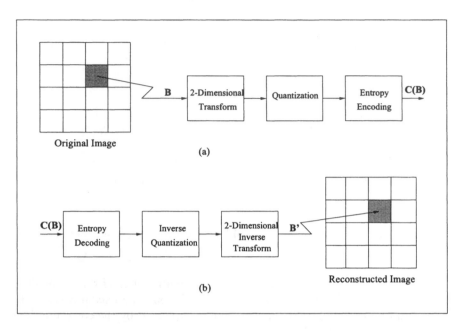

Fig. 3.7 Transform coding-based (a) compression and (b) decompression.

structed image quality. This is possible because the human visual system has perceptual masking effects, so that the high-frequency components are not as sensitive to reconstruction errors as compared to their low-frequency counterparts. If the quantization process is not too coarse, then the reconstructed image can be perceptually similar to the original one.

The general framework for transform coding-based image compression systems is depicted in Fig. 3.7(a). Usually the input image is first divided into a number of smaller rectangular blocks B. Each of these blocks are then independently transformed, using the chosen linear transformation technique. The transformed coefficients are quantized and entropy encoded into bit-stream $c(B)$ in order to achieve compression. During the decompression, as shown in Fig. 3.7(b), the compressed bit stream $c(B)$ is first entropy-decoded to generate the quantized coefficients. This is followed by inverse quantization in order to generate an approximation of the transformed coefficients. The inverse transformation is applied on these coefficients to reconstruct the image block B'. The composition of the reconstructed image blocks forms the reconstructed image, as shown in Fig. 3.7(b).

In transform coding, the selection of the transformation technique is a major decision. The main motivation behind transformation from the spatial domain to another domain (usually frequency domain) is to represent the data in a more compact form in the transformed domain. The optimum transformation also minimizes the mean squared error of the reconstructed image. The *Karhunen–Loeve* Transform (KLT) [5, 10] has been proven to

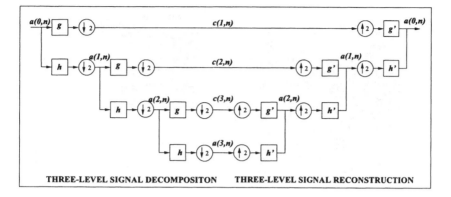

Fig. 3.8 Three-level multi-resolution wavelet decomposition and reconstruction of a signal.

be optimal in terms of the compaction efficiency, by representing the image using few principal components containing a significant portion of the image information. KLT packs the most energy of an image block in the least number of transformed coefficients. It completely decorrelates the pixels, and hence minimizes the spatial redundancy in the image block.

Although KLT is optimum, it is not efficient for practical implementations. The basis functions of KLT are input data-dependent, because they are formed by the eigenvectors of the autocorrelation matrix of the input signal. There is no fast algorithm for practical implementation of KLT, because of its dependency on the input source signal. As a result, we have to choose a suboptimal transform, so that the basis functions are not signal-dependent and a fast algorithm can exist in order to have a practical implementation. A number of suboptimal transforms like the Discrete Fourier Transform (DFT), Discrete Cosine Transform (DCT), Discrete Sine Transform (DST), and Discrete Hadamard Transform (DHT), to name a few, have been used in digital image compression [6, 10]. Of these the DCT is the most popular block-based transform, because its performance is very close to that of KLT and a number of fast algorithms exist for DCT [13]. DCT is the basis for most of the image and video compression algorithms, especially the still image compression standard JPEG in lossy mode and the video compression standards MPEG-1, MPEG-2, MPEG-4, H.263, etc. [14].

3.8.3 Wavelet coding

Representation of a signal using Fourier series in terms of the sinusoids is well known in the signal processing community, provably for more than a century, and is known to be effective for *stationary* as well as *nonstationary* signals. The non-stationary signals are not statistically predictable, especially in the regions of discontinuities. In a typical image, discontinuities occur at the

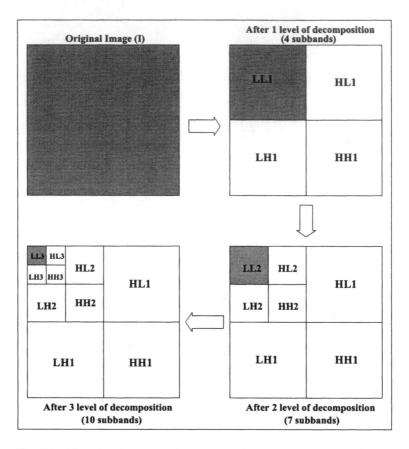

Fig. 3.9 Three level multiresolution wavelet decomposition of an image.

edges. The basics of wavelet representation of signals have been discussed in Section 2.2.7, using Eq. (2.32) and Fig. 2.7. In this section, we introduce how the wavelet transformation is applied in image coding. Wavelet coding is a transform coding technique that is not limited to the block-based implementation only. Usually the wavelet transform is performed on the whole image. Wavelet transform decomposes the input signal into low-frequency and high-frequency subbands.

In 1989, Mallat [15] proposed the multiresolution approach for wavelet decomposition of signals using a pyramidal FIR filter structure of QMF filter pairs, which practically mapped the wavelet decomposition into the subband coding paradigm. Once we express the wavelet decomposition in terms of FIR filters, the same general principles of subband coding of digital images applies. In multiresolution analysis, it can be proven that the decomposition of signals using discrete wavelet transform can be expressed in terms of FIR filters [16] as

$$c_{m,n}(f) = \sum_k a_{m-1,k}(f)g_{2n-k} \qquad (3.11)$$

and

$$a_{m,n}(f) = \sum_k a_{m-1,k}(f)h_{2n-k}, \qquad (3.12)$$

where g and h are the high-pass and low-pass discrete FIR filters whose coefficients are related as $g_i = (-1)^i h_{-i+1}$. If the input signal $f(t)$ is given in discrete sampled form, say $a_{0,n}(f)$, to indicate original discrete samples at resolution 0, then the above equations describe a multiresolution subband decomposition of samples into $a_{m,n}(f)$ and $c_{m,n}(f)$ at level m using the subband decomposed samples $c_{m-1,n}(f)$ at level $m-1$, with a low-pass FIR filter h and high-pass FIR filter g. The output subbands in every level are formed by retaining every other filtered output sample, which results in decimation of the output by a factor of 2. These filters are called the analysis filters. Using the corresponding synthesis filters h' and g', it can be shown that the signal $a_{0,n}$ can be exactly reconstructed in m levels using the formula

$$a_{m-1,i}(f) = \sum_n a_{m,n}(f)h'_{2n-i} + \sum_n c_{m,n}(f)g'_{2n-i}. \qquad (3.13)$$

Figure 3.8 depicts the multiresolution decomposition approach using the analysis filters g and h, and reconstruction of the same using synthesis filters g' and h'.

Image compression techniques using Discrete Wavelet Transform (DWT) have received wide attention in recent years [17, 18]. Using a separable two-dimensional filtering function, two-dimensional DWT can be computed by applying one-dimensional DWT row-wise and column-wise independently. In Fig. 3.9, we show an example of hierarchical wavelet decomposition of an image into ten subbands after three levels of decomposition. After the first level of decomposition, the original image is decomposed into four subbands $LL1$, $HL1$, $LH1$, and $HH1$. The $LL1$ subband is the low-frequency subband which can be considered as a 2:1 subsampled (horizontally and vertically) version of the original image I, and its statistical characteristic is similar to the original image as shown by the shaded regions in Fig. 3.9. Here $HL1$, $LH1$, and $HH1$ are called the high-frequency subbands, where $HL1$ and $LH1$ correspond to the horizontal and vertical high frequencies, respectively. $HH1$ constitutes the high frequencies that are not in either horizontal or vertical orientations. Each of these spatially oriented (horizontal, vertical, or diagonal) subbands mostly contain information of local discontinuities in the image, and the bulk of the energy in each of the high-frequency subbands are concentrated in the vicinity of areas which correspond to edge activity in the original image.

Since the low-frequency subband $LL1$ has similar spatial and statistical characteristics as the original image, it can be further decomposed into four subbands $LL2$, $HL2$, $LH2$, and $HH2$. Continuing the same method for decomposition in $LL2$, the original image is decomposed into 10 subbands $LL3$, $HL3$, $LH3$, $HH3$, $HL2$, $LH2$, $HH2$, $HL1$, $LH1$, and $HH1$ after three levels of pyramidal multiresolution subband decomposition, as shown in Fig. 3.9. The same procedure can continue to further decompose $LL3$ into higher levels.

Using the right wavelet filters and choosing an effective quantization strategy for each subband can yield good compression performance. Each decomposed subband may be encoded separately using a suitable coding scheme. We can allocate different bit-rates to different subbands. Because of the hierarchical nature of the subbands in wavelet decomposition, a smaller number of bits need to be allocated to the high-frequency subbands in a lower level as compared to the high-frequency subbands in upper levels. This helps maintain good fidelity of the reconstructed image and thereby achieves good compression. Experimental results show that we can even allocate zero bits to the $HH1$ subband and still maintain good reconstructed quality in most of the natural images.

3.9 IMAGE COMPRESSION STANDARD: JPEG

JPEG is the acronym for *Joint Photographic Experts Group*. It is the first international image compression standard for continuous-tone still images, including both gray scale and color images [7]. The goal of this standard is to support a variety of applications for compression of continuous-tone still images (i) of different sizes, (ii) in any color space, (iii) in order to achieve compression performance at or near the state of the art, (iv) with user-adjustable compression ratios, and (v) with very good to excellent reconstructed quality. Another goal of this standard is that it should have manageable computational complexity for widespread practical implementation. JPEG defines the following four modes of operation [7].

1. *Sequential Lossless Mode*: Compress the image in a single scan, and the decoded image is an exact replica of the original image.

2. *Sequential DCT-Based Mode*: Compress the image in a single scan using DCT-based lossy compression technique. As a result, the decoded image is not an exact replica but an approximation of the original image.

3. *Progressive DCT-Based Mode*: Compress the image in multiple scans and also decompress the image in multiple scans, with each successive scan producing a better quality image.

4. *Hierarchical Mode*: Compress the image at multiple resolutions for display on different devices.

The three DCT-based modes (2, 3, and 4) in JPEG provide lossy compression, because the precision limitation to digitally compute DCT (and its inverse) and the quantization process introduce distortion in the reconstructed image. For sequential lossless mode of compression, predictive coding (DPCM) is used instead of the DCT-based transformation and also there is no quantization involved. The simplest form of sequential DCT-based JPEG is called the **baseline JPEG** algorithm. We shall describe the JPEG *lossless* algorithm and the *baseline* JPEG algorithm in greater detail in the following two sections.

3.10   THE JPEG LOSSLESS CODING ALGORITHM

Lossless JPEG compression is based on the principles of predictive coding. In this scheme, the value of a pixel X is first predicted by using one or more of the previously encoded adjacent pixels A, B, and C as shown in Fig. 3.10(a). It then encodes the difference between the original pixel and its predicted value, usually called the *prediction error* or *prediction residual*, by either Huffman coding or binary arithmetic coding (QM-coder) [7].

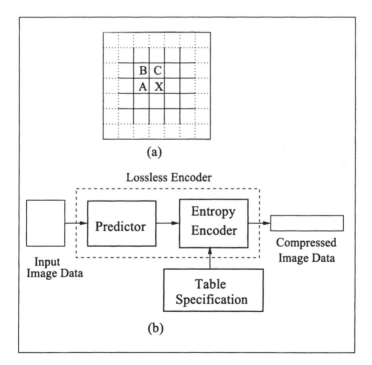

Fig. 3.10   JPEG lossless model with (a) 3-pixel prediction neighborhood and (b) encoder diagram.

There are eight possible options for prediction as shown in Table 3.2. Options 1 to 3 are one-dimensional predictors, while options 4 to 7 deal with two dimensions. Depending upon the nature of the image, one predictor may yield better compression result as compared to another. However, experimental results on various kinds of images show that on the average their performance are relatively close to each other [19]. The chosen option for prediction is indicated in the header of the compressed file, so that both the encoder and decoder use the same function for prediction.

Table 3.2 Prediction functions in lossless JPEG

Option	Prediction function	Type of prediction
0	No prediction	Differential Coding
1	$X_p = A$	1-D Horizontal Prediction
2	$X_p = B$	1-D Vertical Prediction
3	$X_p = C$	1-D Diagonal Prediction
4	$X_p = A + B - C$	2-D Prediction
5	$X_p = A + \frac{1}{2}(B - C)$	2-D Prediction
6	$X_p = B + \frac{1}{2}(A - C)$	2-D Prediction
7	$X_p = \frac{1}{2}(A + B)$	2-D Prediction

Table 3.3 Categories of prediction error values

Category	Prediction error value
0	0
1	$-1, +1$
2	$-3, -2, +2, +3$
3	$-7, \ldots, -4, +4, \ldots, +7$
4	$-15, \ldots, -8, +8, \ldots, +15$
5	$-31, \ldots, -16, +16, \ldots, +31$
6	$-63, \ldots, -32, +32, \ldots, +63$
7	$-127, \ldots, -64, +64, \ldots, +127$
8	$-255, \ldots, -128, +128, \ldots, +255$
9	$-511, \ldots, -256, +256, \ldots, +511$
10	$-1023, \ldots, -512, +512, \ldots, +1023$
11	$-2047, \ldots, -1024, +1024, \ldots, +2047$
12	$-4095, \ldots, -2048, +2048, \ldots, +4095$
13	$-8191, \ldots, -4096, +4096, \ldots, +8191$
14	$-16383, \ldots, -8192, +8192, \ldots, +16383$
15	$-32767, \ldots, -16384, +16384, \ldots, +32767$
16	$+32768$

In the lossless mode, the standard allows precision P of the input source image to be 2 bits to 16 bits wide. Since there is no previously encoded pixel known to the encoder when it encodes the very first pixel in the very first row of the image, it is handled differently. For a given input precision P and a point transform parameter P_t, the predicted value for the first pixel in the first line is 2^{P-P_t-1}. By default, we can assume $P_t = 0$. For details of the point transform parameter, the reader is advised to consult the JPEG standard [7]. For all other pixels (except the first one) in the first line, we use option 1 for prediction function. Except for the first line, option 2 is used to predict the very first pixel in all other lines. For all other pixels, we select one of the eight options for prediction function from Table 3.2. Once a predictor is selected, it is used for all other pixels in the block.

In lossless JPEG standard, the prediction error values are computed *modulo* 2^{16} to take into consideration the full precision allowed in this mode. These error values are first represented as a pair of symbols (*CATEGORY*, *MAGNITUDE*). The first symbol *CATEGORY* represents the category of the error value. The second symbol *MAGNITUDE* represents the Variable-Length Integer (VLI) for the prediction error value. CATEGORY represents the number of bits to encode *MAGNITUDE* in terms of VLI. All the possible prediction error values, *modulo* 2^{16}, and their corresponding categories are shown in Table 3.3. Only the *CATEGORY* in the symbol pair for each prediction error value is Huffman coded.

The codeword for the symbol pair (*CATEGORY*, *MAGNITUDE*) is formed in two steps. First it assigns the Huffman code of the *CATEGORY*. This Huffman code is then appended with additional *CATEGORY* number of bits to represent the *MAGNITUDE* in VLI. If the prediction error value is positive, the *MAGNITUDE* is directly binary represented by a VLI using *CATEGORY* number of bits and hence it starts with bit 1. If the error value is negative, the VLI is 1's complement of its absolute value and hence it starts with bit 0.

For example, the prediction error value "25" is represented by the pair (5, 25) because the number 25 belongs to category 5 in Table 3.3 and hence 25 is represented by a 5-bit VLI. If the Huffman code for category 5 is "011," then the binary codeword for the error value 25 will be "01111001." The first three bits correspond to the Huffman code "011" for category 5 and next 5 bits "11001" is the VLI for 25. Similarly, the prediction error value -25 will be represented as "01100110." Here the last 5 bits '00110' is the 1's complement of "11001" to represent -25 and, since -25 belongs to the same category 5, the first three bits of the codeword correspond to Huffman code of category 5.

Use of the *CATEGORY* of the error values greatly simplifies the Huffman coder. Without this categorization, we would require to use a Huffman table with 2^{16} entries for all the 2^{16} possible symbols of prediction error values. Detailed information for implementation of the JPEG lossless coding can be found in Annex H of the JPEG standard [7].

3.11   BASELINE JPEG COMPRESSION

Among the four modes of the JPEG family, the baseline JPEG compression algorithm is most widely used. It is defined for compression of continuous-tone images with one to four components. The number of components for gray scale images is one, whereas a color image can have up to four color components. The baseline JPEG allows only 8-bit samples within each component of the source image. An example of a four-component color image is a CMYK (cyan, magenta, yellow and black) image which is used in many applications such as printing, scanning etc.

A color image for display has three color components RGB (red, green and blue). In a typical color image, the spatial intercomponent correlation between the red, green, and blue color components is significant. In order to achieve good compression performance, the correlation between color components is first reduced by converting the RGB image into a decorrelating color space. In baseline JPEG, a three-color RGB image is first transformed into a Luminance-Chrominance (L-C) color space such as YCbCr, YUV, CIELAB, etc. The advantage of converting an image into Luminance-Chrominance color space is that the luminance and chrominance components are very much decorrelated between each other. Moreover, the chrominance channels contain many redundant information and can easily be subsampled without sacrificing any visual quality of the reconstructed image.

3.11.1   Color space conversion

In this section, we consider color space conversion only from RGB to YCbCr and vice versa. There are several ways to convert from RGB to YCbCr color space. Here we adopt the CCIR (International Radio Consultative Committee) Recommendation 601-1. This is the typical method for color conversion used in baseline JPEG compression. According to CCIR 601-1 Recommendation, the transformation from RGB to YCbCr is done based on the mathematical expression

$$
\begin{pmatrix} Y \\ Cb \\ Cr \end{pmatrix} = \begin{pmatrix} 0.29900 & 0.58700 & 0.11400 \\ -0.16874 & -0.33126 & 0.50000 \\ 0.50000 & -0.41869 & -0.08131 \end{pmatrix} \begin{pmatrix} R \\ G \\ B \end{pmatrix}.
$$

Color space conversion from RGB to YCbCr using the above transformation may result in negative numbers for Cb and Cr, while Y is always positive. In order to represent Cb and Cr as unsigned 8-bit integers, they are level-shifted by adding 128 to each sample followed by rounding and saturating the value in the range [0, 255]. Hence the above transformation can be expressed as

$$\begin{pmatrix} Y \\ Cb \\ Cr \end{pmatrix} = \begin{pmatrix} 0.29900 & 0.58700 & 0.11400 \\ -0.16874 & -0.33126 & 0.50000 \\ 0.50000 & -0.41869 & -0.08131 \end{pmatrix} \begin{pmatrix} R \\ G \\ B \end{pmatrix} + \begin{pmatrix} 0 \\ 128 \\ 128 \end{pmatrix},$$
(3.14)

in order to produce 8-bit unsigned integers for each of the components in the YCbCr domain. Accordingly, the inverse transformation from YCbCr to RGB is done as

$$\begin{pmatrix} R \\ G \\ B \end{pmatrix} = \begin{pmatrix} 1.0 & 0.0 & 1.40210 \\ 1.0 & -0.34414 & -0.71414 \\ 1.0 & 1.77180 & 0.0 \end{pmatrix} \begin{pmatrix} Y \\ Cb \\ Cr \end{pmatrix} - \begin{pmatrix} 0 \\ 128 \\ 128 \end{pmatrix}.$$
(3.15)

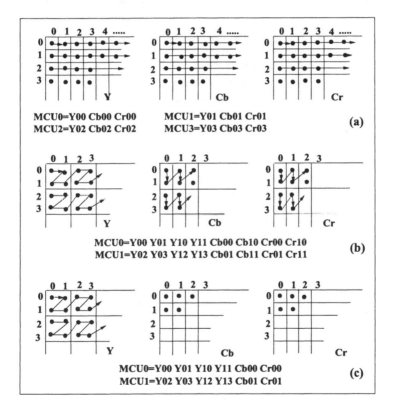

Fig. 3.11 Definition of MCUs for (a) YCbCr 4:4:4, (b) YCbCr 4:2:2, (c) YCbCr 4:2:0.

After the color space conversion, most of the spatial information of the image is contained in the luminance component (Y). The chrominance components (Cb and Cr) contain mostly redundant color information, and we lose little information by subsampling these components both horizontally and/or vertically. We can subsample the chrominance components by simply throwing away every other sample in each row and/or each column, if desired. If we subsample the redundant chrominance components both horizontally and vertically, the amount of data required to represent the color image is reduced to half because each chrominance component now has only half resolution both in horizontal and vertical directions. This color format is called 4:2:0 color subsampling format.

Baseline JPEG also supports 4:2:2 and 4:4:4 color formats. Each chrominance component in the 4:2:2 color format has the same vertical resolution as the luminance component, but the horizontal resolution is halved by dropping alternate samples in each row. In the 4:4:4 format, both the chrominance components Cb and Cr have identical vertical and horizontal resolution as the luminance component. Hence no subsampling is done here. The subsampling operation to generate the 4:2:0 or 4:2:2 color format is the first lossy step.

3.11.2 Source image data arrangement

In the previous section we have seen that the dimension of each of the color components Y, Cb, and Cr could be different, depending upon the color subsampling format. Each color component is divided into 8×8 nonoverlapping blocks. Selecting one or more such data blocks from each of the color components, we can form what is called a *minimum coded unit* (MCU) in JPEG. The standard defines the arrangement of the data blocks in either interleaved or noninterleaved scanning order of the color components. In a noninterleaved scan, the data blocks in each color component are stored and processed separately in raster scan order, left-to-right and top-to-bottom. In interleaved order, data blocks from all the color components appear in each MCU. Definition of the MCUs for 4:4:4, 4:2:2, and 4:2:0 formats of YCbCr images in interleaved scan is shown in Fig. 3.11.

Each dot in Fig. 3.11 represents an 8×8 data block. In 4:4:4 format interleaved scan, each MCU consists of a data block from each of the Y, Cb, and Cr component as shown in Fig. 3.11(a). The order of processing these blocks is in the scan order from left-to-right and top-to-bottom. For example, the first MCU consists of the first data block Y00 from the Y component followed sequentially by the first data blocks Cb00 from the Cb component and Cr00 from the Cr component as shown in Fig. 3.11(a). The next MCU consists of Y01, Cb01, and Cr01, respectively. After all the MCUs consisting of the 8×8 data blocks from the first row (as depicted in Fig. 3.11(a)) are encoded, the second row of 8×8 blocks are scanned in a similar fashion. This procedure is continued until the last 8×8 block in the raster scan is encoded.

In 4:2:2 format, each MCU consists of a 2×2 unit of four data blocks from the Y component followed by a 2×1 unit of two data blocks from each of the Cb and Cr components. The corresponding order of processing is shown in Fig. 3.11(b). In 4:2:0 format, each MCU consists of 2×2 units of four data blocks from the Y component followed by one from each of the Cb and

Cr components, and the corresponding order of processing is illustrated in Fig. 3.11(c).

3.11.3 · The baseline compression algorithm

The baseline JPEG algorithm follows the principles of block-based transform coding. Block diagram of the baseline JPEG algorithm for a gray scale image with a single component is shown in Fig. 3.12. For a color image, the same algorithm is applied to each 8 × 8 data block based on the source image data arrangement described in Section 3.11.2.

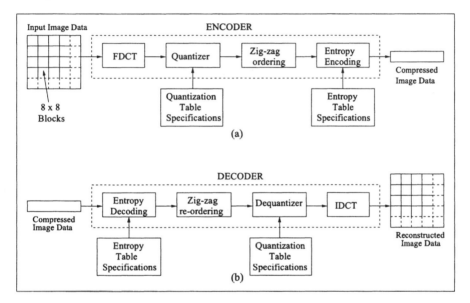

Fig. 3.12 JPEG baseline (a) compression and (b) decompression.

The image component is first divided into nonoverlapping 8 × 8 blocks in the raster scan order left-to-right and top-to-bottom as depicted in Fig. 3.12(a). Each block is then encoded separately by the *Encoder*, shown by the broken box in Fig. 3.12(a). The first step is to level shift each pixel in the block to convert into a signed integer, by subtracting 128 from each pixel. Each level shifted pixel in 8 × 8 block is then transformed into the frequency domain via forward DCT (FDCT). The FDCT of 8 × 8 block of pixels $f(x, y)$ for $(x, y = 0, 1, \ldots, 7)$ is defined as

$$F(u, v) = \frac{1}{4} C(u) C(v) \sum_{x=0}^{7} \sum_{y=0}^{7} f(x, y) \cos \left[\frac{\pi(2x + 1)u}{16} \right] \cos \left[\frac{\pi(2y + 1)v}{16} \right],$$

$$(3.16)$$

for $u = 0, 1, \ldots, 7$ and $v = 0, 1, \ldots, 7$, where

$$C(k) = \begin{cases} \frac{1}{\sqrt{2}} & \text{for } k = 0 \\ 1 & \text{otherwise.} \end{cases}$$

The transformed 8×8 block now consists of 64 DCT coefficients. The first coefficient $F(0,0)$ is the DC component of the block, while the other 63 coefficients are the AC components $AC_{u,v} = F(u,v)$ of the block as shown in Fig. 3.13. The DC component $F(0,0)$ is essentially the sum of 64 pixels in the input 8×8 pixel block multiplied by the scaling factor $\frac{1}{4}C(u)C(v) = \frac{1}{8}$, as in Eq. (3.16).

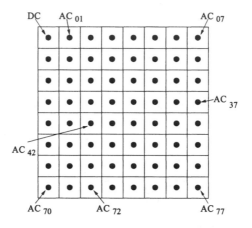

Fig. 3.13 DC and AC components of the transformed block.

The next step in the compression process is to quantize the transformed coefficients. This step is primarily responsible for losing information, and hence introduces distortion in the reconstructed image. That is the reason why baseline JPEG is a lossy compression. Each of the 64 DCT coefficients are uniformly quantized. The 64 quantization step-size parameters for uniform quantization of the 64 DCT coefficients form an 8×8 *Quantization Matrix*. Each element in the *Quantization Matrix* is an integer between 1 and 255. Each DCT coefficient $F(u,v)$ is divided by the corresponding quantizer step-size parameter $Q(u,v)$ in the *Quantization Matrix* and is rounded to the nearest integer as

$$F_q(u,v) = Round\left(\frac{F(u,v)}{Q(u,v)}\right). \tag{3.17}$$

The JPEG standard does not define any fixed *Quantization Matrix*, and it is the prerogative of the user to select the matrix. There are two quantization matrices provided in Annex K of the JPEG standard for reference, but not as a requirement. These two quantization matrices are shown in Tables 3.4 and 3.5, respectively.

Table 3.4   Luminance Quantization Matrix

16	11	10	16	24	40	51	61
12	12	14	19	26	58	60	55
14	13	16	24	40	57	69	56
14	17	22	29	51	87	80	62
18	22	37	56	68	109	103	77
24	35	55	64	81	104	113	92
49	64	78	87	103	121	120	101
72	92	95	98	112	100	103	99

Table 3.5   Chrominance Quantization Matrix

17	18	24	47	99	99	99	99
18	21	26	66	99	99	99	99
24	26	56	99	99	99	99	99
47	66	99	99	99	99	99	99
99	99	99	99	99	99	99	99
99	99	99	99	99	99	99	99
99	99	99	99	99	99	99	99
99	99	99	99	99	99	99	99

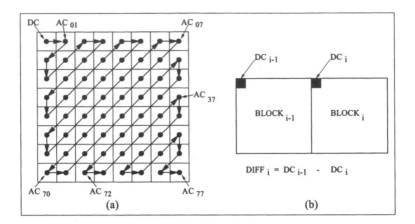

Fig. 3.14 Encoding of quantized DCT coefficients, with (a) zig-zag ordering of AC coefficients, and (b) differential coding of DC.

Table 3.4 is the *Luminance Quantization Matrix* for quantizing the transformed coefficients of the luminance component of an image. Similarly, Table 3.5 is the *Chrominance Quantization Matrix* for quantizing the transformed coefficients of the chrominance components of the image. These two quantization tables have been designed based on the psychovisual experiments by Lohscheller [20] to determine the visibility thresholds for 2-D basis functions. These tables may not be suitable for all kinds of images, but they provide reasonably good result for most natural images with 8-bit precision for luminance and chrominance samples. If the elements in these tables are divided by 2, we get perceptually lossless compression, whereby the reconstructed image is indistinguishable from the original one by human eyes. When the quantization tables are designed based on the perceptual masking properties of the human eye, many of the small DCT coefficients (high-frequency samples) are zeroed out to aid significant compression. This is done by using larger quantization step-size parameters for higher-frequency AC components, as depicted in Tables 3.4 and 3.5.

Quality of the reconstructed image and the achieved compression can be controlled by a user, by selecting a quality factor Q_JPEG to tune the elements in the quantization tables, as proposed by the *Independent JPEG Group* and implemented in their software [21]. The value of Q_JPEG may vary from 1 to 100. The quantization matrices in Tables 3.4 and 3.5 have been set for $Q\_JPEG = 50$. For other Q_JPEG values, each element in both the tables are simply scaled by a factor α defined as [21]

$$
\alpha = \begin{cases} \frac{50}{Q\_JPEG} & \text{if } 1 \leq Q\_JPEG \leq 50, \\[2ex] 2 - \frac{Q\_JPEG}{50} & \text{if } 50 \leq Q\_JPEG \leq 100, \end{cases} \tag{3.18}
$$

subject to the condition that the minimum value of the scaled quantization matrix elements $\alpha Q(u, v)$ is 1. For the best reconstructed quality, Q_JPEG is set to 100.

After quantization of the DCT coefficients, the quantized DC coefficient is encoded by differential encoding. The DC coefficient DC_i of the current block is subtracted from the DC coefficient DC_{i-1} of the previous block and the difference

$$DIFF_i = DC_{i-1} - DC_i \qquad (3.19)$$

is encoded as shown in Fig. 3.14(b). This is done to exploit the spatial correlation between the DC values of the adjacent blocks.

Encoding of the AC coefficients is not straightforward. Instead of encoding each AC coefficient in the block, only the significant (nonzero) coefficients are encoded in an efficient manner such that the runs of zeros preceding a nonzero value is embedded into the encoding. Usually there are few significant low-frequency AC coefficients in the whole 8×8 block, and most of the higher-frequency coefficients are quantized to zeros. In order to exploit this property, the AC coefficients are ordered in a particular irregular order sequence as shown in Fig. 3.14(a). This irregular ordering of the AC coefficients is called the *zig-zag ordering*. It is done to keep the low-frequency coefficients together, and it forms long runs of zeros corresponding to the higher-frequency quantized coefficients. This zig-zag sequence is then broken into runs of zeros ending in a nonzero value.

Before we explain the entropy encoding procedure, let us demonstrate the results of level shifting, DCT, quantization, and zig-zag ordering with an example 8×8 block extracted from a natural image.

110	110	118	118	121	126	131	131
108	111	125	122	120	125	134	135
106	119	129	127	125	127	138	144
110	126	130	133	133	131	141	148
115	116	119	120	122	125	137	139
115	106	99	110	107	116	130	127
110	91	82	101	99	104	120	118
103	76	70	95	92	91	107	106

Example: One 8×8 data block

−18	−18	−10	−10	−7	−2	3	3
−20	−17	−3	−6	−8	−3	6	7
−22	−9	1	−1	−3	−1	10	16
−18	−2	2	5	5	3	13	20
−13	−12	−9	−8	−6	−3	9	11
−13	−22	−29	−18	−21	−12	2	−1
−18	−37	−46	−27	29	−24	−8	−10
−25	−52	−58	−33	−36	−37	−21	−22

Level shifted 8 × 8 data block

−89.00	−63.47	18.21	−6.85	7.50	13.45	−7.00	0.13
74.14	−2.90	−19.93	−21.04	−17.88	−10.81	8.29	5.26
−63.65	3.10	5.08	14.82	10.12	9.33	1.31	−0.62
3.73	2.85	6.67	8.99	−3.38	1.54	1.04	−0.62
2.50	0.57	−4.46	0.52	3.00	−2.89	−0.32	1.33
7.52	−1.80	−0.63	−0.10	0.41	−3.21	−2.74	−2.07
−3.40	0.43	0.81	0.28	−0.40	−0.19	−0.58	−1.09
−2.26	−0.88	1.73	0.23	−0.21	−0.12	1.23	1.61

DCT coefficients of the above 8 × 8 block

−6	−6	2	0	0	0	0	0
6	0	−1	−1	−1	0	0	0
−5	0	0	1	0	0	0	0
0	0	0	0	0	0	0	0
0	0	0	0	0	0	0	0
0	0	0	0	0	0	0	0
0	0	0	0	0	0	0	0
0	0	0	0	0	0	0	0

Results of DCT coefficients quantized by *Luminance Quantization Matrix*

The entropy encoding procedure for the differentially encoded DC coefficient is identical to the entropy encoding of the prediction error values, as explained in Section 3.10 for lossless JPEG. For 8-bit images in baseline JPEG, the DCT coefficients fall in the range $[−1023, +1023]$. Since the DC coefficient is differentially encoded, the differential value of DC falls in the range $[−2047, +2047]$. Assuming that the DC coefficient of the previous block is $−4$

as an example, we get the differential DC value of the present block to be
-2. Using Table 3.3, we find that this belongs to category 2 and hence -2 is
described as (2, "01"). If the Huffman code of category 2 is "011," then -2 is
coded as "01101," where the last two bits "01" represent the variable-length
integer (VLI) code of -2. There are two Huffman tables (Tables K.3 and K.4)
for encoding the DC coefficients in Annex K of the baseline JPEG standard
for reference. But the user can choose any table and add them as part of the
header of the compressed file [7]. Table K.3 is supplied for coding the Luminance DC differences as a reference. Table K.4 is supplied for Chrominance
DC differences.

After zig-zag ordering of the AC coefficients in the example, the resulting
sequence becomes
" -6 6 -5 0 2 0 -1 0 0 0 0 0 -1 0 0 -1 1 0 0 0 0 0 0 0 0 0 0 0 0 0 0 0 0 0
0 0 0 0 0 0 0 0 0 0 0 0 0 0 0 0 0 0 0 0 0 0 0 0 0 0."
This sequence of AC coefficients can be mapped into an *intermediate sequence* of combination of two symbols $symbol_1$ and $symbol_2$. Here $symbol_1$
is represented by a pair ($RUNLENGTH$, $CATEGORY$), where $RUNLENGTH$ is
the number of consecutive zeros preceding the nonzero AC coefficient being
encoded and $CATEGORY$ is the number of bits to represent the VLI code of
this nonzero AC coefficient. Again $symbol_2$ is a single piece of information
designated ($AMPLITUDE$), which is encoded by the VLI code of the nonzero
AC coefficient. Accordingly, the zig-zag sequence in the example can be compactly represented as

(0, 3)(-6), (0, 3)(6), (0, 3)(-5), (1, 2)(2), (1, 1)(-1), (5, 1)(-1), (2, 1)(-1),
(0, 1)(1), (0, 0).

The first significant (nonzero) AC coefficient in the zig-zag sequence is found to
be -6. It is represented as (0, 3)(-6) because it precedes with no run of zeros
(i.e., $RUNLENGTH = 0$) and the $AMPLITUDE = -6$ belongs to $CATEGORY$
$= 3$. Similarly, the following two nonzero coefficients 6 and -5 are represented as (0, 3)(6) and (0, 3)(-5), respectively. The next significant coefficient 2 is represented by (1, 2)(2) because it precedes a zero coefficient (i.e.,
$RUNLENGTH = 1$) and $AMPLITUDE = 2$ belongs to $CATEGORY = 2$. Again,
the next significant symbol is represented as (1, 1)(-1). The following significant coefficient -1 is represented as (5, 1)(-1) because it precedes five
zeros (i.e., $RUNLENGTH = 5$) and $AMPLITUDE = -1$ belongs to $CATEGORY$
$= 1$. Following the same procedure, the next two nonzero coefficients -1
and 1 are represented by (2, 1)(-1) and (0, 1)(1), respectively. There are no
other nonzero coefficients in the remaining of the zig-zag sequence. A special
symbol (0, 0) is used to indicate that the remaining elements in the zig-zag
block are all zeros. Each ($RUNLENGTH$, $CATEGORY$) pair is encoded using a
Huffman code, while the corresponding $AMPLITUDE$ is encoded by the VLI
code.

There are two special symbols in encoding the zig-zag sequence of AC coefficients, namely, (0, 0) and (15, 0). The first special symbol (0, 0) is referred as EOB (end-of-block), to indicate that the remaining elements in the zig-zag block are zeros. The other special symbol (15, 0) is also referred as ZRL (Zero-Run-Length) and is used to indicate a run of 16 zeros. Maximum length of a run of zeros allowed in baseline JPEG is 16. If there are more than 16 zeros, then the run is broken into a number of runs of zeros of length 16. For example, consider 57 zeros before a nonzero coefficient, say −29. This will be represented by (15, 0) (15, 0) (15, 0), (9, 5)(−29). Here the first three (15, 0) pairs represent 48 zeros and (9, 5)(−29) represents 9 zeros followed by the coefficient −29 which belongs to category 5.

The baseline JPEG allows a maximum of four Huffman tables, – that is, two for encoding AC coefficients and two for encoding DC coefficients. In luminance–chrominance image data, usually two Huffman tables (one for AC and one for DC) each are used for encoding the luminance and chrominance data. The Huffman tables used during the compression process are stored as header information in the compressed image file, in order to uniquely decode the coefficients during the decompression process. There are two Huffman tables (Tables K.5 and K.6) for encoding the AC coefficients, and two others (Tables K.3 and K.4) for encoding the DC coefficients in Annex K of the baseline JPEG standard for reference. The users can choose any table of their choice and store it as part of the header of the compressed file [7]. Tables K.3 and K.5 are recommended for luminance DC differences and AC coefficients. Tables K.4 and K.6 are recommended for corresponding chrominance channels.

Let us now allocate the variable-length codes in the last example. The codewords for (0, 0), (0, 1), (0, 3), (1, 1), (1, 2), (2, 1) and (5, 1), from Table K.5, are 1010, 00, 100, 1100, 11011, 11100, and 1111010, respectively. VLI codes for the nonzero AC coefficients 1, -1, 2, -5, 6, and -6 are 1, 0, 10, 010, 110, and 001, respectively. Codeword for the differential DC value is 01101. The compressed bit-stream for the 8 × 8 block is shown below, and it requires only 52 bits as opposed to the 512 bits required by the original 8 × 8 block of 8-bit pixels. We have

'01101 100001 100110 100010 1101110 11000 11110100 111000 001 1010',

where the first five bits "01101" represent the DC coefficient and the other 47 bits represent the AC coefficients. Therefore, we achieve approximately 10:1 compression using the baseline JPEG to compress the block.

3.11.4 Decompression process in baseline JPEG

Decompression is the inverse process to decode the compressed bit-stream, in order to properly reconstruct the image. Block diagram of the baseline decompression algorithm is provided in Fig. 3.12(b). During the decompression

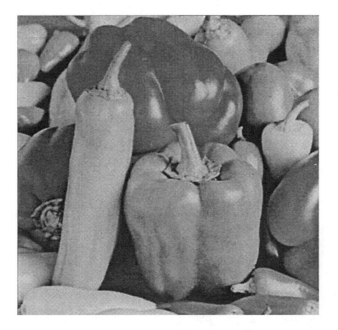

Fig. 3.15   Original pepper image.

process, the system first parses the header of the compressed file in order to retrieve all the relevant information, namely, image type, number of components, format, quantization matrices, and the Huffman tables that were used to compress the original image, etc.

After parsing the header information, the decompression algorithm is applied on the compressed bit-stream as shown in Fig. 3.12(b). The *entropy decoding* step in Fig. 3.12(b) decodes the bit-stream of the compressed data using the Huffman tables that were used during the compression process. The purpose of this step is to regenerate the zig-zag ordered sequence of the quantized DCT coefficients. This zig-zag sequence is then reordered by the *zig-zag reordering* step to create the 8 × 8 block of quantized DCT coefficients. Each DCT coefficient in the quantized block is inverse-quantized as

$$F'(u,v) = F_q(u,v) * Q(u,v), \qquad (3.20)$$

where $Q(u,v)$ is the quantization step-size parameter from the same quantization table that was used during the compression process. After inverse-quantization, the DCT coefficients $F'(u,v)$ are inverse transformed to spatial domain data via inverse DCT (IDCT). The IDCT of an 8 × 8 block $F'(u,v)$, for $u, v = 0, 1, \ldots, 7$, is defined as

$$f(x, y) = \frac{1}{4} \sum_{u=0}^{7} \sum_{v=0}^{7} C(u)C(v)F'(u, v) \cos\left[\frac{\pi(2x+1)u}{16}\right] \cos\left[\frac{\pi(2y+1)v}{16}\right]$$

(3.21)

for $x = 0, 1, \ldots, 7$ and $y = 0, 1, \ldots, 7$.

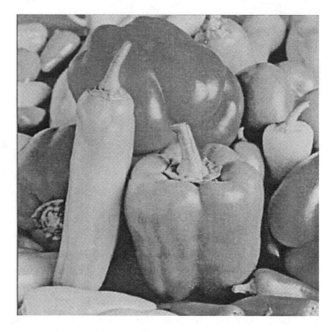

Fig. 3.16   Pepper image compressed with quality factor 75.

After decompression of all the MCUs from the compressed bit-stream, the image components are reconstructed. For a gray scale image, there is only one component and no color transformation is required. For color image, the reconstructed Y, Cb, and Cr components are inverse-transformed to the RGB color space. We show in color the famous *Pepper* image in Fig. 3.15. When compressed, using the baseline JPEG algorithm with quality factor $Q\_JPEG = 75$, the reconstructed image is found to be perceptually almost identical to the original image. This is demonstrated in Fig. 3.16. When we compress the same image with a quality factor $Q\_JPEG = 10$, we can see prominent artifacts in the image as shown in Fig. 3.17. Such artifacts, caused by lossy JPEG compression/decompression, are called *blocking* artifacts. This happens because of the discontinuities created at the 8×8 block boundaries, since these blocks are compressed and decompressed independently.

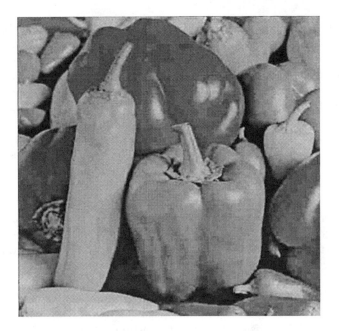

Fig. 3.17 Pepper image compressed with quality factor 10.

3.11.5 JPEG2000: Next generation still picture coding standard

Goal of the JPEG2000 [22, 23] standardization activity is to advance imaging applications in the new era of Internet and wireless communication. This new standard is expected to address the areas where the current JPEG standard fails to produce the best quality or performance requirements.

The current JPEG standard for still image compression is very much suitable for compressing images at 0.5 bits per pixel or higher. However, the reconstructed image quality significantly degrades at lower bit rates. Reconstructed quality of a JPEG compressed image is unacceptable below 0.25 bits per pixel. JPEG results in poor compression performance when applied to bi-level images for compound documents, such as facsimile, scan, and text-type imagery. Current JPEG standard has 44 different modes of operation, with many of these modes being very application-specific and not widely used in practice. As a result, the interchangeability between the different modes of JPEG applications is a difficult proposition.

JPEG2000 is targeted for more compression efficiency in terms of compression ratio and image quality, especially at very low bit-rates (below 0.25 bits per pixel). JPEG2000 will have a single common decompression architecture to encompass different modes and types of applications, so that it is suitable for greater interchange between applications encompassing different features. The same decompression architecture will be suitable both for bi-level and continuous tone images, because the JPEG2000 system is capable of compressing and decompressing images with various dynamic ranges between 1 to 16 bits for each color component. This standard is expected to handle new paradigms of distributed imaging applications, especially Internet imaging. JPEG2000 will provide an open systems approach to imaging applications. The interesting feature of this new standard is that the same algorithm can be used for both lossless and lossy compression of still images.

Unlike DCT in current JPEG, the JPEG2000 coding algorithm is being defined based on the principles of Discrete Wavelet Transform (DWT), which offers multiresolution and efficient progressive encoding/decoding system. Progressive decoding can be achieved in terms of resolution, while being progressive in terms of visual quality from the same encoded bit-stream and selectable during the decoding time. This capability is particularly suitable for client–server applications such as World Wide Web and many other distributed networking environments. This is also suitable for retrieval, archival, print, and color facsimile-type applications.

There are two types of wavelet filters to accomplish DWT in the JPEG2000 standard. One type of wavelet filters generates noninteger values for the transformed coefficients, which are mainly used for lossy image compression and cannot be used for lossless image compression. The other type of wavelet filters generates integer-transformed coefficients, which are used mainly for lossless compression. However, they can be used in lossy mode also, when the transformed coefficients are quantized after wavelet transformation. In current JPEG, the steps in lossless mode of compression are entirely different from the lossy mode. In JPEG2000 a common algorithm is used in both lossy and lossless modes, based on the selection of corresponding wavelet filters. JPEG2000-compressed images are very much suitable for transmission through a noisy environment like wireless channels, because of the error resilience features embedded into the bit stream.

This technology will enable regions of particular interest in an image to be encoded with greater fidelity (*Region of Interest* coding) compared to other areas in the image, and it will also enable random access to the compressed data for manipulation of the images in the compressed domain. The random access of the code-stream will allow operations such as rotation, translation, scaling, filtering, etc., without decompressing the whole image. The file format of JPEG2000 is expected to handle the features of metadata such as *Watermarking* of images, *Intellectual Property Rights* as per the WIPO (World Intellectual Property Organization) compliant, *Content Registration*, JPEG *Registration Authority*, etc. The plan of this standard is to provide appropriate interfaces with MPEG-4, in order to insert and extract still pictures to/from moving video and maintain corresponding Intellectual Property information. JPEG2000 is a good candidate for usage in multimedia data mining, because of the metadata information that can be handled using this standard.

3.12 TEXT COMPRESSION

Text compression is inherently lossless in nature. Like image and video compression, there is no standard committee devoted to define text compression standards under the auspices of an international standard body. However, industry adopted text compression schemes, mainly based on the principles of text processing and string matching. We shall describe some of them here.

Dictionary-based coding techniques are particularly suitable for compressing text datatypes. Typically, redundancy in text appears in the form of common words, which repeat quite often, in addition to the statistical redundancy of individual characters. In order to achieve significantly enhanced compression performance, it is desirable to exploit both these aspects of redundancy. We can handle the redundancy of frequently appearing common words by constructing a *dictionary* and replacing each common word in the text file by an *index* to the dictionary. This approach is popularly known as the *dictionary-based coding* scheme. The dictionary could be *static* or *dynamic*.

In *static dictionary coding*, the dictionary is fixed during both compression and decompression. The simplest example of this scheme is to express (or encode) the words "Sunday," "Monday," ..., "Saturday" by the indices $1, 2, \ldots, 7$. A *dynamic dictionary coding*, however, builds a *dictionary* dynamically using the message itself that is being encoded or decoded. The basic idea behind most of the dynamic dictionary-based robust lossless text compression schemes is to first *parse* the text (which can be considered as a string of characters) into a sequence of *substrings* and then generate compressed codes of these substrings. Jacob Ziv and Abraham Lempel described efficient dynamic dictionary encoders, popularly known as LZ77 [24] and LZ78 [25], by replacing a group of characters of the text (*phrases*) with a pointer to where they have occurred earlier in the portion of the text that has already been encoded. Many variations of these algorithms have been developed after that. They are collectively called the *Ziv–Lempel* or *Lempel–Ziv* (LZ) family, namely, LZSS [26], LZW [27], LZC [28], LZWAJ [29], etc. For example, LZSS, a variation of LZ77, is the basis of the text compression engine in popularly used compression utilities like *zip, gzip, pkzip, winzip*. The LZW algorithm, a variant of LZ78 scheme, is the core of the *Unix compress* utility.

There exist other categories of text compression algorithms. Some of the popular ones include variants of a technique called *Prediction by Partial Matching* (PPM) [30, 31]. PPM is a statistical compression scheme based on context modeling of the symbols. The already encoded portion of the text is used as context to determine the probability of the symbol being encoded. It relies on the *Arithmetic coding scheme* [32] to achieve good compression performance. Although there are a number of variations of the PPM algorithm for text compression, such as PPMA, PPMB, PPMC, etc., none of them are supported by any underlying theory. However, the PPM algorithms are relatively slow as compared to the LZ family of algorithms.

A comparatively recent development in context based text compression is the *block-sorting* scheme based on the Burrows and Wheeler Transform (BWT) [33]. This is analogous to transformation-based image compression schemes. The text is first divided into a number of blocks. Each block is then transformed into a form more amenable to compression. The transformation is done by permuting the characters in each block, so that the characters occurring in a similar context get aligned near each other. The permuted block is then compressed using a suitable coder, which exploits the locality of context of the symbols in the permuted block. During decompression, the decoder first decodes the permuted block which is then inverse-transformed (BWT) in order to reconstruct the original text.

3.12.1 The LZ77 algorithm

LZ77 is the first form of Ziv–Lempel coding proposed by Ziv and Lempel in 1977 [24]. In this approach a fixed-size buffer, containing the previously encoded character sequence that precedes the current coding position, can be considered as a dictionary. The encoder matches the input sequence through a sliding window, as illustrated in Fig. 3.18. The window is divided into two parts, namely, (i) a *search window* that consists of the already encoded character sequence, and (ii) a *lookahead buffer* that contains the character sequence to be encoded as shown in Fig. 3.18.

In order to encode a sequence in the lookahead buffer, the *search window* is scanned to find the longest match in it with a prefix of the lookahead buffer. The match can overlap with the lookahead buffer, but obviously cannot be the lookahead buffer itself. Once the longest match is found, it is coded as a triple $<offset,length,C(char)>$, where *offset* is the distance of the first character of the longest match in the search window from the lookahead buffer, *length* is the length of the match, and $C(char)$ is the binary codeword of the first mismatching symbol *char* that follows the match in the lookahead buffer. The window is shifted left by $length + 1$ symbols to begin the next search.

3.12.1.1 **Example 3–LZ77 coding:** Let the character sequence to be encoded be given as $\cdots baabacbaacbcdbcdbcac\cdots$. We assume that the size of the *search window* is 8 and that of the *lookahead buffer* is 6. Let us assume that the substring *baabacba* in the search window has already been encoded and the substring *acbcdb* in the lookahead buffer is to be encoded, as shown in Fig. 3.18(a). After scanning the search window, the longest match is found to be the substring '*acb*' of length 3 at a distance 4 from the lookahead buffer. The character following the prefix '*acb*' in the lookahead buffer is '*c*'. Hence the triple to output is $< 4, 3, C(c) >$, where $C(c)$ is the codeword for the character *c*. Since the match length is 3, we shift the window left by 4 characters.

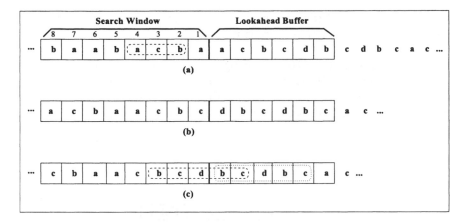

Fig. 3.18 LZ77 coding: An example with sliding window.

Now the first character in the lookahead buffer is '*d*' as illustrated in Fig. 3.18(b), and there is no match for '*d*' in the search window. Hence we output the triple $< 0, 0, C(d) >$ and shift the sliding window by one.

The longest match in the sliding window is the substring '*bcdbc*' as depicted in Fig. 3.18(c). It is to be noted that the matching substring starts in character position 3 in the search window, and it overlaps with the first two characters *bcdbc* in the lookahead buffer. Hence we output the triple $< 3, 5, C(a) >$ and shift the sliding window left by 6 characters to continue.

There are many variations of LZ77 coding, mainly to further improve the performance or implementation efficiency of the scheme. Popular compression softwares like Zip and PKZip use a variation of the LZ77 coding scheme, called LZSS coding [26].

3.12.2   The LZ78 algorithm

LZ78 is the other key algorithm in the LZ family proposed by Ziv and Lempel in 1978 [25]. Instead of using the previously encoded sequence of symbols (or string) in the sliding window as the implicit dictionary, the LZ78 algorithm explicitly builds a dictionary of string patterns dynamically in both the encoder and decoder. The encoder searches this dictionary to find the longest match with the prefix of the input string and encodes it as a pair $< i, C(S) >$, where i is the index of the matched substring in the dictionary and $C(S)$ is the codeword of the first symbol S following the matched portion of the input. A new entry is then added to the dictionary, corresponding to the matched substring concatenated by the symbol S. The codeword $C(S)$ is usually a Huffman-type variable-length code of the source symbol S.

In order to achieve further compression, the index i in the output pair can be encoded using some Huffman-type variable-length binary encoding by exploiting the statistics of the indices. But for the sake of simplicity of explanation, we avoid detailed discussion here.

3.12.2.1 **Example 4–LZ78 encoding:** Let us consider the sequence of symbols *bacababbaabbabbaaacbbc*. Initially the dictionary is empty. Since the first input symbol *b* has no match in the dictionary, the encoder outputs the pair $< 0, C(b) >$ and inserts the first entry *b* into the dictionary with index 1 as shown in Table 3.6.

Table 3.6   Dictionary after Step 1

Encoder output	Index	Entry
$< 0, C(b) >$	1	*b*

Similarly, the next input symbol *a* has no match in the dictionary. Hence the encoder outputs the pair $< 0, C(a) >$ and inserts new entry *a* at index 2 in the dictionary as indicated in Table 3.7.

Table 3.7   Dictionary after Step 2

Encoder output	Index	Entry
$< 0, C(b) >$	1	*b*
$< 0, C(a) >$	2	*a*

Because the next input symbol *c* has no match in the dictionary, the encoder outputs the pair $< 0, C(c) >$ and inserts the new entry *c* at index 3 as shown in Table 3.8.

Table 3.8   Dictionary after Step 3

Encoder output	Index	Entry
$< 0, C(b) >$	1	*b*
$< 0, C(a) >$	2	*a*
$< 0, C(c) >$	3	*c*

Now the input symbol *a* matches with entry 2 in the dictionary, but *ab* fails to generate a match. So the encoder outputs the pair $< 2, C(b) >$ and inserts new entry *ab* at index 4 in the dictionary, as indicated in Table 3.9.

Table 3.9 Dictionary after Step 4

Encoder output	Index	Entry
$< 0, C(b) >$	1	b
$< 0, C(a) >$	2	a
$< 0, C(c) >$	3	c
$< 2, C(b) >$	4	ab

The next two symbols ab match with entry 4 in the dictionary, but abb does not have any match. So the encoder outputs the pair $< 4, C(b) >$ and inserts a new entry abb at index 5 in the dictionary, as shown in Table 3.10.

Table 3.10 Dictionary after Step 5

Encoder output	Index	Entry
$< 0, C(b) >$	1	b
$< 0, C(a) >$	2	a
$< 0, C(c) >$	3	c
$< 2, C(b) >$	4	ab
$< 4, C(b) >$	5	abb

Table 3.11 Final LZ78 dictionary

Encoder output	Index	Entry
$< 0, C(b) >$	1	b
$< 0, C(a) >$	2	a
$< 0, C(c) >$	3	c
$< 2, C(b) >$	4	ab
$< 4, C(b) >$	5	abb
$< 2, C(a) >$	6	aa
$< 1, C(b) >$	7	bb
$< 5, C(a) >$	8	$abba$
$< 6, C(c) >$	9	aac
$< 7, C(c) >$	10	bbc

Continuing the above procedure the encoder generates the output pairs $< 2, C(a) >$, $< 1, C(b) >$, $< 5, C(a) >$, $< 6, C(c) >$ and $< 7, C(c) >$, and builds the dictionary accordingly. The final dictionary is depicted in Table 3.11. The encoded output of the sequence is $< 0, C(b) >$, $< 0, C(a) >$,

$< 0, C(c) >, < 2, C(b) >, < 4, C(b) >, < 2, C(a) >, < 1, C(b) >, < 5, C(a) >,$
$< 6, C(c) >, < 7, C(c) >.$

3.12.2.2 Example 5–LZ78 decoding:

We now decode the encoded data to explain how the LZ78 decoding process works. The decoder also dynamically builds a dictionary, which is the same as that built by the encoder. Initially the dictionary contains nothing. Since the first input pair to the decoder is $< 0, C(b) >$, it first decodes the symbol b from the codeword $C(b)$. As the decoded index is 0, it outputs the symbol b and inserts the first entry $< 1, b >$ in the dictionary as shown in Table 3.6.

The next input pair to the decoder is $< 0, C(a) >$. As a result, the decoder outputs the symbol a and inserts the next entry $< 2, a >$ in the dictionary as indicated in Table 3.7. The following input pair being $< 0, C(c) >$, the decoder outputs the symbol c and inserts the next entry $< 3, c >$ in the dictionary as shown in Table 3.8.

The next input pair is $< 2, C(b) >$, which indicates that the new output is the pattern for entry 2 in the dictionary concatenated by the decoded symbol b. Since entry 2 represents a, the output will be ab. A new pattern ab is now inserted in index 4 of the dictionary.

The following input pair is $< 4, C(b) >$. As a result, the decoder outputs the string abb and inserts it in the dictionary in entry 5. Analogously, the decoder reads the next pair $< 2, C(a) >$ and generates the output aa, inserting it in the dictionary in entry 6. Continuing in a similar fashion, the subsequent decoder outputs are bb, $abba$, aac and bbc; and these are inserted in the dictionary at indices 7, 8, 9, and 10, respectively. The final dictionary is identical to the one generated in Table 3.11. The final decoder output is $bacababbaabbabbaaacbbc$, and it exactly matches with the original input sequence.

Generally the LZ78 algorithm is easier for implementation and less memory-consuming, as compared to the LZ77. This is because of the simpler data structure used in LZ78 to output sequence of pairs only, as opposed to the triples in LZ77. There exist a number of variations of the LZ78 algorithm, the most popular being the algorithm by Welch [27] known as the LZW algorithm. We describe this algorithm in the following section.

3.12.3 The LZW algorithm

The inclusion of the explicit codeword $C(S)$ of the symbol S along with the index i, in the output $< i, C(S) >$ of the LZ78 encoding algorithm, is often found to be very wasteful. The inefficiency is overcome in the LZW algorithm, by omitting $C(S)$ and transmitting the index i only. This is accomplished by initializing the dictionary with a list of single symbol patterns, to include all the symbols of the source alphabet. In each step, the index of the longest match from the input in the dictionary is output and a new pattern is inserted in the dictionary. This new pattern is formed by concatenating the longest match with the next character in the input stream. As a result, the last symbol (or character) of this new pattern is encoded as the first character of the next one.

3.12.3.1 **Example 6–LZW encoding:** The LZW encoding algorithm is explained below with an example to encode the string *babacbabababcb*.

Table 3.12 LZW dictionary for encoding

Index	Pattern	Derived as
1	*a*	
2	*b*	initial
3	*c*	
4	*ba*	$2 + a$
5	*ab*	$1 + b$
6	*bac*	$4 + c$
7	*cb*	$3 + b$
8	*bab*	$4 + b$
9	*baba*	$8 + a$
10	*abc*	$5 + c$

The dictionary generation is shown in Table 3.12. Initially, the dictionary consists of single symbol (or character) patterns *a*, *b*, and *c* from the input alphabet $\{a, b, c\}$. The index of the patterns in the dictionary are 1, 2, and 3, respectively.

After receiving the first character *b*, the encoder finds the match at index 2. But the pattern *ba*, with the first two characters, does not have a match in the current dictionary. Hence the encoder outputs index 2 to encode the first character *b*, and inserts the new pattern *ba* to index 4 in the dictionary.

The second input character *a* has a match in the dictionary with index 1, but *ab* formed by the second and third characters does not have a match. As a result, the encoder outputs index 1 to encode *a* and inserts the new pattern *ab* in the dictionary at index 5.

Now the next two characters *ba* match with the pattern at index 4 in the dictionary, but *bac* does not. Hence the encoder outputs index 4 to encode *ba*, and it inserts the new pattern *bac* into the dictionary at index 6.

The following character *c* now matches with index 3, but *cb* does not. Hence the encoder outputs index 3 to encode *c*, and it inserts *cb* in the dictionary to index 7.

The subsequent two characters *ba* have a match at index 4, but *bab* does not. Hence the encoder outputs the index 4 to encode *ba*, and it inserts the new pattern *bab* in the dictionary to index 8.

The next three characters *bab* have a match in the dictionary to index 8, but *baba* does not. Hence the encoder now outputs the index 8 to encode *bab*, and it inserts the new pattern *baba* in the dictionary at index 9.

The following two characters *ab* now match with the pattern at index 5 in the dictionary, but *abc* does not. Hence the encoder outputs index 5 to encode *ab*, and it inserts the new pattern *abc* in the dictionary to index 10.

The subsequent two characters *cb* have a match at index 7 in the dictionary. Hence the encoder outputs the index 7 to encode *cb*, and it stops. As a result, the output of the LZW encoder is 2 1 4 3 4 8 5 7.

It should be noted that statistical probabilities of appearance of the pointers from the LZW encoder can be further exploited by using Huffman-coding type variable length entropy encoding schemes. This may result in further reduction of the output data, and hence it can enhance the text compression performance.

3.12.3.2 **Example 7–LZW decoding:** Here we take the same encoder output from Example 6, and decode it using the LZW algorithm. The input to the decoder is 2, 1, 4, 3, 4, 8, 5, 7.

Like the encoder, the decoder starts with the initial dictionary having three entries for *a*, *b*, *c* and indices 1, 2, 3. After visiting the first index 2, the decoder outputs the corresponding pattern *b* from the dictionary.

The next output is *a*, corresponding to the second input index 1. At this point, the decoder inserts a new pattern *ba* in the dictionary to index 4. This new pattern *ba* is formed by concatenating the first character *a* of the current output pattern *a* at the end of the last output pattern *b*.

The next input index is 4, which corresponds to the pattern *ba* in the dictionary. Hence the decoder outputs *ba*, and it inserts the new pattern *ab* in the dictionary to index 5. The new pattern *ab* is again formed by concatenating the first character *b* of the current output pattern *ba* at the end of the last output pattern *a*.

The next input index is 3, which corresponds to *c* in the current dictionary. The decoder hence outputs *c* and inserts a new pattern *bac* in the dictionary to index 6. This pattern *bac* has been formed by concatenating *c* at the end of the previous output or matching pattern *ba*.

The next output of the decoder is *ba* because of the input index 4. The decoder now inserts the new pattern *cb* in the dictionary to index 7. This pattern is again formed by concatenating the first character *b* of the current output *ba* at the end of the previous output *c*. At this point, the dictionary has only 7 entries as shown in Table 3.13. So far the decoding process was straightforward.

The next input to the decoder is index 8. But the dictionary does not have any pattern at index 8. This tricky situation arises during decoding, if a pattern has been encoded using the pattern immediately preceding it during the encoding process. As a result, the last character of the pattern is the same as the first character. Hence the decoder creates the output by concatenating the first character of the previous output with the previous output itself. Since the previous output was *ba*, the decoder outputs *bab* in the current decoding

Table 3.13 LZW dictionary for decoding

Index	Pattern	Derived as
1	*a*	
2	*b*	initial
3	*c*	
4	*ba*	$2 + a$
5	*ab*	$1 + b$
6	*bac*	$4 + c$
7	*cb*	$3 + b$

step and inserts this new pattern in the dictionary to index 8. The following input index 5 corresponds to the pattern *ab*, and hence the decoder outputs *ab* and inserts the new pattern *baba* in the dictionary at index 9. This pattern *baba* is formed by concatenating the first character *a* of the current output *ab* at the end of the previous output *bab*.

The next input index 7 corresponds to the pattern *cb*. The decoder outputs *cb* and obviously inserts the new pattern *abc* in the dictionary and stops. At this point the final dictionary is exactly identical to the final dictionary that was formed during the encoding process as shown in Table 3.12 in the previous example.

3.12.4   Other applications of Lempel–Ziv coding

LZ coding techniques are not necessarily applicable to text compression only. Variants of the LZ coding techniques have been found to be effective to compress many other datatypes. They can be effectively used to compress general-purpose data effectively, for archival and storage. LZ coding techniques can be applied to compress databases (both numeric and text), graphical charts, geographical maps, and many other special kinds of images. The LZ-based coding schemes have also been adopted in many international coding standards.

LZW-based coding has been found to be effective to losslessly compress different kinds of images. The widely used image file format 'GIF' (Graphical Interchange Format) is an implementation of the LZW algorithm. This is very similar to the popular *compress* utility in UNIX. GIF is very effective in compressing computer-generated graphical images and pseudo-color or color-mapped images. TIFF (Tag Image File Format) is another industry standard based on LZ coding. This is useful for compressing *dithered binary images*, which simulate gray scale images through a variation of the density of black dots. The CCITT (previously ITU-T) *Recommendation V.42 bis* is a compression standard of data over a telephone network. The compression mode of this standard uses the LZW algorithm to compress data to be transmitted through the modem.

3.13   CONCLUSIONS AND DISCUSSION

In this chapter we have introduced the fundamental principles behind multimedia data compression. Data compression has great potential in the near future to improve the efficiency of data mining systems, by exploiting the benefits of compact and shorter representation of data. This is particularly important because data mining techniques typically deal with large databases, and data storage management is a big issue for managing such large databases. However, the data mining community has hitherto failed to take advantage of the knowledge in the area of data compression and develop special data mining techniques based on the principles behind data compression. Nevertheless, there have been limited efforts at usage of data compression to reduce the high dimensionality of multimedia datasets, with applications for mining multimedia information in a limited manner. Multimedia data mining is covered in detail in Chapter 9.

We have discussed various issues of multimedia data compression, along with some theoretical foundations. We presented some basic source coding algorithms, often used in data compression, in order to introduce this area of development to the readers. We have described the principles behind the popular algorithms for image and text type multimedia data. We avoided discussion on compression of other datatypes such as video, audio, and speech because it is beyond the scope of this book. The advantages of data compression are manifold and will enable more multimedia applications at reduced costs, thereby aiding its usage by a larger population, with newer applications, in the near future.

REFERENCES

1. C. E. Shannon and W. Weaver, *The Mathematical Theory of Communication.* Urbana, IL: University of Illinois Press, 1949.

2. C. E. Shannon, "Certain results in coding theory for noisy channels," *Information Control*, vol. 1, pp. 6–25, 1957.

3. C. E. Shannon, "Coding theorems for a discrete source with a fidelity criterion," Technical Report, IRE National Convention Record, 1959.

4. B. McMillan, "The basic theorems of information theory," *Annals of Mathematics and Statistics*, vol. 24, pp. 196–219, 1953.

5. A. N. Netravali and B. Haskell, *Digital Pictures.* New York: Plenum Press, 1988.

6. A. K. Jain, *Fundamentals of Image Processing.* Englewood Cliffs, NJ: Prentice-Hall, 1989.

7. W. B. Pennenbaker and J. L. Mitchell, *JPEG: Still Image Data Compression Standard.* New York: Chapman & Hall, 1993.

8. R. Hunter and A. H. Robinson, "International digital facsimile standard," *Proceedings of IEEE*, vol. 68, pp. 854–867, 1980.

9. D. A. Huffman, "A method for the construction of minimum redundancy codes," *Proceedings of the IRE*, vol. 40, pp. 1098–1101, 1952.

10. R. J. Clarke, *Transform Coding of Images.* New York: Academic Press, 1985.

11. I. T. Jolliffe, *Principal Component Analysis.* New York: Springer-Verlag, 1986.

12. D. Hand, H. Mannila and P. Smyth, *Principles of Data Mining.* Cambridge, MA: The MIT Press, 2001.

13. K. R. Rao and P. Yip, *Discrete Cosine Transform - Algorithms, Advantages, Applications.* San Diego, CA: Academic Press, 1990.

14. M. Ghanbari, *Video Coding: An Introduction to Standard Codecs*, vol. 42 of *Telecommunications Series.* London, United Kingdom: IEEE, 1999.

15. S. G. Mallat, "A theory for multiresolution signal decomposition: The wavelet representation," *IEEE Transactions on Pattern Analysis and Machine Intelligence*, vol. 11, pp. 674–693, 1989.

16. I. Daubechies, *Ten Lectures on Wavelets.* CBMS, Philadelphia: Society for Industrial and Applied Mathematics, 1992.

17. M. Antonini, M. Barlaud, P. Mathieu, and I. Daubechies, "Image coding using wavelet transform," *IEEE Transactions on Image Processing*, vol. 1, pp. 205–220, 1992.

18. J. M. Shapiro, "Embedded image coding using zerotrees of wavelet coefficients," *IEEE Transactions on Signal Processing*, vol. 41, pp. 3445–3462, 1993.

19. T. Acharya and A. Mukherjee, "High-speed parallel VLSI architectures for image decorrelation," *International Journal of Pattern Recognition and Artificial Intelligence*, vol. 9, pp. 343–365, 1995.

20. H. Lohscheller, "A subjectively adapted image communication system," *IEEE Transactions on Communications*, vol. 32, pp. 1316–1322, 1984.

21. "C source code of JPEG encoder research 6b," Sixth public release of the Independent JPEG group's free JPEG software, The Independent JPEG Group, *ftp://ftp.uu.net/graphics/jpeg/jpegsrc_v6b_tar.gz*, March 1998.

22. "Information technology - JPEG2000 Image Coding System," Final Committee Draft Version 1.0 ISO/IEC JTC 1/SC 29/WG 1 N1646R, March 2000.

23. D. S. Taubman and M. W. Marcellin, *JPEG2000: Image Compression Fundamentals, Standards and Practice.* Boston, USA: Kluwer Academic Publishers, 2002.

24. J. Ziv and A. Lempel, "A universal algorithm for sequential data compression," *IEEE Transactions on Information Theory*, vol. 23, pp. 337–343, 1977.

25. J. Ziv and A. Lempel, "Compression of individual sequences via variable-rate coding," *IEEE Transactions on Information Theory*, vol. 24, pp. 530–536, 1978.

26. J. A. Storer and T. G. Syzmanski, "Data compression via textual substitution," *Journal of the ACM*, vol. 29, pp. 928–951, 1982.

27. T. Welch, "A technique for high-performance data compression," *IEEE Computer*, vol. 17, pp. 8–19, 1984.

28. T. C. Bell, J. G. Cleary, and I. H. Witten, *Text Compression.* Englewood Cliffs, NJ: Prentice-Hall, 1990.

29. T. Acharya and J. F. JáJá, "An on-line variable-length binary encoding of text," *Information Sciences*, vol. 94, pp. 1–22, 1996.

30. J. G. Cleary and I. H. Witten, "Data compression using adaptive coding and partial string matching," *IEEE Transactions on Communications*, vol. 32, pp. 396–402, 1984.

31. A. Moffat, "Implementing the PPM data compression scheme," *IEEE Transactions on Communications*, vol. 38, pp. 1917–1921, 1990.

32. I. H. Witten, R. M. Neal, and J. G. Cleary, "Arithmetic coding for data compression," *Communications of the ACM*, vol. 30, pp. 520–540, 1987.

33. M. Burrows and D. J. Wheeler, "A block-sorting lossless data compression algorithm," Technical Report 124, Digital Equipment Corporation, Palo Alto, CA, May 1994.

4
String Matching

4.1 INTRODUCTION

Text probably got much more attention compared to other media datatypes, in research and development for information retrieval and data mining, because of the wealth of work done in the area of searching patterns in text files during the last three decades. This resulted in the growth of text processing softwares, text information retrieval systems, digital libraries, etc. The single most important reason for this growth is the development of numerous classical algorithms and their efficient implementations in string matching [1, 2]. The results in string matching algorithms influenced the development of text-based search engines, and these are being widely used in the *World Wide Web.*

Text mining is becoming a very practical and important area of development. Given the practical importance of classification and search of patterns in large collection of text data in the Internet, newswire, electronic media, digital library, large textual databases, and their ability to generate knowledge from these vast resources, the development in the area of text mining continues to increase. Development of string matching algorithms also influenced the areas of computational biology, and molecular biology, along with the success of the Human Genome Project. String matching algorithms have been used in DNA search, DNA sequencing, and many other problems in Bioinformatics as well. In our judgment, understanding of the principles in string matching is important for further development in data mining and its applications in multimedia as well as Bioinformatics.

The remaining part of this section introduces the preliminaries of string matching. Classical linear order string matching algorithms are described in Section 4.2. The use of string matching in Bioinformatics is highlighted in Section 4.3. Issues in approximate string matching are dealt with in Section 4.4. Compressed string matching is considered in Section 4.5. Finally, Section 4.6 concludes the chapter.

4.1.1 Some definitions and preliminaries

Before we proceed to detailed algorithmic description, it is essential to prepare the readers with some basic definitions.

Alphabet: Symbols, or characters, are considered to be the basic elemental building blocks in string matching. An *alphabet* is a specific set of symbols. It is usually a finite set. For instance, $\Sigma = \{a, b, c, d, e\}$ is an alphabet containing symbols a, b, c, d, and e.

String: A *string* is a sequence of instances of *symbols*, or characters, over a finite alphabet Σ. For instance, both '$b\,a\,a\,c\,b\,c\,b\,a$' and '$a\,d\,a\,e\,a\,b\,e\,d\,e\,e\,d$' are strings over the alphabet $\Sigma = \{a, b, c, d, e\}$.

The *length* of a string s, say, is the number of instances of the symbols or characters in the string. The string s may be expressed as $s = s_1 s_2 \cdots s_m$, where each s_i is an instance of a symbol, or character, from the alphabet and m is the length of the string s. Often length of the string is represented as $|s|$. An *empty* string, ϵ, is a special string with length 0. The concatenation of two strings $x = x_1 x_2 \cdots x_p$ and $y = y_1 y_2 \cdots y_q$, denoted by $x\,y$, is equal to the string $x_1 x_2 \cdots x_p y_1 y_2 \cdots y_q$. The length of $x\,y$ is $p + q$, where p and q are the lengths of strings x and y, respectively. As an example, the concatenation of two string '$s\,t\,r\,a\,i\,g\,h\,t$' and '$f\,o\,r\,w\,a\,r\,d$' is '$s\,t\,r\,a\,i\,g\,h\,t\,f\,o\,r\,w\,a\,r\,d$'. The concatenation of the empty string ϵ with any string is that string itself.

Substring: A string $x = x_1 x_2 \cdots x_k$ is a *substring* of another string $y = y_1 y_2 y_3 \cdots y_n$, if and only if there exists an i, $0 < i \leq n$, so that $y_{i+j-1} = x_j$ for $j = 1, 2, \ldots, k$.

As an example, the string '$b\,a\,d$' is a substring of a string '$d\,a\,b\,a\,d\,a\,b\,a$'. Hence the substring of a string can be formed by deleting zero or more characters from the beginning and/or end of the string. The empty string is a special substring of any string, and hence it is the shortest length substring of any string. The longest substring of a string is the string itself.

Suffix: The *suffix* of a string s is a substring formed by deleting zero or more characters from the beginning of s. Hence y is a suffix of string s, if there exists a substring x such that $s = x\,y$. In other words, suffix of $s = s_1 s_2 \cdots s_n$ is any substring $s_{n-j} s_{n-j+1} \cdots s_n$ where $0 \leq j \leq n$. The empty string ϵ is the shortest suffix and the string itself is the longest suffix of any string. Any suffix other than the empty string and the string itself is called a *proper suffix*. As an example, '*oil*' is the proper suffix of a string '*turmoil*'. This is pictorially depicted in Fig. 4.1(a).

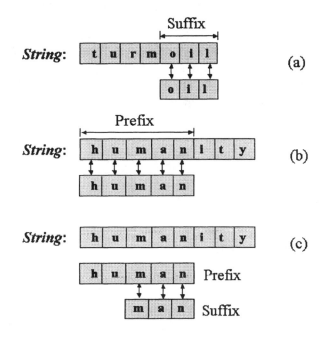

Fig. 4.1 Examples of (a) suffix, (b) prefix, and (c) suffix of prefix of a string.

Prefix: The *prefix* of a string s is a substring formed by deleting zero or more characters from the end of s.

Hence x is a prefix of s if there exist a substring y so that $s = xy$. In other words, prefix of $s = s_1 s_2 \cdots s_n$ is any substring $s_1 s_2 \cdots s_k$, where $0 \le k \le n$. The empty string ϵ is the shortest prefix and the string itself is the longest prefix of any string. Any prefix other than the empty string and the string itself is called a *proper prefix*. As an example, '*human*' is the proper prefix of the string "*humanity*." This is pictorially depicted in Fig. 4.1(b).

It is interesting to note that the substring '*man*' is a suffix of a prefix of the string "*humanity*," as pictorially depicted in Fig. 4.1(c).

Factor: A string y is a factor of a string s if s can be represented as $s = xyz$, where x and y are the prefix and suffix of s. The substring '*man*' is a factor of the string '*humanity*'. In other words, a factor of a string is a *suffix* of a *prefix* or *prefix* of a *suffix* of a string.

4.1.2   String matching problem

String matching essentially is the technique of finding the occurrence of a particular string, called a pattern, in another string called the text. The *String matching problem* can be formulated as follows.

Let us assume that a pattern $p = p_1 p_2 \cdots p_m$ of length m and a text $t = t_1 t_2 \cdots t_n$ of length n are two strings formed over the same finite alphabet Σ such that $m < n$. We say that the pattern p occurs in text t at the beginning of text location k if $1 \le k \le n - m$ and $t_{k+i-1} = p_i$ for $1 \le i \le m$. The *string matching problem* is the problem of finding all the text locations where the given pattern p occurs in the given text t. The string matching problem has been depicted pictorially in Fig. 4.2.

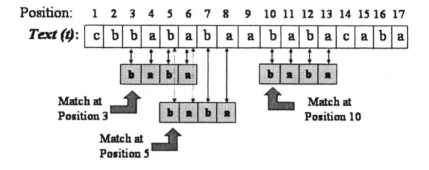

Fig. 4.2   The string matching problem.

Example 1:   Let us assume a text string $t = \ 'cbbababaababacaba'$ and a pattern $p = \ 'baba'$ over the finite alphabet $\Sigma = \{a, b, c\}$ as shown in Fig. 4.2. The pattern '$baba$' occurs in text locations 3, 5, and 10, respectively. Note that locations 3 and 5 overlap each other. A valid string matching algorithm should be able to recognize such overlapping occurrences as well.

There are different interesting variations of the string matching problem. In many applications, the search pattern may not be a simple sequence of characters or symbols. It could be fully or partially specified. If all the symbols or characters p_i for $1 \leq i \leq m$ in the pattern $p = p_1 p_2 \cdots p_m$ are definitely known, the pattern is called a fully specified pattern. If one or more symbol p_j for any $1 \leq j \leq m$ in the pattern is not specifically known, the pattern can be called a partially specified pattern. An unspecified symbol in the pattern can be denoted by a "don't care" or a "wild card" character.

As an example, let us assume an alphabet $\Sigma = \{A, B, C, D\}$. A pattern $P = {}'BCCA'$ is fully specified. However a pattern $P = BC * A$ is partially specified because the third symbol $*$ in P is not known. If $*$ can be any of the symbols from the alphabet Σ, the occurrence of pattern P could be the occurrence of any one of the possible patterns '$BCAA$', '$BCBA$', '$BCCA$', and '$BCDA$'. This unspecified symbol $*$ in P is call the *fixed length don't care (FLDC)* character. However if the pattern P consists of a don't care character ϕ which can be any substring $\{\$, \$\$, \$\$\$, \ldots\}$ of any arbitrary length, then the don't care character ϕ is called the *variable length don't care (VLDC)* character. As an example, let us assume that the partially specified pattern is $P = {}'BC\phi A'$. Since ϕ can contain any pattern from the infinite set of substrings $\{\$, \$\$, \$\$\$, \ldots\}$, the possible occurrences of the pattern in the text will be any matched substring beginning with the prefix 'BA' and ending with the suffix A – for example, 'BCA', '$BCAAA$', '$BCABCBDBCDDBA$', etc. Partially specified pattern matching is useful in searching for text information when the pattern is partially known.

The pattern may also consist of a finite set of sequences instead of just a single string. Here the pattern matching problem can be extended to search for occurrence(s) of any one of the members of the set in the text, while reading the text once only. The patterns of interest may contain wild cards as explained above. They may also contain regular expressions. Use of regular expressions in patterns can be very powerful, because a set of search patterns can be expressed by using a regular expression in the form of a simple string as well as concatenations, unions, and repetitions of other subexpressions. Obviously, the algorithms to solve such problems are very complex, and they still remain a challenge in computer science.

The matching criteria can also vary by permitting slight limited difference between a pattern and its occurrences in the text. This type of pattern matching is popularly known as *approximate matching* and is particularly useful in information retrieval, text processing, and molecular and computational biology. Approximate matching is a powerful tool in automatic detection of spelling errors in texts, distance measures in DNA analysis, DNA sequence and matching, etc. The progress in simple and approximate string matching may have significant influence in text mining and Bioinformatics as well.

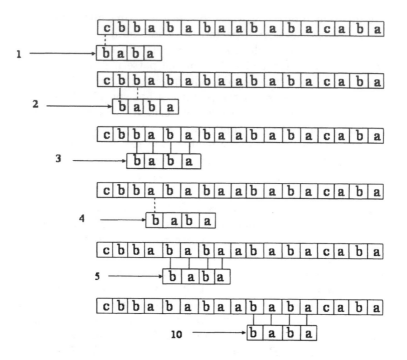

Fig. 4.3 Example of brute force approach to string matching.

4.1.3   Brute force string matching

In a brute force approach, the string matching algorithm compares a pattern character by character in each and every location of the text. Starting at the beginning of the text string, we compare the characters of the pattern one after another with the corresponding characters in the text, until a mismatch is found or the complete pattern is exhausted. If the pattern is exhausted, we claim to have found a match at the beginning of the text. If a mismatch of character is detected before the pattern is exhausted, then the pattern does not occur at the beginning of the text. We start the matching all over again at the next character in the text, and continue the same procedure.

Example 2:   We illustrate how the brute force pattern matching algorithm finds occurrences of a pattern '*baba*' in a text '*cbbababaababacaba*' in Fig. 4.3. The algorithm starts by comparing the first character "*b*" of the pattern with the first character '*c*' of the text string. The broken line connecting them shows that these two characters don't match. Hence the pattern gets shifted to the second character location in the text, in order to start the pattern comparison all over again from the second character location in the string. In the second step, the first character "*b*" of the pattern is compared with the second character 'b' of the text. Since they are the same, this is shown by connecting them with a solid line. Now the second character of the pattern "a" is compared with the next character 'b' in the text, and they are shown to be connected by a broken line as they mismatch in this location. Hence the pattern matching starts all over again at text character location 3 now. We can see that all the four consecutive characters 'b', 'a', 'b', and 'a' in pattern p are now matched with the consecutive four character in the text starting in location 3, and they are shown to be connected by solid lines. Hereby we have found the first occurrence of the pattern in the text at location 3. The pattern is now shifted to restart the matching process from text character location 4. The first character "b" does not match with the character 'a' in location 4, and hence the pattern is shifted to location 5. Here we find that the pattern '$b\,a\,b\,a$' matches with the consecutive four characters in the text starting in location 5 and hence determines an occurrence of the pattern in location 5 of the text. Continuing in the same manner, the other occurrences of the pattern is obtained at text character location 10, as shown in Fig. 4.3. We now formally describe the brute force algorithm for pattern matching.

BRUTE-FORCE-STRING-MATCHING (p, t)

1. Compute pattern length, $m \leftarrow |p|$;

2. Compute text length, $n \leftarrow |t|$;

3. Initialize text pointer, $s \leftarrow 1$;

4. Initialize pattern pointer, $i \leftarrow 1$;

5. **if** $p_i = t_{s+i}$ (i.e., ith character in pattern matches with $(s+i)$th character in text) **then** increment pattern pointer, $i \leftarrow i + 1$,
   else go to step 7;

6. **if** $(i \leq m)$ **then** go to step 5;

7. **if** $i > m$ (i.e., search is successful) **then** print "Pattern occurs at text position" s;

8. Increment text pointer, $s \leftarrow s + 1$ for next search;

9. **if** $s \leq n - m + 1$ (i.e., the text is not exhausted) **then** go to step 4 to repeat above.

The above brute force approach requires the input text string to be buffered, because the text needs to be backtracked whenever there is an unsuccessful match with a symbol in the pattern. The computational complexity of the algorithm is $O(m * n)$ in the worst case. However, there are efficient algorithms for string matching, which take only a linear order of computational complexity $O(m + n)$ in the worst case. Moreover, there is no need of buffering, because these algorithms do not backtrack in the event of occurrence of a mismatch in a pattern symbol.

4.2 LINEAR-ORDER STRING MATCHING ALGORITHMS

String matching algorithms with linear-order computational complexity are very useful in many practical text-based applications such as edit, search and retrieval of text, and development of search engine, and therein lies its possible influence in text data mining. In this section, we first discuss a practical approach of developing a linear-order string matching algorithm with finite automata, in order to avoid the problem of buffering due to backtracking in the text itself. This definition of finite automaton and its property of not backtracking when there is a mismatch has influenced the development of the Knuth–Morris–Pratt algorithm [1] in 1977 as the first linear-order algorithm with computational complexity $O(m + n)$. This was followed by flurries of activity in the computer science community to develop efficient linear-order algorithms for string matching, along with exploration of simple implementation of them. In the remaining part of this section, we describe some of the classical linear order algorithms that established the foundation of research and development in string matching. These include the Boyer–Moore [2], Boyer–Moore–Horspool [3], and Karp–Rabin [4, 5] algorithms.

4.2.1 String matching with finite automata

Finite automata has been used as a tool in string matching. For every pattern p, we can always build a *finite automaton*, which we call a *string-matching automaton* for the corresponding pattern. The string-matching automaton is built from the pattern as a preprocessing step before matching. The text is then scanned through the automaton to find occurrences of the pattern in the text. A finite automaton M can be considered as a 5-tuple $(Q, q_0, S, \Sigma, \delta)$, where

- Q is a finite set of *states* of the automaton,

- $q_0 \in Q$ is a special state called the *start state*,

- $S \subseteq Q$ is a distinguished set of states called the *stop states*,

- Σ is the finite input *alphabet*, and

- δ is a function from $Q \times \Sigma$ into Q, called the *transition function* of the automaton M.

To understand string matching with finite automata, it is not necessary for readers to have a complete understanding of the automata theory. The

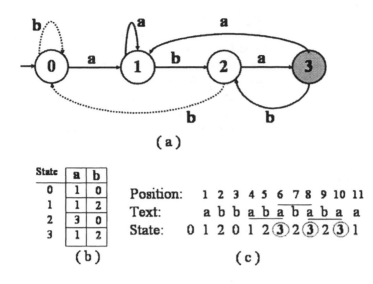

(a)

State	a	b
0	1	0
1	1	2
2	3	0
3	1	2

(b)

Position: 1 2 3 4 5 6 7 8 9 10 11

Text: a b b a b a b a b a a

State: 0 1 2 0 1 2③2③2③1

(c)

Fig. 4.4 Finite automata: (a) state diagram, (b) state transition table, and (c) pattern matching example.

automaton M always begins at the start state q_0 and reads the characters of the string sequentially one at a time. If the automaton M is in a state q_i and reads a character or symbol $\sigma \in \Sigma$, it makes a transition from state q_i to another state, say q_j, and we denote the transition as $q_j = \delta(q_i, \sigma)$. If the state $q_j \in S$, we say that the automaton M has accepted the string scanned so far. The finite automaton can be represented by a state-transition diagram as shown in Fig. 4.4(a). We explain the finite state diagram for a pattern '$a\,b\,a$' with three types of nodes as follows:

- A *start* node. This represents the start state q_0 of M. In Fig. 4.4(a), state 0 is the start state.

- A *stop* node. In simple string matching there is only one stop node and the machine transits to this state when a valid occurrence of the pattern appears in the string. In Fig. 4.4(a), state 3 represents the stop state. This is specially indicated by the shaded node in Fig. 4.4(a).

- Finite number of *internal* or *read* nodes. These are the nodes representing the states of the machine other than the start or stop nodes. The machine reads only one character or symbol of the string in each of these nodes.

Example 3:   We illustrate an example of string matching with finite automaton in Fig. 4.4. In this example, we assume that the pattern is $p =$ "$a\,b\,a$" and the text to be searched is $t =$ '$a\,b\,b\,a\,b\,a\,b\,a\,b\,a\,a$' over the alphabet $\Sigma = \{a, b\}$. State diagram of the finite automaton is shown in Fig. 4.4(a) with four states $Q = \{0, 1, 2, 3\}$ of which $q_0 = 0$ is the *start* state and $S = 3$ is the *stop* state. The state transition function δ is explained through the tabular representation in Fig. 4.4(b). The text and the corresponding state of the automaton, after it scans each character of the text, is shown in Fig. 4.4(c). As indicated in Fig. 4.4(c), there are three occurrences of the pattern $p =$ "$a\,b\,a$" in the text $t =$ '$a\,b\,b\,a\,b\,a\,b\,a\,b\,a\,a$' because the automaton goes to the stop state at character positions 6, 8, and 10 in the text. Since the pattern length is 3, the matched locations of the pattern in the text correspond to character positions 4, 6 and 8 respectively The matched patterns in the string are marked by two underlines and one overline in the text of Fig. 4.4(c).

4.2.1.1 Computational complexity: Once the state diagram (or the state transition table) of the finite automaton of a pattern is constructed, we can scan the text to search for the pattern by comparing each text character only once, not requiring any backtrack when there is a mismatch. Hence we can find all the occurrences of the pattern in the text of length n in $O(n)$ time. This is a major improvement as compared to the naive brute force approach to pattern matching of Section 4.1.3. However, there is an overhead for preprocessing the pattern in terms of time and space complexity in order to (a) construct the state diagram or the state transition table for the pattern and (b) store the table in the memory for pattern matching. The state transition table contains m entries for a pattern of length m and for each of the symbol in the alphabet Σ. As a result, the preprocessing requires $O(m * |\Sigma|)$ time to construct the state transition table. Hence total computational complexity for string matching using the finite automaton becomes $O(n + m * |\Sigma|)$. However, m is usually much smaller compared to n. Therefore for small alphabet Σ the computational complexity, on the average, becomes linear in order.

4.2.2   Knuth–Morris–Pratt algorithm

The linear-order $O(m + n)$ algorithm proposed by Knuth, Morris, and Pratt [1] is the oldest and one of the most popular classical algorithms for string matching. The fundamental idea behind this algorithm is to avoid backtracking on the text when a mismatch occurs, by exploiting the knowledge of the matched substring in the text prior to the mismatch. During the search process, all the characters in the text are read forward sequentially one after another. Unlike constructing the state transition table by preprocessing the pattern in $O(m|\Sigma|)$ time, as in the finite automata based technique, the Knuth–Morris–Pratt algorithm first creates an auxiliary table *Next* with m entries in $O(m)$ time by analyzing the pattern p. This *Next* table is then used to shift the text forward by $Next(i)$ characters in the event of a mismatch at the ith character in the pattern in $O(n)$ time, where $Next(i)$ is the ith entry in this table. Hence the overall complexity of the algorithm is $O(m+n)$. We have explained this through a diagram in Fig. 4.5.

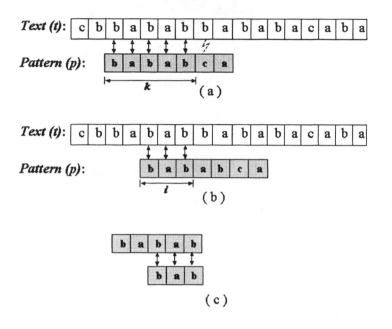

(a)

(b)

(c)

Fig. 4.5 Generation of the *Next* table. (a) First k characters of p matches with the text, (b) p is shifted by $k - i$ positions right, because (c) first i characters of p is also suffix of the first k matched characters.

As described in Fig. 4.5(a), if there is a mismatch at the jth symbol of the text with the $(k+1)$th symbol (p_{k+1}) of the pattern $p = p_1 p_2 \cdots p_m$, then the prefix $p_1 p_2 \cdots p_k$ is the same as the substring $t_{j-k} t_{j-k+1} \cdots t_{j-1}$ in the text, which is same as the suffix of the text matched so far. Hence we can decide how much the text needs to be shifted forward in the event of a mismatch, by observing the already-matched portion of the pattern only. This shift is dependent on the structure of the pattern and the position of mismatch in the pattern. Therefore the *Next* table is independent of the text, and it can be generated by analyzing the pattern itself before scanning the text. In order to determine the kth entry in the *Next* table, we just need to find the longest overlap of a proper prefix of pattern p with a suffix of the already-matched portion of the pattern p as shown in Fig. 4.5(c). Precisely,

$$Next(k) = \max\{i : i < k \text{ and } p_1 p_2 \cdots p_i = p_{k-i+1} p_{k-i+2} \cdots p_k\}. \quad (4.1)$$

To reiterate, the value of $Next(k)$ is the maximum $i < k$, such that the prefix $p_1 p_2 \cdots p_i$ of the pattern $p = p_1 p_2 \cdots p_m$ is a suffix $p_1 p_2 \cdots p_{k-1}$, that is, $p_1 p_2 \cdots p_i = p_{k-i+1} \cdots p_{k-1}$. The value $Next(k)$ is assigned to be 1 if such

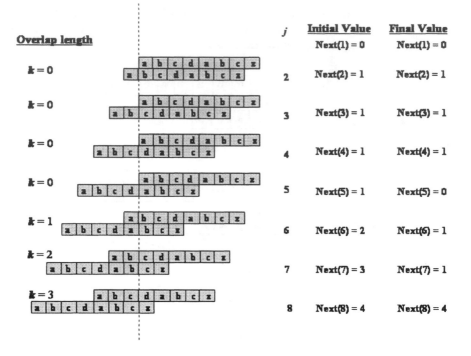

The table accompanying the figure:

		j	Initial Value Next(1) = 0	Final Value Next(1) = 0
Overlap length				
k = 0		2	Next(2) = 1	Next(2) = 1
k = 0		3	Next(3) = 1	Next(3) = 1
k = 0		4	Next(4) = 1	Next(4) = 1
k = 0		5	Next(5) = 1	Next(5) = 0
k = 1		6	Next(6) = 2	Next(6) = 1
k = 2		7	Next(7) = 3	Next(7) = 1
k = 3		8	Next(8) = 4	Next(8) = 4

Fig. 4.6   Generation of the *Next* table for pattern $p = $ "$abcdabcz$."

a prefix does not exist, indicating a prefix that is an empty string ϵ only. To compute $Next(k)$, the pattern $p_1 p_2 \cdots p_{k-1}$ is overlapped with itself by sliding one copy of itself over another, character by character from left to right, until all the overlapping characters match or there is none left to slide. The overlapping substring then defines the desired prefix, and $Next(k)$ is the length of the overlapping prefix plus 1. We demonstrate this with an example in Fig. 4.6 to compute the *Next* table for the pattern $p = $ "$abcdabcz$."

The *Next* value for the first character of the pattern is always 0 because there is no mismatching substring prior to the first character. In Fig. 4.6, we show the pattern overlapped with itself. The left-hand side of the vertical line shows the substring $p_1 p_2 \cdots p_{j-1}$ as well as the overlapping of the longest prefix of this substring with its suffix, for the computation of $Next(j)$. For $j = 2, 3, 4,$ and 5, the overlap length is 0 because only the empty string ϵ can be the longest prefix, which is also a suffix of all the substrings 'a', 'ab', 'abc', and '$abcd$', respectively, as shown in Fig. 4.6. Hence the initial values of $Next(2)$, $Next(3)$, $Next(4)$ and $Next(5)$ are 1's. For $j = 6$, 'a' is the longest prefix that is also a suffix of the substring '$abcda$'. Since the overlap length is 1, the value of $Next(6)$ becomes 2. For $j = 7$, the longest prefix of the substring '$abcdab$' is 'ab', that is also a suffix of '$abcdab$'. Now the value of $Next(7)$ is 3, because the overlap length is 2. Similarly 'abc' is the longest prefix and also a suffix of the substring '$abcdabc$' for $j = 8$, and accordingly the value of $Next(8)$ is 4.

These $Next(j)$ values can be considered during the string matching in the event of a mismatch of the jth character of a pattern with the ith character of the text, and accordingly the pattern is shifted so that the next character in the text after mismatching t_{i+1} can now be aligned with $p_{Next(j)+1}$ in the pattern to continue the forward matching without backtracking.

We may further improve the *Next* table by considering the actual symbol causing a mismatch. Let us consider the above example with the initial *Next* table as shown in Fig. 4.6. If there is a mismatch between a text character t_i and pattern symbol p_7 (i.e., the second 'c' in the pattern), then the next comparison is done between the same t_i and p_3 ($= p_{Next(7)}$). However, the comparison will fail again because p_3 is also the same character 'c' and will shift the comparison to p_1 as $Next(3) = 1$. Hence we can further improve the *Next* table by taking the actual symbol causing the mismatch into consideration. The modified $Next(k)$ (final value) is expressed as

$$Next(k) = \max\{i : \ i < k \text{ and } p_1 p_2 \cdots p_i = p_{k-i+1} p_{k-i+2} \cdots p_k \text{ and } x_i \neq x_k\}.$$
(4.2)

Using this definition, the final values of the new *Next* table are computed as shown in Fig. 4.6. For example, the initial value of $Next(5)$ is 1. However, $p_5 = p_1 =$ 'a', and hence we replace the initial value of $Next(5)$ by the value of $Next(1)$ that is 0. Similarly, initial value of $Next(6)$ is 2. Since $p_6 = p_2 =$ 'b' and $p_6 \neq p_1$ ($=p_{Next(2)}$), the final value of $Next(6)$ is 1. Iterating this procedure for all the entries in the *Next* table, we generate the final values of *Next* as depicted in Fig. 4.6. The formal algorithm to generate the *Next* table is shown below.

GENERATE-NEXT-TABLE (p)

1. Initialize pattern pointer, $j \leftarrow 1$;

2. Initialize overlap length of the patterns, $k \leftarrow 0$;

3. Initialize *Next* table, $Next(1) \leftarrow 0$ (special value for mismatch at p_1);

4. **while** $(k > 0$ and $p_j \neq p_k)$ **do** $k \leftarrow Next(k)$;

5. Increment pattern pointer, $j \leftarrow j + 1$;

6. Increment overlap length, $k \leftarrow k + 1$;

7. **if** $(p_j = p_k)$ **then** $Next(j) \leftarrow Next(k)$ **else** $Next(j) \leftarrow k$;

8. **if** $(j < m)$ **then** go to step 4;

9. Stop.

The string matching algorithm using the above *Next* table is described below.

KNUTH–MORRIS–PRATT-STRING-MATCHING $(p, t, Next)$

1. Initialize the pattern index, $j \leftarrow 1$;

2. Initialize the text index, $k \leftarrow 1$;

3. Set length of the pattern, $m \leftarrow |p|$;

4. Set length of the text, $n \leftarrow |t|$;

5. **while** $j > 0$ and $p_j \neq t_i$ (i.e., there is a mismatch) **do**
   shift pattern pointer $(j \leftarrow Next(j))$;

6. Advance text pointer, $i \leftarrow i + 1$;

7. Advance pattern pointer, $j \leftarrow j + 1$;

8. **if** $j \geq m$ (i.e., match is successful) **then**
   print "pattern occurs at text index" $i - m$
   else shift pattern pointer, $j \leftarrow Next(j)$.

9. **if** $i \leq n$ and $j \leq m$ (i.e., matching is not complete) **then**
   go to step 5 to continue pattern matching
   else Stop.

Example 4:   An example of pattern matching with the Knuth–Morris–Pratt algorithm is shown in Fig. 4.7. We consider finding the occurrences of a pattern $p =$ "$babab$" in a text $t =$ '$ababababababaababababa$'. First we compute the next table [0, 1, 0, 1, 3] for the pattern $p =$ "$babab$" as shown in Fig. 4.7(a). Matching details are depicted in Fig. 4.7(b). The indices i and j represent, respectively, the character positions in text and the pattern being matched. The symbol "y" for $t_i = p_j$ represents a match of the text character t_i with the corresponding pattern character p_j. The symbol "Y" indicates occurrence of the pattern p ending at the text position i shown by a circle. The symbol "N" represents mismatch of t_i and corresponding p_j. Whenever the result of comparison $t_i = p_j$ is either Y or N, j is replaced by $Next(j)$. For $i = 1$ and $j = 1$ in the figure, we witness the first mismatch. This is indicated by the symbol "N" and hence the value of $j = 1$ is replaced by $j = Next(1) = 0$. Both i and j are incremented and the characters p_j and t_i are compared, until there is a mismatch or occurrence of the end of the pattern in the text. We witness the end of occurrence of the pattern at $i = 6$ and hence the text location 2 is marked by a down arrow $(\downarrow)$ to indicate the beginning of the first occurrence of the pattern in the text. Similarly, the pattern occurs in the text beginning at indices 4, 6 and ending at indices 8 and 10, respectively. At $i = 12$, the text character t_{12} doesn't match with the corresponding pattern character p_5, and hence $j = 5$ is replaced by $Next(5) = 3$. Again t_{12} doesn't match with p_3 and hence j is replaced by $Next(3) = 0$ again. Both i and j are incremented and matching continues forward. The next pattern occurrence is obtained after we find the character match at $i = 17$, and hence the match occurs beginning at $i = 13$.

4.2.2.1 Computational complexity: The computational complexity of Knuth–Morris–Pratt algorithm is $O(n)$ in both the worst and average cases for the pattern matching phase. By analyzing the matching algorithm, it can be shown that the assignment $j \leftarrow Next(j)$ in step 5 never exceeds the total execution of the increment operation $i \leftarrow i+1$ in step 6. The pattern is therefore shifted to the right for a total of at most n times, and hence the computation complexity of the matching phase is $O(n)$. Similarly, we can show that the processing time for initialization of the *Next* table is of the same order $O(m)$. As a result, the worst case overall computational complexity of the algorithm is $O(m + n)$. The worst case computation time happens when a Fibonacci string pattern is matched in a text.

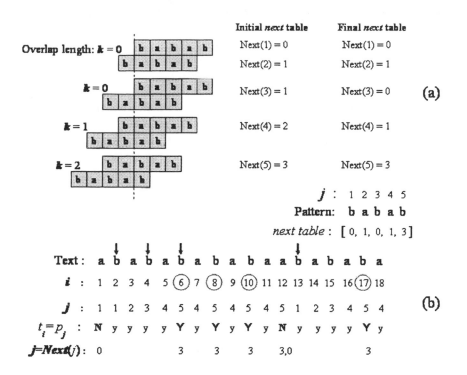

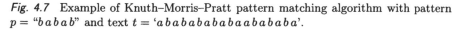

Fig. 4.7 Example of Knuth–Morris–Pratt pattern matching algorithm with pattern $p =$ "$babab$" and text $t =$ '$abababababaababab a$'.

4.2.3 Boyer–Moore algorithm

Boyer and Moore proposed their algorithm for string matching [2] around the same time that Knuth, Morris, and Pratt came out with theirs, in 1977. Both the algorithms became historically famous in the research and development of string matching, mainly because of their application to text processing. Although the computational complexity of both the algorithms is on the average linear, but Boyer–Moore algorithm is likely to be more efficient than the Knuth–Morris–Pratt algorithm for a relatively longer pattern p and reasonably large alphabet Σ.

The key insight of the Boyer–Moore algorithm is that some of the characters in the text can be skipped entirely without comparing them with the pattern, because it can be shown that they can never contribute to an occurrence of the pattern in the text. In Boyer–Moore algorithm, although the text is scanned left to right, comparisons of the pattern and the text are done backwards right to left along the search window while reading the longest suffix of the search window that is also a suffix of the pattern.

The first comparison is made between the last pattern character p_m and the text character t_m, where m is the length of the pattern p. If p_m mismatches with t_m and the character t_m does not at all appear in pattern p, then it is a wastage in comparing the first $m - 1$ characters of the pattern with the first $m-1$ characters of the text since the pattern cannot occur in any of the first m positions of the text. As a result, the pattern can be shifted safely m places to the right so that the next comparison happens between p_m and t_{2m}. Consider searching for a pattern, say "$a\,b\,a\,b\,z$", in a text which does not contain the character 'z' in any of its positions. The total number of comparisons in the text will then be only $\frac{n}{5}$ instead of n. This is a significant performance improvement as compared to prefix comparison-based string matching, such as Knuth–Morris–Pratt or the finite automaton-based algorithms.

In general, if p_m does not match with t_i and t_i does not appear in the pattern $p = p_1 p_2 \cdots p_m$, then we simply ignore comparing all the previous $m - 1$ text characters and shift the pattern m places to the right of t_i in the text. This is illustrated with an example in Fig. 4.8(a) for a pattern "$b\,c\,b\,a\,b$" of length five, aligned with the text beginning at index 12. Here $p_5 = $ 'b' does not match with $t_{16} = $ 'd' and 'd' does not appear in any position of the pattern '$b\,c\,b\,a\,b$'. Hence the pattern is shifted right by five places and aligned with the text beginning at index 17, as shown in Fig. 4.8(b), such that further comparison resumes from this location.

On the other hand, if $p_m \neq t_i$ and t_i does appear in the pattern such that the rightmost appearance of t_i in pattern is p_{m-j}, then the pattern can safely be shifted by j places to the right of t_i in the text in order to align p_{m-j} with t_i. Thereafter, comparison of p_m starts again with t_{i+j}. As an example, $p_m = p_5 = $ 'b' does not match with $t_i = t_{21} = $ 'c' as shown in Fig. 4.8(b). However, 'c' appears in the pattern and its rightmost appearance is $p_{m-j} = p_2 = $ 'c'. Hence the pattern '$b\,c\,b\,a\,b$' is shifted right by $j = 3$ places in order to align

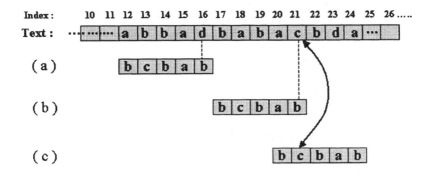

Fig. 4.8 Example of skipping character comparisons in Boyer–Moore algorithm for pattern matching. (a) Current pattern position, (b) pattern completely shifted right because '*d*' does not appear in the pattern, (c) pattern is shifted by three positions to align with character '*c*'.

$p_2 = $ '*c*' with $t_{21} = $ '*c*', as indicated by the curved arrow in Fig. 4.8(c), and further comparison of p_5 resumes with text character $t_{i+j} = t_{24}$.

If a match is found between p_m and t_i, then the preceding characters in the text from t_i are compared sequentially right to left with the corresponding positions in the pattern until there is a mismatch or the pattern is completely matched. If the pattern gets completely matched, this implies that the pattern occurs at location i. Hence the pattern is shifted by one place to the right, and the matching procedure resumes.

The number of positions to slide forward, upon mismatch, depends on the character t_i being matched with the rightmost character p_m of the pattern. These numbers can be stored in an array or table, say *skip* with $|\Sigma|$ entries in the table, where Σ is the alphabet over the text and the pattern. The entry for a symbol $\sigma \in \Sigma$ in the *skip* table is $skip(\sigma) = m - j$ when p_j is the rightmost occurrence of σ in pattern p, and $skip(\sigma) = m$ if σ does not appear in the pattern at all. Hence we can compute the *skip* table using the following algorithm.

GENERATE-SKIP-TABLE(Σ, p)

1. Set pattern length, $m \leftarrow |p|$;

2. Initialize *skip* table, $skip(\sigma) = m$ for all symbols $\sigma \in \Sigma$;

3. Initialize pattern index, $j \leftarrow 1$;

4. **for** jth character p_j in the pattern, set $skip(p_j) \leftarrow m - j$;

5. Increment pattern index, $j \leftarrow j + 1$;

6. **if** $j \leq m$ (i.e., the pattern is not complete) **then** go to step 4;

7. Stop.

The nature of shift of the pattern has been explained with an example in Fig. 4.9 to find the occurrences of the pattern string 'match' in the text string 'one of them matches and others mismatch from'. The procedure requires only 19 character comparisons, as opposed to 44 or more comparisons by Knuth–Morris–Pratt or the finite automaton-based string matching algorithms.

When a match is found between p_m and t_i, subsequent comparisons are made with preceding characters in the text from t_i sequentially right-to-left with the corresponding positions in the pattern. If a mismatch is found at p_j (i.e., $p_j \neq t_{i-m+j}$), then the suffix $u = p_{j+1}p_{j+2} \cdots p_m$ of length $m - j$ of the pattern is said to match with the text substring $u = t_{i-m+j+1} \cdots t_i$. If the rightmost occurrence of the mismatching character t_{i-m+j} in the pattern is p_{m-k}, then the pattern is then shifted by k positions right from the mismatching position in the text to align p_{m-k} with t_{i-m+j} and the matching procedure resumes further. However, the shift will be only one position right if $j < m - k$, in order to avoid negative shift to align p_{m-k} with t_{i-m+j}.

It is also possible that a greater shift is obtained, as compared to the above case, when a mismatch occurs after a partial match of a substring. The idea is to find a suffix $u = p_{j+1}p_{j+2} \cdots p_m$, occurring in another pattern, as a factor of p. Then the pattern can be shifted safely forward to the right, so that $u = t_{i-m+j+1} \cdots t_i$ in the text matches with the next occurrence of u in the pattern. If no such factor exists in the pattern, we cannot safely move the whole pattern right to the mismatching character. In this case, the algorithm computes the longest prefix v of p that is also a proper suffix of u. The pattern is then shifted by $m - |v|$ positions to align with v in the text. The possible shift can be precomputed from the pattern itself and stored in an array or '*shift*' table.

During the search stage, the shift for mismatch at pattern location p_j and mismatching text character t_i is chosen as $\max\{skip(t_i), \ shift(j)\}$.

The Boyer–Moore search algorithm has worst-case computational complexity of the order $O(m * n)$. However, it is sublinear on the average case. Many

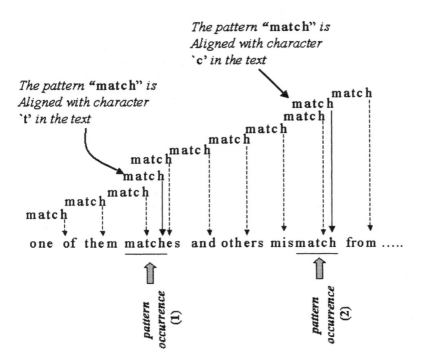

Fig. 4.9 Example of Boyer–Moore pattern matching.

variations of Boyer–Moore idea have been proposed to define worst-case algorithms of linear order [2]. Although it theoretically provides high-performance, the Boyer–Moore (as well as Knuth–Morris–Pratt) algorithm requires complicated preprocessing of the pattern before beginning the actual search of occurrences of the pattern in the string. Hence the Boyer–Moore algorithm, in spite of its promise of sublinear performance on the average, has not been used in many applications in its original form.

Horspool was the first to propose a very simplified version of the Boyer–Moore algorithm [3], by dispensing the processing and use of the *shift* array all together. It uses a variation of the original *skip* array only, and it ensures linear-order computational complexity on the average as well. This is popularly known as the *Boyer–Moore–Horspool* algorithm for string matching.

4.2.4 Boyer–Moore–Horspool algorithm

In the Boyer–Moore–Horspool algorithm [3], we compare the text character t_i with the last character p_m of the pattern. If they match, then we compare the preceding characters of the text with corresponding characters in the pattern sequentially right to left, until we detect either an occurrence of the pattern or a mismatch on a text character. Irrespective of the match, we slide the pattern according to the next occurrence of the character t_i in the pattern. The number of positions to be moved is determined by the value of $skip(t_i)$.

Computation of the skip table in the Boyer–Moore–Horspool algorithm has a subtle difference with the original skip table definition proposed in the Boyer–Moore algorithm. If we carefully observe the $skip$ table generation procedure in the Boyer–Moore algorithm, we find that the value of $skip(p_m)$ is always 0. In the Horspool version, $skip(p_m) = m$ if p_m is unique within the pattern (i.e., the character p_m does not appear in any other location in the pattern); otherwise $skip(p_m) = m - k$, where p_{m-k} is the penultimate (rightmost) appearance of the character p_m in the pattern. The preprocessing algorithm for computation of skip table in the Boyer–Moore–Horspool algorithm is as follows:

GENERATE-SKIP-TABLE(Σ, p)

1. Set pattern length, $m \leftarrow |p|$;

2. Initialize $skip$ table, $skip(\sigma) = m$ for all symbols $\sigma \in \Sigma$;

3. Initialize pattern index, $j \leftarrow 1$;

4. **for** jth character p_j in the pattern, set $skip(p_j) \leftarrow m - j$;

5. Increment pattern index, $j \leftarrow j + 1$;

6. **if** $j \leq m - 1$ **then** go to step 4;

7. Stop.

Note that the preprocessing algorithm for computation of skip table in the Boyer–Moore–Horspool algorithm differs from the computation of the skip table in the Boyer–Moore algorithm only in step 6. Here we now have "**if** $(j < m)$ **then** go to step 4." Since step 4 is iterated here for $j = 1$ to $m - 1$, the value of $skip(p_m)$ is never zero. This value will be m if p_m is unique, while it becomes $m - j$ if p_j is the penultimate appearance of p_m in p. We show in Fig. 4.10 two examples of skip tables, generated for patterns "$a\,b\,c\,d\,e$" and "$a\,e\,c\,d\,e$", using the Boyer–Moore (BM) and Boyer–Moore–Horspool (BMH) algorithms.

The Boyer–Moore–Horspool pattern matching algorithm is formally presented below.

BOYER–MOORE–HORSPOOL-ALGORITHM(t, p, Σ)

1. Initialize pattern length, $m \leftarrow |p|$;

2. Initialize the text length, $n \leftarrow |t|$;

3. Compute *skip* table GENERATE-SKIP-TABLE(Σ, p);

4. Initialize text pointer, $i \leftarrow 0$;

5. Initialize pattern pointer, $j \leftarrow m$;

6. **while** $j > 0$ and $t_{i+j} = p_j$ (i.e., string character matches with pattern character) **do** move pattern pointer to left, $j \leftarrow j - 1$;

7. **if** $j = 0$ (i.e., match is successful) **then** print *"pattern occurs at text index"* $i + 1$;

8. Shift the text pointer, $i \leftarrow i + skip(t_{i+m})$;

9. **if** $i \leq n - m$ (i.e., text not yet fully traversed) **then** go to step 5 to continue matching process.

10. stop.

Alphabet $(\Sigma) = \{a, b, c, d, e, f, g\}$

Pattern 1 = a b c d e   Pattern 2 = a e c d e

Skip Table 1:   Skip Table 2:

$\sigma \in \Sigma$	BM	BMH
a	4	4
b	3	3
c	2	2
d	1	1
e	0	5
f	5	5
g	5	5

$m = 5$

$\sigma \in \Sigma$	BM	BMH
a	4	4
b	5	5
c	2	2
d	1	1
e	0	3
f	5	5
g	5	5

Fig. 4.10 Example of skip tables.

Example 5:   Here we demonstrate the effectiveness of the Boyer–Moore–Horspool algorithm in matching patterns from simple English text. An example is shown in Fig. 4.11. The alphabet considered in this example is $\Sigma = \{a, c, d, e, f, h, i, m, n, o, r, s, t, ' \ '\}$. The symbol ' ' represents the blank character. Since the pattern "match" has only five characters $\{a, c, h, m, t\}$, the rest of the characters in Σ are considered to belong to the *don't care* category as denoted by $ in Fig. 4.11. The broken arrows ($\downarrow$) represent the position where the text character (t_i) mismatches with the corresponding pattern character, and hence the pattern needs to be shifted right by $skip(t_i)$. The value of $skip(t_i)$ is shown as the label of each broken arrow, that is aligned with each mismatching character t_i and the last character of the pattern (i.e., $p_5 = $ 'h').

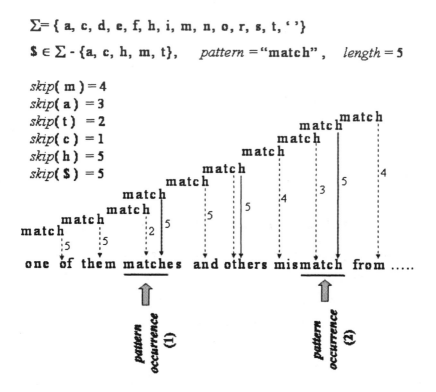

Fig. 4.11 Example of Boyer–Moore–Horspool string matching.

For example, the matching process begins by comparing $t_5 = $ 'o' with $p_5 = $ 'h'. Since they mismatch, the pattern is shifted by 5 positions right because $skip(o) = 5$. Now the text character $t_{10} = $ 'e' is compared with $p_5 = $ 'h'. Since they mismatch, the pattern is again shifted by 5 positions right because $skip(e) = 5$. Subsequently, $t_{15} = $ 't' mismatches with 'h' and the pattern is shifted by 2 because $skip(t) = 2$. Now the text character under consideration is $t_{17} = $ 'h', which matches with the rightmost character of the pattern. Hence all the preceding characters are compared, and we find a complete match of the pattern. Hence occurrence of the pattern beginning at text position 13 is reported. The pattern is now shifted right by $skip(h) = 5$ positions.

Continuing in this manner, we find the second occurrence of the pattern at location 35 as shown in Fig. 4.11.

It should be noted that the total number of character comparisons in this example is 19, which is the same as the number of comparisons required by the original Boyer–Moore algorithm shown in Fig. 4.9. Moreover, Boyer–Moore–Horspool algorithm is not only simpler for implementation, it also requires less preprocessing overhead and often provides better average computation performance.

4.2.5   Karp–Rabin algorithm

In Karp–Rabin algorithm [4, 5], instead of directly comparing the pattern characters with the text characters, the text is first pre-processed to map into a sequence of integers. Here each character position in the text is mapped into an integer, and this sequence of numbers is then compared with a fixed integer representing the pattern. In general, if there are d symbols in the alphabet Σ, then each symbol or character can be considered as a digit in the radix-d notation for number representation. Hence we can map the pattern $p = \text{``}p_1 p_2 \cdots p_m\text{''}$ into a radix-d integer number I^p whose decimal equivalent is

$$I^p = p_1 * d^{m-1} + p_2 * d^{m-2} + \cdots + p_{m-1} * d^1 + p_m * d^0. \qquad (4.3)$$

Similarly we generate a radix-d integer number I_i^t for each character location t_i in text $t = \text{`}t_1 t_2 t_3 \cdots t_n\text{'}$, whose decimal equivalent is

$$I - i = t_i * d^{m-1} + t_{i+1} * d^{m-2} + \cdots + t_{i+m-2} * d^1 + t_{i+m-1} * t^0. \qquad (4.4)$$

Example 6:   For the purpose of simple explanation, let us assume that the alphabet consists of the decimal digits $\Sigma = \{0, 1, 2, 3, 4, 5, 6, 7, 8, 9\}$. With this decimal notation, we can assume that a string of m consecutive symbols or characters is equivalent to an m-digits decimal number. The character string '5 2 8 3 7 0 3 1' can be considered to be the decimal number $52,837,031$. We provide a simple pattern matching example, using Karp–Rabin algorithm, in Fig. 4.12.

Here we consider a pattern $p = \text{``}3\,4\,3\text{''}$ of length 3 and a text '1 0 3 4 3 4 3 2 0 1' of length 10 over an alphabet $\Sigma = \{0, 1, 2, 3, 4\}$. Hence each symbol in the alphabet is a digit in the 5-radix number system notation. The decimal equivalent of the integer map of the pattern $p = \text{``}3\,4\,3\text{''}$ is the integer

$$I^p = 3 * 5^2 + 4 * 5^1 + 3 * 5^0 = 98.$$

The corresponding integer map, with 3-symbols length substring in first 8 character positions in the text, is $I^t = \{28, 19, 98, 119, 98, 117, 85, 51\}$ as shown in Fig. 4.12. We do not consider the integer map in the last two symbol positions because the pattern length is 3 and there will never be a match beginning either at position 9 or 10. As shown by dotted arrows, the first integer 28 is

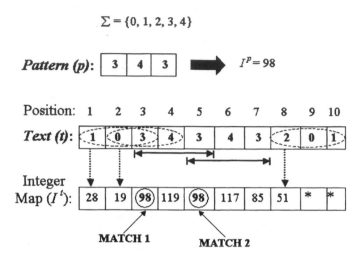

Fig. 4.12   Example of Karp–Rabin string matching.

obtained by taking the decimal equivalent of the first three consecutive symbols starting at position 1 (*i.e.*, $1 * 5^2 + 0 * 5^1 + 3 * 5^0 = 28$). Analogously, the second integer 19 is obtained from the three consecutive symbols starting at the second position, and continuing in a similar manner the last integer 51 in position 8 is obtained by decimal number representation with the three consecutive symbols starting at position 8. Upon scanning the integer map and comparing each decimal with the integer number 98 (representing the pattern), we find two matches at positions 3 and 5, respectively. These, indeed, are the valid matches when compared with the original text string. We can compute I^p in time $O(m)$, because we can express it as

$$I^p = ((\cdots(p_1 * d + p_2) * d + p_3) * d + \cdots + p_{m-1}) * d + p_m. \tag{4.5}$$

This can be recursively computed in m steps, with 1 multiplication and 1 addition in each step, as follows.

1. Initialize integer map and pattern index, $I^p \leftarrow 0$, $i = 1$;

2. Update integer map and increment pattern index, $I^p \leftarrow I^p * d + p_i$, $i \leftarrow i + 1$;

3. **if** $i \leq m$ (i.e., pattern not completed) **then**
   go to step 2 to continue computation;

4. Return integer I^p.

Here the first integer map I_1^t for the first text character (t_1) can be computed as

$$I_1^t = ((\cdots (t_1 * d + t_2) * d + t_3) * d + \cdots + t_{m-1}) * d + t_m$$

in $O(m)$ time. The remaining integer map, for the rest of the characters $t_2, t_3, \cdots, t_{n-m+1}$ in the text, can be computed in $O(n - m)$ time. This is because I_{i+1}^t can be computed incrementally from the value of I_i^t using

$$I_{i+1}^t = (I_i^t - d^{m-1} * t_i) * d + t_{i+m}. \tag{4.6}$$

It is obvious that the multiplication factor d^{m-1} can be precomputed in $O(m)$ in the worst case.

As an example, $I_5^t = 98$ represents the integer map of the substring '3 4 3' beginning at position 5 in the text as shown in Fig. 4.12. To compute the next integer map I_6^t, we need to drop the high-order digit $t_5 = 3$ from the substring and add the low-order digit $t_8 = 2$ as

$$I_6^t = (I_5^t - 5^2 * t_5) * 5 + t_8 = (98 - 25 * 3) * 5 + 2 = 117.$$

After the above preprocessing, I^t is scanned from left to right and compared with I^p to find all occurrences of pattern p in text t. Hence the Karp–Rabin algorithm can be computed in $O(m + n)$ time. However, there is a practical problem with the above simplified approach for string matching, because of the limited precision of digital computers for both processing and storage of the numbers I^p and I_i^t. If the alphabet $d = |\Sigma|$ and m are large, each necessary arithmetic computation for I^p and I_i^t with limited precision digital computer cannot be performed in constant time. This problem has been solved by adopting a hash function to compute the integers to represent the signature of a substring, in order to represent them within the permitted precision. The hash function permits generation of a signature so that I_{i+1}^t can be derived easily from I_i^t.

The hash function is carefully chosen by adopting the *modulo-q* operation, selecting q in such a manner that $d * q$ fits within the precision of a single computer word, where d is the size of the alphabet Σ. Adjusting the recurrence Eq. (4.6) to work with *modulo-q*, we get

$$I_{i+1}^t = (I_i^t - k * t_i) * d + I_{i+m}^t \pmod{q}, \tag{4.7}$$

where $k \equiv d^{m-1} \pmod{q}$. The distributive property of the *mod* function, namely,

$$(x + y) \pmod{z} = (x \pmod{z} + y \pmod{z}) \pmod{z}, \tag{4.8}$$

allows only the remainders to be stored after each stage of computation and helps to keep the results small enough to fit within the allowed precision of

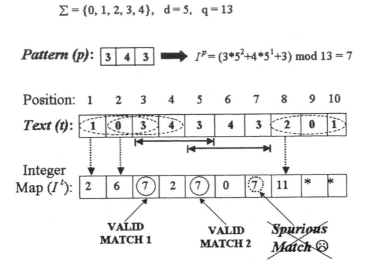

$\Sigma = \{0, 1, 2, 3, 4\}, \quad d = 5, \quad q = 13$

Pattern (p): 3 4 3 ⟹ $I^p = (3*5^2 + 4*5^1 + 3) \bmod 13 = 7$

Fig. 4.13 Example of Karp–Rabin string matching algorithm with modulo operation.

a computer word. In Fig. 4.13, we demonstrate an example of the above modulo-based matching operation.

The problem with the above approach is that the *modulo* operation is a many-to-one function, and hence not unique. As a result, it can generate *spurious* matches in addition to desired valid matches in the string as shown in Fig. 4.13. For a large value of q, however, the appearance of spurious matches will be significantly smaller. Therefore when a potential match is detected, the substring is directly compared with the original pattern to check the validity of the match. The algorithm is formally explained below.

KARP–RABIN-STRING-MATCHING ALGORITHM(p, t)

1. Set pattern length, $m \leftarrow |p|$;

2. Initialize integer map for pattern, $I^p \leftarrow 0$;

3. Initialize integer map for text, $I_1^t \leftarrow 0$;

4. Set $k \leftarrow d^{m-1} \pmod{q}$;

5. **for** $j \leftarrow 1$ to m **do**
   $I^p \leftarrow (I^p * d + p_j) \pmod{q}, \ I_1^t \leftarrow (I_1^t * d + t_j) \pmod{q}$;

6. Initialize text pointer, $i \leftarrow 1$;

7. **if** $I_i^t \neq I^p$ (i.e., mismatch in current text position) **then**
   go to step 9 to continue at the next text position;

8. **if** $t_i t_{i+1} \cdots t_{i+m-1} = p_1 p_2 \cdots p_m$ (i.e., match at text position i) **then**
   print "Valid match at location" i;

9. **if** $i \leq n - m$ (i.e., text not completely scanned) **then**
   $I_{i+1}^t \leftarrow (I_i^t - k * t_i) * d + I_{i+m}^t$ (mod q) (i.e., compute hash function at
   position $i + 1$);

10. Increment text pointer, $i \leftarrow i + 1$;

11. **if** $i \leq n - m + 1$ (i.e., text not complete) **then**
    go to step 7 to continue;

12. Stop.

Karp and Rabin proposed an algorithm [5] in 1987 to reduce the probability of occurrence of spurious matches, by randomly selecting a prime q on the occurrence of a spurious match, reinitializing the integer map after the spurious match location, and thereafter continuing with the search.

4.3   STRING MATCHING IN BIOINFORMATICS

From information theoretic perspective, the DNA can be considered as a string or sequence of symbols, where each symbol is one of the four bases *adenine* [A], *cytosine* [C], *guanine* [G] and *thymine* [T]. Hence the alphabet in DNA string search can be assumed to be $\Sigma = \{A, C, T, G\}$. Let us consider a DNA fragment '*AGATACGATATATACGATATAGA*', in which we would like to search for a string '*ATATA*'. Here we show the application of Knuth–Morris–Pratt algorithm and Boyer–Moore–Horspool algorithm in matching the DNA substring '*ATATA*' in the DNA fragment '*AGATACGATATATACGATATAGA*'.

Example 7:   We apply the Knuth–Morris–Pratt algorithm to match the DNA substring '*ATATA*' in the DNA fragment '*AGATACGATATATACGATATAGA*'. The *Next* table for pattern "*ATATA*" is the same as the *Next* table for pattern "*babab*" of Example 4 as derived in Fig. 4.7. The matching process to find the occurrences of DNA string '*ATATA*' in DNA fragment '*AGATACGATATATACGATATAGA*' is depicted in Fig. 4.14.

Example 8:   Here we consider the Boyer–Moore–Horspool algorithm for the same DNA search, to detect occurrences of the DNA string '*ATATA*' in

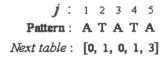

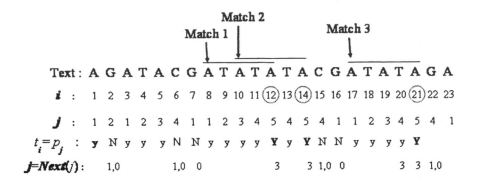

Fig. 4.14 Example of searching the DNA string '*ATATA*' in the DNA fragment '*AGATACGATATATACGATATAGA*' with Knuth–Morris–Pratt algorithm.

the DNA fragment '*AGATACGATATATACGATATAGA*'. The matching process is illustrated in Fig. 4.15. The character $t_5 =$ '*A*' is compared with the last character of the pattern $p_5 =$ '*A*', and they are found to be the same. The comparison continues right to left until we detect a mismatch at $t_2 =$ '*G*' with $p_2 =$ '*T*'. The pattern is shifted by 2 because $skip(A) = 2$. Continuing this process, we find three occurrences of the pattern "*ATATA*" in the DNA fragment '*AGATACGATATATACGATATAGA*' as shown in Fig. 4.15. Total number of character comparisons required in this example is 23.

The principles and results of string matching have been used to solve many problems in Bioinformatics. In the following section we describe the concepts and principles behind approximate string matching algorithms and their solutions. The concept of approximate string matching is also a very powerful tool in DNA sequencing, alignment, homologue search, and many other similar problems in Bioinformatics. We described these problems and their solutions in greater detail in Chapter 10.

$\Sigma = \{A, C, G, T\}$

pattern = "ATATA", *length* = 5

$skip(A) = 2$
$skip(C) = 5$
$skip(G) = 5$
$skip(T) = 1$

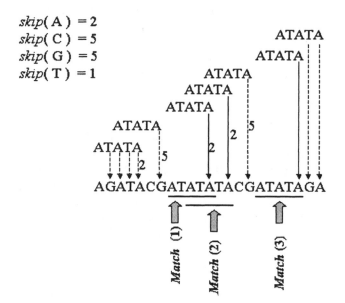

Fig. 4.15 Example of Boyer–Moore–Horspool string matching using DNA.

4.4 APPROXIMATE STRING MATCHING

In the preceding sections we considered exact matching of patterns in text. However, the string matching problem becomes challenging when the pattern is not an exact one. This may be partially specified, as discussed in Section 1.11. A generalization of the string matching problem is *Approximate String Matching*.

The approximate string matching problem deals with finding the occurrences of substrings in a text $t = t_1 t_2 \cdots t_n$ which are similar to a given pattern $p = p_1 p_2 \cdots p_m$. By the word similar, we mean to allow for a limited number $k > 0$ of *differences* between the pattern and its occurrence in the text. Before proceeding further, let us provide some basic definitions of difference, also termed *distance*.

4.4.1   Basic definitions

There are many definitions of *"difference"*, such as *Hamming distance, Levenshtein distance, Edit distance*, etc. There are other complex measures of '*difference*', mainly in computational biology, but most of the popular and useful algorithms have been developed based on the *Levenshtein distance*.

4.4.1.1 Hamming distance: This is always measured between two strings of equal length. Hamming distance between two strings is equal to the number of symbol positions at which they differ. For example Hamming distance between strings $D =$ '*SUNDAY*' and $D' =$ '*MONDAY*' is 2 because they differ in the first two character positions only.

4.4.1.2 Levenshtein distance: A string $X = x_1 x_2 \cdots x_p$ can be transformed to another string $Y = y_1 y_2 \cdots y_q$ by applying one or more of the following three 'edit operations' in each character of the string, namely, *insertion, deletion*, and *substitution*. The *Levenshtein distance* $d(X, Y)$ between the strings X and Y is the minimum number of edit operations required to transform the string X into Y, or vice versa. For example, the *Levenshtein distance* between two strings $D =$ '*SATURDAY*' and $D' =$ '*SUNDAY*' is $d(D, D') = 3$, because we can delete characters '*A*' and '*T*' and substitute '*R*' in '*SATURDAY*' by '*N*' to convert '*SATURDAY*' to '*SUNDAY*'.

4.4.1.3 Edit distance: If the string $X = x_1 x_2 \cdots x_p$ can be transformed to $Y = y_1 y_2 \cdots y_q$ by applying one or more *insertion* and *deletion* operations only, then the *edit distance* between X and Y is the minimum number of *insertion* and/or *deletion* operations required to transform the string X into Y, or vice versa. For example, the *edit distance* between $D =$ '*SATURDAY*' and $D' =$ '*SUNDAY*' is $d(D, D') = 4$ because we can delete characters '*A*', '*T*', and '*R*' in '*SATURDAY*' and then insert '*N*' to convert '*SATURDAY*' to '*SUNDAY*'. Although the substitution operation is not directly applied to measure the *edit distance*, it can be accomplished by applying a *deletion* operation followed by an *insertion* operation in a character position.

4.4.1.4 k-Approximate string matching problem: With the above definition of *difference* or *distance function(s)*, we can formally define the approximate string matching problem as follows.

Given a pattern $p = p_1 p_2 \cdots p_m$ of length m characters, text $t = t_1 t_2 \cdots t_n$ of length n, where $0 < m \leq n$, a positive integer k, and a *distance function* d, find all the substrings y of text t such that

$$d(p, y) \leq k. \tag{4.9}$$

When the distance function d represents the Hamming distance, the problem is called an approximate string matching with *k-mismatches*. When d

represents the edit distance, it is called an approximate string matching with *k-differences* or *k-errors*.

4.4.2 Wagner–Fischer algorithm for computation of string distance

The popular Wagner–Fischer algorithm [6] for computation of distance between two strings is based on the dynamic-programming approach [7]. Accordingly, distances between the prefixes of the strings are successively computed from the previous values until the final result.

Let us assume that we are interested in computing the distance between two strings $p = p_1 p_2 \cdots p_m$ and $t = t_1 t_2 \cdots t_n$. Also, let us assume that $d_{i,j}$ represents the distance between the prefixes $p(i) = p_1 p_2 \cdots p_i$ and $t(j) = t_1 t_2 \cdots t_j$ of strings p and t, where i is the length of prefix $p(i)$ and j is length of prefix of $t(j)$, respectively. Hence

$$d_{i,j} = d(p(i),\ t(j))$$

and $d_{m,n}$ is the distance between the two strings $p = p_1 p_2 \cdots p_m$ and $t = t_1 t_2 \cdots t_n$. Let us assume that $w(p_i,\ t_j)$ represents the cost of symbol substitution from p_i to t_j if $p_i \neq t_j$, $w(p_i,\ \epsilon)$ is the cost of deleting symbol p_i, and $w(\epsilon,\ t_j)$ is the cost of inserting symbol t_j in a string. During computation of the string distance, the values of $d_{i,j}$ are recorded in a two-dimensional array $d[m+1,\ n+1]$. The value of $d_{i,j}$ is computed using the recurrence formula

$$d_{i,j} = \min\{d_{i-1,j-1} + w(p_i,\ t_j),\ d_{i-1,j} + w(p_i,\ \epsilon),\ d_{i,j-1} + w(\epsilon,\ t_j)\}. \quad (4.10)$$

The boundary conditions for this recurrence relation are as follows.

$$d_{0,0} = 0,$$

$$d_{i,0} = \sum_{k=1}^{i} w(p_k,\ \epsilon) \quad \text{for } 1 \leq i \leq m,$$

$$d_{0,j} = \sum_{k=1}^{j} w(\epsilon,\ t_j) \quad \text{for } 1 \leq j \leq n. \quad (4.11)$$

For Levenshtein distance, we assume unit values for each *deletion, insertion,* and *substitution* operations. The corresponding cost values are expressed as

$$w(p_i,\ \epsilon) = 1,$$

$$w(\epsilon, t_j) = 1,$$

$$w(p_i, t_j) = \begin{cases} 1 & \text{if } p_i \neq t_j \\ 0 & \text{if } p_i = t_j \end{cases}. \quad (4.12)$$

Hence, for Levenshtein distance, the boundary computation are done as follows.

$$d_{0,0} = 0,$$

$$d_{i,0} = i \quad \text{for} \quad 1 \le i \le m,$$

$$d_{0,j} = j \quad \text{for} \quad 1 \le j \le n. \tag{4.13}$$

Using the array d, it is possible to determine a minimal-cost trace and hence a least-cost editing sequence from string p to string t. The algorithm can be expressed as follows.

LEAST-COST-TRACE-COMPUTATION($d[m+1, n+1]$, p, t)

1. Initialize $i \leftarrow m$, for string p of length m;

2. Initialize $j \leftarrow n$, for string t of length n;

3. **if** $(d_{i,j} = d_{i-1,j} + w(p_i, \epsilon))$ **then**
   compute $i \leftarrow i - 1$ and go to step 7 to continue;

4. **if** $(d_{i,j} = d_{i,j-1} + w(\epsilon, t_j))$ **then**
   compute $j \leftarrow j - 1$ and go to step 7 to continue;

5. print (i, j) for symbol substitution from p_i to t_j;

6. compute $i \leftarrow i - 1$, $j \leftarrow j - 1$;

7. **if** $i > 0$ and $j > 0$ (i.e., scanning not complete) **then**
   go to step 3 to continue cost computation;

8. Stop.

4.4.2.1 Example 9:

Let us consider two strings $p = $ '$SUNDAY$' and $t = $ '$SATURDAY$'. The length of these two strings are 6 and 8, respectively. Hence we compute the values in the array $d[7, 9]$ based on the recurrence formula for $d_{i,j}$ for $i = 0$ to 6 and $j = 0$ to 8. Entries in the two-dimensional array $d[7, 9]$ are shown in Fig. 4.16(a).

Here the value of $d_{m,n} = d_{6,8} = 3$. Hence the string distance (Levenshtein distance) between the strings '$SATURDAY$' and '$SUNDAY$' is 3. The minimal-cost trace and hence the least-cost editing sequence can be generated from the completed distance array. Accordingly, by applying LEAST-COST-TRACE-COMPUTATION for $d[7, 9]$, the following trace T is generated by listing the output of the algorithm in reverse order.

$$T = \{(1, 1), (2, 4), (4, 6), (5, 7), (6, 8)\}.$$

The transformation of the string '$SUNDAY$' to '$SATURDAY$' is depicted in Fig. 4.16(b). The characters in p (i.e., '$SUNDAY$' in this example) untouched by edges are substituted (i.e., 'N' is substituted by 'R'), and this is indicated by a broken arrow. The characters in t (i.e., '$SATURDAY$' in this example) untouched are inserted (i.e., 'A' and 'T').

	S	A	T	U	R	D	A	Y
	0	1	2	3	4	5	6	7	8
S	1	0	1	2	3	4	5	6	7
U	2	1	1	2	2	3	4	5	6
N	3	2	2	2	3	3	4	5	6
D	4	3	3	3	3	4	3	4	5
A	5	4	3	4	4	4	4	3	4
Y	6	5	4	4	5	5	5	4	3

(a)

SUNDAY

SATURDAY

(b)

Fig. 4.16 Wagner–Fischer algorithm showing (a) matrix computation for distance function and (b) transformation, of the string 'SUNDAY' to 'SATURDAY'.

4.4.2.2 *Longest common subsequence problem:* A *longest common subsequence* of two strings is a subsequence, common to both strings, having the maximal length. Given two strings p and t, with $|p| = m$ and $|t| = n$, where $0 < m \le n$, the *longest common subsequence problem* is to find the longest common subsequence $lcs(p, t)$ of two strings p and t as well as its length $|lcs(p, t)|$.

After computation of the complete *distance array* and finding the least-cost trace T, it is fairly straightforward to find the $lcs(p, t)$. The constituents of the $lcs(p, t)$ are p_i, or equivalently t_j, such that $(i, j) \in T$ and $p_i = t_j$. So in above example, the longest common subsequence for strings $p =$ '*SUNDAY*' and $t =$ '*SATURDAY*' is

$$lcs(p, t) = p_1 p_2 p_4 p_5 p_6 = t_1 t_4 t_6 t_7 t_8 = \text{'SUDAY'}.$$

The longest common subsequence has been used in many application areas, such as detection and correction of spelling error. It has also been used in Bioinformatics for molecular sequence matching, both for exact match and for common substrings up to k-mismatches [8].

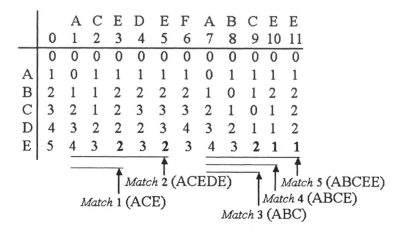

Fig. 4.17   Example of text search with k-mismatches for $k = 2$.

4.4.3   Text search with k-differences

The dynamic programming approach for computation of *Levenshtein distance* between two strings provides the foundation of text searching with k-differences or k-errors. Here we search for occurrences of the pattern p in text t, with a maximum difference of k characters between the pattern and a text substring in text t. The only difference of this approach with Levenshtein distance computation is that we must allow for a substring occurrence to begin at any text position. This is achieved by adjusting the boundary condition in Eq. (4.13) to $d_{0,j} = 0$ for all $j = 0$ to n, because the minimum distance between the empty string ϵ and any substring of t is 0. The computation of the recurrence relation to generate all other $d_{i,j}$ are identical to that of the Levenshtein distance by Eq. (4.13). Upon completion of the computation of all the entries in the array $d[m + 1, n + 1]$, any value not exceeding k in the last row m indicates a position in the text where a substring having at most k-differences with the pattern ends.

4.4.3.1 **Example 10:**   Let us consider two strings, namely, a pattern $p =$ "*ABCDE*" and a text $t =$ '*ACEDEFABCEE*'. The complete distance array corresponding to these two strings is shown in Fig. 4.17. For $k = 2$, we find from row 5 of the array that there are five occurrences of the pattern "*ABCDE*" with up to 2-differences in the text, ending at text positions 3, 5, 9, 10, and 11. The corresponding matching text substrings are '*ACE*', '*ACEDE*', '*ABC*', '*ABCE*', and '*ABCEE*', respectively.

4.5 COMPRESSED PATTERN MATCHING

One important operation that is fundamental to many database applications is to be able to search a large database to find the occurrence of pattern(s). In order to exploit the benefits of data compression, to conserve internal processor storage and computation resources, it is naturally desirable to perform pattern matching directly on compressed data without inherently decompressing it. We call this the *compressed pattern matching* problem.

Extra overhead caused by data compression is a major bottleneck in its use in many applications, where data need to be retrieved and manipulated often based on the pattern search operation. One way to correct this problem is to develop string or pattern matching techniques to operate directly on compressed data. Although effective data compression techniques have been around for almost half a century, little work has been addressed in this direction.

Let $c(t)$ denote a compressed text string corresponding to a text t. The *compressed pattern matching problem* is to find the occurrence(s) of a pattern p in t by searching directly into the compressed text $c(t)$.

The compressed pattern matching problem becomes even more challenging when the pattern is not fully specified, because of appearance of don't care character(s) in it. The problem of searching a compressed text using Huffman coding type tree-based coding or run-length encoding seems superficially straightforward. The idea is to apply any well-known string search algorithm [1, 3, 5, 9] on $c(t)$ with respect to the compressed pattern $c(p)$. A close examination of the algorithm reveals that such an approach is not very practical in many applications. If we use Huffman encoding of Section 3.6.2, an *implicit decompression* process has to be performed to determine the *character boundary* (that is the starting bit of each encoded symbol). We have demonstrated this with an example in Fig. 4.18.

Acharya [10] designed hardware algorithms to handle this problem, by generating a signal to indicate the boundary of a character in the compressed text where the linear pattern matching takes place. If a potential match is found in the compressed text, it is further checked to determine whether a character boundary signal is detected as well. If a character boundary is detected in conjunction with the occurrence of the compressed pattern, then the occurrence of the pattern is considered to be a valid match as depicted in the block diagram of Fig. 4.18. Acharya [10] also proposed how to handle the compressed patter matching problem, in these hardware algorithms, even when the patterns are partially specified with either *fixed-length don't care characters* (FLDC)

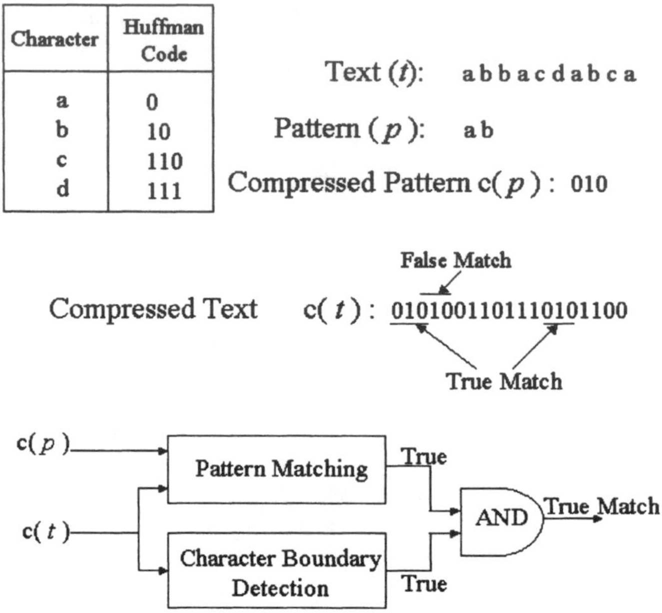

Character	Huffman Code
a	0
b	10
c	110
d	111

Text (t):   a b b a c d a b c a

Pattern (p):   a b

Compressed Pattern c(p) : 010

False Match

Compressed Text   c(t) : 0101001101110101100

True Match

c(p)

Pattern Matching — True

c(t)

Character Boundary Detection — True

AND) True Match

Fig. 4.18 Example of compressed pattern matching using Huffman code.

or *variable-length don't care characters* (VLDC). The same working principle can be applied to any tree-based code such as Shannon–Fano code [11], Elias Code [12], etc.

The compressed pattern matching problem with Lempel–Ziv codes (of Section 3.12) is very difficult, due to the fact that for Lempel–Ziv codes a substring may have multiple encoding in the compressed file [10]. Some attention has recently been paid to the search of patterns in text compressed with variations of Lempel–Ziv coding. The first algorithm for pattern search in LZ78 coded files was proposed in [13]. A randomized algorithm to determine whether a pattern is present in an LZ77 compressed text was presented in Ref. [14]. However, these algorithms are very complex. There is tremendous need for further research and development in this area of compressed pattern matching, for practical applications and their usage in data mining in the near future. Acharya proposed a general formulation for compressed pattern matching in Lempel–Ziv codes in two steps. The first step is to preprocess the given pattern to be searched using the "*Codebook*" generated during Lempel–Ziv compression of the text. The compressed matching is done in the second step, using a graph generated in the pattern preprocessing step [10].

Although the computational complexity of these methods are polynomial in nature, still it is very high for any practical implementation. Hence development of computationally efficient algorithms for pattern matching in compressed domain remains a challenge. Development of these algorithms especially suitable for data mining applications will be even more interesting to explore and offer promises for performance of future data mining systems.

4.6 CONCLUSIONS AND DISCUSSION

In this chapter, we presented fundamentals of string matching algorithms and their applications in different domains. We have presented several classical and pioneering algorithms in this area of study. We have also introduced the concept of the compressed pattern matching problem, in order to explore how pattern matching can be employed directly in compressed databases without involving explicit decompression. In addition to the description of the algorithms, we have presented a number of examples in each case to demonstrate clearly how they work.

The area of compressed pattern matching being still nascent, we wanted to motivate readers to pay attention in this direction in order to make significant progress in text mining and data mining applications in general. The results of string matching have paved the way for many text processing applications, including search, edit, and indexing of text databases. The search engines for the World Wide Web have been designed based on the results from string matching research. Text based search and retrieval systems are being used in text mining and Web mining applications as well. These issues are covered in further detail in Chapter 9.

The principles of string matching have been widely used in Bioinformatics for DNA sequence search, sequencing, alignment, etc. The concepts behind approximate string matching have been particularly useful for homology search and related problems in large genome databases. All these are described in greater detail in Section 10.3.4 of Chapter 10.

REFERENCES

1. D. Knuth, J. Morris, and V. Pratt, "Fast pattern matching in strings," *SIAM Journal of Computing*, vol. 6, pp. 323–350, 1977.

2. G. A. Stephen, *String Searching Algorithms*. Singapore: World Scientific, 2001.

3. R. N. Horspool, "Practical fast searching in strings," *Software–Practice and Experience*, vol. 10, pp. 501–506, 1980.

4. R. M. Karp and M. O. Rabin, "Efficient randomized pattern matching algorithms," Tech. Rep. TR-31-81, Harvard University Center for Research in Computing, 1981.

5. R. M. Karp and M. O. Rabin, "Efficient randomized pattern matching algorithms," *IBM Journal of Research and Development*, vol. 31, pp. 249–60, 1987.

6. R. A. Wagner and M. J. Fischer, "The string-to-string correction problem," *Journal of the ACM*, vol. 21, pp. 168–73, 1974.

7. R. Bellman and S. Dreyfus, *Applied Dynamic Programming*. Princeton, NJ: Princeton University Press, 1962.

8. R. Arratia, L. Gordon, and M. Waterman, "An extreme value theory for sequence matching," *The Annals of Statistics*, vol. 14, pp. 971–993, 1986.

9. R. Boyer and J. A. Moore, "A fast string searching algorithm," *Communications of the ACM*, vol. 20, pp. 762–772, 1977.

10. T. Acharya, *VLSI Algorithms and Architectures for Data Compression*. PhD thesis, Department of Computer Science, University of Central Florida, Orlando, FL, August 1994.

11. R. M. Fano, *Transmission of Information*. Cambridge, MA: MIT Press, 1949.

12. P. Elias, "Universal codeword sets and representations of the integers," *IEEE Transactions on Information Theory*, vol. 21, pp. 194–203, 1975.

13. A. Aho, G. Benson, and M. Farach, "Let sleeping files lie: Pattern matching in z-compressed files," *Journal of Computer and Systems Sciences*, vol. 52, no. 2, 1996.

14. M. Farach and M. Thorup, "String matching in Lempel–Ziv compressed strings," *Algorithmica*, vol. 20, no. 4, 1998.

5

Classification in Data Mining

5.1 INTRODUCTION

As the quantity and variety of data available increases, there arises a commensurate need for robust, efficient, and versatile data exploration techniques that can be supervised or unsupervised. Classification, as explained in Section 1.8, is a method of categorizing or assigning class labels to a pattern set under the supervision of a *teacher*. Decision boundaries are generated to discriminate between patterns belonging to different classes. The patterns are initially partitioned into training and test sets, and the classifier is trained on the former. The test set is used to evaluate the generalization capability of the classifier. Examples of classification from diverse domains include (i) medical patients based on the disease, (ii) a set of images containing a red rose, from an image database, (iii) a set of documents describing "data mining", from a document database, (iv) equipment malfunction based on cause, and (v) loan applicants based on their likelihood of payment. For example, in the latter case the problem is to predict a new applicant's loan eligibility given old data about the customers (like age, salary, profession, location) and their payment patterns.

A decision tree classifier is one of the most widely used supervised learning methods used for data exploration. It is easy to interpret and can be re-represented as *If-then-else* rules. It approximates a function by piecewise constant regions and does not require any prior knowledge of the data distribution. This classifier works well on noisy data. A decision tree aids in data exploration in the following manner [1].

- It reduces a volume of data by transformation into a more compact form, that preserves the essential characteristics and provides an accurate summary.

- It discovers whether the data contains well-separated classes of objects, such that the classes can be interpreted meaningfully in the context of a substantive theory.

- It maps data in the form of a tree so that prediction values can be generated by backtracking from the leaves to its root. This may be used to predict the outcome for a new data or query.

The concept of decision trees was popularized by Quinlan with ID3 [2], which stands for *Interactive Dichotomizer 3*. Systems based on this approach use an information theoretic measure, like entropy, for assessing the discriminatory power of each attribute. The most important feature of decision trees is their capability to break down a complex decision-making process into a collection of simpler decisions, thereby providing an easily interpretable solution [3]. ID3 is a popular and efficient method of making decisions for classification of *symbolic* data and is generally not suitable in cases where numerical values are to be operated upon. Since most real-life problems deal with nonsymbolic (numeric, continuous) data, they must be discretized prior to attribute selection. Classification and Regression Trees (CART) [4] and C4.5/C5.0 [5], however, do not require such prior discretization. Here the thresholds are dynamically computed depending on the conditions along a path, and they often result in the multiple use of a particular attribute with different thresholds. This can, however, lead to an increased accuracy at the cost of reduced comprehensibility.

The major decision tree algorithms are grouped as (i) classifiers from the machine learning community: ID3, C4.5, CART; and (ii) classifiers for large databases [6]: SLIQ, SPRINT, SONAR, RainForest. Generally, a pruning phase is followed by a building phase. During the building phase the algorithm recursively splits nodes, using the best splitting attribute for that node. It is found that smaller, imperfect decision trees generally achieve better accuracy. Hence leaf nodes are recursively pruned to prevent over-fitting.

As discussed in Section 2.2.3, the advantages of artificial neural networks (ANNs) for classification include the learning of complicated, or highly nonlinear, class boundaries, fast application, and handling of a large number of features. Like decision trees, they are also nonparametric. The major disadvantages of ANNs encompass a slow training time, harder interpretation, and a difficult implementation in terms of the optimal number of nodes. Some of the popular ANN models, used for classification, include multilayer perceptron and radial basis function networks [7].

Both decision trees and ANNs are the most commonly used tools for pattern classification. Note that the decision tree approach is *monothetic*. It considers the utility of individual attributes one at a time and may miss the case when multiple attributes are weakly predictive separately but become strongly predictive in combination. However, neural approaches are *polythetic*. Here multiple attributes can be considered simultaneously.

Probabilistic learning [8] is used to calculate explicit probabilities for the hypotheses and is among the most practical approaches to certain types of learning problems. When this is incremental, each training example can be used to incrementally increase or decrease the probability that a hypothesis is correct. Prior knowledge can also be combined with the observed data. One can use probabilistic prediction to infer multiple hypotheses, weighted by their probabilities. Even when Bayesian methods are computationally intractable, they can provide a standard of optimal decision making against which other methods can be measured.

Instance-based learners work on the basis of minimum distance from instances or prototypes [8]. Some typical models include the k-nearest neighbor classifier, radial basis function networks, and case-based reasoning. Nearest-neighbor classifiers typically define the proximity between instances, find the neighbors of a new instance, and then assign to it the label for the majority class of its neighbors. Case-based reasoning [9] is generally used when the attributes are more complicated than simple real-valued.

Support vector machines (SVMs) are a general class of learning architectures, inspired by the statistical learning theory, that performs *structural risk minimization* on a nested set structure of separating hyperplanes [10]. Given a training data, the SVM learning algorithm generates the optimal separating hyperplane in terms of generalization error. SVMs have been found to be very useful in handling data mining problems.

Section 5.2 of this chapter deals with different decision tree classifier models. Issues related to overfitting, pruning, and rule extraction are discussed in this context. Fusion of decision trees and ANNs is also presented. This is followed by Bayesian classifiers, instance-based learners, and support vector machines in Sections 5.3–5.5, respectively.

A problem with ID3 is that it cannot provide any information about the intersection region where the pattern classes are overlapping. This can be handled using fuzzy decision trees. Section 5.6 describes a method of designing fuzzy ID3 and extracting linguistic rules from this for encoding a fuzzy MLP [11, 12]. This generates a fuzzy knowledge-based network. Note that knowledge-based networks provide for initial embedding of prior knowledge about the domain. This is a desirable feature for data mining. Use of fuzzy sets enables uncertainty handling in this framework. Fuzzy decision trees provide a way of encoding a fuzzy knowledge-based network. Details on methodologies involving other soft computing tools are provided in Section 8.2.3.

The fuzzy ID3 formulates a scheme for automatic linguistic discretization of continuous attributes, based on quantiles. A novel concept of measuring the goodness of a decision tree, in terms of its compactness (size) and efficient performance, is provided. Linguistic rules are evaluated using quantitative indices. The knowledge encoding of the network incorporates the frequency

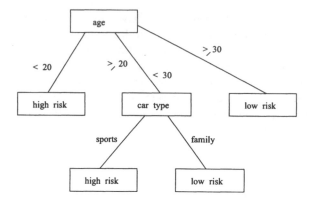

Fig. 5.1   A decision tree.

of samples and depth of the attributes in the fuzzy decision tree. Fuzziness measures, in terms of class memberships, are used at the node level of the tree to take care of overlapping classes. The effectiveness of the network, in terms of recognition scores, structure of decision tree, performance of rules, and network size, is demonstrated on real life data. The chapter is concluded in Section 5.7.

5.2   DECISION TREE CLASSIFIERS

A decision tree classifier splits a dataset on the basis of discrete decisions, using certain thresholds on the attribute values. Figure 5.1 depicts a typical decision tree demonstrating the risk factor associated with rash driving. There is a root node on top of the tree structure, indicating the feature (or attribute) that is split first for highest discrimination. The internal nodes of the tree represent simple decision rules on one or more attributes, while the leaf nodes are the predicted class labels. Tree traversal along the left branch in the figure indicates that persons with *age* < 20 involve the *high* risk category, while the right branch depicts that people with *age* > 30 are associated with *low* risk irrespective of the *car type*. The third (middle) branch, on the other hand, is traversed for 30 > *age* ≥ 20 and leads to a second split on attribute *car type* before arriving at a final decision.

   An object X is, therefore, classified by passing it through the tree starting at the root node. The test at each internal node along the path is applied to the attributes of X, to determine the next branch along which X should go down. The label at the leaf node at which X ends up is output as its classification. An object is *misclassified* by a tree if the classification output by the tree is not the same as the object's correct class label. The proportion of objects correctly classified by a decision tree is known as its *accuracy*, whereas the proportion of misclassified objects is the *error*. There exist several well-known tree learning algorithms in literature [1, 6]. Some of these are ID3 [2], its successor C4.5 [5], CART [4], SLIQ [13], SPRINT [14], SONAR [15], and RainForest [16].

Greedy top-down construction is the most commonly used method for tree growing. A hierarchical model is constructed top-down, starting from the entire data, partitioning it into subsets, and recursing the partitioning procedure using a splitting rule. When more than one tree can describe a dataset perfectly, one needs metrics to quantify the *goodness* of trees.

The process of tree building starts with an empty tree and the entire training set, and it broadly proceeds as follows until no more splits are possible.

1. If all the training examples at the current node t belong to category C_i, create a leaf node with the class (category) C_i.

2. Otherwise, score each one of the set of possible splits S, using a *goodness measure*.

3. Choose the best split S^* as the test at the current node.

4. Create as many child nodes as there are distinct outcomes of S^*, and partition the training data using S^* into the child nodes.

5. A child node t is said to be *pure* if all the training samples at t belong to the same class. Repeat the previous steps on all impure child nodes.

Tree construction can proceed by maximizing global *mutual information* of the whole tree, or by locally optimizing *information gain*. Sometimes distance measures like the *Gini index* of diversity [Eq. (5.2)] is also used. Both locally optimizing information gain as well as distance-based splitting criteria are found to produce small, shallow and accurate trees. In order to split at a node, the algorithm proceeds as follows:

- Intuitively pick an attribute that best separates instances of the different classes.

- Quantify the intuitive factor for measuring the separability: Define an impurity $I(S)$ of an arbitrary set S consisting of l classes. It can be

    - Information entropy, measured as

$$Entropy(S) = -\sum_{i=1}^{l} p_i \log p_i, \qquad (5.1)$$

where p_i is the relative frequency of class i in S (*a priori* probability). This has a value of zero when all the patterns belong to only one class, and it has a value of one when all the classes are in equal number.

      − Gini index, expressed as

$$Gini(S) = 1 - \sum_{i=1}^{l} p_i^2. \tag{5.2}$$

- Compute the information gain on partitioning S into r subsets. This is measured as the impurity of S *less* the sum of weighted impurity of each subset. For example,

$$Gain(S, S_1, \ldots, S_r) = I(S) - \sum_{j=1}^{r} \frac{|S_j|}{|S|} I(S_j), \tag{5.3}$$

    where $|S|$ is the cardinality of S, and $I(S)$ is the intuitive factor defined as either $Entropy(S)$ or $Gini(S)$ using eqns. (5.1)-(5.2).

- The attribute that provides the largest information gain is chosen to split the node. However, one needs to enumerate all possible splitting points for each attribute.

It has been observed [1] that the Gini index has difficulty when there are a relatively large number of classes. This index emphasizes equal-sized off-springs with purity of all children. Information gain, on the other hand, is biased towards attributes with a large number of possible values. They typically produce trees that are extremely deep and difficult to interpret. However, nothing definite can be said about the consistent superiority of one measure over the other. Measures like information gain and Gini index are all concave (never reporting a worse goodness value after trying a split than before splitting), so that there is no natural way of assessing where to stop further expansion of a node. Techniques like *minimum description length* (Section 5.2.5) are often used to decide which splits to prefer over others, and also for pruning.

A *regression tree* is a decision tree with continuous class labels. It approximates a function with piece-wise constant regions. When computing the split criteria for regression trees, one determines the predicted value for a set S as the average of all values in S. The error is the square root of the sum of square of difference of each member of S from the predicted average. The objective is to pick the smallest average error. The splits are made on categorical attributes.

One of the main difficulties of inducing a recursive partitioning structure is knowing when to stop, with a *right*-sized tree. For moderate-sized problems, the critical issues are generalization accuracy. For very large tree classifiers, on the other hand, the critical issue is optimizing structural properties like height and balance of the tree. The tree quality typically depends more on good stopping rules than on splitting rules [1]. Pruning is a method widely used for obtaining right-sized trees. It proceeds by building a complete tree (in which splitting no leaf node further will improve the accuracy on the training data) and then removing subtrees that are not contributing significantly towards generalization accuracy. This method is better than stop-splitting rules by partly compensating for the suboptimality of greedy tree induction. For example, consider a very good node T_2 a few levels below a not-so-good node T_1. Here a stop-splitting rule will stop tree growth at T_1, whereas pruning may give a high rating for, and retain, the whole subtree at T_1. Typically, pruning is found to be more beneficial for accuracy with increasing skewness in class distribution and/or increasing sample size.

The advantages of decision trees include reasonable training time, fast application, easy interpretation, easy implementation, and ability to handle large number of features. Since they do not make any assumptions about the underlying data distribution, they are specially suited for exploratory knowledge discovery. Their major demerits include an inability to handle complicated relationships between features, generation of simple axis-parallel decision boundaries, and their problems with lots of missing data. Sample size versus dimensionality of a dataset greatly influences the quality of trees constructed from it. The shortcomings of decision tree models, as well as solutions to alleviate them, have been extensively reported in literature [1].

In the remaining part of this section we describe some decision tree classifier models and discuss issues related to their overfitting, rule extraction, and fusion with neural networks.

5.2.1 ID3

ID3 uses an information theoretic approach. The procedure is that at any point one examines the feature that provides the greatest gain in information or, equivalently, the greatest decrease in entropy. Entropy is measured by Eq. (5.1).

The general case is that of N labeled patterns partitioned into sets belonging to classes C_i, $i = 1, 2, 3, \ldots, l$. The population in class C_i is n_i. Each pattern has n input features and each feature can take on two or more values.

5.2.1.1 Algorithm The ID3 prescription for synthesizing an efficient decision tree can be stated as follows:

1. Calculate the initial value of entropy

$$Entropy = \sum_{i=1}^{l} -(n_i/N) \log_2(n_i/N) = \sum_{i=1}^{l} -p_i \, \log_2 \, p_i, \qquad (5.4)$$

   where N is the total number of labeled patterns.

2. Select that feature which results in the maximum decrease in entropy or gain in information, according to Eq. (5.3), to serve as the root node of the decision tree.

3. Build the next level of the decision tree providing the greatest decrease in entropy.

4. **repeat** steps 1 through 3. Continue the procedure until all subpopulations are of a single class and the system entropy is zero.

At this stage, one obtains a set of leaf nodes (subpopulation) of the decision tree, where the patterns are of a single class. Note that there can be some nodes which cannot be resolved any further.

Table 5.1 Sample dataset for ID3, along with a split on *height*

Height	Hair	Eyes	Class	Height	Hair	Eyes	Class
tall	blond	brown	C_1		blond	brown	C_1
tall	dark	blue	C_1		dark	blue	C_1
tall	dark	brown	C_1	tall	dark	brown	C_1
short	dark	blue	C_1		red	blue	C_2
short	blond	brown	C_1		blond	blue	C_2
tall	red	blue	C_2		dark	blue	C_1
tall	blond	blue	C_2	short	blond	brown	C_1
short	blond	blue	C_2		blond	blue	C_2

5.2.1.2 Example 1: Let us illustrate the tree formation with a simple example. Table 5.1 provides a sample dataset of eight patterns, containing three attributes (height, hair color, eye color) and two output classes (C_1, C_2). The initial value of entropy is computed by Eq. (5.4) as

$$-\frac{5}{8}\log_2\frac{5}{8} - \frac{3}{8}\log_2\frac{3}{8} = 0.954 \text{ bits.}$$

Splitting on the basis of attribute height leads to five samples along the *tall* branch and three along the *short* branch, as depicted in columns 5 to 8 of the table, having corresponding entropies of

$$-\frac{2}{5}\log_2\frac{2}{5} - \frac{3}{5}\log_2\frac{3}{5} = 0.971 \text{ bits}$$

and

$$-\frac{1}{3}\log_2\frac{1}{3} - \frac{2}{3}\log_2\frac{2}{3} = 0.918 \text{ bits,}$$

respectively. The information gain with *height* is evaluated, using Eq. (5.3), as

$$0.954 - \left[\frac{5}{8} * (0.971) + \frac{3}{8} * (0.918)\right] = 0.954 - 0.951 = 0.003 \text{ bits.}$$

Similarly, the corresponding gains based on attributes *hair* and *eyes* are 0.454 and 0.347 bits, respectively. Maximizing, we find that the split with *hair* gives the largest information gain. Hence attribute *hair* is chosen as the root node. This procedure is continued in subsequent levels of the resultant tree for the remaining attributes. It is found at the second level that a split on attribute *eyes* yields a larger information gain and all nodes are resolved (or pure). This completes the tree building procedure.

5.2.2 IBM IntelligentMiner

Here the decision tree uses the Gini index. If a dataset S contains examples from l classes, $gini(S)$ is defined by Eq. (5.2). If a dataset S is split into two subsets S_1 and S_2, then the Gini index $Gini(S)$ is defined as

$$Gini_{split}(S) = \frac{|S_1|}{|S|} Gini(S_1) + \frac{|S_2|}{|S|} Gini(S_2). \qquad (5.5)$$

The attribute that provides the smallest $Gini_{split}(S)$ is chosen to split the node.

5.2.3 Serial PaRallelizable INduction of decision Trees (SPRINT)

SPRINT [14] is a decision-tree classifier for data mining. It is able to handle large disk-resident training sets, with no restrictions on training-set size, and is easily parallelizable. One list is maintained for each attribute in the dataset. The entries in an *attribute list* consist of the attribute value, class value, and record ID (*RID*). The algorithm uses a hash tree proportional to the training set size to store the RIDs.

5.2.3.1 Example 2: Let a sample dataset as in Table 5.2 provide risk factors (*high, low*) for the numeric attribute *Age* and the categorical attribute *car type*.

Table 5.2 A sample attribute list for SPRINT

age	car type	risk	RID
23	family	high	0
17	sports	high	1
43	sports	high	2
68	family	low	3
32	truck	low	4
20	family	high	5

Lists for continuous (numeric) attributes are in sorted order and may be disk-resident. Each leaf-node has its own set of attribute lists representing the training examples belonging to that leaf. The Gini index of Eq. (5.2) is used to evaluate the split points, using only the class frequencies in the process. For each attribute the algorithm evaluates splits using the attribute list, and keeps that split with the lowest Gini index.

Let us refer to the data of Table 5.2. The initial attribute lists for the root node are given in Tables 5.3 and 5.4 corresponding to attributes *age* and *car type*, respectively.

Table 5.3   Initial numeric attribute list for root node

age	risk	RID
17	high	1
20	high	5
23	high	0
32	low	4
43	high	2
68	low	3

Table 5.4   Initial categorical attribute list for root node

car type	risk	RID
family	high	0
sports	high	1
sports	high	2
family	low	3
truck	low	4
family	high	5

The split is evaluated for every value in each attribute list, for determining the optimal choice at a given tree-node. While performing the splits, the attribute lists of every node must be divided among the two children. The building phase proceeds by initializing the root node of the tree, while a node α that can be split exists. For each attribute A_j, all possible splits are evaluated on A_j. Then the best split is used to split node α.

In case of continuous attribute A_j, splits of the form $value(A_j) < v$ are considered. From Table 5.3, we find the class frequencies for the root node to be 4, 2 for risk *high*, *low*, respectively. The split $age < 20$ generates class histograms with frequencies of 1, 0 for risk *high*, *low*, respectively, in case of left child [RID = 1], and histogram frequencies 3, 2 for risk *high*, *low*, respectively, in case of right child [RID = 5, 0, 4, 2, 3]. This results in a Gini value of 0.4. It is found that the lowest Gini value of 0.222 is obtained for the split *age* < 32. This is depicted in Table 5.5 with RID = 1, 5, 0 along the left branch (*high* risk) and RID = 4, 2, 3 along the right (*low* risk).

Since every record is vertically partitioned over all attribute lists, here each attribute list needs to be distributed across the children separately through a hash-join with that of the splitting attribute. The record identifier, which is duplicated into each attribute list, establishes the connection between the vertical parts of the record. Since during the hash-join each attribute list is read and distributed sequentially, the initial sort order of the attribute list is preserved. In the example under consideration the hash table maintains the mapping of RIDs 0, 1, 5 to the left child for the split *age* < 32. The corresponding attribute list for *car type* is given in Table 5.6.

On the other hand, in case of categorical attributes the algorithm considers splits of the form $value(A_j) \in \{v_1, \ldots, v_n\}$. Here we have *car type* $\in \{family, sports, truck\}$. Considering Table 5.4, the class frequencies for risk *high, low*, corresponding to the root node, are found to be 2,1 [RID = 0, 5, 3]; 2,0 [RID = 1, 2]; and 0,1 [RID = 4] for *car type* v_i in *family, sports, truck*, respectively. A split on *car type* in *sports* results in class frequencies of 2, 0 [RID = 1, 2] for risk *high, low*, respectively, in case of left child, and 2, 2 [RID = 0, 3, 4, 5] for risk *high, low*, respectively, in case of right child (not in *sports*). This yields a Gini value of 0.333. The lowest Gini value of 0.267 is obtained for the split on *car type* in *truck*.

Table 5.5 Numeric attribute list for split on *age* < 32

Left child			Right child		
age	risk	RID	*age*	risk	RID
17	high	1	32	low	4
20	high	5	43	high	2
23	high	0	68	low	3

Table 5.6 Attribute list for *car type* with split on *age* < 32

Left child			Right child		
car type	risk	RID	*car type*	risk	RID
family	high	0	sports	high	2
sports	high	1	family	low	3
family	high	5	truck	low	4

5.2.3.2 Algorithm   The algorithm is summarized as follows:

- Each node of the decision tree classifier requires us to efficiently examine all possible splits on each value of each attribute.

- After choosing a split attribute, it needs to partition all data into its subset.

- While evaluating splits on numeric attributes, it sorts on attribute value and incrementally computes the Gini index.

- While splitting on categorical attributes, it finds the Gini index for each subset and chooses the best; for large datasets, a greedy method is used.

Some of the drawbacks of SPRINT include [16] (i) an increase in the size of the training database while maintaining the attribute list at each node, (ii) a large cost to keep these attribute lists sorted, and (iii) involvement of a costly hash-join between vertically separated parts of a record through the record identifier.

5.2.4 RainForest

Studies have shown that no algorithm is uniformly most accurate over all datasets. Hence a unifying generic framework RainForest [16] has been developed for classification tree construction. It yields scalable versions of a wide range of classification algorithms and offers performance improvements above a factor of three over SPRINT, the fastest available scalable classification algorithm. Unlike SPRINT, RainForest requires a certain minimum amount of main memory proportional to the set of distinct values in a column of the input relation. However, given the current main memory costs, this requirement is readily met in most, if not all, workloads. This generic algorithm can be specialized to obtain scalable versions of most classification and regression tree construction algorithms available in the literature.

5.2.5 Overfitting

A tree T overfits if there is another tree T' that gives a higher error on the training data while giving a lower error on unseen test data. Such an overfitted tree does not generalize to unseen instances. This situation generally occurs when the data contains noise or irrelevant attributes, and the training set size is small. Overfitting can reduce the accuracy drastically, even around 10-25% as reported in [17]. Smaller consistent decision trees typically have higher generalization accuracy than larger consistent trees.

Let us explain the concept of overfitting (poor generalization) in the context of a two-class problem. A classifier with excellent performance over a training dataset may have poor generalization over an unseen test set, since its decision

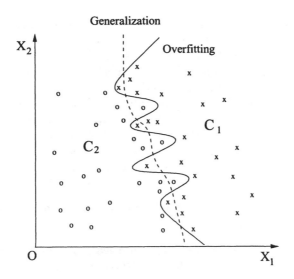

Fig. 5.2 Overfitting and generalization for decision boundaries in classification.

boundary overfits the training data as depicted in Fig. 5.2. On the other hand, a decision boundary with good generalization provides consistently good performance over both the training and test sets. This is also illustrated in the figure.

There are two popular approaches to prevent overfitting.

- Stop growing the tree beyond a certain point (pre-prune). For this purpose, one can use the statistical significance χ^2 or information gain, to assess the goodness of a split.

- First overfit and then post-prune. Here the tree building is divided into two phases, namely, growing and pruning.

Since it is hard to decide when to stop growing the tree, the second approach is more widely used. Although post-pruning requires more computations, it eventually generates a more reliable tree.

There exist three broad criteria for finding the correct final tree size. These are (i) cross-validation with separate test data, (ii) use of some criteria function, like Minimum Description Length (MDL), to choose the best size, and (iii) computation of statistical bounds, using all data for training but applying statistical tests to choose the right size.

Cross-validation consists of partitioning the dataset into two disjoint parts. The training set is used for building the tree, while a validation set is used for pruning the tree. The rule of the thumb is to keep two-thirds for training and to keep the remaining one-third for validation. The tree is evaluated on the validation set, keeping count of the correctly labeled data at each leaf as well as internal nodes. Starting bottom-up, the algorithm prunes nodes with error less than its children. However, if the training dataset size is limited, k-fold cross-validation [18] is used.

Pruning using the MDL principle views a decision tree as a means for efficiently encoding the classes of records in the training set. The best tree is considered as the one that can encode records using the fewest number of bits. The cost of encoding a tree includes one bit for encoding the type of each node (e.g., leaf or internal), the cost C_{split} for encoding the attribute and value for each split, and the cost $N' \times E$ of encoding the N' records in each leaf (E being entropy). The problem is to compute the minimum cost subtree at the root of a built tree. Pruning proceeds in a bottom-up fashion. The basic steps are as follows:

- Suppose $_{min}C_\alpha$ is the cost of encoding the minimum cost subtree rooted at α.

- Compute $_{min}C_\alpha$ as $N'E + 1$ if α is a leaf, and $\min\{N'E + 1, C_{split} + 1 +_{min} C_{\alpha_1} +_{min} C_{\alpha_2}\}$ if α has children α_1 and α_2.

- Prune the children of a node α if $_{min}C_\alpha = N'E + 1$.

5.2.6   PrUning and BuiLding Integrated in Classification (PUBLIC)

This is an improved decision tree classifier [19] that integrates the pruning phase with the initial building phase. In PUBLIC, a node is not expanded in the building phase if it is determined that it will be pruned in the subsequent pruning phase. Before a node is expanded, the algorithm computes a lower bound on the minimum cost subtree rooted at the node. This estimate, based on the records contained in the leaf, is then used by PUBLIC to identify the nodes that are certain to be pruned later, such that no effort is initially expended on splitting them. Since building a subtree usually requires repeated scans over the data, a significant reduction in I/O and improvement in performance is realized by minimizing this wastage of effort. However, there exists a trade-off between the accuracy of the estimate and the actual cost involved.

5.2.7   Extracting classification rules from trees

The knowledge encoded by the decision tree can be extracted in the form of IF-THEN rules. One rule is created for each path from the root to a leaf, with each attribute-value pair along a path forming a conjunction. The leaf node holds the class prediction. Rules being easier for humans to understand, their usefulness in improving understandability and subsequent role in better human–machine interaction cannot be ignored. For example, sample rules can be of the form

IF $age \leq 30$ AND $student = yes$ THEN $buys\_computer = yes$;
IF $31 \leq age \leq 40$ THEN $buys\_computer = yes$;
IF $age \leq 30$ AND $credit\_rating = fair$ THEN $buys\_computer = no$.

An example of a rule extracted from the decision tree of Fig. 5.1 is
IF $30 > age \geq 20$ AND *car type = sports* THEN *driving risk = high.*

Tree-based pruning limits the kind of pruning involved. When a node is
pruned, all subtrees under it have to be pruned as well. One can also use
rule-based pruning. Here, for each leaf of the tree, a rule is extracted using
a conjunction of all tests upto the root. Then, based on the validation set,
one independently prunes tests from each rule in order to generate the highest
accuracy for that rule. The rules are maintained sorted, in decreasing order
of their accuracy.

5.2.8   Fusion with neural networks

Decision trees and neural networks are the most commonly used non-parametric
tools for pattern classification [20]. While in decision trees the number of tuples becomes smaller as the path between the root node and a new node
increases, the decision boundaries of the neural net are formed by considering
all the available input tuples as a whole. Hence a neural net can be expected
to generate fewer rules, but with larger number of antecedent conditions [21].
In recent years, enormous work has been done in an attempt to combine the
advantages of neural networks and decision trees [22]–[24].

Sethi [22] proposed a procedure for mapping a decision tree into a multilayered feed-forward neural network with two hidden layers. The mapping rules
are as follows. (a) The number of neurons in the first hidden layer equals to
the number of internal nodes in the tree. Each of these neurons implements
one of the decision functions of the internal nodes. (b) The number of neurons
in the second hidden layer equals the number of leaf nodes in the tree. (c)
The number of neurons in the output layer equals to the number of distinct
classes. Ivanova and Kubat [23] have directly mapped a decision tree into a
three-layered network, such that each conjunction (in a rule) is modeled by a
hidden node. The input domain is partitioned into a set of non-overlapping
intervals of attributes, which are then mapped to input nodes of the network.
Setiono and Liu [24] computed binary training patterns from the decision
rules and attribute intervals. These are used to train a feed-forward network,
which is then pruned to generate an optimal topology.

Determination of the optimal size of an artificial neural network (ANN)
is a problem of considerable importance, as this has a significant impact on
the effectiveness of its performance. In general, it is desirable to have small
networks. This is because increasing the number of hidden nodes or links may
improve the approximation quality of an ANN at the expense of deteriorating
its generalization capability (due to the resulting redundancy). One way of
improving the generalization behavior of an ANN is to use knowledge-based
networks [25, 26]. Decision trees provide a way of extracting crude domain
knowledge from a large dataset, which can be directly encoded into an ANN
to formulate a knowledge-based network. Further details on knowledge-based
networks are provided in Section 8.2.3.

5.3   BAYESIAN CLASSIFIERS

Statistical methods constitute one of the oldest learning paradigms in the literature [27], and work under the assumption that the underlying pattern generating mechanism is faithfully represented by a statistical model. Given that there are l possible hypotheses (pattern classes) $h_1, h_2, \ldots, h_l$, and an arbitrary pattern belongs to hypothesis h_i with *a priori* probability $p_i \geq 0$, we have $\sum_{i=1}^{l} p_i = 1$. A decision rule assigns an unknown pattern $\mathbf{X}$ to a class h, such that the average loss incurred in the process is as small as possible.

5.3.1   Bayesian rule for minimum risk

Bayes' theorem provides a way of computing the probability of a particular event $\mathbf{X}$, given some set of observations. For training pattern or sample $\mathbf{X}$, the *posteriori* probability of a class or hypothesis h, $P(h|X)$, is expressed as

$$P(h|X) = \frac{P(X|h)P(h)}{P(X)}, \tag{5.6}$$

where $P(h) = \frac{|h|}{N}$ is the estimated *a priori* probability of h (given $|h|$ and N are the number of patterns in class h and the total number of patterns, respectively, and assuming that all hypotheses are equally likely), $P(X/h)$ is the *posterior* probability of $\mathbf{X}$ conditioned on h, and $P(X)$ is the prior probability of $\mathbf{X}$ (and is constant).

The maximum posteriori (MAP) hypothesis is used to assign to the class h having maximum $P(h/X)$. It is expressed as

$$h_{MAP} \equiv arg \max_{h \in H} P(h|X) = arg \max_{h \in H} P(X|h)P(h),$$

where H is the set of hypotheses.

Given the probability distribution of the data, Bayesian classifiers are able to perform efficiently with the minimum error rate [8]. Here the expected loss (or conditional risk) of making a decision is the *minimum*. This statistically optimal classification rule is a generally accepted standard against which the performance of other classification algorithms is often compared. However, the practical difficulties involved include the requirement of initial knowledge about many probabilities and a significant computational cost.

5.3.2   Naive Bayesian classifier

The naive Bayesian classifier represents each pattern $\mathbf{X}$ as an n-dimensional vector of attribute values $[a_1, a_2, \ldots, a_n]$. Given that there are l classes $C_1, C_2, \ldots, C_l$, the classifier predicts an unknown sample $\mathbf{X}$ as belonging to the class having the highest posterior probability conditioned on $\mathbf{X}$. In other words, $\mathbf{X}$ is assigned to class C_i if and only if

$$P(C_i|X) > P(C_j|X) \tag{5.7}$$

for $1 \leq j \leq l$ and $j \neq i$. Using Eq. (5.6), we get

$$P(C_i|X) = \frac{P(X|C_i)P(C_i)}{P(X)}.$$

In order to reduce the computational expenses involved, the classifier makes the naive or simplified assumption that the n attributes are *conditionally independent* of one another. The class-conditional independence is expressed as

$$P(C_i|X) \infty P(C_i) \prod_{j=1}^{n} P(a_j|C_i).$$

As $P(X)$ is constant for all classes, and $P(C_i) = \frac{|C_i|}{N}$, one needs to maximize just $P(X|C_i)$. Therefore, we compute

$$P(X|C_i) = \prod_{j=1}^{n} P(a_j|C_i). \qquad (5.8)$$

This greatly reduces the computation costs, since it only counts the class distribution.

If the ith attribute is categorical, $P(a_j|C_i)$ is estimated as the relative frequency of samples having value a_j as the jth attribute in class C_i. If, on the other hand, the jth attribute is continuous, then $P(a_j|C_i)$ is generally estimated through a Gaussian density function. Both cases are computationally easy.

When the Gaussian distribution is assumed, we have the normal density functions given by

$$P(X|C_i) = \frac{1}{(2\pi)^{\frac{n}{2}}|\Sigma_i|^{\frac{1}{2}}} \exp\left[-\frac{1}{2}(\mathbf{X} - \mathbf{m}_i)^T \Sigma_i^{-1}(\mathbf{X} - \mathbf{m}_i)\right], \qquad (5.9)$$

for $i = 1, 2, \ldots, l$, where $\mathbf{m}_i$ and Σ_i are the mean vector and the covariance matrix, respectively, for the ith class.

Bayesian classifiers are very simple, requiring only a single scan of the data, thereby providing high accuracy and speed for large databases. Their performance is comparable to that of decision trees and neural networks. However there arise inaccuracies due to (a) the simplified assumptions involved and (b) a lack of available probability data or knowledge about the underlying probability distribution. Bayesian classifiers have the minimum error rate, unless there are inaccuracies in their assumptions.

5.3.2.1 Example 3: Let Table 5.7 depict the attribute-class information related to a simple classification example, for which one needs to design the naive Bayesian classifier. Consider a numeric two-attribute two-class problem, to predict the classification of a new sample $\mathbf{X} = [a_1, a_2] = [1, 1]$. We compute

Table 5.7 Sample dataset for naive Bayesian classifier

Attributes		Class
a_1	a_2	
1	0	C_1
0	0	C_1
2	1	C_2
1	2	C_2
0	1	C_1

the *a priori* probabilities $P(C_1) = \frac{3}{5}$ and $P(C_2) = \frac{2}{5}$. The conditional probabilities $P(a_j|C_i)$ are estimated, for every attribute value given in the new sample **X**, as $P(a_1 = 1|C_1) = \frac{1}{3}$, $P(a_1 = 1|C_2) = \frac{1}{2}$, $P(a_2 = 1|C_1) = \frac{1}{3}$, and $P(a_2 = 1|C_2) = \frac{1}{2}$, respectively. Assuming conditional independence of attributes, the conditional probabilities of Eq. (5.8) become

$$P(X|C_1) = P(a_1 = 1|C_1) * P(a_2 = 1|C_1) = \frac{1}{3} * \frac{1}{3} = \frac{1}{9}$$

and

$$P(X|C_2) = P(a_1 = 1|C_2) * P(a_2 = 1|C_2) = \frac{1}{2} * \frac{1}{2} = \frac{1}{4}.$$

This is used to evaluate

$$P(C_1|X) = \frac{1}{9} * \frac{3}{5} = \frac{1}{15}$$

and

$$P(C_2|X) = \frac{1}{4} * \frac{2}{5} = \frac{1}{10}.$$

Maximizing, we find that $P(C_2|X)$ is larger. Hence the sample **X** is predicted to be in class C_2.

5.3.3 Bayesian belief network

A Bayesian network is a directed acyclic graph whose nodes represent random variables of interests, while the edges reflect the direct (causal) influence. It provides a graphical model of causal relationships, based on which learning can be performed. The conditional probabilities for the nodes are given all possible combinations of their parents. A Bayesian network is also termed a Belief or Probabilistic net [28]. It provides an efficient and effective representation of a probability distribution, in terms of the dependencies among the attributes. The nodes are statistically independent of their nondescendants, given the state of their parents. This implies that one can compute conditional probabilities of nodes, given the observed values of some nodes.

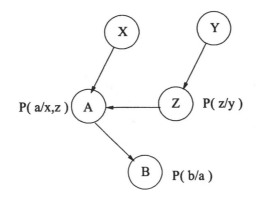

Fig. 5.3 A belief network.

5.3.3.1 Example 4: Figure 5.3 depicts a belief network consisting of five nodes X, Y, Z, A, B. Here X directly influences A, while Y also influences A through Z. Each node has a number of discrete states. For example, node X can take up states $\{x_1, x_2, \ldots\}$, collectively denoted as $\mathbf{x}$.

5.4 INSTANCE-BASED LEARNERS

These *nearest neighbor* rules are based on the concept of minimum distance classification from "instances" and can involve either a single prototype or multiple prototypes [8]. When the patterns of a class tend to cluster tightly about a typical representative pattern for that class, we use a single prototype from which to compute the minimum distance. Let $\mathbf{m}_i$ be the prototype for the $i = 1, \ldots, l$ classes, such that the distance between an arbitrary pattern vector $\mathbf{X}$ and the ith prototype is given by D_i.

When a non-Euclidean metric like the *Mahalanobis distance* is used, the corresponding minimum distance classifier is termed the Mahalanobis classifier. Here

$$D_i^2 = (\mathbf{X} - \mathbf{m}_i)^T \Sigma_i^{-1} (\mathbf{X} - \mathbf{m}_i), \qquad (5.10)$$

where $\sum_i$ is the covariance matrix of the underlying Gaussian (or normal) distribution for class i. When the Euclidean distance is used, we have

$$D_i^2 = \|\mathbf{X} - \mathbf{m_i}\|^2 = \mathbf{X}'\mathbf{X} - 2(\mathbf{m}_i'\mathbf{X} - \frac{1}{2}\mathbf{m}_i'\mathbf{m}_i). \qquad (5.11)$$

5.4.1 Minimum distance classifiers

In this category of decision rules, one does not make assumptions of an underlying statistical distribution. The minimum distance classifier computes the distance of an unlabeled pattern $\mathbf{X}$ from the prototype of each class, and

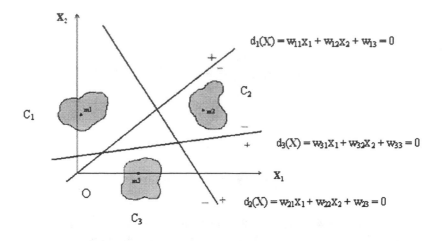

Fig. 5.4   Decision boundaries d_i for a three-class problem.

it assigns the pattern to that class to which it is closest. Ties are resolved arbitrarily. In other words, one generates a linear discriminant function

$$\min(D_i^2) = \max(d_i) = \max(\mathbf{m}_i'\mathbf{X} - \frac{1}{2}\mathbf{m}_i'\mathbf{m}_i),$$

from Eq. (5.11), where the decision boundary is $d_i(\mathbf{X}) = \mathbf{w}_i'\mathbf{X}$, for $i = 1, \ldots, l$, such that $w_{ij} = m_{ij}$, $j = 1, \ldots, n$, and $w_{i,n+1} = -\frac{1}{2}\mathbf{m}_i'\mathbf{m}_i$. Figure 5.4 illustrates the concept of the minimum distance based decision boundaries, generated for a three-class problem with single prototypes.

When each class is characterized by multiple prototypes, the minimum distance is computed from all of these as before. Let the ith class contain N_i prototypes $\mathbf{m}_i^1, \ldots, \mathbf{m}_i^{N_i}$, such that the distance

$$D_i = \min_k ||\mathbf{X} - \mathbf{m}_i^k|| \qquad (5.12)$$

for $k = 1, \ldots, N_i$. The unlabeled pattern $\mathbf{X}$ is classified into the ith class if $D_i < D_j$ for all $j \neq i$. The piecewise linear discriminant function $d_i = \max_k\{(\mathbf{m}_i^k)'\mathbf{X}) - \frac{1}{2}(\mathbf{m}_i^k)'\mathbf{m}_i^k\}$ for $k = 1, \ldots, N_i$.

Instance-based learners are also called *lazy* learners because they store all the training samples. This may present difficulties when learning from very large datasets. On the other hand, decision trees and neural networks are termed *eager* learners since they are able to construct a generalization model, before receiving unknown or new samples to classify. Although lazy learners are faster at training, they are slower during application. They incur expensive computational costs when the number of stored samples or instances, with which to compare a given unlabeled sample, is large.

In this framework let us now present the k-nearest neighbor classifier, regression, radial basis function network, and case-based reasoning. The last two can, again, be categorized as soft computing approaches.

5.4.2 k-nearest neighbor (k-NN) classifier

Here all the instances correspond to pattern points in the n-dimensional space. The nearest neighbors are typically defined in terms of Euclidean distance. The target function could be either discrete- or real-valued. In case of discrete values, the algorithm assigns to a point $\mathbf{X}$ the label or class for the majority of its k-nearest neighbors from a sample pattern set $\mathbf{m}_i \in \{\mathbf{m}_1, \ldots, \mathbf{m}_{l'}\}$ of known classification, where $l' \geq l$ and each of these instances belongs to one of the l classes. A nearest-neighbor (NN) classification rule assigns an unlabeled pattern $\mathbf{X}$ to the class of its nearest neighbor, where $\mathbf{m}_i \in \{\mathbf{m}_1, \ldots, \mathbf{m}_{l'}\}$ is a nearest neighbor to $\mathbf{X}$ if the distance

$$D(\mathbf{m}_i, \mathbf{X}) = \min_j\{D(\mathbf{m}_j, \mathbf{X})\}, \tag{5.13}$$

for $j = 1, 2, \ldots, l'$. A Voronoi diagram defines the decision surface induced by a 1-NN for a typical set of training examples. A k-NN ($k > 1$) rule consists of determining the k-nearest neighbors to $\mathbf{X}$ and using the *majority* of equal classifications in this group as the classification of $\mathbf{X}$.

For $k = 1$, the error rate is never worse than twice the Bayes' rate (which holds for unlimited number of samples). For large k, the algorithm is computationally more expensive, as compared to a decision tree or neural network, and requires efficient indexing. Moreover, it assigns equal weight to each attribute, thereby accommodating no feature selection. Different approaches to attain scalability for data mining incorporate (i) indexing to find k-nearest neighbors, (ii) an R-tree family, which works well up to 20 dimensions, (iii) a Pyramid tree for high-dimensional data, and (iv) clustering to reduce the dataset size.

5.4.2.1 Example 5:   Figure 5.5 demonstrates the k-NN rule for $k = 5$. Considering the five nearest neighbors around $\mathbf{X}$, marked by the dotted line, we observe that there are three instances (patterns) from class C_2 and two from class C_1. Taking a majority vote enables assignment of $\mathbf{X}$ to C_2.

5.4.3   Locally weighted regression

The objective is to learn a new regression equation by weighting each training instance based on its distance from a new instance. The regression equation can be expressed as $\hat{f}(x) = w_0 + w_1 a_1(x) + \cdots + w_n a_n(x)$. The algorithm tries to find the w_is to minimize the error

$$E(X) \equiv \frac{1}{2} \sum_{x \in X} (f(x) - \hat{f}(x))^2.$$

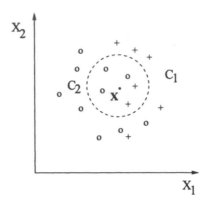

Fig. 5.5   A k-nearest neighbor rule for $k = 5$.

It constructs an explicit approximation of f over a local region surrounding query instance X_q. The target function f is approximated near X_q using the linear function

$$E(X_q) \equiv \frac{1}{2} \sum_{x \in k-NN\_of\_X_q} (f(x) - \hat{f}(x))^2 K(D(X_q, x)). \tag{5.14}$$

The squared error is minimized using a distance-decreasing weight K.

5.4.4   Radial basis functions (RBFs)

The RBFs are related to distance-weighted regression and artificial neural networks. In the framework of instance based learners, we can represent Eq. (2.25) as

$$y = f(x) \equiv w_0 + \sum_{j=1}^{m} w_j K(D(\mu_j, x)), \tag{5.15}$$

where each μ_j is an instance from the training data and $K(D(\mu_j, x))$ is the Gaussian kernel function of Eq. (2.24). Here the contribution of an instance is non-negligible only if the input region falls in the region of the instance. The training of an RBF can be summarized as follows:

- Choose the m kernel points μ_js and the parameters of K – for example, the variance σ_j of the distribution.

- Choose the weights so as to minimize the error on the training data.

Every instance can be chosen as a kernel point, making all variances the same. Otherwise the instances can be clustered, excluding the target function, by using c-means or expectation maximization (EM)-like clustering algorithm [6] and choosing a representative within each cluster.

5.4.5   Case-based reasoning (CBR)

Cases are the symbolic representation of some typical situations, already experienced by the system. These are more complex than the simple training patterns of nearest-neighbor classifiers in the Euclidean space. The instances are conceptualized pieces of knowledge, representing an experience that teaches a lesson for achieving the goals of the system. CBR involves [9]

- adapting old solutions to meet new demands,

- using old cases to explain new situations or to justify new solutions, and

- reasoning from precedents to interpret new situations.

The system learns and becomes more efficient as a byproduct of its reasoning activity.

Examples of CBR encompass medical diagnosis and law interpretation, where the knowledge available is incomplete and/or evidence is sparse. Unlike traditional knowledge-based systems, a case-based system proceeds through a process of (i) remembering one or a small set of concrete instances or cases and (ii) basing decisions on comparisons between the new situation and the old ones. The basic operations include

- Case selection, where the cases belong to the set of examples encountered, and

- Case generation, where the constructed cases need not be any of the available examples.

Challenges in CBR include finding a good similarity metric, developing efficient techniques for indexing training cases, and methods for combining solutions. Some of the existing case selection methods [29] are k-NN based, using (i) condensed nearest neighbor (CNN), (ii) instance-based learning with case growing or pruning (e.g., IB3), and (iii) instance-based learning with feature weighting (e.g., IB4).

5.4.6   Granular computing and CBR

As mentioned in Section 2.3.2, granular computing [30] is an approach under soft computing. An information granule is a group of similar objects clubbed together by an indiscernibility relation. Granular computing is, therefore, performed using the information granules and not the data points (objects). This helps achieve information compression, leading to a computational gain. Here the cases are considered to be informative patterns or prototypes, characterizing the problem.

In the rough-fuzzy framework used in Ref. [31], cases are represented as information granules or clusters. These involve a reduced number of relevant features with variable size that (i) have less storage requirements, (ii) are amenable to fast retrieval, and (iii) are suitable for mining data with large dimension and size. Fuzzy sets help in the linguistic representation of patterns, providing a fuzzy granulation of the feature space. Rough sets help in generating dependency rules to model the *informative* or *representative* regions in the granulated feature space. Fuzzy membership functions corresponding to these representative regions are stored as the cases.

5.5 SUPPORT VECTOR MACHINES

The Support Vector Machine (SVM) [32, 10] has recently become very popular as a high-performance classifier in several domains including pattern recognition, data mining and Bioinformatics. It has strong theoretical foundations and a good generalization capability. Another advantage of SVM is that, as a by-product of learning, it obtains a set of support vectors (SVs) which characterizes a given classification task or compresses a labeled dataset. Often the number of SVs is only a small fraction of the original dataset.

The basic idea is to construct a hyperplane as the decision surface such that the margin of separation between positive and negative examples is maximized. The *structural risk minimization* principle is used for the purpose. Here the error rate of a learning machine is considered to be bounded by the sum of the training error rate and a term depending on the Vapnik–Chervonenkis (VC)[1] dimension. Given a labeled set of N training samples (X_i, y_i), where $X_i \in R^n$ and $y_i \in \{-1, 1\}$, the discriminant hyperplane is defined as

$$f(X_q) = \sum_{i=1}^{N} y_i \alpha_i K(X_q, X_i) + b. \qquad (5.16)$$

Here $K(.)$ is a kernel function and the sign of $f(X_q)$ determines the membership of query sample X_q. Constructing an optimal hyperplane is equivalent to determining all nonzero α_is, which correspond to the support vectors, and the bias b.

A limitation of the SVM design algorithm, particularly for large datasets, is the need to solve a quadratic programming (QP) problem involving a dense $N \times N$ matrix, where N is the number of points in the dataset. Since most QP routines have quadratic complexity, SVM design requires huge memory and computational time for large data applications. However, approaches also exist for circumventing these shortcomings [33].

A simple method to solve the SVM QP problem has been described by Vapnik [10]. Here a 'chunking' algorithm uses the fact that the solution of the SVM problem remains the same if one removes the points that correspond to

---

[1]The VC dimension of a system is defined as the largest set S of data samples for which the system can implement all possible $2^{|S|}$ dichotomies on S, where dichotomy implies a two-class categorization.

zero Lagrange multipliers of the QP problem (the non-SV points). The large QP problem can thus be decomposed into a series of smaller QP subproblems, whose ultimate goal is to identify all the nonzero Lagrange multipliers (SVs) while discarding the zero Lagrange multipliers (non-SVs). At every step, chunking solves a QP subproblem that consists of (a) the nonzero Lagrange multiplier points from the previous step and (b) a chunk of q other points. At the final step, the entire set of nonzero Lagrange multipliers are identified, thereby solving the large QP problem. Several variations of the algorithm exist depending upon the method of forming the chunks [32]. Chunking greatly reduces the training time as compared to batch learning of SVMs. However, it may not suitably handle large-scale training problems due to slow convergence of the chunking steps, when q new points are chosen randomly.

Active learning has recently become a popular paradigm for reducing the sample complexity of large-scale learning tasks [34]. Instead of learning from randomly selected samples, here the learner has the ability to select its own training data. This is done iteratively, and the output of a step is used to select examples for the next step. In the context of SVMs, active learning has been used to speed up chunking algorithms [35]. The points that split the current version space into two halves having equal volumes are selected at each step, as they are likely to be the active SVs. This active learning strategy queries for a single point at each step. However, a gain in computational time can be obtained by querying multiple instances at a time. A major limitation of this greedy method is that the selection of a new point is influenced only by the current hypothesis (separating hyperplane) available. Hence learning may be severely hampered if (i) a 'bad' example is queried, which drastically worsens the current hypothesis, and (ii) the current hypothesis itself is far from the optimal hypothesis (in the initial phase of learning), so that the examples queried are less likely to be the actual SVs.

5.6 FUZZY DECISION TREES

In this section we embark on a soft computing-based hybridization of decision trees with fuzzy sets. A decision tree that incorporates fuzzy set theoretic concepts at the input, output, and/or node levels can be termed a fuzzy decision tree. The data can be presented in fuzzy terms, the output decision may be provided as fuzzy membership values, and the measure determining the separability (or splitting) at the node level can be fuzzified.

The fusion of fuzzy sets with decision trees enables one to combine the uncertainty handling and approximate reasoning capabilities of the former with the comprehensibility and ease of application of the latter. This enhances the representative power of decision trees *naturally* with the knowledge component inherent in fuzzy logic, leading to better robustness, noise immunity, and applicability in uncertain or imprecise contexts.

Fuzzy decision trees [36] assume that all domain attributes or linguistic variables have predefined fuzzy terms, determined in a data-driven manner using fuzzy restrictions. The impurity factor, used for splitting a node, is modified for fuzzy representation, and a pattern can have nonzero match to one or more leaves. Techniques for the design of fuzzy decision trees have been reported in the literature [36]–[43].

Ichihashi et al. [37] extract fuzzy reasoning rules viewed as fuzzy partitions. An algebraic method to facilitate incremental learning is also employed. The intuitive factor used for splitting a node, which provides the maximal information gain, is defined as

$$Entropy = -\sum_{i=1}^{l} \frac{\sum_{j=1}^{N} \mu_{ij}}{N} \log_2 \frac{\sum_{j=1}^{N} \mu_{ij}}{N}, \tag{5.17}$$

where μ_{ij} is the membership of the jth pattern point to the ith decision class (leaf) and N is the total number of data objects. This uses a normalized version of fuzzy entropy, instead of the classical entropy component involved in the conventional expression of Eq. (5.4). If the relative frequency of a class i is greater than a threshold, then it is termed a leaf and labeled by the corresponding class with probability $\frac{\sum_{j=1}^{N} \mu_{ij}}{N}$.

Xizhao and Hong [38] discretize continuous attributes using fuzzy numbers and possibility theory. Pedrycz and Sosnowski [39], on the other hand, employ context-based fuzzy clustering for this purpose. Yuan and Shaw [40] induce a fuzzy decision tree by reducing classification ambiguity with fuzzy evidence. The input data are fuzzified using triangular membership functions around cluster centers obtained using Kohonen's feature map [44]. Wang et al. [41] present optimization principles of fuzzy decision trees based on minimizing the total number and average depth of leaves, proving that the algorithmic complexity of constructing a minimum tree is NP-hard. Fuzzy entropy and classification ambiguity are minimized at node level, and fuzzy clustering is used to merge branches.

Fuzzy knowledge-based networks [45, 46] typically incorporate fuzziness at the network level, using fuzzy neural networks. We now describe the formulation of a fuzzy knowledge-based network using fuzzy ID3 [11, 12]. Quantitative measures are defined to evaluate the effectiveness of the fuzzy decision tree and the linguistic rules. The novel concept of tree evaluation, in terms of its compactness and performance, enables extraction of only meaningful (less ambiguous) rules. A smaller or compact tree is more efficient in terms of both storage and time requirements, tends to generalize better to unknown test cases, and leads to the generation of more comprehensible linguistic rules. Quantitative evaluation of the linguistic rules not only minimizes human intervention, but also provides aids for knowledge discovery.

Discretization of continuous attributes, based on the distribution of pattern points in the feature space, is made in linguistic terms using quantiles. Unlike other fuzzy decision trees [36], this discretization to boolean form helps

Fig. 3.15   Original pepper image.

Fig. 3.16   Pepper image compressed with quality factor 75.

Fig. 3.17 Pepper image compressed with quality factor 10.

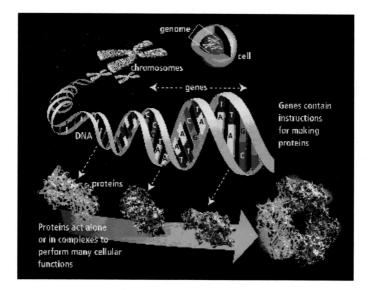

Fig. 10.1 Molecular biology.

in reducing the computational complexity while preserving the linguistic nature of the decision in rule form. New fuzziness measures, in terms of class memberships, are used at the node level of the tree to take care of overlapping classes. The extracted rules are mapped onto a fuzzy knowledge-based network. Unlike [22]–[24], the frequency of samples (representative of a rule) and the depth of the attributes in the decision tree are incorporated during the mapping. The effectiveness of the model is demonstrated on benchmark datasets [12].

5.6.1 Classification

Here we describe the incorporation of fuzziness at the input, output, and node levels of the fuzzy ID3 [12], to handle different forms of uncertainty. Input attributes are automatically discretized in linguistic terms, based on the distribution of pattern points in the feature space. Different forms of fuzzy entropy are computed at the node level, in terms of class membership, to take care of overlapping classes. Pruning is used to minimize noise, resulting in a smaller decision tree with more efficient classification. A new metric, called T-measure, is developed to evaluate the decision tree both in terms of performance and size.

5.6.1.1 Fuzziness at input Any input feature value is described in terms of some combination of overlapping membership values in the linguistic property sets *low* (L), *medium* (M), and *high* (H). An n-dimensional pattern $\mathbf{X}_i = [a_1, a_2, \ldots, a_n]$ is represented as a $3n$-dimensional vector [47]

$$\mathbf{X}_i = [\mu_{low(a_1)}(\mathbf{X}_i), \mu_{medium(a_1)}(\mathbf{X}_i), \mu_{high(a_1)}(\mathbf{X}_i), \ldots, \mu_{high(a_n)}(\mathbf{X}_i)], \tag{5.18}$$

where the μ values indicate the membership functions of the corresponding linguistic functions *low, medium,* and *high* along each feature axis. Each μ value is then discretized, using a threshold (generally 0.5), to enable a convenient mapping in the ID3 framework. This discretization to boolean form speeds up computation by reducing the complexity of the search space. However, the linguistic flavor of the attributes is retained, thereby enabling the extraction of more user-friendly *natural* rules that are then mapped to the fuzzy knowledge-based network.

When the input feature is numerical, we divide it into three partitions (with range [0, 1]) using only two parameters P_{j1} and P_{j2} as depicted in Fig. 5.6. Features in linguistic and set forms can also be handled. *Quantiles* or *partition values*[2] [48] are used in order to minimize the influence of extreme values or noisy patterns.

---

[2]Quantiles or partition values are the values of a variate which divide the total frequency into a number of equal parts.

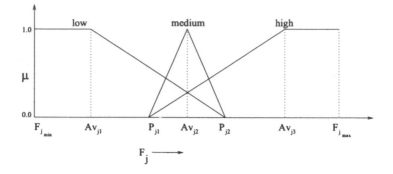

Fig. 5.6 Linguistic input membership functions.

Let $F_{j_{\max}}$ and $F_{j_{\min}}$ denote the maximum and minimum values encountered along feature F_j considering N training patterns $F_{1j}, F_{2j}, \ldots, F_{Nj}$. Let these patterns be sorted in the ascending order of their values along the jth axis. The first quantile (P_{j1}) is the value of F_j that exceeds one-third of the measurements and is less than the remaining two-thirds. The second quantile (P_{j2}) is the value of F_j that exceeds two-thirds of the measurements and is less than the remaining one-third. In order to determine the two quantiles, we divide the measurements into a number of small class intervals of equal width δ and count the corresponding class frequencies f_i. The position of the kth partition value (here quantile, as $k = 1, 2$ for three partitions) is calculated as

$$P_{jk} = l_i + \frac{R_k - cf_{i-1}}{f_i} \cdot \delta, \qquad (5.19)$$

where l_i is the lower limit of the ith class interval, $R_k = \frac{N.k}{3}$ is the rank of the kth partition value, and cf_{i-1} is the cumulative frequency of the immediately preceding class interval, such that $cf_{i-1} \le R_k \le cf_i$. Then, from Fig. 5.6, we have
$Av_{j1} = \frac{F_{j_{\min}} + P_{j1}}{2}, \quad Av_{j2} = \frac{P_{j1} + P_{j2}}{2}, \quad$ and $\quad Av_{j3} = \frac{P_{j2} + F_{j_{\max}}}{2}$.
    The membership values of a pattern along the jth axis, in the corresponding three-dimensional linguistic space of Eq. (5.18), is computed as [12]

$$\mu_{low(a_j)}(\mathbf{X}_i) = \begin{cases} 1 & \text{for } F_{ij} < Av_{j1} \\ \frac{P_{j2} - F_{ij}}{P_{j2} - Av_{j1}} & \text{for } Av_{j1} \le F_{ij} < P_{j2} \\ 0 & \text{otherwise,} \end{cases} \qquad (5.20)$$

$$\mu_{medium(a_j)}(\mathbf{X}_i) = \begin{cases} 0 & \text{for } F_{ij} < P_{j1} \\ \frac{Av_{j2} - F_{ij}}{Av_{j2} - P_{j1}} & \text{for } P_{j1} \le F_{ij} < Av_{j2} \\ \frac{P_{j2} - F_{ij}}{P_{j2} - Av_{j2}} & \text{for } Av_{j2} \le F_{ij} < P_{j2} \\ 0 & \text{otherwise,} \end{cases} \qquad (5.21)$$

$$\mu_{high(a_j)}(\mathbf{X}_i) = \begin{cases} 0 & \text{for } F_{ij} < P_{j1} \\ \frac{F_{ij}-P_{j1}}{Av_{j3}-P_{j1}} & \text{for } P_{j1} \le F_{ij} < Av_{j3} \\ 1 & \text{otherwise.} \end{cases} \qquad (5.22)$$

5.6.1.2 Output membership and fuzzy entropy Consider an l-class problem domain. The membership of the ith pattern in class k, lying in the range $[0,1]$, is defined as [47]

$$\mu_{ik}(\mathbf{X}_i) = \frac{1}{1 + (\frac{z_{ik}}{f_d})^{f_e}}, \qquad (5.23)$$

where z_{ik} is the weighted distance of the training pattern $\mathbf{X}_i$ from class C_k, and the positive constants f_d and f_e are the denominational and exponential fuzzy generators controlling the amount of fuzziness in the class membership set.

Fuzziness is incorporated into the ID3 algorithm at the node level by modifying the conventional decision function, with classical Shannon entropy, by the inclusion of different fuzzy measures. The fuzzy entropy considers the membership of a pattern to a class and helps enhance the discriminative power of an attribute. In order to reduce the effect of noise or exceptions, a node is pruned depending on the number of patterns reaching it. For this purpose, a threshold t is defined as a lower bound on the fraction of patterns allowed in an existing node.

Let us now provide the different fuzzy entropy or fuzziness measures, denoted as *cases a, b, d,* and *e,* respectively, investigated at the node level of the decision tree. Note that μ_{ij}, the membership of the jth pattern to the ith class, is calculated by Eq. (5.23) and p_k is the *a priori* probability of the kth class. Comparison is provided with *cases c* [37] and *f* [49].

Case a [12]:

$$Entropy = -\sum_{i=1}^{l} p_i \log_2 p_i - \frac{1}{N} \sum_{i=1}^{l} \sum_{j=1}^{N} [\mu_{ij} \log_2 \mu_{ij} + (1 - \mu_{ij}) \log_2(1 - \mu_{ij})].$$

$$(5.24)$$

The first term on the right is the classical entropy of Eq. (5.4), while the second term corresponds to fuzzy entropy [47].

Case b: Same as *Case a*, but without pruning.

Case c: Method of Ichihashi et al. using Eq. (5.17).

Case d [12]: *Entropy =*

$$-\sum_{i=1}^{l} \frac{\sum_{j=1}^{N} \mu_{ij}}{N} \log_2 \frac{\sum_{j=1}^{N} \mu_{ij}}{N} - \frac{1}{N} \sum_{i=1}^{l} \sum_{j=1}^{N} [\mu_{ij} \log_2 \mu_{ij} + (1 - \mu_{ij}) \log_2(1 - \mu_{ij})].$$

$$(5.25)$$

This is an amalgamation of the two forms of fuzzy entropy, where the first term on the right corresponds to Eq. (5.17) and the second term relates to the fuzzy entropy part of Eq. (5.24).

Case e [11]:

$$Entropy = -\sum_{i=1}^{l} p_i \log_2 p_i - \frac{1}{N} \sum_{i=1}^{l} \sum_{j=1}^{N} \min(\mu_{ij}, 1 - \mu_{ij}). \qquad (5.26)$$

Here the first term on the right is the classical entropy of Eq. (5.4), while the second term corresponds to a fuzzy measure of the ambiguity present. When the class membership values are zero or one (crisp), the expression boils down to that of classical entropy. The fuzzy measure ensures that pattern points lying in overlapping regions are assigned lower weights during the construction of the decision tree; this is intuitively appealing. The reason for this lower weighting is that such ambiguous patterns (having μ values close to 0.5) lead to an increase in the entropy; thereby placing an impedance to its minimization.
Case f: Conventional ID3 algorithm, using Eq. (5.4).

5.6.1.3 Performance measure for decision tree Decision trees generated by different fuzzy entropy measures may vary in size and structure, and this influences the performance of both the tree and the rules extracted from it. In order to evaluate the efficiency of a decision tree the *T-measure* is introduced [12], keeping in view the following issues:

- The less the depths of the leaf nodes of the tree, the better it is since it takes less time to reach a decision.

- The existence of unresolved terminal nodes is undesirable.

- The distribution of labeled leaf nodes at different depths affects the performance of the tree; a tree whose frequently accessed leaf nodes are at lower depths is more efficient in terms of time.

DEFINITION 5.6.1 *The* **T-measure**, *T, for a decision tree is defined as*

$$T = \frac{2n - \sum_{i=1}^{N_{lnodes}} w_i d_i}{2n - 1}, \qquad (5.27)$$

where

$$w_i = \begin{cases} \frac{N_i}{N} & \text{for a resolved leaf node} \\ \frac{2N_i}{N} & \text{otherwise,} \end{cases} \qquad (5.28)$$

n is the number of binary attributes of a pattern, d_i is the depth of a leaf node, N_{lnodes} is the number of terminal (leaf or unresolved) nodes, N is the total number of patterns in the training set, and N_i is the total number of training set patterns that percolate down to the ith leaf node. The value of T lies in the interval $[0, 1)$. A value 0 for T is undesirable, and a value close to 1 signifies a good decision tree.

Let us demonstrate the evaluation of the T-measure with an example. Consider a two-class problem, with two-dimensional patterns. Let Fig. 5.7 depict

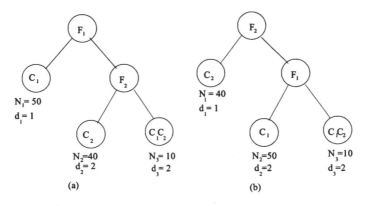

Fig. 5.7 Example demonstrating T-measure computation.

two decision trees generated by two different algorithms. For the decision tree in Fig. 5.7(a), $T = \frac{2 \times 2 - 0.5 \times 1 - 0.4 \times 2 - 0.2 \times 2}{2 \times 2 - 1} = 0.77$, while for the decision tree in Fig. 5.7(b) one obtains $T = \frac{2 \times 2 - 0.5 \times 2 - 0.4 \times 1 - 0.2 \times 2}{2 \times 2 - 1} = 0.73$. Hence we observe that the first decision tree is better than the second, since the fraction of patterns in the node at depth *one* is more in the first case.

Theorem. *The value of T-measure lies within 0 and 1, that is, $0 \le T < 1$.*
Proof: Let us first establish the upper limit. By Eq. (5.28), we have

$$w_i \ge \frac{N_i}{N}, i = 1, 2, \ldots, N_{lnodes} \tag{5.29}$$

and

$$d_i \ge 1, i = 1, 2, \ldots, N_{lnodes}. \tag{5.30}$$

Hence

$$\sum_{i=1}^{N_{lnodes}} w_i d_i \ge \sum_{i=1}^{N_{lnodes}} \frac{N_i}{N}.$$

Since $\sum_{i=1}^{N_{lnodes}} N_i = N$, one obtains

$$\sum_{i=1}^{N_{lnodes}} w_i d_i \ge 1.$$

So

$$2n - \sum_{i=1}^{N_{lnodes}} w_i d_i < 2n - 1,$$

that is,

$$T = \frac{2n - \sum_{i=1}^{N_{lnodes}} w_i d_i}{2n - 1} < 1. \tag{5.31}$$

Now we check the lower bound for T. We have

$$w_i \leq \frac{2N_i}{N}, \quad i = 1, 2, \ldots, N_{lnodes} \tag{5.32}$$

and

$$d_i \leq n, \quad i = 1, 2, \ldots, N_{lnodes}. \tag{5.33}$$

Hence

$$\sum_{i=1}^{N_{lnodes}} w_i d_i \leq \sum_{i=1}^{N_{lnodes}} \frac{2N_i n}{N} = 2n,$$

that is,

$$0 \leq 2n - \sum_{i=1}^{N_{lnodes}} w_i d_i,$$

that is,

$$0 \leq \frac{2n - \sum_{i=1}^{N_{lnodes}} w_i d_i}{2n - 1} = T. \tag{5.34}$$

Thus one obtains

$$0 \leq T < 1. \tag{5.35}$$

5.6.2 Rule generation and evaluation

Here we explain the algorithm for extracting domain knowledge, in the form of rules, using the decision tree generated by the fuzzy ID3 [12]. As explained in Section 5.2.7, the path from the root to a leaf is traversed to generate the rule corresponding to a pattern from that class. In this manner, one obtains a set of rules for all the pattern classes, in the form of intersection of the features or attributes encountered along the traversal paths. The ith attribute is marked as A_i or $\overline{A_i}$ depending on whether the traversal is made along the right or left branch. Each rule is marked by its frequency – that is, the number of pattern points reaching this leaf node. Note that each leaf node that has pattern points corresponding to only one class is termed *resolved*.

5.6.2.1 Example 6: The scheme of extracting the rules from the decision tree is demonstrated with an example. Suppose the training set consists of 21 patterns, from three pattern classes, with three features F_1, F_2, and F_3. After splitting each feature into the three linguistic variables *low, medium,* and *high* by Eq. (5.18), one obtains the nine-dimensional symbolic features L_1, M_1, H_1, L_2, M_2, H_2, L_3, M_3, H_3. Let the sample decision tree be shown in Fig. 5.8, and let the extracted rules be

1. $\overline{L}_1 \wedge \overline{H}_3 \quad \rightarrow \quad C_1; 2,$

2. $L_1 \wedge \overline{M}_3 \wedge \overline{M}_1 \rightarrow C_2; 6,$

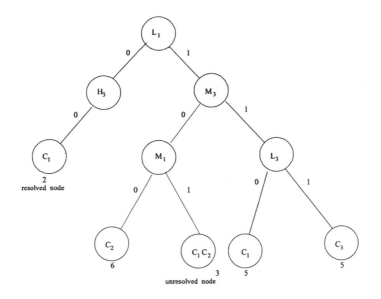

Fig. 5.8 Sample decision tree for rule generation.

3. $L_1 \wedge \overline{M}_3 \wedge M_1 \rightarrow C_1, C_2; 3,$

4. $L_1 \wedge M_3 \wedge \overline{L}_3 \rightarrow C_1; 5,$

5. $L_1 \wedge M_3 \wedge L_3 \rightarrow C_3; 5.$

5.6.2.2 Quantitative measures for rule evaluation The quantitative indices accuracy, user's accuracy, kappa, and confusion, as explained in Section 2.4.2 with reference to ANNs, are used for evaluating the extracted rules. A new measure to estimate the coverage of these rules is designed in the context of decision trees [12].

DEFINITION 5.6.2 **Coverage** *is defined as the ratio between the total number of patterns associated with the rules corresponding to resolved leaf nodes, and the total number of patterns in all the rules and hence the terminal (resolved and/or unresolved) nodes.*

When the rules can perfectly classify all the patterns, then coverage is 1, and when they cannot classify any pattern, then it is 0.

5.6.2.3 Example 7: For example, from Fig. 5.8 we have

$$Coverage = \frac{2+6+5+5}{2+6+3+5+5} = \frac{18}{21}.$$

5.6.3   Mapping of rules to fuzzy neural network

In this section we describe the mapping of the extracted rules to generate an optimal fuzzy knowledge-based neural network. The $3n$-dimensional input vector of Eq. (5.18) is clamped at the input layer to the input nodes $[y_1^0, y_2^0, \ldots, y_{3n}^0]$. Here $y_1^0, \ldots, y_{3n}^0$ refer to the activation values of the $3n$ neurons in the input layer of the network depicted in Fig. 2.3. The l-dimensional output vector, in terms of class membership values (μ) of patterns [Eq. (5.23)], is clamped at the l nodes in the output layer of the MLP. During training, the weights are updated by backpropagating errors with respect to these membership values such that the contribution of uncertain or ambiguous pattern vectors is automatically reduced.

Let r_{ki} be the ith rule for class C_k with frequency f'_{ki}. Each rule is mapped using a single hidden node, modeling the conjunct, that connects the attributes corresponding to the appropriate pattern class. Therefore, one generates at least l hidden nodes in a single hidden layer for an l-class problem. For simplicity, rules involving only one class (pertaining to leaves) are selected and those corresponding to unresolved nodes of the decision tree are discarded. If there are two rules for a single class C_k, then that rule with the highest frequency is considered. Hence we use only l hidden nodes to model l classes. This constraint can of course be relaxed to incorporate other rules, albeit at the cost of increasing the size and computational complexity of the resultant network.

5.6.3.1 Example 8:   The sample rules generated from Fig. 5.8 thus reduce to

1. $L_1 \wedge \overline{M}_3 \wedge \overline{M}_1 \rightarrow C_2; 6,$

2. $L_1 \wedge M_3 \wedge \overline{L}_3 \rightarrow C_1; 5,$

3. $L_1 \wedge M_3 \wedge L_3 \rightarrow C_3; 5.$

5.6.3.2 Network encoding   These rules are used to initially encode an MLP, which then learns in the presence of training data. It is to be noted that these rules just serve as representatives, describing the major characteristics of the pattern classes, and as the starting point of the MLP for further learning. Therefore, the representative rulebase need not be too detailed or accurate; rather, a crude knowledge is sufficient to initiate the training procedure. This is the reason for sacrificing accuracy at the expense of simplicity at the decision tree level, by pruning the nodes and limiting the size of the extracted rulebase. The generalization aspect and other intricacies of the decision boundary are handled after the network mapping phase, during neural learning.

The weight w_{ki}^1, between output node k (class C_k) and hidden node i (rule r_{ki}) is set at $W = \dfrac{f'_{ki}}{\sum_k f'_{ki}}$ where $f'_{ki} = 1$. This indicates the importance of this rule among all other rules determining the whole network. The scheme for mapping weight $w_{ia_j}^0$ between attribute a_j (L_j or M_j or H_j) and hidden

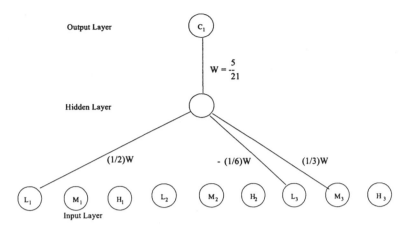

Fig. 5.9 Weight encoding scheme.

node i depends on the importance of feature a_j in the corresponding decision tree. Consider Fig. 5.8. We note from sample rule (2) that the attributes are selected in the order L_1, M_3, L_3 for class C_1. So the weight $w^0_{i a_j}$ is assigned a value $\frac{2[Card(r_{ki})-j+1]}{Card(r_{ki})[Card(r_{ki})+1]} * W$, where $Card(r_{ki})$ indicates the number of features or attributes encountered along the traversal path from the root to the leaf containing the corresponding pattern. In other words, $Card(r_{ki})$ is the number of operands in the conjunct of rule r_{ki} for class C_k. It is to be noted that

$$\sum_{i=1}^{Card(r_{ki})} \left| \frac{2[Card(r_{ki})-j+1]}{Card(r_{ki})[Card(r_{ki})+1]} \right| * W = W. \qquad (5.36)$$

5.6.3.3 *Example 9:* An example illustrating this scheme is provided in Fig. 5.9 for class C_1. Sequentially, for $j = 1, 2, 3$, we obtain

$$w^0_{1L_1} = \frac{2[3-1+1]}{3[3+1]} * W = \frac{1}{2}W,$$

$$w^0_{1M_3} = \frac{2[3-2+1]}{3[3+1]} * W = \frac{1}{3}W$$

and

$$w^0_{1\overline{L}_3} = \frac{2[3-3+1]}{3[3+1]} * W = -\frac{1}{6}W.$$

Here the negative sign in the last expression takes care of the negation of the corresponding attribute L_3.

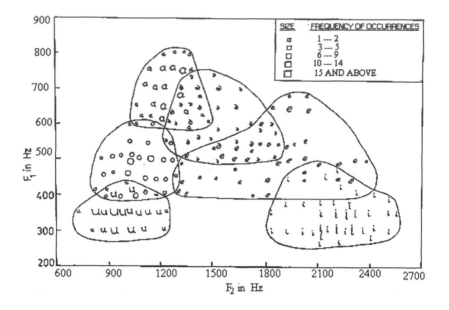

SIZE	FREQUENCY OF OCCURRENCES
▫	1 --- 2
▫	3 --- 5
▫	6 --- 9
▫	10 --- 14
▫	15 AND ABOVE

Fig. 5.10   Vowel diagram in F_1–F_2 plane.

5.6.4   Results

The system was implemented on benchmark datasets, the detailed results of which are available in Ref. [12]. Different sizes of training sets were selected at random, and in each case the remaining data were kept aside as the test set. All results were averaged over 40 runs. The threshold t for pruning a node of the decision tree was set at 0.2 after several experiments.

In this section we provide sample results on two datasets, namely, *Vowel* and *Balance scale*. The *Vowel* data consists of a set of 871 Indian Telugu vowel sounds [47], uttered by three male speakers in the age group of 30 to 35 years, in a Consonant–Vowel–Consonant context. The three features F_1, F_2, and F_3 correspond to the first, second, and third vowel formant frequencies obtained through spectrum analysis of the speech data. Figure 5.10 shows a 2D projection of the 3D feature space of the six vowel classes ∂, a, i, u, e, o in the F_1–F_2 plane, for ease of depiction. The boundaries of the classes in the given data set are ill-defined (fuzzy).

The *Balance scale* data [50] consists of 625 instances generated to model psychological experimental results. There are four numeric attributes corresponding to the *left weight, left distance, right weight,* and *right distance*, and there are three output classes, namely, *tip right, tip left,* and *balanced*.

The fuzzy ID3 (Table 5.8) is used, for the different fuzzy measures involving *cases a to f*, to extract rules that are then quantitatively evaluated (Tables 5.9 and 5.10). These are then used for generating fuzzy knowledge-

Table 5.8 Performance of fuzzy ID3

Case	Train set (%)	Vowel		T	Balance scale		T
		Recognition score (%)			Recognition score (%)		
		Training	Testing		Training	Testing	
a	10	81.1	72.8	.70	89.8	79.4	.81
	20	77.6	71.9	.69	86.0	80.7	.78
	30	75.9	72.6	.68	83.2	80.9	.78
	40	74.7	71.0	.67	84.1	81.1	.78
	50	74.9	73.1	.67	81.9	79.8	.76
b	10	77.2	70.7	.53	92.4	80.2	.52
	20	73.5	68.8	.53	85.6	76.9	.52
	30	69.9	64.5	.53	79.7	76.6	.52
	40	65.6	62.8	.53	77.3	74.7	.52
	50	63.0	61.6	.53	74.3	70.9	.52
c	10	79.5	70.4	.70	90.1	75.2	.52
	20	76.1	70.0	.69	84.5	76.0	.52
	30	74.8	70.4	.70	80.6	75.9	.52
	40	74.1	70.6	.69	76.1	73.9	.52
	50	73.2	73.1	.67	75.1	71.7	.52
d	10	79.0	70.3	.71	89.8	77.6	.52
	20	76.3	71.5	.71	85.2	76.4	.52
	30	74.2	70.3	.69	78.9	75.9	.52
	40	74.5	71.1	.69	76.6	74.1	.52
	50	74.1	70.3	.69	73.0	72.4	.52
e	10	66.0	63.6	.64	71.1	65.4	.75
	20	61.3	64.5	.61	64.7	67.5	.71
	30	58.1	62.3	.60	69.8	68.7	.70
	40	58.9	60.4	.60	68.5	67.0	.68
	50	58.8	60.7	.60	69.2	68.5	.69
f	10	63.3	52.7	.64	71.0	63.8	.75
	20	57.7	51.4	.61	65.7	68.1	.72
	30	57.1	48.1	.60	69.6	68.8	.72
	40	57.2	48.4	.60	69.0	69.1	.70
	50	56.5	44.5	.59	72.7	68.2	.70

Table 5.9   Quantitative measures for evaluating rules in *Vowel* data

Case	Train set (%)	Accuracy (%)	User's accuracy (%)	Kappa	Confusion	Coverage
	10	63.20	72.67	0.67	2.30	0.80
	20	62.70	73.15	0.67	2.37	0.78
a	30	59.74	75.47	0.70	2.37	0.72
	40	59.62	77.14	0.72	2.20	0.73
	50	60.06	75.40	0.70	2.34	0.75
	10	60.33	71.45	0.65	2.54	0.76
	20	60.14	73.58	0.67	2.24	0.79
b	30	60.52	77.63	0.72	2.26	0.73
	40	59.46	79.36	0.75	2.38	0.69
	50	60.18	80.65	0.77	2.06	0.72
	10	70.81	87.14	0.85	1.78	0.78
	20	66.90	84.66	0.81	2.04	0.75
c	30	65.59	84.08	0.81	2.37	0.75
	40	62.62	84.20	0.81	2.32	0.72
	50	60.92	83.00	0.80	2.14	0.70
	10	71.55	86.45	0.83	1.84	0.77
	20	65.26	84.80	0.82	2.07	0.74
d	30	62.04	81.42	0.78	2.27	0.72
	40	62.22	82.82	0.80	2.26	0.71
	50	59.22	83.22	0.80	2.20	0.68
	10	60.69	77.22	0.72	2.19	0.71
	20	59.70	71.80	0.67	1.89	0.60
e	30	53.59	74.64	0.70	1.93	0.54
	40	53.39	73.95	0.69	1.99	0.52
	50	53.27	72.71	0.68	1.92	0.52
	10	60.36	63.00	0.57	2.13	0.73
	20	57.15	66.00	0.60	2.29	0.60
f	30	57.10	66.00	0.61	2.11	0.54
	40	55.72	67.00	0.61	1.97	0.50
	50	55.67	67.00	0.61	2.16	0.47

Table 5.10 Quantitative measures for evaluating rules in *Balance* data

Case	Train set (%)	Accuracy (%)	User's accuracy (%)	Kappa	Confusion	Coverage
	10	84.76	91.72	0.87	1.73	0.92
	20	78.80	89.93	0.85	1.65	0.86
a	30	75.48	88.93	0.83	1.80	0.83
	40	76.26	89.15	0.84	1.85	0.84
	50	73.44	88.62	0.84	1.77	0.80
	10	86.13	97.41	0.96	2.38	0.88
	20	77.06	98.47	0.97	2.62	0.77
b	30	70.13	99.75	1.00	2.93	0.70
	40	66.04	99.60	0.99	2.92	0.66
	50	62.34	100.00	1.00	3.00	0.62
	10	81.78	89.37	0.83	1.78	0.90
	20	77.04	90.34	0.85	1.68	0.84
c	30	73.96	88.70	0.83	1.75	0.81
	40	74.14	87.71	0.81	1.58	0.82
	50	73.37	85.98	0.79	1.68	0.83
	10	73.94	87.01	0.81	1.52	0.82
	20	77.12	89.68	0.84	1.68	0.84
d	30	74.52	87.98	0.81	1.60	0.82
	40	74.10	88.65	0.84	1.70	0.81
	50	73.94	87.01	0.81	1.52	0.82
	10	67.51	71.78	0.53	1.36	0.91
	20	78.92	88.45	0.82	1.70	0.87
e	30	75.59	89.20	0.84	1.75	0.83
	40	74.68	87.90	0.83	1.77	0.83
	50	74.36	87.30	0.82	1.80	0.83
	10	78.00	89.08	0.83	1.72	0.85
	20	77.49	88.34	0.83	1.70	0.86
f	30	75.86	88.42	0.83	1.70	0.84
	40	73.17	88.18	0.83	1.82	0.80
	50	67.51	71.78	0.53	1.36	0.91

based network (Table 5.11). The classification performance is provided for all three stages. Generally the knowledge-based networks result in better performance, in terms of network size and recognition scores. This is natural since the crude domain knowledge is encoded and further refined here, in the presence of training data.

Table 5.11 Performance of knowledge encoded MLP

Dataset	Model	Train set (%)	Recognition scores (%)		No. of links	No. of cycles
			Training	Testing		
Vowel	MLP	10	93.3	78.9	90.5	242
		20	87.5	79.6	91.2	203
		30	82.6	79.4	91.4	106
		40	76.8	77.6	91.8	27
	Knowledge-encoded MLP	10	88.7	78.5	63.6	102
		20	86.0	80.3	68.3	50
		30	82.9	80.2	66.5	35
		40	80.8	79.0	64.2	25
Balance scale	MLP	10	98.3	82.8	46.2	309
		20	91.8	87.5	47.8	331
		30	91.8	87.8	48.4	307
		40	91.3	88.6	47.1	312
	Knowledge-encoded MLP	10	94.8	82.7	39.4	277
		20	91.9	87.3	37.0	272
		30	91.3	89.1	35.7	252
		40	90.0	88.9	38.8	247

Knowledge encoding using linguistic rules extracted from the fuzzy decision tree generally enhances the performance of the knowledge-based system in terms of both network compactness and recognition scores. It is typically observed that the value of T decreases with an increase in size of the training data. This is because an increase in training set size leads to the consideration of a larger number of both noisy and good samples during the decision tree generation. The former influences the formation of a tree of greater depth, with an increased possibility of larger number of unresolved nodes, leading to a lower value of T.

5.7 CONCLUSIONS AND DISCUSSION

In this chapter we have described classification from the perspective of data mining. Different decision tree classifiers have been presented, followed by statistical models like the Bayesian classifier. Next we dealt with Instance-based learners – like the minimum distance classifier, nearest-neighbor classifier, radial basis function, and case-based reasoning – and the Support Vector Machine. Finally, fuzzy decision trees are described.

Greedy splitting heuristics are efficient and adequate for most decision tree applications, but are essentially suboptimal. Crisp decisions that the trees usually output may not be adequate or useful in some settings. Therefore, sometimes results from multiple decision trees are combined to improve upon generalization accuracy. Current research issues involved with decision trees include (i) multiple splits on continuous attributes, using multi-interval discretization of continuous attributes [51], (ii) multi-attribute tests on nodes to handle correlated attributes, using multivariate linear splits as in oblique trees [1], (iii) methods of handling missing values, by either assuming the majority value, or taking the most probable path, (iv) allowing varying costs for different attributes, and (v) generation of *optimal* trees.

The design of a fuzzy knowledge-based network, based on linguistic rules extracted from a fuzzy decision tree [12], has also been described. Its major contributions include: (a) developing a new scheme for automatic linguistic discretization of continuous attributes using quantiles, (b) introducing the novel concept of a quantitative measure T to evaluate the goodness of the decision tree, in terms of its compactness and performance, (c) evaluating quantitatively the extracted linguistic rules with some new indices, (d) mapping the linguistic rules to a fuzzy knowledge-based network, incorporating frequency of samples and depth of attributes in the decision tree, and (e) using new fuzziness measures at the node level of the tree, to handle overlapping classes.

In this soft computing framework we integrate the generic merits of decision trees, like efficient exploration of large data, along with the uncertainty handling capability of fuzzy sets. It enhances the understandability of a decision by providing rules in linguistic form. Thereby, it improves the human–machine interaction in a system.

In the following chapter we move on to another major function of data mining, namely, unsupervised learning or clustering.

REFERENCES

1. S. K. Murthy, "Automatic construction of decision trees from data: A multi-disciplinary survey," *Data Mining and Knowledge Discovery*, vol. 2, pp. 345–389, 1998.

2. J. R. Quinlan, "Induction on decision trees," *Machine Learning*, vol. 1, pp. 81–106, 1986.

3. S. Rasoul Safavian and D. Landgrebe, "A survey of decision tree classifier methodology," *IEEE Transactions on Systems, Man, and Cybernetics*, vol. 21, pp. 660–674, 1991.

4. L. Breiman, J. H. Friedman, R. A. Olshen, and C. J. Stone, *Classification and Regression Trees.* Monterey, CA: Wadsworth and Brooks/Cole, 1984.

5. J. R. Quinlan, *C4.5: Programs for Machine Learning.* San Mateo, CA: Morgan Kaufmann, 1993.

6. J. Han and M. Kamber, *Data Mining: Concepts and Techniques.* San Diego: Academic Press, 2001.

7. S. Haykin, *Neural Networks: A Comprehensive Foundation.* New York: Macmillan College Publishing Co., 1994.

8. J. T. Tou and R. C. Gonzalez, *Pattern Recognition Principles.* London: Addison-Wesley, 1974.

9. J. L. Kolodner, *Case-Based Reasoning.* San Mateo: Morgan Kaufmann, 1993.

10. V. Vapnik, *Statistical Learning Theory.* New York: John Wiley & Sons, 1998.

11. P. K. Singal, S. Mitra, and S. K. Pal, "Incorporation of fuzziness in ID3 and generation of network architecture," *Neural Computing and Applications,* vol. 10, pp. 155–164, 2001.

12. S. Mitra, K. M. Konwar, and S. K. Pal, "Fuzzy decision tree, linguistic rules and fuzzy knowledge-based network: Generation and evaluation," *IEEE Transactions on Systems, Man, and Cybernetics, Part C: Applications and Reviews,* vol. 32, pp. 328–339, 2002.

13. M. Mehta, R. Agrawal, and J. Rissanen, "SLIQ: A fast scalable classifier for data mining," in *Proceedings of 1996 International Conference on Extending Database Technology (EDBT '96)* (Avignon, France), March 1996.

14. J. Shafer, R. Agrawal, and M. Mehta, "SPRINT: A scalable parallel classifier for data mining," in *Proceedings of 1996 International Conference on Very Large Data Bases (VLDB '96)* (Bombay, India), pp. 544–555, September 1996.

15. T. Fukuda, Y. Morimoto, S. Morishita, and T. Tokuyama, "Data mining using two-dimensional optimized association rules: Scheme, algorithms, and visualization," in *Proceedings of 1996 ACM-SIGMOD International Conference on Management of Data (SIGMOD '96)* (Montreal, Canada), pp. 13–23, June 1996.

16. J. Gehrke, R. Ramakrishnan, and V. Ganti, "RainForest–A framework for fast decision tree construction of large datasets," *Data Mining and Knowledge Discovery,* vol. 4, pp. 127–162, 2000.

17. J. Mingers, "An empirical comparison of pruning methods for decision-tree induction," *Machine Learning*, vol. 4, pp. 227–243, 1989.

18. R. O. Duda and P. E. Hart, *Pattern Classification and Scene Analysis*. New York: John Wiley & Sons, 1973.

19. R. Rastogi and K. Shim, "PUBLIC: A decision tree classifier that integrates building and pruning," *Data Mining and Knowledge Discovery*, vol. 4, pp. 315–344, 2000.

20. B. D. Ripley, *Pattern Recognition and Neural Networks*. New York: Cambridge University Press, 1996.

21. H. J. Lu, R. Setiono, and H. Liu, "Effective data mining using neural networks," *IEEE Transactions on Knowledge and Data Engineering*, vol. 8, pp. 957–961, 1996.

22. I. K. Sethi, "Entropy nets: from decision trees to neural networks," *Proceedings of the IEEE*, vol. 78, pp. 1605–1613, 1990.

23. I. Ivanova and M. Kubat, "Initialization of neural networks by means of decision trees," *Knowledge-Based Systems*, vol. 8, pp. 333–344, 1995.

24. R. Setiono and H. Liu, "A connectionist approach to generating oblique decision trees," *IEEE Transactions on Systems, Man, and Cybernetics, Part B: Cybernetics*, vol. 29, pp. 440–444, 1999.

25. L. M. Fu, "Knowledge-based connectionism for revising domain theories," *IEEE Transactions on Systems, Man, and Cybernetics*, vol. 23, pp. 173–182, 1993.

26. G. G. Towell and J. W. Shavlik, "Knowledge-based artificial neural networks," *Artificial Intelligence*, vol. 70, pp. 119–165, 1994.

27. P. A. Devijver and J. Kittler, eds., *Pattern Recognition Theory and Applications*. Berlin: Springer-Verlag, 1987.

28. J. Pearl, "Fusion, propagation and structuring in belief networks," *Artificial Intelligence*, vol. 29, pp. 241–288, 1986.

29. D. W. Aha, D. Kibler, and M. K. Albert, "Instance-based learning algorithms," *Machine Learning*, vol. 6, pp. 37–66, 1991.

30. L. A. Zadeh, "Toward a theory of fuzzy information granulation and its centrality in human reasoning and fuzzy logic," *Fuzzy Sets and Systems*, vol. 19, pp. 111–127, 1997.

31. S. K. Pal and P. Mitra, "Case generation using rough sets with fuzzy representation," *IEEE Transactions on Knowledge and Data Engineering*.

32. C. J. C. Burges, "A tutorial on support vector machines for pattern recognition," *Data Mining and Knowledge Discovery*, vol. 2, pp. 1–47, 1998.

33. P. S. Bradley and O. L. Mangasarian, "Massive data discrimination via linear support vector machines," *Optimization Methods and Software*, vol. 13, pp. 1–10, 2000.

34. D. Cohn, L. Atlas, and R. Ladner, "Improving generalization with active learning," *Machine Learning*, vol. 15, pp. 201–221, 1994.

35. S. Tong and D. Koller, "Support vector machine active learning with application to text classification," *Journal of Machine Learning Research*, vol. 2, pp. 45–66, 2001.

36. C. Z. Janikow, "Fuzzy decision trees: Issues and methods," *IEEE Transactions on Systems, Man, and Cybernetics*, vol. 28, pp. 1–14, 1998.

37. H. Ichihashi, T. Shirai, K. Nagasaka, and T. Miyoshi, "Neuro fuzzy ID3: A method of inducing fuzzy decision trees with linear programming for maximizing entropy and algebraic methods," *Fuzzy Sets and Systems*, vol. 81, no. 1, pp. 157–167, 1996.

38. W. Xizhao and J. Hong, "On the handling of fuzziness for continuous-valued attributes in decision tree generation," *Fuzzy Sets and Systems*, vol. 99, pp. 283–290, 1998.

39. W. Pedrycz and A. Sosnowski, "Designing decision trees with the use of fuzzy granulation," *IEEE Transactions on Systems, Man, and Cybernetics - Part A*, vol. 30, pp. 151–159, 2000.

40. Y. Yuan and M. J. Shaw, "Induction of fuzzy decision trees," *Fuzzy Sets and Systems*, vol. 69, pp. 125–139, 1995.

41. X. Wang, B. Chen, G. Qian, and F. Ye, "On the optimization of fuzzy decision trees," *Fuzzy Sets and Systems*, vol. 112, pp. 117–125, 2000.

42. I. J. Chiang and J. Y. J. Hsu, "Integration of fuzzy classifiers with decision trees," in *Proceedings of Asian Fuzzy Systems Symposium*, pp. 266–271, 1996.

43. I. Hayashi, T. Maeda, A. Bastian, and L. C. Jain, "Generation of fuzzy decision trees by fuzzy ID3 with adjusting mechanism of AND/OR operators," in *Proceedings of International Conference on Fuzzy Systems (FUZZ-IEEE 98)*, pp. 681–685, 1998.

44. T. Kohonen, *Self-Organization and Associative Memory*. Berlin: Springer-Verlag, 1989.

45. S. Mitra, R. K. De, and S. K. Pal, "Knowledge-based fuzzy MLP for classification and rule generation," *IEEE Transactions on Neural Networks*, vol. 8, pp. 1338–1350, 1997.

46. M. Banerjee, S. Mitra, and S. K. Pal, "Rough fuzzy MLP: Knowledge encoding and classification," *IEEE Transactions on Neural Networks*, vol. 9, pp. 1203–1216, 1998.

47. S. K. Pal and S. Mitra, *Neuro-fuzzy Pattern Recognition: Methods in Soft Computing*. New York: John Wiley & Sons, 1999.

48. G. R. Davies and D. Yoder, *Business Statistics*. London: John Wiley & Sons, Inc., 1937.

49. Y. H. Pao, *Adaptive Pattern Recognition and Neural Networks*. Reading, MA: Addison-Wesley, 1989.

50. C. Blake and C. Merz, "UCI repository of machine learning databases," 1998. University of California, Irvine, Dept. of Information and Computer Sciences, *http://www.ics.uci.edu/~mlearn/MLRepository.html*.

51. U. Fayyad and K. Irani, "Multi-interval discretization of continuous-values attributes for classification learning," in *Proceedings of 13th International Joint Conference on Artificial Intelligence (IJCAI '93)* (Chambery, France), pp. 1022–1029, 1993.

6
Clustering in Data Mining

6.1 INTRODUCTION

Clustering is a useful technique for the discovery of some knowledge from a dataset. It maps a data item into one of several clusters, where clusters are natural groupings of data items based on similarity metrics or probability density models. Clustering pertains to unsupervised learning, when data with class labels are not available.

For example, when introducing a new product in the market, one groups or clusters the existing customers based on time series of payment history such that similar customers lie in the same cluster. The key requirement is the need for a good measure of similarity between the instances or patterns. This can help to identify micro-markets and develop separate policies for each. Analogously, one can group students of similar intelligence levels together so that efficient teaching strategies may be developed for each cluster.

The problem is to group N patterns into c desired clusters, such that the data points within clusters are more similar than across clusters. Some sample applications of clustering lie in customer segmentation, market basket customer analysis, attached mailing in direct marketing, and clustering of companies with similar growth.

Clustering is also very important in multimedia data mining, in order to cluster similar multimedia contents together for efficient indexing and storage in multimedia databases. For example, similar pictures can be clustered together for efficient indexing; thus, when a query is requested using a query image or image description, then all the similar images can be effectively retrieved.

Clustering of data is broadly based on two approaches, namely, hierarchical and partitive [1, 2]. In partitional algorithms, the goal is to find a partition of c clusters that optimizes the chosen partitioning criterion. If a global optimality is desired, then one needs to exhaustively enumerate all partitions. Heuristic methods like the c-means and c-medoids have been designed to circumvent this problem. In the c-means algorithm [3], each cluster is represented by the center of gravity of the cluster. This need not essentially correspond to an object of the given pattern set. In the c-medoids algorithm [4], on the other hand, each cluster is represented by one of the representative objects in the cluster located near the center. A few variants of the c-means algorithm differ in (i) the selection of the initial c means, (ii) dissimilarity calculations, and (iii) strategies to calculate the cluster means.

Partitioning Around Medoids (PAM) [4] starts from an initial set of medoids, and it iteratively replaces one of the medoids by one of the nonmedoids if it improves the total distance of the resulting clustering. Although PAM works effectively for small data, it does not scale well for large datasets. The algorithms CLARA [4], CLARANS [5] (using randomized sampling), and the focusing technique for spatial data structures [6] are capable of dealing with the scalability issue.

Hierarchical methods can again be categorized as *agglomerative* and *divisive* algorithms, corresponding to bottom-up and top-down strategies, to build a hierarchical clustering tree (*dendogram*). The optimal number of clusters is usually determined based on a validation index. There exist several clustering algorithms and validation indices in literature [1, 7], but they conventionally deal with numerical or quantitative data.

One of the major challenges to data mining [8, 9] is handling of *mixed media data*. This implies learning from data that is represented by a combination of various media, like (say) numeric, symbolic, images, text, etc. Symbolic or categorical clustering refers to the clustering of symbolic or categorical data. This is important from the point of view of data mining, where one has to mine for information from a set of symbolic objects. These objects are defined by attributes that can be quantitative (numeric or intervals) as well as qualitative. The similarity and dissimilarity measures between symbolic objects are often determined based on their position, span, and content features [10, 11].

Conceptual clustering [12, 13], from the Machine Learning community, is also applicable to a mixture of numeric, ordinal, and symbolic data. Here the focus is on interpretability or meaningfulness of the generated patterns, so that objects are clustered according to the concepts that they carry. The algorithm preserves cohesiveness within clusters while maintaining clear distinctness between clusters. Nonparametric probabilistic measures are used to determine the groupings.

This chapter is organized as follows. Section 6.2 elucidates the different distance measures and the concept of symbolic objects. The conventional clustering categories are described in Section 6.3. The scalable versions of clustering algorithms, suitable for large data, are provided in Section 6.4. Soft computing-based approaches are dealt with in Section 6.5. Clustering with categorical attributes and symbolic clustering are described in Sections 6.6 and 6.7, respectively. Section 6.8 concludes the chapter.

6.2 DISTANCE MEASURES AND SYMBOLIC OBJECTS

Before moving on to clustering methodologies, let us explain what distance between a pair of objects refers to. In the context of mixed media data, the distance cannot be constrained to the numeric domain. Hence we need to compute distances between binary, nominal, and symbolic objects as well. The‚similarity measure and distance computation is also an integral part of multimedia data indexing, retrieval, and data mining techniques.

6.2.1 Numeric objects

Distances are normally used to measure the similarity or dissimilarity between two data objects X_i and X_j. The larger the similarity, the smaller the dissimilarity and hence the smaller the distance between the pair of objects. In the numeric domain, a popular measure is the Minkowski distance. It is defined as

$$d(X_i, X_j) = (|X_{i_1} - X_{j_1}|^q + (|X_{i_2} - X_{j_2}|^q + \cdots + (|X_{i_n} - X_{j_n}|^q)^{\frac{1}{q}}, \quad (6.1)$$

where q is a positive integer and n is the number of attributes involved. If $q = 1$, then d is termed *Manhattan* distance, while for $q = 2$ it is called the *Euclidean* distance. One can also use weighted distance or other dissimilarity measures [14].

6.2.2 Binary objects

In case of every pair of binary objects, a contingency table is designed. This is depicted in Table 6.1. Let there be two objects, such that location (1,1) of the 2×2 matrix denotes the number of features for which both take on values one. Analogously, location (2,2) corresponds to the number of features for which both X_i and X_j have values zero. Here b, c correspond to the occasions when the values of X_i and X_j mismatch.

The *simple matching coefficient* is used if the binary variable is symmetric. For example, in case of attribute gender, both states *female* and *male* are equally valuable and carry the same weight. Here the distance is invariant and is measured as

$$d(X_i, X_j) = \frac{b + c}{a + b + c + d}. \quad (6.2)$$

Table 6.1 Contingency table for binary variables

	X_j		
X_i	1	0	Sum
1	a	b	$a+b$
0	c	d	$c+d$
Sum	$a+c$	$b+d$	n

When the binary variable is asymmetric, the *Jaccard coefficient* is used. For example, the positive outcome of a disease test is considered more important than a negative outcome. Here the negative match of two zeros (corresponding to d in Table 6.1) is ignored. The measure is noninvariant and is defined as

$$d(X_i, X_j) = \frac{b+c}{a+b+c}. \tag{6.3}$$

6.2.2.1 Example 1: Let us consider an example to illustrate the process using Table 6.2. Let Sam, Mita, and Harry be three objects whose attributes correspond to their gender, symptoms (temperature, cold), and results of four tests. Here gender is a symmetric attribute, while the remaining are all asymmetric. Let the values Y and P be set to 1, and the value N be set to 0. (Here Y, P, and N correspond to symbolic outputs *yes, positive* and *negative*, respectively.) Considering only the asymmetric attributes, using Eq. (6.3), we have

$$d(Sam, Mita) = \frac{0+1}{2+0+1} = 0.33,$$

$$d(Sam, Harry) = \frac{1+1}{1+1+1} = 0.67,$$

and

$$d(Harry, Mita) = \frac{1+2}{1+1+2} = 0.75.$$

Table 6.2 Example to compute distance between binary objects

Name	Gender	Temperature	Cold	Test 1	Test 2	Test 3	Test 4
Sam	M	Y	N	P	N	N	N
Mita	F	Y	N	P	N	P	N
Harry	M	Y	P	N	N	N	N

6.2.3 Categorical objects

Nominal (or categorical) variables are a generalization of binary variables, in that each can take up more than two states. For example, color can be {red, yellow, blue, green}. One can use simple matching, considering p to be the total number of features and m to be the number of matches where X_i and X_j have the same state. Then using Eq. (6.2) we have

$$d(X_i, X_j) = \frac{p - m}{p}. \tag{6.4}$$

Another option would be to use a large number of binary variables, creating a new binary variable for each of the M nominal states.

There can be other types of variables as well. An ordinal variable can be discrete or continuous but, unlike nominal variables, here the order is important. An example of such a variable is rank. An interval variable specifies a lower and upper limit, between which its value lies. Variables can also be of mixed types, where a database may contain a mixture of numeric, symmetric binary, asymmetric binary, nominal, ordinal, and interval variables.

6.2.4 Symbolic objects

Let us now describe *symbolic* objects and the different dissimilarity measures, expressed as the distance between them. Symbolic objects are defined as the logical conjunction of events linking values and variables. The following are two examples of events: $e_1 = [\text{color} = \{\text{white, blue}\}]$, $e_2 = [\text{height} = [1.5\text{-}2.0]]$. Here e_1 indicates that the variable color takes a value either white or blue, while e_2 indicates that the variable height takes a value in the interval between 1.5 and 2.0, that is, $1.5 \le height \le 2.0$. For simplicity, we can drop the variable name and only take the value of that feature variable. Two symbolic objects A and B are written as the Cartesian product of features A_k and B_k, represented by $A = A_1 \times \cdots \times A_n$ and $B = B_1 \times \cdots \times B_n$. Let O_k denote the domain of the kth feature. Then the feature space can be expressed as a Cartesian product $O^{(n)} = O_1 \times \cdots \times O_n$.

The dissimilarity between two symbolic objects A and B is defined in terms of their distance involving position D_p, span D_s, and content D_c components [10, 11]. We have

$$D_p(A_i, B_i) = \cos\left[\left(1 - \frac{|\text{lower limit of } A_i - \text{lower limit of } B_i|}{\text{length of maximum interval along feature } i}\right) * 90\right], \tag{6.5}$$

where the denominator indicates the difference between the highest and lowest values of the ith feature over all the objects. This measure holds for quantitative attributes only. The remaining two measures are defined for both quantitative and qualitative attributes.

$$D_s(A_i, B_i) = \cos \left[\frac{|\text{length of } A_i| + |\text{length of } B_i|}{2 * (\text{span length of } A_i \text{ and } B_i)} * 90 \right], \qquad (6.6)$$

where span length denotes the length of the minimum interval containing both A_i and B_i for quantitative values. The length of a qualitative feature value is the number of its elements, and the span length of two such feature values is the number of elements in their union.

$$D_c(A_i, B_i) = \cos \left[\frac{\text{length of intersection of } A_i \text{ and } B_i}{\text{span length of } A_i \text{ and } B_i} * 90 \right]. \qquad (6.7)$$

Hence the distance $D(A, B)$ becomes

$$D(A, B) = \sum_{i=1}^{n} D(A_i, B_i), \qquad (6.8)$$

where

$$D(A_i, B_i) = D_p(A_i, B_i) + D_s(A_i, B_i) + D_c(A_i, B_i)$$

with D_p, D_s, and D_c normalized to [0,1] as per Eqs. (6.5)–(6.7).

6.3   CLUSTERING CATEGORIES

Clustering consists of partitioning data into *homogeneous* granules or groups, based on some objective function that maximizes the intercluster distances while simultaneously minimizing the intracluster distances. Traditional clustering algorithms can be broadly categorized into two main types [3]. Partitive algorithms like c-means divides the patterns into a set of spherical clusters, while minimizing the objective function. Here the number of clusters is predefined. Hierarchical methods, on the other hand, can again be grouped as agglomerative and divisive. Here no assumption is made about the shape or number of clusters, and a validity index is used to determine termination.

6.3.1   Partitional clustering

It basically involves enumerating c partitions, optimizing some criterion, over t iterations. The most commonly used numeric distance function is the square error, defined as $\sum_{i=1}^{c} \sum_{\mathbf{X} \in U_i} ||\mathbf{X} - \mathbf{m}_i||^2$, where $\mathbf{m}_i$ is the mean of cluster U_i and $\mathbf{X}$ is the pattern vector (data object). The computational complexity of the algorithm is $O(N * c * t)$, where $c, t \ll N$. Generally, this works for well-separated, convex clusters. It is also scalable and efficient for large datasets. Even for very large databases, it is possible to work in a memory-efficient way with a small number of representatives and only periodic disk scans of the actual patterns.

Some of its drawbacks are as follows. It prefers splitting large clusters, and the gain from such splits can offset the merging of small clusters. A mean is not defined for categorical attributes and/or symbolic objects. Hence the algorithm cannot be used in applications involving categorical data, since it typically minimizes a cost function by changing the means of clusters. The algorithm is sensitive to noise and outliers, and it often terminates at a local optimum. The global optimum may, however, be found using techniques such as deterministic annealing and genetic algorithms. Finally, there is an inherent need to specify the value of c.

6.3.1.1 c-means algorithm The algorithm proceeds by partitioning the N objects into c nonempty subsets. During each partition, the centroids or means of the clusters are computed. The main steps of the c-means algorithm [3] are as follows:

- Assign initial means $\mathbf{m}_i$ (also called centroids).

- Assign each data object (pattern point) $\mathbf{X}_k$ to the cluster U_i for the closest mean.

- Compute new mean for each cluster using

$$\mathbf{m}_i = \frac{\sum_{\mathbf{X}_k \in U_i} \mathbf{X}_k}{|c_i|}, \tag{6.9}$$

where $|c_i|$ is the number of objects in cluster U_i.

- Iterate until the criterion function converges, that is, there are no more new assignments.

6.3.1.2 Example 2: Let us consider four two-dimensional samples $\mathbf{X}_1 = (1,1)$, $\mathbf{X}_2 = (2,2)$, $\mathbf{X}_3 = (3,8)$, $\mathbf{X}_4 = (4,8)$, to be clustered using $c = 2$. Let the first two patterns be chosen for initializing the means, as $\mathbf{m}_1 = (1,1)$ and $\mathbf{m}_2 = (2,2)$. The remaining two objects are assigned to U_2 based on their proximity to the closest mean. The cluster mean $\mathbf{m}_2$ then gets updated as

$$\mathbf{m}_2 = \left(\frac{2+3+4}{3}, \frac{2+8+8}{3} \right) = (3,6).$$

The second iteration causes the assignment of $\mathbf{X}_1$, $\mathbf{X}_2$ to cluster U_1 and $\mathbf{X}_3$, $\mathbf{X}_4$ to cluster U_2, with convergence to cluster means

$$\mathbf{m}_1 = \left(\frac{1+2}{2}, \frac{1+2}{2} \right) = (1.5, 1.5)$$

and

$$\mathbf{m}_2 = \left(\frac{3+4}{2}, \frac{8+8}{2} \right) = (3.5, 8).$$

6.3.1.3 Some variants Some of the variants of the conventional c-means algorithm are along the following lines.

1. Initial hierarchical clustering, followed by iterative relocation of patterns to the clusters.

2. ISODATA [3] employs splitting and merging operations on clusters, splitting if the sample variance in a cluster is more than a threshold while merging when the distance between the centroids of a pair of clusters is less than a threshold.

3. Instead of means, one could use c-modes (Section 6.6.3) to accommodate symbolic objects. This involves using new dissimilarity measures, and a frequency-based method to update modes of clusters.

4. Scalability of the algorithm is enhanced by retaining essential objects in main memory, while compressing or summarizing elements belonging to tight subclusters (using a clustering feature) and discarding redundant data. Hence large data are modeled only by the clustering feature and the retained objects in main memory.

6.3.1.4 Partitioning Around Medoids (PAM) The algorithm uses the most centrally located object in a cluster, the medoid, instead of the mean. Note that a medoid, unlike a mean, is essentially an existing data object from the cluster. It is closest to the corresponding mean. The basic steps are outlined as follows:

- Arbitrarily choose c objects as the initial medoids or seed points.

- Assign each remaining data object (pattern) to the cluster for the closest medoid.

- Replace each of the medoids by one of all the nonmedoids (causing the greatest reduction in square error), as long as the quality of clustering improves.

- Iterate until the criterion function converges.

For large N and c, the c-medoids [4] is computationally more costly than the conventional c-means. Here the computational complexity is $O((1 + \beta)c(N - c)^2)$, where β is the number of successful swaps (replacements). However, in the presence of noise and outliers, c-medoids is found to be more robust. This is because of the inherent robustness of medoids, as compared to means, with respect to noise. It is invariant to translations and orthogonal transformations of objects and is generally not influenced either by the order of presentation of objects or by the initial choice of seed points.

6.3.1.5 Example 3:   Let us compare the working of PAM to that of c-means on the sample two-dimensional clustering problem. At the end of the first iteration, the cluster medoids are computed as $\mathbf{m}_1 = (1,1)$ and $\mathbf{m}_2 = (3,8)$ [closest to the mean $(3,6)$].

6.3.1.6 Model-based clustering   These methods aim to optimize the match between the given data and some mathematical model. Here the data are often assumed to be generated from c probability distributions, typically Gaussian or *Normal* around the cluster centers. This can also be termed as the probabilistic version of c-means clustering. One needs, however, to find the distribution parameters.

Expectation Maximization (EM) [15] is a popular iterative refinement algorithm that belongs to the category of model-based clustering. It differs from the conventional c-means algorithm in that each pattern point belongs to a cluster according to some weight (probability of membership). In other words, there are no strict boundaries between clusters. New means are computed based on weighted measures. It provides a statistical model of the data and is capable of handling the associated uncertainties. The algorithm can be characterized as follows:

- Initialize c cluster centers.

- Iterate between the two steps.

  - Expectation step: Assign each data point $\mathbf{X}_i$ to the cluster U_k with probability

$$P(X_i \in U_k) = p(U_k|X_i) = \frac{p(U_k)p(X_i|U_k)}{p(X_i)}, \qquad (6.10)$$

    where $p(X_i|U_k) = N(m_k, E_k(X_i))$ follows the Normal distribution around mean $\mathbf{m}_k$ with expectation E_k.

  - Maximization step: Estimate model parameters

$$m_k = \frac{1}{N} \sum_{i=1}^{N} \frac{X_i P(X_i \in U_k)}{\sum_j P(X_i \in U_j)}. \qquad (6.11)$$

In practice the algorithm converges fast, but may not reach the global optima. Convergence is guaranteed for certain forms of optimization functions. The computational complexity is $O(c * N * n * t)$, where n is the number of input features.

6.3.2 Hierarchical clustering

This method creates hierarchical nested partitions of the dataset, using a tree-structured dendogram and some termination criterion. A matrix of similarity

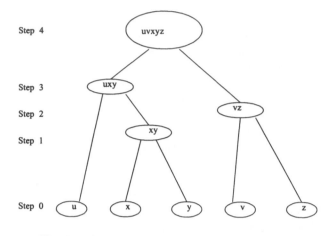

Fig. 6.1 A dendogram for hierarchical clustering.

or dissimilarity is provided between every pattern pair. The decomposition of the dendogram can be bottom-up, starting from individual data objects at the leaves as separate clusters and *agglomeratively* progressing upwards by merging the closest objects (or groups) into clusters. The top-down strategy, on the other hand, proceeds from a single cluster at the root and involves *divisive* splits while progressing down to the leaves. The merge or split decisions, if not properly made, may lead to low-quality clusters. Typically, the agglomerative strategy is more commonly used. However, in case of large databases, this method is not very practical since it scales at least quadratically with the number of data objects, that is, $O(N^2)$.

In agglomerative hierarchical clustering, the dendrogram shows how the clusters are merged hierarchically. A clustering of the data objects at any stage is obtained by cutting the dendrogram at the desired level, whereby each connected component in the tree corresponds to a cluster.

6.3.2.1 Example 4:   Let there be five data objects u, v, x, y, z. The dendogram of a hierarchical clustering, involving these objects, is depicted in Fig. 6.1. The merging of clusters proceeds in a sequence xy, vz, uxy, $uvxyz$ of four steps. The splitting for the divisive method would follow the reverse sequence. Although this method does not require the number of clusters c to be prespecified, it needs a termination condition.

6.3.2.2 Distance measure   Generally, the distance matrix is used as the clustering criterion. The algorithm repeatedly merges closest clusters until the number of clusters becomes c. The distance involved can be either of the following:

- $d_{mean}(U_i, U_j) = ||\mathbf{m}_i - \mathbf{m}_j||$ in the centroid approach, preferring break of large, nonhyperspherical clusters.

- $d_{\min}(U_i, U_j) = \min_{\mathbf{X} \in U_i, \mathbf{X'} \in U_j} ||\mathbf{X} - \mathbf{X'}||$ in the minimum spanning tree approach, which is sensitive to outliers and slight change in position.

Analogically, there can be $d_{average}(U_i, U_j)$ and $d_{\max}(U_i, U_j)$.

The merging can follow the *single linkage* strategy, which combines two clusters such that the minimum distance between two points $\mathbf{X}$, $\mathbf{X'}$ from two different clusters U_i, U_j is the least. The disadvantage includes confusion created by overlapping objects. *Complete linkage*, on the other hand, merges two clusters U_i, U_j when all points in one cluster are "close" to all points in the other. This method is, however, sensitive to outliers. Several other hierarchical merging strategies are reported in the literature [1].

6.3.3   Leader clustering

This is another approach that is found to be useful in data mining. The leader clustering algorithm [2] chooses a *leader* as a representative (center) of a cluster, such that it is also its member. The algorithm depends on a threshold value to determine whether an object is similar (close) enough to the leader in order to lie in the same partition. If the threshold (or tolerance) is large, then more objects are grouped into less numbers of clusters, and vice versa. The main steps of the leader clustering algorithm are outlined below.

1. Initialize threshold θ; initialize the first cluster center $\mathbf{m}_1$ by the first pattern. This is a leader.

2. **for** each of the remaining patterns $\mathbf{X}$ **repeat** steps 3–6.

3. Find nearest cluster U_i.

4. **if** distance $||\mathbf{X} - \mathbf{m}_i|| < \theta$ **then** go to step 5 **else** go to step 6.

5. Update cluster center $\mathbf{m}_i$.

6. Generate new cluster center (leader).

The algorithm involves a single database scan, and it is required to store only the leaders (or cluster centers). It is incremental and robust to outliers, but is dependent on the order of pattern presentation. Moreover, one does not need to prespecify the number of clusters c. The algorithm is found to be suitable for use in large data.

6.4   SCALABLE CLUSTERING ALGORITHMS

Scalable algorithms were designed mainly by the Database community for working on very large datasets. Here the time and space complexities of the algorithms are of utmost concern. The number of database scans required is a good indicator of the algorithm's feasibility. Often feature extraction becomes useful for visualization. One could proceed by using an incremental (on-line) clustering that generates cluster representatives in a single database scan. A divide-and-conquer strategy may be applied by clustering a part of the data at a time in the main memory, generating their representatives, and finally merging these for all blocks of the data.

Some of the popular scalable algorithms include CLARA and CLARANS (Partitional), DBSCAN (Density-based), BIRCH (Hierarchical or Leader), CLIQUE (Grid-based), and CURE (Hierarchical). They are described below in this section.

6.4.1   Clustering large applications

This encompasses partitional algorithms like CLARA [4] and CLARANS [5].

6.4.1.1   Clustering LARge Applications (CLARA)   Here PAM is used to choose medoids from multiple random samples of data, returning the best clustering as the output. The computational complexity is $O(cs^2 + c(N - c))$ for a sample size s. Note that CLARA [4] considers *selected* sample datasets for the medoids, while conventionally PAM searches for the best c medoids from the entire data. However, CLARA cannot find the best clustering if any sampled medoid is not among the best c medoids. This is the trade-off for efficiency. Moreover, if s is not large enough, the effectiveness is lower; and if s is too large, the efficiency is not good.

6.4.1.2   Clustering Large Applications based on RANdomized Search (CLARANS)
Unlike CLARA that is confined to a fixed sample initially chosen, CLARANS [5] draws a sample with some randomness at each stage of the search. Each cluster is represented by a medoid. Multiple scans of the database are required by the algorithm. Here the clustering process searches through a graph, where each node is represented by a set of c medoids. Two nodes are termed as neighbors if they only differ by one medoid. Hence each node has $c * (N - c)$ neighbors.

The main steps are as follows:

- Initially, a node of c medoids is chosen randomly.

- Replace one of the c medoids at random, by selecting a neighbor node randomly.

- Assign data objects (pattern points) to the cluster with the closest medoid, by calculating average distance for this node; this requires one scan of the database.

- **if** the criterion function does not improve **then** revert back to the old medoid (node); **else** set the current node to be the neighbor node.

- **repeat** for a fixed number of times.

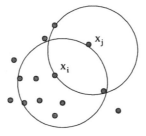

Fig. 6.2 Concept of density-reachable points.

CLARANS has been experimentally shown to be more effective than PAM and CLARA. It enables the detection of outliers. The computational complexity is $O(N^2)$. However the clustering quality is dependent on the sampling method used, and for large N the quality cannot be guaranteed.

6.4.2 Density-based clustering

This method clusters based on a local criterion such as density-connected points. The major features of the clustering include the abilities to (i) discover clusters of arbitrary shape and (ii) handle noise. The algorithm requires just one scan through the database. However, density parameters are needed for the termination condition. Some of the interesting studies in this direction are DBSCAN [16], OPTICS [17], DENCLUE [18], and CLIQUE [19].

Density-Based Spatial Clustering of Applications with Noise (DBSCAN) [16] discovers clusters of arbitrary shape in spatial databases in the presence of noise. The clusters are regarded as dense regions of objects in the data space, separated by regions of low density or noise. The objective is to determine the maximal set of *density-connected* points. The user is required to specify two parameters to define the minimum density. These are the ϵ-neighborhood (maximum radius) of an object and the minimum number of objects $MinPts$ within this. Let $MinPts = 5$ and $\epsilon = 1$ centimeter. Consider Fig. 6.2. A point $\mathbf{X}_i$ is directly *density-reachable* from a point $\mathbf{X}_j$ with respect to ϵ and $MinPts$, if

1. $\mathbf{X}_i$ belongs to $N_\epsilon(\mathbf{X}_j)$, that is, $d(\mathbf{X}_i, \mathbf{X}_j) \leq \epsilon$, where N_ϵ is called a neighborhood function and $N_\epsilon(\mathbf{X}_j)$ contains the points belonging to the neighborhood of $\mathbf{X}_j$, and

2. core point condition $|N_\epsilon(\mathbf{X}_j)| \geq MinPts$ holds.

A point $\mathbf{X}_i$ is density-reachable from a point $\mathbf{X}_j$ with respect to ϵ and $MinPts$ if there is a chain of points $\mathbf{X}_1, \ldots, \mathbf{X}_{N'}$, $\mathbf{X}_1 = \mathbf{X}_j$, $\mathbf{X}_{N'} = \mathbf{X}_i$ such that $\mathbf{X}_{k+1}$ is directly density-reachable from $\mathbf{X}_k$. A point $\mathbf{X}_i$ is density-connected to a point $\mathbf{X}_j$ with respect to ϵ and $MinPts$ if there is a point $\mathbf{X}_k$

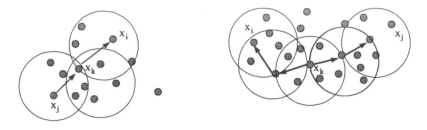

Fig. 6.3   Concept of density-connected points.

such that both $\mathbf{X}_i$ and $\mathbf{X}_j$ are density-reachable from $\mathbf{X}_k$ with respect to ϵ and *MinPts*. This is depicted in Fig. 6.3.

The algorithm is outlined as follows:

- Arbitrarily select a point $\mathbf{X}_i$.

- Retrieve all points density-reachable from $\mathbf{X}_i$ with respect to ϵ and *MinPts*.

- **if** $\mathbf{X}_i$ is a core point **then** a cluster is formed.

- **if** $\mathbf{X}_i$ is a border point **then** no points are density-reachable from $\mathbf{X}_i$ and DBSCAN visits the next data point of the database.

- **repeat** the process **until** all the data objects (pattern points) have been processed.

The computational complexity of the algorithm is $O(N \log N)$. Using spatial access methods, DBSCAN is found to be efficient even for very large spatial databases. A generalized version of the algorithm has been recently developed [20] to cluster point objects as well as spatially extended objects.

A parallel version of DBSCAN, called PDBSCAN, has also been reported [21]. The main program of PDBSCAN, the master, starts a clustering slave on each available computer in the network and distributes the whole dataset into partitions onto the slaves. Every slave concurrently clusters only its local data. The basic steps of the algorithm are as follows:

1. Divide the database DB into c partitions $S_1, S_2, \ldots, S_c$, such that $DB = \bigcup_{i=1}^{c} S_i$ and $S_i \cap S_j = \Phi$, for $i \neq j$. The partition S_i is distributed on slave computer C_i, where $i = 1, 2, \ldots, c$.

2. Process the c partitions concurrently using DBSCAN on the available computers $C_1, C_2, \ldots, C_c$.

3. Merge the clustering results obtained from the partitions $S_i, i = 1, 2, \ldots, c$, into a clustering result for DB.

Since the run-time of DBSCAN only depends on the size of the input data, the partitions should be almost of equal size if we assume all computers to have the same processing performance. Otherwise, the data may be distributed on computers according to their efficiency. In order to minimize communication costs, the nearby objects need to be organized on the same computer.

6.4.3 Hierarchical clustering

A major weakness of agglomerative clustering methods is that they do not scale well, the time complexity being at least $O(N^2)$ for N data objects. Moreover, they can never undo what was done in a previous step. Hence there have been integration of hierarchical with distance-based clustering, for suitably handling large datasets. These include (i) BIRCH [22], which uses a tree structure to store clustering features, and incrementally adjusts the quality of subclusters; (ii) CURE [23], which selects well-scattered points from the cluster and then shrinks them towards the center of the cluster by a specified fraction; and (iii) CHAMELEON [24], which performs hierarchical clustering using dynamic modeling.

6.4.3.1 Balanced Iterative Reducing and Clustering Using Hierarchies (BIRCH)
The algorithm [22] pre-clusters data points using a clustering feature tree (CF-tree). A CF-tree is height-balanced, storing the clustering features (CF) (summarized or condensed representations) for the application of a hierarchical clustering. The clustering feature is defined as

$$CF = (N, ls, ss),$$

where ls is the linear sum and ss is the square sum of N data points in a cluster or leaf.

The basic steps of the algorithm are as follows:
for each point

1. The CF-tree is traversed to find the closest cluster.

2. **if** the cluster is within a *threshold* **then** the point is absorbed into the cluster. The corresponding CF representation is updated.

3. Otherwise, the point starts a new cluster with its own CF representation (involving insertion and/or node split).

BIRCH requires only a single scan of the data, with the computational complexity being $O(N)$. The rebuilding process of the CF-tree is similar to insertion and node split of B+ trees. The algorithm is linearly scalable for large data and is capable of handling noise. The cluster summaries stored in the CF-tree are given to the hierarchical clustering algorithm for further processing. BIRCH can also be viewed as an extension of the leader algorithm (Section 6.3.3), since each point either is assigned to the cluster of the closest CF or is used to form a new cluster.

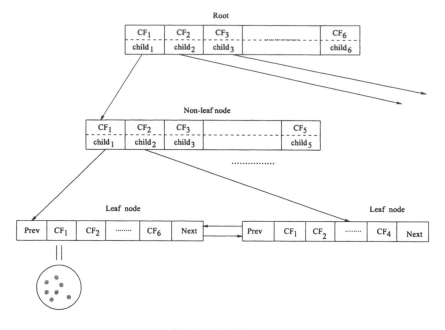

Fig. 6.4 A CF-tree.

However, it works for spherical clusters of uniform size and considers only limited available memory. The weakness of the algorithm is that it handles only numeric data and is sensitive to the order of the pattern point insertions.

6.4.3.2 Example 5: For example, let there be three points $(3, 4)$, $(2, 6)$, $(4, 5)$ in a cluster. Then we have the clustering feature of the corresponding node to be

$$CF = (3, (3+2+4, 4+6+5), (3^2+2^2+4^2, 4^2+6^2+5^2)) = (3, (9, 15), (29, 77)).$$

The non-leaf nodes store sums of the CFs of their children. The parameters involved are the branching factor (maximum number of children per non-leaf node) and the threshold (maximum diameter of cluster stored at leaf node). Figure 6.4 depicts a CF-tree.

6.4.3.3 Clustering Using Representatives (CURE) Hierarchical clustering of large data typically uses a small number of representatives to represent a cluster. If it is centroid-based, then only one point is used. This involves too little information and can result in hyperspherical clusters. In a representative-object-based (minimum spanning tree) approach, on the other hand, one uses every point to represent a cluster. This involves too much information and can often be misleading.

CURE [23] uses a random sampling of original objects. A partitioning of the samples is made, followed by correct labeling. A small number of scattered representative points k are chosen. These are distributed over the cluster, such that each point in the cluster is close to one representative and the distance between clusters is the smallest distance between the representatives. This enables the capturing of the physical shape and geometry of the cluster. Farthest point heuristic is used to scatter the points over the cluster, and this is followed by shrinking it uniformly around its mean to dampen the effects of outliers. Availability of more than one representative point per cluster enables handling of nonspherical shapes. The algorithm is scalable for large databases, with a computational complexity of $O(N)$.

6.4.4 Grid-based methods

Grid-based clustering quantizes the pattern space into a finite number of cells, which form a multiresolution grid structure on which the operations are performed. These algorithms typically involve fast processing time since they are dependent only on the number of cells in each dimension of the quantized space and are typically independent of the number of actual data objects. This category of clustering algorithms encompasses STING [25] and CLIQUE [19].

6.4.4.1 Statistical Information Grid-based method (STING) The algorithm STING [25] divides the spatial area into rectangular cells using hierarchical structure, storing the statistical parameters of each numeric feature of the objects (like maximum, minimum, mean, etc.) within the cells. There are usually several levels of rectangular cells corresponding to different levels of resolution, each cell at a higher level being partitioned to form a number of cells at the next lower level in a top-down approach. The complexity of cluster generation is $O(N)$, while the complexity of response time of a query is $O(g)$, where $g << N$ is the number of grid cells at the lowest level.

The quality of clustering depends on the granularity at the lowest level of the grid structure: A finer granularity leads to an increased processing cost. The spatial relationship between neighboring cells at a particular level is not, however, considered in the hierarchy. This results in an isothetic shape of resulting clusters, with only horizontal and vertical cluster boundaries, such that no diagonal boundary can be detected.

6.4.4.2 Clustering In QUEst (CLIQUE) The algorithm CLIQUE [19] integrates density-based and grid-based clustering methods. It is scalable to high-dimensional data in large databases. The algorithm is insensitive to the order of input tuples and does not presume any data distribution. However, accuracy may be degraded at the expense of its simplicity.

The algorithm finds clusters in all (nonoverlapping, rectangular) subspaces of the original pattern space. A unit in n-dimensions is defined as an intersection of one interval from each dimension. A cluster is expressed as a set of connected dense units in n-dimensions. It is assumed that if an n-dimensional unit is dense, then so are its projections in the $(n-1)$-dimensional space. An *A priori*-like algorithm (described in Section 7.2.1) is used to generate candidate n-dimensional dense units. This enables generation of a minimal description for each of the clusters. In other words, it determines the maximal region that covers the clusters of connected dense units, followed by a minimal cover for each cluster.

6.4.5   Other variants

Recent research indicates that the concepts of proximity or clustering may not be meaningful in high dimensional data, mainly due to their inherent sparsity problem. A generalized projected clustering method [26] is designed to circumvent this problem by constructing clusters in arbitrarily aligned subspaces of lower dimensionality. The arbitrarily ORiented projected CLUSter generation (ORCLUS) technique searches for hidden subspaces with clusters which are created by inter-attribute correlations. The discovery of such correlations lead to projections which are not parallel to the original axis system. Extended cluster feature vectors are used to make the algorithm scalable for very large databases.

6.5   SOFT COMPUTING-BASED APPROACHES

In this section we concentrate on clustering, using different soft computing tools. These encompass fuzzy sets, neural networks, wavelets, rough sets, and evolutionary algorithms, the basics of which have been described in Section 2.2.

6.5.1   Fuzzy sets

Information granules can be viewed as collections of objects (patterns) drawn together by the criteria of indistinguishability, similarity or functionality, as in discretization or fuzzy partitioning. Fuzzy sets help in the semantics attachment to these granules (or clusters) of data. They also enable the determination and description of meaningful associations between the granules. In this section we describe some fuzzy clustering algorithms used for data mining.

6.5.1.1   Fuzzy c-means (FCM)   This is a fuzzification of the c-means algorithm, proposed by Bezdek [27]. It partitions a set of N patterns $\{\mathbf{X}_k\}$ into

c clusters by minimizing the objective function

$$J = \sum_{k=1}^{N} \sum_{i=1}^{c} (\mu_{ik})^{m'} ||\mathbf{X}_k - \mathbf{m}_i||^2, \qquad (6.12)$$

where $1 \leq m' < \infty$ is the fuzzifier, $\mathbf{m}_i$ is the ith cluster center, $\mu_{ik} \in [0, 1]$ is the membership of the kth pattern to it, and $||.||$ is the distance norm, such that

$$\mathbf{m}_i = \frac{\sum_{k=1}^{N} (\mu_{ik})^{m'} \mathbf{X}_k}{\sum_{k=1}^{N} (\mu_{ik})^{m'}} \qquad (6.13)$$

and

$$\mu_{ik} = \frac{1}{\sum_{j=1}^{c} \left(\frac{d_{ik}}{d_{jk}} \right)^{\frac{2}{m'-1}}}, \qquad (6.14)$$

$\forall i$, with $d_{ik} = ||\mathbf{X}_k - \mathbf{m}_i||^2$, subject to $\sum_{i=1}^{c} \mu_{ik} = 1, \forall k$, and $\sum_{k=1}^{N} \mu_{ik} > 0$, $\forall i$. The algorithm proceeds as follows.

1. Pick the initial means $\mathbf{m}_i$, $i = 1, \ldots, c$. Choose values for fuzzifier m' and threshold ϵ. Set the iteration counter $t = 1$.

2. **repeat** steps 3 and 4, by incrementing t, **until** $|\mu_{ik}(t) - \mu_{ik}(t-1)| > \epsilon$.

3. Compute μ_{ik} by Eq. (6.14) for c clusters and N data objects.

4. Update means $\mathbf{m}_i$ by Eq. (6.13).

Note that for $\mu_{ik} \in [0, 1]$ the objective function of Eq. (6.12) boils down to the hard c-means case, whereby a *winner-take-all* strategy is applied in place of membership values in Eq. (6.9).

6.5.1.2 Context-based clustering The conditional fuzzy c-means algorithm [28] uses a context, while performing fuzzy clustering. The aim is to determine the structure in a data set $\{\mathbf{X}_k\}$ for a given context or domain knowledge which is represented by a fuzzy set B defined over y_k, that is, $B(y_k)$. This introduces some focus and granularity in the search. It consists of a constraint-based optimization of the objective function of Eq. (6.12), such that $\mathbf{m}_i$ is given by Eq. (6.13) but Eq. (6.14) is modified to

$$\mu_{ik} = \frac{B(y_k)}{\sum_{j=1}^{c} \left(\frac{d_{ik}}{d_{jk}} \right)^{\frac{2}{m'-1}}}. \qquad (6.15)$$

6.5.1.3 Fuzzy c-medoids This is a fuzzification of the c-medoids algorithm and is outlined as follows [29]:

1. Pick the initial medoids $\mathbf{m}_i$, $i = 1, \ldots, c$.

2. **repeat** steps 3 and 4 **until** convergence.

3. Compute μ_{ik} for $i = 1, \ldots, c$ and $k = 1, \ldots, N$.

4. Compute new medoids

$$\mathbf{m}_i = \mathbf{X}_q,$$

where

$$q = arg \min_{1 \leq j \leq N} \sum_{k=1}^{N} (\mu_{ik})^{m'} \|\mathbf{X}_j - \mathbf{X}_k\|^2 \qquad (6.16)$$

refers to that j for which the minimum value of the expression is obtained.

Note that this boils down to the hard c-medoids with $\mu_{ik} = 1$, if $i = q$, and $\mu_{ik} = 0$ otherwise.

6.5.1.4 Granular clustering

The granular clustering algorithm [30] organizes findings about data in the form of a collection of information granules, called hyperboxes. A compatibility measure guides the construction (growth) of the clusters. Indices like volume, compatibility measure, inclusion, overlap, normalized length, and sparsity are developed to describe the hyperboxes and express the relationships between such information granules. The family of the information granules result in a granular signature of the data. Abstraction is achieved through condensation of original data elements into granules, whose location and granularity reflects the essence of the structure of data. The basic steps of the algorithm consist of

- finding the two closest information granules to build a new granule embracing them, thereby condensing the data while reducing the dataset;

- repeating the first step until enough data condensation has been accomplished, as determined by a terminating criterion or a validation mechanism.

The indices *sparsity* and *overlap* are found to be useful in understanding the relevance of the variables, particularly their discriminatory abilities.

6.5.2   Neural networks

Neural network models based on variations of the self-organizing map (SOM) [31] are mainly used for clustering large datasets. The SOM is depicted in Fig. 2.4. It also results in good visualization of the results. The Adaptive Resonance Theory (ART) network [32] can also be viewed as a neural implementation of leader clustering (described in Section 6.3.3).

6.5.2.1 Construction of large SOM This was designed by Kohonen et al. [33]. The models of the larger map are initialized using the smaller ones, while pointers are initialized from the data to the models. The main steps of the algorithm are as follows:

- Initialize models of a very small SOM.

- Teach this small SOM.

- **repeat until** the desired map size is obtained.

The larger map can be fine-tuned with a parallel batch-map algorithm, which is typically used for faster computation. Let us consider Eq. (2.23). Assuming that the convergence to some ordered state is true, the expectation values of $\mathbf{m}_i(t+1)$ and $\mathbf{m}_i(t)$ for $t \to \infty$ become equal. Hence, in the stationary state, one has

$$E_t\{\alpha(t)[\mathbf{X}(t) - \mathbf{m}_i(t)]\} = 0, \quad \forall i,$$

where $E_t\{.\}$ is the expectation value over the index of regression t. For a finite batch of $\mathbf{X}(t)$, we have

$$\mathbf{m}_i = \frac{\sum_t \alpha(t)\mathbf{X}(t)}{\sum_t \alpha(t)}. \tag{6.17}$$

Consider the Voronoi set $V_i = \{\mathbf{X}| \ ||\mathbf{X} - \mathbf{m}_i||$ is minimum$\}$ such that $n_i = |V_i|$ is the number of samples of $\mathbf{X}(t)$ falling into V_i. Then the batch-map algorithm is outlined as follows:

1. Initialize the centers $\mathbf{m}_i$, $\forall i$.

2. **for** a finite set of samples $\mathbf{X}(t)$, compute a step of vector quantization

$$\overline{\mathbf{X}}_i = \frac{\sum_{\mathbf{X}(t) \in V_i} \mathbf{X}(t)}{n_i}, \quad \forall i. \tag{6.18}$$

3. Carry out one smoothing step

$$\mathbf{m}_i = \frac{\sum_j n_j \alpha \overline{\mathbf{X}}_j}{\sum_j n_j \alpha}, \quad \forall i, \tag{6.19}$$

where α is regarded as time invariant for simplicity.

4. **repeat** steps 2 and 3 **until** $\mathbf{m}_i$ becomes stationary.

The parallelization of the batch-map algorithm is possible due to the localized nature of the search for the winner. Here the data are distributed into several processors, and each executes the batch-map algorithm in parallel.

The algorithm has been applied to a large document database of patent abstracts [33] containing classes of 21 subsections, with 68,40,568 documents, and an initial dimension of 7,33,179 (number of different words) that is reduced to 500 using feature selection methods. The initial size of the SOM is 435. This later grows to a final size involving 10,02,240 nodes. The classification accuracy is found to be 64%.

6.5.2.2   Clustering of SOM   This is a two-level approach described in Ref. [34]. The SOM is used to produce prototypes, which are then clustered using agglomerative and partitive methods. It is reported to have better performance than direct clustering, by resulting in a reduction in the computation time.

6.5.2.3 Dynamic self-organizing maps   The dynamic self-organizing map (GSOM) [35] grows the nodes of the network according to the need of resolution. A spread factor is used to control the generation of maps with different dimensionality for different regions of interest in the feature space. Initially, one starts with a small map having a low spread factor. Hierarchical clustering is then done to achieve finer resolution for *interesting* clusters.

6.5.3   Wavelets

WaveCluster [36] uses a hybridization of grid and density-based approaches to cluster using wavelet transformation. The low-pass filter, inherent in the transform, helps to remove the outliers. It is possible to identify clusters at different levels of accuracy (i.e., fine or coarse) by using multiresolution. This implies that there are less clusters at a coarser resolution.

Multidimensional spatial data are considered as a multidimensional signal, and wavelet transform is applied to convert it to a number of frequency subbands. Convolution, with an appropriate kernel function as shown in Eqs. (3.11) and (3.12) as an example, results in a transformed space where the natural clusters become more distinguishable. A down sampling of the signal by two is made by skipping alternate signal samples. This results in the scales becoming coarser. However, at each scale the spatial relationships are preserved because of the inherent space-time localization principles of Discrete Wavelet Transform.

Consider Fig. 3.9. The high-frequency parts of the signal correspond to the boundaries of the clusters. Here the subbands LHi, HLi, and HHi refer to the horizontal, vertical, and diagonal features, respectively, constituting the high-frequency edge or discontinuity information at level i ($i = 1, 2, 3$). The low-frequency parts, with high amplitude, correspond to regions where the patterns (objects) are concentrated. This involves the actual clusters, falling in the average subband LLi. Details on the hierarchical decomposition of the subbands has been provided in Section 3.8.3. The main steps of the algorithm are as follows:

1. Quantize the feature space, and then assign objects to the units.

2. Apply wavelet transform on the feature space.

3. Find the connected components (clusters) in the (average) subband of the transformed feature space, at different levels.

4. Assign labels to the units.

5. Make the lookup table (map units in the transformed space to the original feature space).

6. Map the objects to the clusters.

WaveCluster is fast, with a linear time complexity $O(N)$, because of the finite length of filters. It efficiently handles large, high-dimensional spatial databases. Since the average subbands give approximations of the original feature space at different scales, this helps the algorithm to find clusters at different levels of details. It is possible to discover clusters with arbitrary shapes and complex structures. Outliers can be successfully handled using the inherent low-pass filter. No input parameter specifications are required, and the algorithm is insensitive to the order of input pattern presentation. WaveCluster is claimed to outperform the algorithms BIRCH, CLARANS, and DBSCAN.

6.5.4 Rough sets

Here the c-means algorithm is extended by viewing each cluster as an interval or rough set [37]. As mentioned in Section 2.2.6, a rough set Y is characterized by its lower and upper approximations $\underline{B}Y$ and $\overline{B}Y$, respectively. This permits overlaps between clusters. Adapting Eq. (6.9), the centroid $\mathbf{m}_i$ of cluster U_i is computed as

$$
\mathbf{m}_i = \begin{cases} w_{low} \dfrac{\sum_{\mathbf{x}_k \in \underline{B}U_i} \mathbf{x}_k}{|\underline{B}U_i|} + w_{up} \dfrac{\sum_{\mathbf{x}_k \in (\overline{B}U_i - \underline{B}U_i)} \mathbf{x}_k}{|\overline{B}U_i - \underline{B}U_i|} & \text{if } \overline{B}U_i - \underline{B}U_i \neq \emptyset \\[2em] w_{low} \dfrac{\sum_{\mathbf{x}_k \in \underline{B}U_i} \mathbf{x}_k}{|\underline{B}U_i|} & \text{otherwise,} \end{cases}
$$

(6.20)

where the parameters w_{low} and w_{up} correspond to the relative importance of the lower and upper approximations, respectively. Here $|\underline{B}U_i|$ indicates the number of pattern points in the lower approximation of cluster U_i, and $|\overline{B}U_i - \underline{B}U_i|$ is the number of elements in the rough boundary lying between the two approximations.

Note that the expression boils down to Eq. (6.9) when the lower approximation is equal to the upper approximation, implying an empty boundary region. In order to determine whether an object $\mathbf{X}_k$ belongs to the upper or lower approximation of clusters, one computes the difference in its distance $d(\mathbf{X}_k, \mathbf{m}_i) - d(\mathbf{X}_k, \mathbf{m}_j)$ from cluster centroid pairs $\mathbf{m}_i$ and $\mathbf{m}_j$. If this is less than some threshold, then $\mathbf{X}_k \in \overline{B}U_i$ and $\mathbf{X}_k \in \overline{B}U_j$ and $\mathbf{X}_k$ cannot be a member of any lower approximation. Otherwise, $\mathbf{X}_k \in \underline{B}U_i$ such that distance $d(\mathbf{X}_k, \mathbf{m}_i)$ is minimum over the c clusters. A major disadvantage of this algorithm is the involvement of too many user-defined parameters.

6.5.5   Evolutionary algorithms

Evolutionary algorithms have been applied for optimally selecting the initial
seed points (centroids) in c-means clustering [2]. Each solution string (chromosome) represents a valid c-partition of the N patterns. Here the length of
the string is $c * n$, where n is the dimensionality of the patterns. A partition
may also be encoded as a string of length N where the ith element denotes
the cluster number of pattern $\mathbf{X}_i$. The squared error value associated with
a solution is translated into its fitness value, with a smaller error implying
a larger fitness. The evolutionary operators selection, crossover, and mutation are applied to generate successive populations of solutions, until some
termination criterion is satisfied. Selection ensures that highly fit individuals
participate in the evolution with a higher probability. Crossover and mutation
help in exploring the search space randomly.

Simulated Annealing [38], which updates a solution stochastically to permit
its escape from local minimum, and Tabu Search [39], which searches in the
vicinity of the current solution by storing possible solution vectors in a list
while exploring the best solution found so far, have also been employed for
determining optimal partitions.

Genetic algorithms (GA) have also been used for medoids-based clustering
[2]. Here each chromosome consists of c parameters corresponding to the c
medoids, with the parameter values corresponding to their record IDs in the
database. The strings are not binary, as in conventional GAs (Section 2.2.5),
but consist of integer values lying between 1 and N where N is the total
number of objects in the dataset. The fitness of each individual is inversely
proportional to the dissimilarity of the clusters. The selection procedure is
the same as that of the conventional GAs.

Random Respectful Recombination (RRR) crossover operator is applied.
Here the parameter values, which are common in both the parent individuals,
are transported to the offsprings. The remaining parameter values of the
offspring are chosen randomly from the rest of the parameter values of the
parents.

6.5.5.1 Example 6: For example, with $c = 5$ and $N = 100$ and parent
chromosomes 7 19 43 67 89 and 8 19 39 67 92, we find that the common values
are 19, 67. These constitute the first two values in case of both offsprings.
The remaining slots are randomly filled up with the values 8, 43, 89 and 89,
7, 39 from the parents, resulting in the children 19 67 | 8 43 89 and 19 67 | 89
7 39.

Mutation tries to replace the parameter value of a chromosome by another
object (record number) not already present in it. First a random (integer)
number in the range $[1, \ldots, N]$ is generated. If this is different from the
existing numbers in the current chromosomes, it replaces the old number by
this new one.

6.5.5.2 *Example 7:* For example, a mutation on the 2nd gene of the parent 7 |19| 43 67 89 with the generation of a random number 34 produces an offspring chromosome given by 7 |34| 43 67 89.

6.5.5.3 *Procedure* The c-medoids algorithm, using GAs, involves the following steps.

1. Choose an initial population of c medoids.

2. Compute the dissimilarity (distance) of the clusters from the chromosomes.

3. Assign fitness values to the individuals, with more dissimilarity implying less fitness.

4. Generate new population of medoids by performing selection, crossover and mutation.

5. **if** termination criterion is satisfied **then** go to step 6 **else** go to step 2.

6. Return the best fit chromosome.

Clustering Large Applications based on Simulated Annealing (CLASA) applies simulated annealing to select better medoids [40]. Simulated annealing, unlike GAs, stochastically anneals a single chromosome with the help of a temperature parameter. A *cooling* schedule of the temperature is undertaken, as the search space is explored for determining the optimum set of medoids.

6.6 CLUSTERING WITH CATEGORICAL ATTRIBUTES

Traditional algorithms, suited for numeric or quantitative features, do not work well for categorical or nominal attributes. Viewing the feature space as points with (0/1) values of attributes does not solve the problem. The Jaccard coefficient of Eq. (6.3) is often used for handling binary values. However, it becomes hard to reflect the properties of the neighborhood of the points and the algorithms fail to capture the natural clustering of datasets. When using a traditional algorithm, involving centroids, as the cluster size grows, the number of attributes appearing in the mean goes up. Their values in the mean also decrease in a *ripple* effect. Thus it becomes very difficult to distinguish between two points.

Often one builds a weighted hyper-graph, with frequent itemsets involving categorical attributes. A hyper-edge in this graph represents a frequent item. The weight of the edge is the average of confidences of all association rules generated from its itemset. This hyper-graph partitioning algorithm is used to cluster items by minimizing the sum of weights of hyper-edges.

Some of the clustering algorithms, working on categorical attributes, include STIRR [41], ROCK [42], CACTUS [43], and c-modes [44].

6.6.1   Sieving Through Iterated Relational Reinforcements (STIRR)

STIRR [41] is based on nonlinear dynamic systems. It seeks a similarity based on co-occurrences of items in the same column. Each distinct value of each column becomes a node. The algorithm assigns weight to each node (either uniformly or randomly), such that the sum of all weights is one. An iterative approach is followed for assigning and propagating weights on the categorical values. However, it is difficult to analyze the stability of this method.

Table 6.3   Sample transactions set to demonstrate STIRR

Item purchased	Intermediate node	Transaction ID
A	α	1
A	α	2
B	β	3
B	α	4
C	α	1
C	β	3

6.6.1.1   Example 8:   Let us consider an example in Table 6.3, demonstrating the relation between transactions of items purchased in a store, to illustrate how STIRR works. Figure 6.5 depicts the resulting undirected graph linking the items with the corresponding transactions. The intermediate nodes refer to the association or relationship between the items and the transactions, thereby defining possible clusters on the basis of similarity. The weights of the items, clusters, and transactions are represented by w_A, w_B, w_C; w_α, w_β; and w_1, w_2, w_3, w_4; respectively. These are initialized randomly. The subsequent weight update expression is given as $w_B = w_\alpha + w_4 + w_\beta + w_3$ or $w_B = w_\alpha.w_4 + w_\beta.w_3$. Upon convergence, clusters of transactions get reinforced by the larger weight values at the intermediate nodes.

6.6.2   Robust Hierarchical Clustering with Links (ROCK)

ROCK [42] uses the number of *common neighbors* between two data points in order to measure their similarity. Here common neighbors refer to nodes that differ from each other in only one item. As it uses a global knowledge of the similarity of data points in order to measure distances, the decision on which points to merge in a single cluster becomes very robust. It is basically a hierarchical clustering for categorical attributes, suitable for analyzing (say) market basket customers. A novel concept of cross-links is used for merging clusters. A similarity function $sim(T_i, T_j)$ captures the closeness or interconnectivity between transactions T_i and T_j. A pair of patterns T_i and T_j are

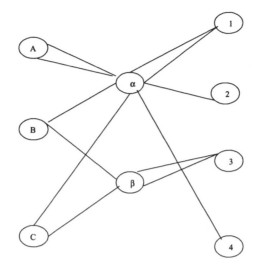

Fig. 6.5 Example demonstrating STIRR.

termed neighbors if $sim(T_i, T_j) \geq \theta$, where θ is a user-specified threshold, and $link(T_i, T_j)$ determines their number of common neighbors. A goodness measure is used to evaluate the clustering. Random sampling is employed for scaling up to large datasets.

6.6.2.1 Example 9: Let us consider an example with two clusters of transactions, at any point of time of the hierarchical clustering, involving items $< 1, 2, 3, 4, 5 >$ and $< 1, 2, 6, 7 >$, respectively, for $\theta = \frac{2}{3}$. Let the individual transactions be expressed as two natural partitions consisting of $\{1, 2, 3\}$ $\{1, 2, 4\}$ $\{1, 2, 5\}$ $\{1, 3, 4\}$ $\{1, 3, 5\}$ $\{1, 4, 5\}$ $\{2, 3, 4\}$ $\{2, 3, 5\}$ $\{2, 4, 5\}$ $\{3, 4, 5\}$ and $\{1, 2, 6\}$ $\{1, 2, 7\}$ $\{1, 6, 7\}$ $\{2, 6, 7\}$, respectively. We define

$$sim(T_i, T_j) = \frac{|T_i \cap T_j|}{|T_I \cup T_j|} \geq 0.5.$$

Here the transactions $\{1, 2, 6\}$ and $\{1, 2, 7\}$ are found to have five links (common neighbors, namely, $\{1, 2, 3\}, \{1, 2, 4\}, \{1, 2, 5\}, \{1, 6, 7\}, \{2, 6, 7\}$), validating their existence in the same cluster. On the other hand, transactions $\{1, 2, 3\}$ and $\{1, 2, 6\}$ are seen to have three links only (namely, $\{1, 2, 4\}$, $\{1, 2, 5\}, \{1, 2, 7\}$), implying less similarity and hence their existence in different clusters.

6.6.3 *c*-modes algorithm

An approach in Ref. [45] has used the *c*-means algorithm to cluster categorical data. Here multiple category attributes are converted into binary form, with a 0/1 indicating the absence (or presence) of a category, and then the binary attributes are treated as numeric in the c-means framework. However, as mentioned earlier, this approach needs to handle a large number of binary attributes because the datasets often involve categorical attributes with hundreds or thousands of categories. This inevitably increases both computational and space costs of the c-means algorithm when used for data mining. The other drawback is that the cluster means, expressed as real values between 0 and 1, do not essentially indicate the characteristics of any of the clusters.

The c-modes algorithm [44] is capable of handling categorical or nominal attributes. It uses a partitional approach and proceeds along the lines of the c-means. However, the cluster means are replaced with their modes. Note that a mode is another measure of central tendency in a dataset, referring to that pattern or object having the maximum frequency of occurrence in a cluster. For example, the two modes of the set $\{(x, y), (x, z), (z, y), (y, z)\}$ are (x, y) and (x, z). New dissimilarity measures are used to deal with categorical objects. A frequency-based method is used to update the modes of the clusters. A mixture of categorical and numerical data can be handled by the c-prototypes method [44]. This has applications in real-world databases involving mixed-type objects. As in the c-means, both these algorithms produce locally optimal solutions that are dependent on the initial modes and the order of presentation of objects in the dataset.

The basic steps of the c-modes algorithm are outlined as follows:

1. Select c initial modes.

2. Allocate an object to the cluster whose mode is the nearest to it. Update the mode of the cluster after each allocation.

3. After all objects have been allocated to clusters, retest the dissimilarity of objects against the current modes. If an object is found such that its nearest mode belongs to another cluster, reallocate the object to that cluster and update the modes of both clusters.

4. **repeat** step 3 **until** no object has changed clusters after a full cycle test of the whole dataset.

The major differences between CLARA (since PAM can use any dissimilarity measures, it can cluster objects with categorical attributes) and the c-prototypes algorithm include the following. (i) CLARA clusters based on samples, whereas c-prototypes directly works on the whole large dataset. (ii) CLARA optimizes its clustering result at the sample level, and hence may not produce a good clustering if the sample is biased; whereas the c-prototypes algorithm guarantees at least a locally optimal clustering. (iii) The efficiency of CLARA depends on the sample size, while the c-prototypes algorithm has no such restrictions.

6.7 HIERARCHICAL SYMBOLIC CLUSTERING

Symbolic objects include linguistic, nominal, boolean, and interval-type of features, along with quantitative attributes. Clustering in this domain involves the use of symbolic dissimilarity between the objects. In this section we outline conceptual clustering [12, 13] and a hierarchical symbolic clustering algorithm [46, 47] with different validity indices for determining the optimal number of meaningful clusters. The novelty of the method lies in transforming the different clustering validity indices, like Normalized Modified Hubert's statistic, Davies–Bouldin index, and Dunn's index, from the quantitative domain to the symbolic framework. The effectiveness of the algorithm is quantitatively evaluated on real-life benchmark datasets.

6.7.1 Conceptual clustering

Conceptual clustering [12, 13] is based on *Category Utility CU* of a cluster U_k, defined as the average over the l clusters. It is expressed as

$$\frac{\sum_{k=1}^{l} CU_k}{l}, \tag{6.21}$$

where

$$CU_k = P(U_k) * \left(\sum_i \sum_j P(a_i = V_{ij}|U_k)^2 - \sum_i \sum_j P(a_i = V_{ij})^2 \right). \tag{6.22}$$

Here $P(U_k)$ is the *a priori* probability of cluster U_k, $P(a_i = V_{ij})$ is the probability of feature a_i taking on value V_{ij}, and $P(a_i = V_{ij}|U_k)$ is the conditional probability of $a_i = V_{ij}$ in cluster U_k. This represents an increase in the number of feature values that can be correctly guessed for cluster $U_k(P(a_i = V_{ij}|U_k)^2)$, over the expected number of correct guesses, given that no class information is available $[P(a_i = V_{ij})^2]$.

The objective is to generate maximally cohesive clusters (high intraclass similarity) while achieving maximum separability (high interclass dissimilarity) among the clusters in a partition. Probabilistic measures, to evaluate the goodness of the partitioning, are expressed as [13]

$$M_{dk} = \sum_{i,j \in \{a_i\}_d} (P(a_i = V_{ij}|U_k)^2 - P(a_i = V_{ij})^2) \tag{6.23}$$

and

$$Var(U(k), U(l)) = \frac{1}{n} \sum_i \sum_j (P(a_i = V_{ij}|U_k) - P(a_i = V_{ij}|U_l))^2. \tag{6.24}$$

Here M_{dk} is the increase in predictability of an object $\mathbf{X}_d$ to cluster U_k. *Cohesion* of a partition structure is measured as the sum of the M_{dk} values of all objects in the dataset, while $Var(U(k), U(l))$ is the variance of distribution match between clusters U_k and U_l in a given partition. *Distinctness* of a partition is taken as the average variance between clusters in that partition. Another popular conceptual clustering algorithm is COBWEB [48], which builds an incremental classification tree.

6.7.2   Agglomerative symbolic clustering

The agglomerative algorithm [46, 47] typically involves a repetition of the steps (i) assignment of pattern vector $\mathbf{X}$ to a cluster, (ii) all intercluster distance computation, and (iii) merging pairs of clusters which are closest to each other, until there is only one cluster left. Like typical hierarchical methods, the partitioning at any stage depends on the previously found clusters.

Let us now define two different measures for within-cluster and between-cluster distances in the symbolic framework. Let $\{\mathbf{X}_1, \ldots, \mathbf{X}_{c_k}\}$ be a set of symbolic objects lying in a cluster U_k. Then the *average distance* within the cluster U_k is expressed as

$$S_a(U_k) = \frac{\sum_{i,i'} D(\mathbf{X}_i, \mathbf{X}_{i'})}{|c_k|(|c_k| - 1)}, \tag{6.25}$$

where $\mathbf{X}_i, \mathbf{X}_{i'} \in U_k$, $i \neq i'$, $|c_k|$ is the number of samples in cluster U_k, and D indicates the symbolic dissimilarity of Eq. (6.8). The *between-cluster* distance is defined as

$$d_a(U_k, U_l) = \frac{\sum_{i,j} D(\mathbf{X}_i, \mathbf{X}_j)}{|c_k||c_l|}, \tag{6.26}$$

where $\mathbf{X}_i \in U_k$, $\mathbf{X}_j \in U_l$, such that $k \neq l$. We have used S_a and d_a in our computations, in terms of the symbolic dissimilarity D of Eq. (6.8). The algorithm is as follows.

1. Let the initial number of clusters be N, with each cluster having a weight (number of objects) of 1. Therefore $\mathbf{X}_i \in U_i$, $i = 1, \ldots, N$.

2. Compute the weighted dissimilarities between all pairs of clusters in the dataset as

$$d_{aw}(U_i, U_j) = d_a(U_i, U_j) \left(\frac{|c_i| \cdot |c_j|}{|c_i| + |c_j|} \right)^{0.5}. \tag{6.27}$$

Note that the weighting term on the r.h.s. of Eq. (6.27) yields a value $\sqrt{50}$ for $|c_i| = |c_j| = 100$, while it results in $\sqrt{0.5}$ for $|c_i| = |c_j| = 1$ (singleton clusters). Hence the dissimilarity is highlighted for larger clusters. However, for $|c_i| = 100$, $|c_j| = 1$, we have $100/101 \simeq 1$, naturally implying a higher dissimilarity than that for $|c_i| = |c_j| = 1$. So there is a greater probability of merging a pair of smaller clusters as compared to larger clusters.

3. Determine the mutual pair (clusters) having the lowest average weighted dissimilarity $d_{a_{w_{min}}}$ by Eq. (6.27). Form a composite cluster U_k by merging the individuals of this pair, such that $|c_k| = |c_i| + |c_j|$. Reduce the number of clusters by 1.

4. **repeat** steps 2 and 3 **until** the number of clusters equals 1.

5. Compute cluster validity index V_t by Eqs. (6.29)–(6.32). Determine the stage t_0, with clusters $c = c_0$, for $c = 2, \ldots, \sqrt{N}$, at which V_t is optimum. This indicates the optimal number of clusters.

6.7.3   Cluster validity indices

To select the best among different partitioning, each of these can be evaluated using some validity index. Several validation methods have been proposed in the literature [7] for quantitative data. These include Normalized Modified Hubert's statistic, Davies–Bouldin index, and Dunn's index. Since the conventional centroid-based representation is not feasible in the symbolic framework, we modify these expressions using the average scatter S_a [Eq. (6.25)] within a cluster and d_a [Eq. (6.26)] between clusters [46, 47]. The performance is compared with that of the Cluster indicator [10].

6.7.3.1   Hubert's statistic   Let $\mathbf{X}_i$ be the ith object and $L(i) = k$ if $\mathbf{X}_i \in U_k$. The Modified Hubert's statistic is a measure used for determining the optimal number of clusters in the quantitative domain [7]. For a cluster structure in the symbolic framework, it can be expressed in terms of symbolic dissimilarity as

$$\Gamma = \sum_{i=1}^{N-1} \sum_{j=i+1}^{N} D(\mathbf{X}_i, \mathbf{X}_j) d_a(U_{L(i)}, U_{L(j)}). \tag{6.28}$$

If $\mathbf{X}_i$ and $\mathbf{X}_j$ lie in two different clusters, d_a is computed using Eq. (6.26). However, when they belong to the same cluster, $d_a = 0$. From this, we get Normalized Modified Hubert's statistic $\hat{\Gamma}$ as

$$\hat{\Gamma} = \frac{1}{M} \sum_{i=1}^{N-1} \sum_{j=i+1}^{N} \frac{(D(\mathbf{X}_i, \mathbf{X}_j) - \overline{D})(d_a(U_{L(i)}, U_{L(j)}) - \overline{d_a})}{s_D s_{d_a}}. \tag{6.29}$$

Here

$$\overline{D} = \frac{1}{M} \sum_{i=1}^{N-1} \sum_{j=i+1}^{N} D(\mathbf{X}_i, \mathbf{X}_j),$$

$$\overline{d_a} = \frac{1}{M} \sum_{i=1}^{N-1} \sum_{j=i+1}^{N} d_a(U_{L(i)}, U_{L(j)}),$$

$$s_D^2 = \frac{1}{M} \sum_{i=1}^{N-1} \sum_{j=i+1}^{N} D^2(\mathbf{X}_i, \mathbf{X}_j) - \overline{D}^2,$$

and

$$s_{d_a}^2 = \frac{1}{M} \sum_{i=1}^{N-1} \sum_{j=i+1}^{N} d_a^2(U_{L(i)}, U_{L(j)}) - \overline{d_a}^2,$$

where $M = \frac{N(N-1)}{2}$ is the total number of terms under the double summation. The terms s_D and s_{d_a} are the standard deviations of the entries of the matrices D and d_a respectively, while s_D^2 and $s_{d_a}^2$ are the corresponding variances [7]. The optimal partitioning occurs at $c = c_0$ for which $\Delta(\Delta\hat{\Gamma})$ is minimum. This corresponds to a sharp change in slope (also called *knee*) of the piecewise linear graph for Normalized modified Hubert's statistic, in case of well-separated clusters.

6.7.3.2 Davies–Bouldin index

The Davies–Bouldin index is a function of the ratio of the sum of within-cluster distance to between-cluster separation. The best clustering, for $c = c_0$, minimizes

$$\frac{1}{c} \sum_{k=1}^{c} \max_{l \neq k} \left\{ \frac{S_a(U_k) + S_a(U_l)}{d_a(U_k, U_l)} \right\}, \tag{6.30}$$

for $1 \leq k, l \leq c$. Here the within-cluster distance is minimized and the between-cluster separation is maximized. The index is expressed in the symbolic framework, using Eqs. (6.25) and (6.26).

6.7.3.3 Dunn's index

Like Davies–Bouldin index, Dunn's index is designed to identify sets of clusters that are compact and well separated. We maximize

$$\min_k \left\{ \min_{l \neq k} \left\{ \frac{d_a(U_k, U_l)}{\max_j S_a(U_j)} \right\} \right\}, \tag{6.31}$$

for $1 \leq j, k, l \leq c$. Here also the symbolic intercluster separation is maximized, while minimizing symbolic intracluster distances.

6.7.3.4 Cluster indicator

The cluster indicator value at the tth iteration is defined as

$$CI_t = \frac{R_t}{R_{t+1}}, \tag{6.32}$$

where

$$R_t = \frac{\min_{k \neq l} d_a^t(U_k, U_l)}{\min_{k' \neq l'} d_a^{t+1}(U_{k'}, U_{l'}) + \min_{k'' \neq l''} d_a^{t-1}(U_{k''}, U_{l''})}. \tag{6.33}$$

This is maximized over different iterations for $t = 2, \ldots, N - 2$. Note that initially, at $t = 0$, there are N singletons. At $t = 1$, the pair of closest clusters are merged, resulting in $N - 1$ clusters. Therefore, at the tth iteration we have $N - t$ clusters.

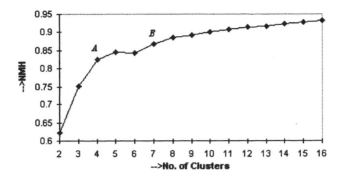

Fig. 6.6 Plot of Hubert's statistic for *Zoo* data.

6.7.4 Results

The symbolic clustering algorithm was implemented [46, 47] on benchmark symbolic data, namely, *Zoo, Auto Import,* and *Mushroom* [49]. The results were compared with that of conceptual clustering, and the measures *Cohesiveness* and *Distinctness* of Eqs. (6.23) and (6.24) were used for this purpose.

In this section we provide sample results for the *Zoo* data consisting of 100 instances of animals with 17 features and 7 output classes. The name of the animal constitutes the first attribute. There are 15 boolean features corresponding to the presence of hair, feathers, eggs, milk, backbone, fins, or tail; and whether airborne, aquatic, predator, toothed, breathes, venomous, domestic, catsize. The character attribute corresponds to the number of legs lying in the set {0,2,4,5,6,8}.

The validity indices used, Cohesion and Distinctness values, the number of elements in each cluster (in parentheses), and the individual elements according to their sequential order of entry in the corresponding cluster are provided in Table 6.4. The symbolic clustering algorithm provided four clusters for the *Zoo* data with validity indices CI, Normalized Modified Hubert's statistic, Davies–Bouldin, and Dunn's, while Conceptual clustering generated two clusters (merging clusters 2, 3, and 4 into cluster 2 here). It is observed that the resulting partitions in the symbolic clustering are semantically meaningful and are very similar to those obtained by Kohonen's self-organizing feature map [35]. A plot of Hubert's statistic for the data, in Fig. 6.6, shows a sharp *knee* corresponding to four clusters. The Cohesion and Distinctness measures indicate better partitioning for four clusters.

Table 6.4 Symbolic clustering and evaluation of Zoo data

Index	Cohesion, distinctness	Cluster	Animals
CI, Normalized Modified Hubert's, Davies–Bouldin, and Dunn's	458.43, 0.58	1 (41)	aardvark, bear, girl, boar, cheetah, leopard, lion, raccoon, wolf, lynx, mongoose, polecat, puma, mink, platypus, dolphin, porpoise, seal, sealion, antelope, buffalo, deer, elephant, giraffe, oryx, gorilla, wallaby, calf, goat, pony, reindeer, pussycat, cavy, hamster, fruitbat, vampire, squirrel, hare, vole, mole, opossum.
		2 (21)	bass, catfish, piranha, chub, herring, carp, haddock, seahorse, sole, dogfish, pike, tuna, stingray, frog, toad, newt, tuatara, pitviper, slowworm, scorpion, seasnake.
		3 (21)	chicken, dove, parakeet, lark, pheasant, sparrow, wren, flamingo, ostrich, tortoise, crow, hawk, vulture, kiwi, rhea, penguin, duck, swan, gull, skimmer, skua.
		4 (17)	clam, seawasp, crab, starfish, crayfish, lobster, octopus, flea, termite, slug, worm, gnat, ladybird, housefly, moth, honeybee, wasp.
Conceptual	132.49, 0.50	1 (41)	aardvark, bear, girl, boar, cheetah, leopard, lion, raccoon, wolf, lynx, mongoose, polecat, puma, mink, platypus, dolphin, porpoise, seal, sealion, antelope, buffalo, deer, elephant, giraffe, oryx, gorilla, wallaby, calf, goat, pony, reindeer, pussycat, cavy, hamster, fruitbat, vampire, squirrel, hare, vole, mole, opossum.
		2 (59)	bass, catfish, piranha, chub, herring, carp, haddock, seahorse, sole, dogfish, pike, tuna, stingray, frog, toad, newt, tuatara, pitviper, slowworm, scorpion, seasnake. chicken, dove, parakeet, lark, pheasant, sparrow, wren, flamingo, ostrich, tortoise, crow, hawk, vulture, kiwi, rhea, penguin, duck, swan, gull, skimmer, skua. clam, seawasp, crab, starfish, crayfish, lobster, octopus, flea, termite, slug, worm, gnat, ladybird, housefly, moth, honeybee, wasp.

6.8   CONCLUSIONS AND DISCUSSION

In this chapter we have described clustering from the viewpoint of mining both homogeneous and heterogeneous data. Different distance measures have been defined for symbolic objects involving quantitative, binary, nominal (categorical) and ordinal attributes. Partitional and hierarchical methods, along with some scalable versions of clustering algorithms have been discussed. Use of soft computing-based approaches, involving fuzzy sets, neural networks, rough sets, genetic algorithms, and wavelets, are highlighted. Finally, clustering of symbolic objects has been outlined. Clustering has useful applications in data mining, pattern recognition, image segmentation, and Web mining.

Segmentation is a process of partitioning an image space into nonoverlapping meaningful homogeneous regions. The success of an image analysis system depends on the quality of segmentation. Remote sensing image data, containing observations from the Indian Remote Sensing (IRS) satellite for the city of Kolkata, India, has been segmented using fuzzy clustering based on thresholding [50]. The data contain images of four spectral bands and consist of six categories, namely, clear water (ponds, fisheries), turbid water (the river Ganga flowing through the city), concrete (buildings, roads, airport tarmac), habitation (concrete structures of lower density), vegetation (crop, forest areas), and open spaces (barren land, playgrounds). A rough–fuzzy hybridization of the EM algorithm [51], employing pixel classification, has been used to segment the multispectral satellite images into different landcover types.

The importance of clustering to Web mining, specifically in the domains of Web Content and Web Usage mining, make Web clustering an interesting topic of research. This includes clustering of Web documents, snippets and access logs. Usually the Web involves overlapping clusters. So a crisp usage of metrics is better replaced by fuzzy sets that can reflect, in a more natural manner, the degree of belongingness/membership to a cluster. A review of robust methods used for fuzzy Web clustering is presented in Ref. [52]. A robust algorithm is one whose performance is minimally affected in the presence of outliers. The algorithms considered include fuzzy c-means (FCM), fuzzy trimmed c-prototype, fuzzy c-least medians, and relational fuzzy c-means clustering, along with some techniques used to make them robust. These issues are further elaborated in Section 9.5.

The importance of symbolic clustering in real-world data is all the more evident, considering the availability of large volumes of mixed-media data that are distributed over the Internet. It enables efficient handling of heterogeneous data such as linguistic, nominal, boolean, interval, shape, color, etc. Partitioning of such data demands the use of symbolic measures for determining the similarity and dissimilarity between objects. The validity indices, expressed here in the symbolic framework, are generally found to provide better partitioning as compared to Conceptual clustering.

The determination of the optimal number of clusters is an open problem. The number of meaningful clusters selected, however, depends on the application domain. For example, if one desires plain clustering or segmentation, then one should go for coarser granules. On the other hand, if the goal is data condensation for data mining, then one should concentrate on finer granules as representative points.

REFERENCES

1. A. K. Jain and R. C. Dubes, *Algorithms for Clustering Data.* Englewood Cliffs, NJ: Prentice-Hall, 1988.

2. A. K. Jain, M. N. Murty, and P. J. Flynn, "Data clustering: A review," *ACM Computing Surveys*, vol. 31, pp. 264–323, 1999.

3. J. T. Tou and R. C. Gonzalez, *Pattern Recognition Principles.* London: Addison-Wesley, 1974.

4. L. Kaufman and P. J. Rousseeuw, *Finding Groups in Data: An Introduction to Cluster Analysis.* New York: John Wiley & Sons, 1990.

5. R. Ng and J. Han, "Efficient and effective clustering method for spatial data mining," in *Proceedings of 1994 International Conference on Very Large Data Bases (VLDB '94)* (Santiago, Chile), pp. 144–155, September 1994.

6. M. Ester, H. P. Kriegel, and X. Xu, "Knowledge discovery in large spatial databases: Focusing techniques for efficient class identification," in *Proceedings of 4th International Symposium on Large Spatial Databases (SSD '95)* (Portland, OR), pp. 67–82, August 1995.

7. J. C. Bezdek and N. R. Pal, "Some new indexes for cluster validity," *IEEE Transactions on Systems, Man, and Cybernetics, Part-B*, vol. 28, pp. 301–315, 1998.

8. J. Han and M. Kamber, *Data Mining: Concepts and Techniques.* San Diego: Academic Press, 2001.

9. S. Mitra, S. K. Pal, and P. Mitra, "Data mining in soft computing framework: A survey," *IEEE Transactions on Neural Networks*, vol. 13, pp. 3–14, 2002.

10. K. Chidananda Gowda and E. Diday, "Unsupervised learning through symbolic clustering," *Pattern Recognition Letters*, vol. 12, pp. 259–264, 1991.

11. K. Chidananda Gowda and T. V. Ravi, "Divisive clustering of symbolic objects using the concepts of both similarity and dissimilarity," *Pattern Recognition*, vol. 28, pp. 1277–1282, 1995.

12. R. Wilson and T. R. Martinez, "Improved heterogeneous distance functions," *Journal of Artificial Intelligence Research*, vol. 6, pp. 1–34, 1997.

13. G. Biswas, J. B. Weinberg, and D. H. Fisher, "ITERATE: A conceptual clustering algorithm for data mining," *IEEE Transactions on Systems, Man, and Cybernetics, Part C: Applications and Reviews*, vol. 28, pp. 219–230, 1998.

14. P. A. Devijver and J. Kittler, eds., *Pattern Recognition Theory and Applications*. Berlin: Springer-Verlag, 1987.

15. P. Bradley, U. M. Fayyad, and C. Reina, "Scaling clustering algorithms to large databases," in *Proceedings of 4th International Conference on Knowledge Discovery and Data Mining* (California), pp. 9–15, AAAI, 1998.

16. M. Ester, H. P. Kriegel, J. Sander, and X. Xu, "A density-based algorithm for discovering clusters in large spatial databases," in *Proceedings of 1996 International Conference on Knowledge Discovery and Data Mining (KDD '96)* (Portland, OR), pp. 226–231, August 1996.

17. M. Ankerst, M. Breunig, H. P. Kriegel, and J. Sander, "OPTICS: Ordering points to identify the clustering structure," in *Proceedings of 1999 ACM-SIGMOD International Conference on Management of Data (SIGMOD '99)* (Philadelphia, PA), pp. 49–60, June 1999.

18. A. Hinneburg and D. A. Keim, "An efficient approach to clustering in large multimedia databases with noise," in *Proceedings of 1998 International Conference on Knowledge Discovery and Data Mining (KDD '98)* (New York), pp. 58–65, August 1998.

19. R. Agrawal, J. Gehrke, D. Gunopulos, and P. Raghavan, "Automatic subspace clustering of high dimensional data for data mining applications," in *Proceedings of 1998 ACM-SIGMOD International Conference on Management of Data (SIGMOD '98)* (Seattle, WA), pp. 94–105, June 1998.

20. J. Sander, M. Ester, H. P. Kriegel, and X. Xu, "Density-based clustering in spatial databases: The algorithm GDBSCAN and its applications," *Data Mining and Knowledge Discovery*, vol. 2, pp. 1–27, 1998.

21. X. Xu, J. Jaeger, and H. P. Kriegel, "A fast parallel clustering algorithm for large spatial databases," *Data Mining and Knowledge Discovery*, vol. 3, pp. 263–290, 1999.

22. T. Zhang, R. Ramakrishnan, and M. Livny, "BIRCH: An efficient data clustering method for very large databases," in *Proceedings of 1996 ACM-SIGMOD International Conference on Management of Data (SIGMOD '96)* (Montreal, Canada), pp. 103–114, June 1996.

23. S. Guha, R. Rastogi, and K. Shim, "An efficient clustering algorithm for large databases," in *Proceedings of 1998 ACM-SIGMOD International Conference on Management of Data (SIGMOD '98)* (Seattle, WA), pp. 73–84, June 1998.

24. G. Karypis, E. H. Han, and V. Kumar, "CHAMELEON: A hierarchical clustering algorithm using dynamic modelling," *Computer*, vol. 32, pp. 68–75, 1999.

25. W. Wang, J. Yang, and R. Muntz, "STING: A statistical information grid approach to spatial data mining," in *Proceedings of 1997 International Conference on Very Large Data Bases (VLDB '97)* (Athens, Greece), pp. 186–195, August 1997.

26. C. C. Aggarwal and P. S. Yu, "Redefining clustering for high-dimensional applications," *IEEE Transactions on Knowledge and Data Engineering*, vol. 14, pp. 210–225, 2002.

27. J. C. Bezdek, *Pattern Recognition with Fuzzy Objective Function Algorithms.* New York: Plenum Press, 1981.

28. W. Pedrycz, "Conditional fuzzy c-means," *Pattern Recognition Letters*, vol. 17, pp. 625–632, 1996.

29. R. Krishnapuram, A. Joshi, O. Nasraoui, and L. Yi, "Low complexity fuzzy relational clustering algorithms for web mining," *IEEE Transactions on Fuzzy Systems*, vol. 9, pp. 595–607, 2001.

30. W. Pedrycz and A. Bargiela, "Granular clustering: A granular signature of data," *IEEE Transactions on Systems, Man, and Cybernetics, Part B: Cybernetics*, vol. 32, pp. 212–224, 2002.

31. T. Kohonen, *Self-Organization and Associative Memory.* Berlin: Springer-Verlag, 1989.

32. G. A. Carpenter and S. Grossberg, "The ART of adaptive pattern recognition by a self organizing neural network," *IEEE Computer*, pp. 77–88, March 1988.

33. T. Kohonen, S. Kaski, K. Lagus, J. Salojarvi, J. Honkela, V. Paatero, and A. Saarela, "Self organization of a massive document collection," *IEEE Transactions on Neural Networks*, vol. 11, pp. 574–585, 2000.

34. J. Vesanto and E. Alhoniemi, "Clustering of the self-organizing map," *IEEE Transactions on Neural Networks*, vol. 11, pp. 586–600, 2000.

35. D. Alahakoon, S. K. Halgamuge, and B. Srinivasan, "Dynamic self organizing maps with controlled growth for knowledge discovery," *IEEE Transactions on Neural Networks*, vol. 11, pp. 601–614, 2000.

36. G. Sheikholeslami, S. Chatterjee, and A. Zhang, "WaveCluster: A multi-resolution clustering approach for very large spatial databases," in *Proceedings of 1998 International Conference on Very Large Data Bases (VLDB '98)* (New York), pp. 428–439, August 1998.

37. P. Lingras and C. West, "Interval set clustering of Web users with rough k-means," Technical Report No. 2002-002, Dept. of Mathematics and Computer Science, St. Mary's University, Halifax, Canada, 2002.

38. S. Kirkpatrick, C. D. Gelatt Jr., and M. P. Vecchi, "Optimization by simulated annealing," *Science*, vol. 220, pp. 671–680, 1983.

39. F. Glover and M. Laguna, *Tabu Search*. Boston: Kluwer Academic Publishers, 1997.

40. S. C. Chu, J. F. Roddick, and J. S. Pan, "A comparative study and extensions to k-medoids algorithms," in *Proceedings of Fifth International Conference on Optimization: Techniques and Applications* (Hong Kong, China), pp. 1708–1717, 2001.

41. D. Gibson, J. M. Kleinberg, and P. Raghavan, "Clustering categorical data: An approach based on dynamical systems," in *Proceedings of 1998 International Conference on Very Large Data Bases (VLDB '98)* (New York), pp. 311–323, August 1998.

42. S. Guha, R. Rastogi, and K. Shim, "ROCK: A robust clustering algorithm for categorical attributes," in *Proceedings of 1999 International Conference on Data Engineering (ICDE '99)* (Sydney, Australia), pp. 512–521, March 1999.

43. V. Ganti, J. E. Gehrke, and R. Ramakrishnan, "CACTUS: Clustering categorical data using summaries," in *Proceedings of 1999 International Conference on Knowledge Discovery and Data Mining (KDD '99)* (San Diego, CA), 1999.

44. Z. Huang, "Extensions to the k-means algorithm for clustering large data sets with categorical values," *Data Mining and Knowledge Discovery*, vol. 2, pp. 283–304, 1998.

45. H. Ralambondrainy, "A conceptual version of the k-means algorithm," *Pattern Recognition Letters*, vol. 16, pp. 1147–1157, 1995.

46. K. Mali and S. Mitra, "Clustering of symbolic data and its validation," in *Advances in Soft Computing–AFSS 2002* (N. R. Pal and M. Sugeno,

eds.), Lecture Notes in Artificial Intelligence, pp. 339–344, Heidelberg: Springer-Verlag, 2002.

47. K. Mali and S. Mitra, "Clustering and its validation in a symbolic framework," *Pattern Recognition Letters*, 2003 (to appear).

48. D. Fisher, "Improving inference through conceptual clustering," in *Proceedings of 1987 AAAI Conference* (Seattle, WA), pp. 461–465, July 1987.

49. C. Blake and C. Merz, "UCI repository of machine learning databases," 1998. University of California, Irvine, Dept. of Information and Computer Sciences, *http://www.ics.uci.edu/~mlearn/MLRepository.html.*

50. S. K. Pal, A. Ghosh, and B. UmaShankar, "Segmentation of remotely sensed images with fuzzy thresholding, and quantitative evaluation," *International Journal of Remote Sensing*, vol. 21, pp. 2269–2300, 2000.

51. S. K. Pal and P. Mitra, "Multispectral image segmentation using rough set initialized EM algorithm," *IEEE Transactions on Geoscience and Remote Sensing*, vol. 40, pp. 2495–2501, 2002.

52. A. Joshi and R. Krishnapuram, "Robust fuzzy clustering methods to support web mining," in *Proceedings of ACM-SIGMOD Workshop on Data Mining and Knowledge Discovery*, August 1998.

7

Association Rules

7.1 INTRODUCTION

Rule mining constitutes another major function of data mining. Here the relationship between attributes is expressed in the form of rules, thereby enhancing the understandability of the underlying information to users. As explained in Section 1.10, rules can broadly be of three types, namely, association rules, dependency rules and classification rules. In this chapter we dwell on association rules.

Let us consider a database of customer transactions T, where each transaction is a set of items. The objective is to find all rules of the form $X \Rightarrow Y$, which correlate the presence of one set of items X with another set of items Y. An example of such a rule is

98% of people who purchase diapers and baby food also buy baby soap.

For this purpose, one needs to ensure that (i) support of X and Y are greater than a user threshold s, and (ii) conditional probability (confidence) of Y given X is greater than a user threshold c.

A rule must have some minimum user-specified *Confidence*. A rule

$$1 \ \& \ 2 \Rightarrow 3$$

is defined to have 90% confidence if when a customer bought items 1 and 2, in 90% of those cases, the customer also bought item 3. A rule must also have some minimum user-specified *Support*. This implies that the rule $1 \ \& \ 2 \Rightarrow 3$

should hold in some minimum percentage of transactions, in order to have business value.

There can be any number of items in the consequent and antecedent parts of a rule. It is also possible to specify constraints on rules, such as finding only those rules involving expensive imported products.

Sample applications of association rules include

- Market basket analysis.

- Attached mailing in direct marketing.

- Fraud detection for medical insurance and credit cards.

- Department store floor or shelf planning.

An association rule can generally be viewed as being defined over attributes of a relation and has the form $C_1 \Rightarrow C_2$, where C_1 and C_2 are conjunctions of conditions and each condition is either $a_i = v_i$ or $a_i \in [l_i, u_i]$ with v_i being a value (for categoric or numeric) and u_i, l_i being upper and lower bound values (for numeric) from the domain of the attribute a_i. The support of the rule $C_1 \Rightarrow C_2$ is the same as the support of the conjunction $C_1 \wedge C_2$, while its confidence is the ratio of the supports of conditions $C_1 \wedge C_2$ and C_1.

The different types of association rules can be categorized as follows.

1. Boolean: Here the association is between presence or absence of items.

2. Quantitative: Here the attribute values are partitioned into intervals, such as the age or income of an individual.

3. Categorical: Here an attribute is categorical, like the make of a car.

4. Single dimensional: A sample rule is of the form
   $buys(X, \text{``computer''}) \Rightarrow buys(X, \text{``}financial\_management\_software\text{''})$.

5. Multidimensional: A sample rule is of the form
   $age(X, \text{``}30\ldots39\text{''}) \wedge income(X, \text{``}42K\ldots48K''\text{''})$
   $\Rightarrow buys(X, \text{``}high\_resolution\_TV\text{''})$.

6. Multilevel: This involves rules with attributes at different levels of abstraction in a concept hierarchy.

   (a) Considering "$laptop\_computer$" to be at a lower level in the concept hierarchy, as compared to "$computer$," we have rules of the form
       $age(X, \text{``}30\ldots39\text{''}) \Rightarrow buys(X, \text{``}laptop\_computer\text{''})$ and
       $age(X, \text{``}30\ldots39\text{''}) \Rightarrow buys(X, \text{``}computer\text{''})$, or

   (b) when the attributes span across multiple hierarchies, involving concepts "$computer$" and "$printer$", we can have a cross-level rule involving "$computer$" and "$b/w\_printer$" (at a lower level in the

second hierarchy) of the form
"computer" ⇒ *"b/w_printer"*.

In the following sections we provide an overview on the different kinds of association rules and their mining, as reported in the literature. Section 7.2 deals with some efficient algorithms for mining association rules, using the candidate generation and test methods. Section 7.3 gives some insight into depth-first search methods for rule mining. The concept of interestingness of rules is provided in Section 7.4. In Sections 7.5–7.8 we describe multilevel rules, online generation of rules, generalized rules, and scalable mining of rules, respectively. Section 7.9 deals with some other variants of association rule mining. Fuzzy association rules are reviewed in Section 7.10. Finally, Section 7.11 concludes the chapter.

7.2 CANDIDATE GENERATION AND TEST METHODS

In this section we describe the *A priori* algorithm [1, 2] and some of its variants, including the partition algorithm [3].

7.2.1 A priori algorithm

This algorithm computes *frequent itemsets* from a transactions database over multiple iterations. Each iteration involves (i) candidate generation and (ii) candidate counting and selection. Utilizing the knowledge about infrequent itemsets, obtained from previous iterations, the algorithm prunes *a priori* those candidate itemsets that cannot become frequent. After discarding every candidate itemset that has an infrequent subset, the algorithm enters the candidate counting step.

Table 7.1 Sample transactions to demonstrate association rule mining

Transaction ID	Purchased items
1	{1, 2, 3}
2	{1, 3}
3	{1, 4}
4	{2, 5, 6}

7.2.1.1 Example 1: Let us consider an example in Table 7.1, depicting the items purchased by customers in four transactions. For a minimum support of 50% (here, two transactions) and a minimum confidence of 50%, we have the following rules

(i) $1 \Rightarrow 3$ with 50% support and 66% confidence;

(ii) $3 \Rightarrow 1$ with 50% support and 100% confidence.

The objective is to generate confident rules, having at least the minimum confidence. The problem decomposition proceeds as follows:

- Find all sets of items that have minimum support, typically using the *Apriori* algorithm [1, 2]. This is the most expensive phase of the search, and involves lots of research for reducing the complexity.

- Use the *frequent itemsets* to generate the desired rules. Given m items there can be potentially 2^m frequent itemsets.

Consider Table 7.2. For the rule $1 \Rightarrow 3$, we have

$$Support = Support(\{1, 3\}) = 50\%$$

and

$$Confidence = \frac{Support(\{1, 3\})}{Support(\{1\})} = 66\%.$$

Table 7.2   Computation of frequent itemsets

Frequent itemset	Support (%)
$\{1\}$	75
$\{2\}$	50
$\{3\}$	50
$\{1, 3\}$	50

The *A priori* algorithm is outlined as follows. Let F_k be the set of frequent itemsets of size k, let C_k be the set of candidate itemsets of size k, and let F_1 be the set of large items. We start from $k = 1$.

1. **for** all items in frequent itemset F_k **repeat** steps 2–4.

2. Generate new candidates C_{k+1} from F_k.

3. **for** each transaction T in the database, increment the count of all candidates in C_{k+1} that are contained in T.

4. Generate frequent itemsets F_{k+1} of size k from candidates in C_{k+1} with minimum support.

The final solution is $\bigcup_k F_k$.

A key observation is that every subset of a frequent itemset is also frequent. This implies that a candidate itemset in C_{k+1} can be pruned if even one of its subsets is not contained in F_k.

Table 7.3 Example transactions database for frequent itemset generation

Transaction ID	Purchased items
1	{1, 3, 4}
2	{2, 3, 5}
3	{1, 2, 3, 5}
4	{2, 5}

Table 7.4 Stages of Apriori algorithm demonstrating frequent itemset generation

C_1	Count	Support (%)	F_1	C_2	Count	Support (%)	F_2
{1}	2	50	–	{2, 3}	2	50	–
{2}	3	75	{2}	{2, 5}	3	75	{2, 5}
{3}	3	75	{3}	{3, 5}	2	50	–
{4}	1	25	–	–	–	–	–
{5}	3	75	{5}	–	–	–	–

7.2.1.2 Example 2:   Let us explain the *A priori* algorithm with an example database of transactions provided in Table 7.3. Consider Table 7.4, with a minimum *Support* > 50%. After the first scan of the database, we have the candidate itemsets C_1 along with their corresponding *Supports*, as
{1} : 50%, {2} : 75%, {3} : 75%, {4} : 25%, and {5} : 75%.
The frequent itemsets F_1 consist of {2}, {3}, and {5}, each with *Support* of 75%.

Now the candidate itemsets C_2 are {2,3}, {2,5}, {3,5}, with *Supports* of 50%, 75%, 50%, respectively.

The corresponding frequent itemset F_2 becomes {2,5} with a *Support* of 75%.

The rules generated are

$2 \Rightarrow 5$ with $Confidence = \frac{Support\{2,5\}}{Support\{2\}} = 100\%$ and

$5 \Rightarrow 2$ with $Confidence = \frac{Support\{2,5\}}{Support\{5\}} = 100\%.$

However, in this method, multiple passes have to be made over the database for each different value of minimum support and confidence. This number can be as large as the longest frequent itemset. For very large databases of transactions, this may involve considerable input–output (I/O) and lead to unacceptable response times for online queries. Moreover, the potential number of frequent itemsets is exponential to the number of different items, although the actual number of frequent itemsets can be considerably smaller.

Constraints are sometimes specified to focus only on the interesting portions of a database. An example could be to find the association rules where the prices of items are at most 200 dollars ($max < 200$). Incorporating constraints can result in efficiency. The anti-monotonicity property ensures that when an itemset violates the constraint, so does any of its supersets (say, $min > X$ or $max < X$). The *A priori* algorithm uses this property for pruning the rulebase.

7.2.2   Partition algorithm

The main characteristics of the partition algorithm [3] are given below.

- Logically divide the horizontal database into a number of nonoverlapping partitions, which can be accommodated in main memory.

- Each partition is read, and locally frequent itemsets are generated.

- All locally frequent itemsets are merged, and a second pass is made through all the partitions.

- Global counts of all chosen itemsets are obtained.

A key observation, here, is that a globally frequent itemset must be locally frequent in at least one of the non-overlapping partitions. This implies that all frequent itemsets are guaranteed to be found. It minimizes I/O by scanning the database only twice. In the first pass, it generates the set of all potentially or locally frequent itemsets, while in the second pass it counts their global support. However, the Partition algorithm may enumerate too many false positives (itemsets locally frequent in some partition but not globally frequent) in the first pass. Moreover, if this local frequent set does not fit in main memory then additional database scans are required.

7.2.3   Some extensions

There exist some other variants of the *A priori* algorithm. These include (i) consideration that a high confidence may not essentially imply high correlation, (ii) incorporation of correlations, and (iii) pruning of the large number of mined rules.

The DHP algorithm [4] involves hashing in the framework of the *A priori* algorithm. It tries to reduce the number of candidates by collecting approximate counts in the previous level. Here a k-itemset is considered to be in C_k only if it is hashed into a bucket satisfying the minimum support criterion. However, like *A priori*, it requires as many database passes as the longest itemset.

The method in Refs. [5] and [6] finds all frequent itemsets using random sampling. A *negative border* is indicative of infrequent itemsets, whose subsets are all frequent. The major steps are as follows.

- Scan the database to count support for frequent itemsets, and for itemsets in a negative border.

- If no itemset in the negative border is frequent, then no more passes over the database is needed.

- Otherwise, scan the database to count support for candidate itemsets generated from the negative border.

The negative border is useful in increasing the efficiency of generation of large itemsets and in derivation of *negative* association rules.

Dynamic Itemset Counting [7] dynamically counts the support for all supersets of an itemset (with frequent subsets) if, during a pass, an itemset becomes frequent. It counts candidates of varying lengths as the database scan progresses and is thereby able to reduce the number of scans over the *A priori* algorithm.

7.3   DEPTH-FIRST SEARCH METHODS

The *A priori* algorithm is a breadth-first search technique that exhaustively evaluates all possible combinations of itemsets at a particular level. An efficient variation of this is a depth-first search algorithm *Eclat* [8], used for association rule mining. A search tree is generated in terms of the itemsets using depth-first traversal. This results in an efficient utilization of the memory and has applicability to the handling of large data.

Often the *A priori* algorithm needs to generate a huge number of candidate sets. For example, in order to discover a frequent pattern of size 100, such as $\{a_1, \ldots, a_{100}\}$, it needs to generate more than $2^{100} \approx 10^{30}$ candidates. Moreover, it may need to repeatedly scan the database while checking a large set of candidates using pattern matching.

The Frequent-Pattern growth (FP-growth) algorithm avoids this candidate generation phase all together, by employing a divide-and-conquer strategy [9]. It *compresses* the database representing frequent (or representative) items into a Frequent-Pattern tree (FP-tree), while retaining the itemset association information. The compressed database is divided into a set of conditional (or projected) databases, each associated with one frequent item. Finally, each compressed database is mined separately.

Example 3:   Let us consider Tables 7.3 and 7.4 for describing the FP-growth algorithm. In the first scan of the transactional database we obtain the list of items, sorted in descending order on their counts as

$$L = \{(2,3), (3,3), (5,3), (1,2), (4,1)\},$$

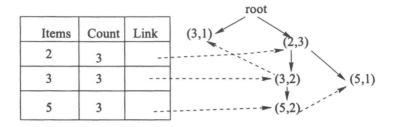

Items	Count	Link
2	3	--
3	3	---
5	3	--

Fig. 7.1   An example FP-tree.

where the number following the comma indicates the count. Considering only those items having minimum support of 3, for simplified understanding, we have

$$L' = \{(2,3),(3,3),(5,3)\}.$$

The resultant FP-tree of Fig. 7.1 is constructed as follows. First the *root* node is created. The database is scanned a second time, and the items in each transaction are processed in the order given in L' while creating a branch corresponding to each transaction. For example, the scan of the first transaction $\{1,3,4\}$ of Table 7.3 yields the item $\{3\}$, as only it has minimum support. This leads to the leftmost branch of the tree with node $(3,1)$, with item $\{3\}$ being linked to the *root*. The second transaction $\{2,3,5\}$ is found to be in proper order as L', and it generates a branch from the *root* with three nodes $(2,1)$, $(3,1)$, and $(5,1)$. The third transaction $\{1,2,3,5\}$ yields the itemset $\{2,3,5\}$ according to L', and it shares the second branch of the tree. Hence the counts along these three nodes are incremented by one along the entire path, now resulting in nodes $(2,2)$, $(3,2)$, and $(5,2)$. The fourth transaction $\{2,5\}$, being again in order as L', is used to generate the rightmost branch of the tree with a common prefix for item $\{2\}$. Therefore, the nodes along this path from the *root* now become $(2,3)$ and $(5,1)$.

Tree traversal is facilitated by constructing an *item header table*, as shown in Fig. 7.1, so that each item points to its node(s) of occurrence in the tree through a chain of dotted links. Now mining of frequent patterns in databases reduces to recursively mining the FP-tree. The algorithm starts from the last item in list L', as an initial suffix pattern, and constructs its *conditional pattern base* or sub-database consisting of the set of *prefix paths* in the FP-tree co-occurring with it.

Example 4:   Here we demonstrate the tree traversal method for generating frequent itemsets. Let us start from item $\{5\}$. Based on the node-link connections from the root of Fig. 7.1, the two paths selected are $\{(2,3),(5,1)\}$ and $\{(2,3),(3,2),(5,2)\}$. We observe that the samples with a frequent item $\{5\}$ are $\{(2,2),(3,2),(5,2)\}$ for transaction IDs 2, 3, and $\{(2,1),(5,1)\}$ for transaction ID 4, from Table 7.3. The frequent patterns generated, observing minimum support from both these patterns, are therefore $\{(2,3),(5,3)\}$ or simply the itemset $\{2,5\}$.

Analyzing item $\{3\}$, we obtain paths $\{(3,1)\}$ and $\{(2,3),(3,2)\}$ from the root. However these lead to no frequent patterns. Hence the solution of the FP-growth method is the set of frequent itemsets $\{2,5\}$.

Instead of finding long frequent patterns, the FP-growth method resorts to searching recursively for shorter ones followed by a concatenation of the suffix. The use of the least frequent item as a suffix serves to significantly reduce the search costs. The FP-growth method is efficient and scalable for mining long frequent patterns. It is found to be faster [9] than the *Tree-projection* algorithm, which recursively projects a database into a tree of projected databases, as well as the *A priori* algorithm.

7.4 INTERESTING RULES

Unlike accuracy, which involves evaluating the performance of a large number of rules exhibiting typical behavior for a particular situation, *interestingness* measures the deviation from prior expectation of the general information inherent in these prevalent rules. Mining's payoff is in extracting such *surprising* phenomena that lie hidden in the data. The concept of surprisingness is explained from the information theoretic viewpoint in Section 3.2.1. Now let us outline what makes a rule surprising. It

- does not match prior expectation and

- cannot be trivially derived from simpler rules.

It is evident that rules having very low *interestingness* values need not be examined, as they are likely to contain well-known aspects about the domain. So we need some kind of measure to evaluate this interestingness, which can again be objective or subjective [10]. While objective measures categorize the interestingness of a pattern in terms of its structure and the underlying data used in the discovery process, the subjective measures additionally incorporate the views of the person inspecting the pattern. These lead to the development of parameters like unexpectedness and actionability. A rule is interesting to a user if it is unexpected (or surprising) and if (s)he can act on the knowledge provided by the rule to her/his advantage.

The different interestingness measures are provided below. Note that these are in addition to the quantitative measures of Section 2.4.2, used for evaluating the performance of rules.

1. *Simplicity:* This is desirable for human comprehension, as a more complex rule structure implies that it is more difficult to interpret and is

therefore less interesting. It is measured in terms of the rule length or the number of decision tree nodes or leaves.

2. *Certainty*: This is the reliability (or accuracy) in classification rules. It is measured as

$$confidence(X \Rightarrow Y) = \frac{no._{-}of_{-}tuples_{-}containing_{-}both_{-}X_{-}and_{-}Y}{no._{-}of_{-}tuples_{-}containing_{-}X}.$$

(7.1)

3. *Utility*: This is measured as

$$support(X \Rightarrow Y) = \frac{no._{-}of_{-}tuples_{-}containing_{-}both_{-}X_{-}and_{-}Y}{total_{-}no._{-}of_{-}tuples}. \quad (7.2)$$

4. *Novelty*: This corresponds to patterns that contribute new information or increased performance. It implies some sort of data exception, which differs from what is expected based on a statistical model or user beliefs.

5. *Interest*: This also provides a measure of the new information provided, and it can be viewed as an estimation of the increase in probability of Y caused by the occurrence of X, that is, $P(Y|X) - P(Y)$. It is expressed as

$$interest(X \Rightarrow Y) = confidence(X \Rightarrow Y) - \frac{no._{-}of_{-}tuples_{-}containing_{-}Y}{total_{-}no._{-}of_{-}tuples}.$$

(7.3)

7.5   MULTILEVEL RULES

Data can be generalized by replacing low-level concepts with their more general high-level concepts from a concept hierarchy. When a rule involves attributes from different levels in such a concept hierarchy, it is termed *Multilevel*. A rule is typically said to be *redundant* if it does not offer any additional information and is less general (namely, at a lower level).

Let us consider an example concept hierarchy of *computer* (support: 10%) at level 1, followed by descendants *laptop* (support: 6%) and *desktop* (support: 4%) at the next lower level 2. There exist several approaches to mine Multilevel rules. These are mentioned below.

- *Uniform minimum support* for all levels: The search avoids examining itemsets containing any item whose ancestors do not have the minimum support. For example, if the minimum support for the levels is 5%, then only the association involving *laptop* can be considered at level 2. However, if the minimum support threshold is set too high, it may miss several meaningful associations occurring at lower abstraction levels.

Moreover, if this threshold is too low, it may lead to the generation of many uninteresting associations at higher abstraction levels.

- *Reduced minimum support* at lower levels: Now let the minimum support at level 2 be reduced to (say) 3%. This overcomes the first problem mentioned above, so that the association involving *desktop* also becomes frequent at level 2.

- *Level-by-level independent*: Each node is examined regardless of whether or not its parent node is frequent. Here both concepts *laptop* and *desktop* are examined.

- *Level-cross filtering by single item*: An item at the ith level is examined if and only if its parent at the $(i-1)$th level is frequent. This may miss associations between low-level items that are frequent based on a reduced minimum support, but whose ancestors do not satisfy (higher) minimum support. For example, if the minimum support at levels 1 and 2 are set at 12% and 3% respectively, then the concepts at level 2 are not examined here since the concept at level 1 (i.e., computer) is not frequent.

- *Controlled level-cross filtering* by single item: Users may choose to lower the level passage threshold at higher concept levels to allow descendants of subfrequent items at lower levels to be examined. For example, if the level passage threshold at level 1 is now set at 8%, then the descendants of the subfrequent concept *computer* (support: 10%) can be involved for determining associations.

- *Level-cross filtering by k-itemset*: A k-itemset at the ith level is examined, if and only if its parent k-itemset at the $(i-1)$th level is frequent. This restriction can lead to filtering out of many valuable patterns. Let us now modify the above example to include the concept pair $(k = 2)$ *computer & printer* (support: 7%) at level 1, followed by descendants *laptop & b/w printer* (support: 1%), *laptop & color printer* (support: 2%), *desktop & b/w printer* (support: 1%), and *desktop & color printer* (support: 3%) at level 2. If the minimum support at levels 1 and 2 are now set at 5% and 2%, respectively, then all 2-itemsets at level 2 can now be examined to determine associations.

7.6 ONLINE GENERATION OF RULES

It is often hard for a user to guess, *a priori*, how many rules might satisfy a given level of support and confidence. In most cases, one finds that the number of redundant rules is significantly larger than the number of essential rules. To circumvent these problems, an online algorithm is described in Ref. [11]. The data are preprocessed and stored such that a graph theoretic search algorithm, with complexity proportional to the size of the output, may be applied for effectively handling repeated online queries. It is independent of the size of the transactional (preprocessed) data. The algorithm is capable of quickly discovering association rules, in compact form, from large itemsets with specific items in the antecedent or consequent.

In most cases, the number of redundant rules is significantly larger than the number of essential rules. This kind of redundancy arises when we consider rules having more than one item in the consequent. For example, if the rule $X \Rightarrow YZ$ is true for a given minimum support and confidence, then rules such as $XY \Rightarrow Z$, $XZ \Rightarrow Y$, $X \Rightarrow Y$, and $X \Rightarrow Z$ are said to be redundant. Mining of nonredundant association rules helps significantly in the reduction of irrelevant noise. The kinds of online queries that this system can support are outlined below.

1. Find all association rules above a certain level of *min_support* and *min_confidence*.

2. At a certain level of *min_support* and *min_confidence*, find all association rules concerned with the set of items X.

3. Find the number of association rules or itemsets in any of the above two cases.

4. Find the level of *min_support* at which exactly k-itemsets exist containing the set of items Z.

5. For a particular level of *min_confidence* c, find the level of *min_support* at which exactly k single-consequent rules exist involving the set of items Z.

An itemset X is said to be *adjacent* to an itemset Y, if one of them can be obtained from the other by adding a single item. An itemset X is called the parent of itemset Y (descendant or child) if the latter can be generated from the former by adding one item. The algorithm proceeds by forming an *adjacency lattice L*, which is a directed acyclic graph. For each vertex $v(J)$ in L which is a descendant of $v(I)$, support $S(J) \leq S(I)$. The number of edges in the adjacency lattice is equal to the sum of the number of items in the primary itemsets. For a given itemset I (including the null set $\{\}$), the algorithm finds all itemsets J such that $v(J)$ is reachable from $v(I)$ by a directed path in the lattice L and satisfies $S(J) \geq s$, where s indicates minimum support.

The adjacency lattice, so generated from the transactions, is then traversed to mine association rules.

7.7   GENERALIZED RULES

Items in a database are often stored as concept hierarchies. Often there exist associations across these hierarchies, resulting in generalized association rules.

Let us consider a hierarchy of *clothes*, categorized as *outwear* (consisting of *jackets* and *pants*) and *shirts*. Let there be another hierarchy of *footwear* grouped as *shoes* and *hiking boots*. In this case, a rule *clothes* ⇒ *footwear* may hold even if the rule *clothes* ⇒ *shoes* does not hold (depending upon the corresponding levels of confidence and support). Approaches to handle such rules are provided in the literature [12, 13].

A graph-based approach [14] is used to discover primitive (conventional), generalized, and multilevel association rules. In a concept hierarchy, the terminal nodes are the database items while the nonterminal nodes are the generalized items. Here the database is scanned only once to construct an *association graph*, which is then traversed to generate all large itemsets. The basic steps of the algorithm are as follows.

- Numbering phase: Here all items are assigned an integer value.

- Large item generation: This consists of determining the items with support not less than a user specified minimum support.

- Association graph construction: This consists of determining the association between large items.

- Association pattern generation: This is done by traversing the association graph.

- Association rule generation: Here one generates all generalized and multilevel rules.

Table 7.5 Transactions demonstrating Bit vector computation

Transaction ID	Itemset
1	CAD
2	ECB
3	ABCE
4	EB

The algorithm scans the database and computes a *Bit vector* for each item. The length of the vector is equal to the number of transactions in the database. If an item appears in the ith transaction, the ith bit of the corresponding bit vector BV_i is set to 1, else it is 0.

Example 5: Table 7.5 depicts a sample set of transactions of items to demonstrate Bit vector generation. Let the minimum support be 50%, that is, 2 transactions. The BVs for items A, B, C, E are (1010), (0111), (1110), (0111), respectively. The support for itemset $\{i_1, \ldots, i_k\}$ is the number of ones in $BV_{i_1} \wedge \ldots \wedge BV_{i_k}$. For every two large items i, j ($i < j$), if the number of ones in $BV_i \wedge BV_j$ achieves the user-specified minimum support, then a directed edge from item i to item j is created in the association graph. Considering itemset $\{i, j\}$ to be a large 2-itemset, sample rules generated from Table 7.5 are $A \Rightarrow C$ (with support 2); $B \Rightarrow C, E$ (with supports 2,3 respectively); and $C \Rightarrow E$ (with support 2).

However, the algorithm assumes that the bit vectors fit in main memory, and thus scalability could be a problem for databases with millions of transactions.

7.8   SCALABLE MINING OF RULES

The idea of scalable mining in large databases is important because the search space is often exponential in the number of database attributes. Most current approaches are iterative in nature, requiring multiple database scans. This makes them very expensive. Use of sampling can be sensitive to data skew, and this can adversely affect the performance of an algorithm. Moreover, most existing approaches use very complicated data structures involving poor locality and thereby incur additional space and computational overheads.

A scalable algorithm, described in Ref. [15], utilizes the structural properties of frequent itemsets to facilitate fast discovery. Efficient lattice traversal techniques are presented to quickly identify all the long frequent itemsets and their subsets (if required). The approach is insensitive to data skew, and the simple intersection operations involved make it an attractive option for direct implementation in distributed systems using SQL. Its main characteristics are as follows.

- It uses a vertical transactions ID (TID)-list, associating each itemset with the list of transactions in which it occurs. All frequent itemsets are enumerated via TID-list intersections.

- The original search space (lattice) is decomposed into smaller sublattices, which can be processed independently in the main memory. One can use prefix-based and maximal-clique[1]-based partition for this purpose.

- Bottom-up, top-down and efficient hybrid searches are used for enumerating the frequent items within each sublattice.

- The algorithm requires only a few database scans, thereby minimizing I/O costs. It also retains linear scalability in the number of transactions.

---

[1]A graph consists of a set of vertices and edges. A graph is complete if there is an edge between all pairs of vertices. A complete subgraph of a graph is called a *clique*.

- Some of the assertions made in the algorithm include the following.

  - All subsets of a frequent itemset are frequent.
  - The maximal frequent itemsets uniquely determine all frequent itemsets.
  - Two itemsets are in the same class if they share a common k length *prefix*.

The algorithm is found to outperform several approaches like *A priori* and Partition (described in Section 7.2).

7.9 OTHER VARIANTS

In this section we dwell on some variants like quantitative association rules, temporal association rules, correlation rules, localized associations, and optimized association rules.

7.9.1 Quantitative association rules

As mentioned earlier, a boolean association rule is an implication written as $X \Rightarrow Y$ among items (or attributes) X and Y. The support of the rule is s, if s tuples contain both X and Y as attributes. The confidence of the rule is c ($c < 1$, expressed as a percentage) if c of all tuples that contain X also contain Y.

A more general form of such rules is the quantitative association rule [16]. A sample quantitative association rule is

10% of married people with age between 50 and 70 have at least 2 cars.

The algorithm involves discretizing the domains of quantitative attributes into intervals, in order to reduce the domain into a categorical one. Here A and B are vectors of intervals, each of which is in one of the attributes in X and Y, respectively. The support of the rule is s, if s tuples fall in intervals of A and B, when projected to attributes X and Y respectively. The confidence of the rule is c, if c of all the tuples that fall in intervals in A also fall in intervals in B.

7.9.2 Temporal association rules

Temporal rules can be used to describe the rich temporal character inherent in the data. Consider a sample rule *diaper* $\Rightarrow$ *baby food*, with a support of 5% and confidence of 87%. The support of this rule may jump to 25% between 6 to 9 PM on weekdays. The problem is to determine how to find rules that follow some interesting user-defined temporal patterns. The challenge is to design efficient algorithms that do much better than finding every rule in every time unit. Approaches in this direction are provided in the literature [17, 18].

7.9.3   Correlation rules

Association rules, typically, do not capture correlations. For example, suppose 90% customers buy coffee, 25% buy tea, and 20% buy both tea and coffee. The rule *tea* $\Rightarrow$ *coffee* has a high support of 0.2 and confidence 0.8. But the items {tea, coffee} are not correlated. The expected support of customers buying both is $0.9 \times 0.25 = 0.225$.

In correlation rules, the correlation between the occurrences of X and Y is expressed as

$$corr_{X,Y} = \frac{P(X \cup Y)}{P(X)P(Y)}, \tag{7.4}$$

where a value < 1 indicates a negative correlation, $= 1$ signifies independence, and > 1 implies a positive correlation between the items, and $P(.)$ refers to the corresponding probability.

Fast itemset counting has been used to find correlated events. This has applications in (i) medicine, to find redundant tests, (ii) cross selling in retail and (iii) banking. These rules help improve the predictive capability of classifiers that assume attribute independence.

7.9.4   Localized associations

Aggarwal et al. [19] have designed an algorithm effective in discovering localized associations, from individual segments, that expose a customer pattern which is more specific than the aggregate behavior. Such personalized associations are applicable to more useful target marketing. For example, those transactions which are drawn from extremely cold geographical regions may contain correlations corresponding to heavy winter apparel, whereas these may not be present in the aggregate data because they are often not present to a very high degree in the rest of the database. An attempt to find such correlations, using global analysis by lowering the support, will result in finding a large number of uninteresting and redundant "correlations" which are created simply by chance throughout the dataset.

The CLustering for ASsociation Discovery (CLASD) algorithm [19] can also be used to segment categorical data. Concepts from both agglomerative and partitional clustering are used in conjunction with random sampling, in order to make it robust, practical, and scalable for very large databases. The *affinity* $A(i, j)$ between two items i and j is expressed as

$$A(i, j) = \frac{sup(\{i, j\})}{sup(\{i\}) + sup(\{j\}) - sup(\{i, j\})}, \tag{7.5}$$

where $sup(X)$ denotes the aggregate support of a set of items X. The *similarity* between a pair of transactions $T = \{i_1, \ldots, i_m\}$ and $T' = \{j_1, \ldots, j_n\}$ is defined as the average affinity of their items. Here

$$Sim(T, T') = \frac{\sum_{p=1}^{m} \sum_{q=1}^{n} A(i_p, j_q)}{m * n}. \qquad (7.6)$$

The overall approach uses a set of cluster representatives or seeds to create the partitions and is always larger than the final number of clusters c. In each iteration, the closest pair of representatives are merged to reduce their number by a factor α. Random sampling is performed on the database to assign the transactions to seeds. The value of the sample size is also increased by a factor α in each iteration. Thus later phases of the clustering benefit from larger sample sizes, and robust computations are possible in later iterations.

7.9.5 Optimized association rules

Association rules are built from atomic conditions. For the atomic condition $a_i = v_i$, if v_i is a value from the domain of attribute a_i, the condition is referred to as *instantiated*; else, if v_i is a variable, the condition is termed as *uninstantiated*. Optimized association rules are permitted to contain uninstantiated attributes. The problem is to determine instantiations, such that either the support or confidence of the rule is maximized. Optimized association rules are generalized [20] by allowing the rules to contain disjunctions over an arbitrary number of uninstantiated attributes, having either categorical or numeric values. Useful information is extracted about seasonal and local patterns involving multiple attributes. Pruning is incorporated using a combination of depth-first search, branch and bound techniques, and a graph search algorithm.

7.10 FUZZY ASSOCIATION RULES

Quantitative association rules, as mentioned in Section 7.9.1, require the specification of appropriate intervals along each attribute. However, these intervals may often not be concise and meaningful enough for human experts to discover nontrivial knowledge. Fuzzy sets can be used from this perspective to represent intervals with non-sharp boundaries, thereby generating fuzzy association rules (introduced in Section 2.3.3). Assignment of meaningful linguistic terms to the fuzzy sets makes these rules more understandable. A sample fuzzy association rule is

10% of married old people have at least several cars.

Algorithms for mining fuzzy association rules are provided in the literature [21]. Typically, an expert is required to provide the fuzzy sets for the

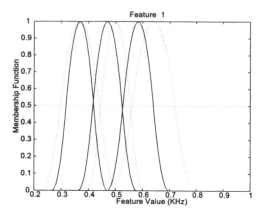

Fig. 7.2   Overlapping fuzzy sets.

quantitative attributes, along with their corresponding membership functions. Sometimes these functions are also determined by clustering and subsequent tuning. Pruning is another feature necessary to retain only the *interesting* rules.

Fuzzy set concepts are integrated with the *A priori* algorithm (Section 7.2.1) to mine interesting fuzzy association rules, using the Fuzzy Transaction Data mining Algorithm (FTDA) [21]. Quantitative values in transactions are transformed to natural and more understandable linguistic terms, which are then filtered to generate fuzzy associations.

Let there be N transactions data each with n attribute values, a set of membership functions, and predefined minimum support s and confidence c. The steps of the FTDA are outlined as follows.

1. Transform the quantitative value a_{ij} of each transaction t^i, $i = 1, \ldots, N$, for each attribute a_j, $j = 1, \ldots, n$, into a fuzzy set μ_{ij_k} represented as

$$\left(\frac{\mu_{ij_1}}{R_{j_1}} + \frac{\mu_{ij_2}}{R_{j_2}} + \ldots + \frac{\mu_{ij_l}}{R_{j_l}} \right),$$

using the given membership functions. Here R_{j_k} is the kth linguistic partition (e.g., *low, medium, high*, etc.) of attribute a_j, μ_{ij_k} is the fuzzy membership value for a_{ij} in region R_{j_k}, and $l(= |a_j|)$ is the number of fuzzy partitions used for a_j.

(**Example:** Consider Fig. 7.2. Let there be a quantitative input feature (in KHz), denoted as a_j. The corresponding value of transaction t^i along this axis is given as a_{ij}. Using fuzzy sets, we split this axis into l overlapping partitions of linguistic terms, say, *low, medium*, and *high*. Let these partitions be represented as R_{j_1} for low, R_{j_2} for medium, and R_{j_3} for high, with centers r_{j_1}, r_{j_2}, r_{j_3}, respectively. The three overlapping membership functions (drawn with solid lines) indicate low, medium, and high regions of the feature axis, from left to right. Here we use π membership functions, as explained in Section 2.2.2.1. The overlap between adjacent partitions is termed p, uniformly for each pair, along the axis. A quantitative feature value a_{ij} is hence mapped to a three-dimensional vector $[\mu_{ij_1}, \mu_{ij_2}, \mu_{ij_3}]$, whose components (lying in $[0,1]$) refer to the membership value to the corresponding linguistic term (low R_{j_1}, medium R_{j_2}, or high R_{j_3}). Note that the membership function at each of the centers $(r_{j_1}, r_{j_2}, r_{j_3})$ has a value of 1.)

2. Calculate the scalar cardinality of each attribute region R_{j_k} in the transaction data as

$$count_{j_k} = \sum_{i=1}^{N} \mu_{ij_k}. \tag{7.7}$$

3. Find $count_j^{\max} = \max_{k=1}^{|a_j|} count_{j_k}$, for $j = 1, \ldots, n$. Let $R_j^{\max}$ be the linguistic partition with $count_j^{\max}$ for attribute a_j.

4. Check whether the $count_j^{\max}$ of each $R_j^{\max}$, $j = 1, \ldots, n$, is larger than or equal to the support s, and then put it in the set of frequent 1-itemsets (F_1). Therefore

$$F_1 = \left\{ R_j^{\max} | count_j^{\max} \geq s \right\} \tag{7.8}$$

for $1 \leq j \leq n$.

5. Set $r = 1$, where r represents the number of items kept in the current frequent itemsets.

6. Generate the candidate set C_{r+1} from F_r in a manner similar to that in the *A priori* algorithm.

7. **for** each newly formed $(r + 1)$-itemset R [corresponding to the $R_j^{\max}$ along jth axis by Eq. (7.8)], with items $(R_1, R_2, \ldots, R_{r+1})$ in C_{r+1}, **do** the following substeps.

   (a) Calculate the fuzzy value of each transaction data t^i in R as $\mu_{iR} = \mu_{iR_1} \wedge \mu_{iR_2} \wedge \ldots \wedge \mu_{iR_{r+1}}$, where μ_{iR_j} is the membership value of t^i in region R_j. If the minimum operator is used for the intersection, we have

$$\mu_{iR} = \min_{j=1}^{r+1} \mu_{iR_j}. \tag{7.9}$$

   (b) Calculate the scalar cardinality of R in the transaction data as

$$count_R = \sum_{i=1}^{N} \mu_{iR}. \tag{7.10}$$

(c) **if** $count_R$ is larger than or equal to the support s **then** put R in F_{r+1}.

8. **if** F_{r+1} is null **then** go to the next step; **else** set $r = r + 1$ and **repeat** steps 6–8.

9. Construct the association rules for all frequent q-itemset R with items $(R_1, R_2, \ldots, R_q)$, $q \geq 2$, using the following substeps.

(a) Form all possible association rules as

$$R_1 \wedge \ldots \wedge R_{k-1} \wedge R_{k+1} \wedge \ldots \wedge R_q \rightarrow R_k, \qquad (7.11)$$

for $k = 1, \ldots, q$.

(b) Calculate the confidence values of all association rules using

$$\frac{\sum_{i=1}^{N} \mu_i S}{\sum_{i=1}^{N} \left(\mu_{iR_1} \wedge \ldots \wedge \mu_{iR_{k-1}} \wedge \mu_{iR_{k+1}} \wedge \ldots \wedge \mu_{iR_q} \right)}.$$

10. Output the rules with confidence values larger than or equal to the predefined confidence c.

The rules mined can serve as meta-knowledge concerning the given transactions. Since each attribute uses only the linguistic term with the maximum cardinality, the number of items remains the same as that of the original attributes. Instead, if in step 4, all the regions with support values larger than the threshold are considered, then the algorithm would generate more rules while also consuming more time. Thus trade-off exists between rule completeness and time complexity.

Determination of appropriate fuzzy sets R_{j_k}, $k = 1, \ldots, l$, for quantitative attribute a_j, is made using clustering. Here optimization of a goodness index is made based on cluster compaction and separation [22]. The number l of such clusters and their corresponding updated centers $r_{j_i}, i = 1, \ldots, l$, are obtained. Let the initial set of overlapping membership functions be indicated by the dotted line in Fig. 7.2. Clustering is used to tune the centers of these functions, thereby translating the membership functions along the feature axis. The final situation, after updating, is depicted by the solid line in the figure.

Initially a quantitative attribute interval is divided into l linguistic subintervals around the cluster centers, with a coverage (or overlapping) of $p\%$ between adjacent linguistic partitions. The non-fuzzy partitioning is obtained as a special case with $p = 0$. For the ith linguistic fuzzy set R_{j_i}, the effective upper and lower bounds $d_{j_i}^+$ and $d_{j_i}^-$ are expressed as

$$d_{j_i}^+ = r_{j_i} + \frac{1}{100} * \left(\frac{100 - p}{2} \right) * (r_{j_{i+1}} - r_{j_i}), \qquad (7.12)$$

$$d_{j_i}^- = r_{j_i} - \frac{1}{100} * \left(\frac{100 - p}{2}\right) * (r_{j_i} - r_{j_{i-1}}), \qquad (7.13)$$

respectively, with a uniform overlap p between each pair of adjacent partitions.

Interestingness measures, based on statistics and information theory, have been designed [22] for fuzzy association rules. Given a database $D = \{t^1, t^2, \ldots, t^N\}$ with N transactions, let (Z, C) be an attribute-fuzzy set pair (itemset) for attribute $Z = X \cup Y$ having associated fuzzy set $C = A \cup B$. Here X *is* A is the antecedent, and Y *is* B the consequent of the fuzzy association rule, such that X and Y are disjoint.

If the rule $(X, A) \Rightarrow (Y, B)$ is interesting, it should have enough *fuzzy support* $FS_{(Z,C)}$ and a high *fuzzy confidence* $FC_{((X,A),(Y,B))}$. These are computed as

$$FS_{(Z,C)} = \frac{\sum_{i=1}^N \prod_{j=1}^m t^i(Z_j, C_j)}{N}, \qquad (7.14)$$

where m is the number of items in itemset (Z, C), and

$$FC_{((X,A),(Y,B))} = \frac{FS_{(Z,C)}}{FS_{(X,A)}}. \qquad (7.15)$$

Fuzzy covariance is based on the co-occurrence of the antecedent (X, A) and consequent (Y, B) and is defined as

$$Cov_{((X,A),(Y,B))} = FS_{(Z,C)} - FS_{(X,A)} * FS_{(Y,B)}. \qquad (7.16)$$

Fuzzy correlation, additionally, takes the pattern distribution into consideration. It is expressed as

$$Corr_{((X,A),(Y,B))} = \frac{Cov_{((X,A),(Y,B))}}{\sqrt{Var_{(X,A)} * Var_{(Y,B)}}}, \qquad (7.17)$$

where $Var_{(X,A)} = FS_{(X,A)^2} - \left(FS_{(X,A)}\right)^2$ and $FS_{(X,A)^2} = \frac{\sum_{i=1}^N \left(\prod_{j=1}^m t^i(X_j, A_j)\right)^2}{N}$ for (X, A). In both these cases, only a positive value implies that the antecedent and consequent are related: The higher the value, the greater their relation.

Let us now describe the information theoretic measures. The *independence entropy* $H_{((X,A);(Y,B))}$ represents the amount of information needed per transaction, using a (false) assumption of independence, when the true probability is $FS_{(Z,C)}$ [Eq. (7.14)] with true entropy $H_{(Z,C)}$ for (Z, C). Here

$$H_{((X,A);(Y,B))} = -FS_{(Z,C)} \log_2 \left(FS_{(X,A)} FS_{(Y,B)}\right) \\ - \left(1 - FS_{(Z,C)}\right) \log_2 \left(1 - FS_{(X,A)} FS_{(Y,B)}\right)$$

and

$$H_{(Z,C)} = -FS_{(Z,C)} * \log_2 FS_{(Z,C)} - \left(1 - FS_{(Z,C)}\right) * \log_2 \left(1 - FS_{(Z,C)}\right).$$

[Note the analogy with the conventional entropy expression of Eq. (5.1)]. Using these, we obtain a good measure of correlation termed *unconditional entropy* UE that is defined as

$$UE_{((X,A),(Y,B))} = H_{((X,A);(Y,B))} - H_{(Z,C)}. \qquad (7.18)$$

This difference is always larger when the dependence is higher.

The *unconditional entropy* $H_{(Y,B)}$ of the consequent (Y, B) is expressed as

$$H_{(Y,B)} = -FS_{(Y,B)} * \log_2 FS_{(Y,B)} - \left(1 - FS_{(Y,B)}\right) * \log_2 \left(1 - FS_{(Y,B)}\right).$$

The conditional probability $P_{((Y,B)|(X,A))}$ is the same as fuzzy confidence $FC_{((X,A),(Y,B))}$ of Eq. (7.15) and is different from $P_{(Y,B)}$. We use

$$H_{((Y,B)|(X,A))} = \quad -FC_{((X,A),(Y,B))} \log_2 \left(FC_{((X,A),(Y,B))}\right) \\ - \left(1 - FC_{((X,A),(Y,B))}\right) \log_2 \left(1 - FC_{((X,A),(Y,B))}\right).$$

The interestingness measure *conditional entropy* $CE_{((X,A),(Y,B))}$ is given as

$$CE_{((X,A),(Y,B))} = H_{(Y,B)} - H_{((Y,B)|(X,A))}. \qquad (7.19)$$

Genetic algorithms are used [23] to tune the fuzzy support s and confidence c, while generating fuzzy rules based on the *A priori* algorithm. The fitness function is chosen to maximize the classification accuracy and minimize the number of fuzzy rules.

Mining of fuzzy generalized rules, expressing associations across higher-level concept hierarchies (fuzzy taxonomies), is described in Ref. [24]. The *A priori* algorithm is extended to handle fuzzy sets in the generalized framework. Linguistic hedges, like *very, more or less*, etc., are incorporated in these rules to extract more meaningful knowledge.

7.11 CONCLUSIONS AND DISCUSSION

Mining of associations among items in large groups of transactions constitutes an integral part of data mining. In this chapter we have described efficient mining of association rules. These include the candidate generation and test methods, and depth-first search methods. The concept of interesting rules has been highlighted. Techniques involving multilevel rules, online generation of rules, generalized rules, and scalable mining of rules have been outlined. Fuzzy association rules have also been described, along with several fuzzy interestingness measures.

Association rules have recently been applied to texture classification and image segmentation [25]. The statistical and structural information of an image are embedded in the local intensity variation patterns of the texture regions. Association rules are used to identify these frequently-occurring patterns in the image, and discover relationships which have significant discriminative power. The frequency of occurrence of these local patterns, within a region, are used as the texture features.

In the following chapter we deal with rule mining in the soft computing framework. A modular strategy enables splitting of the problem into subtasks. This sort of *divide-and-conquer* approach is useful from the context of data mining.

REFERENCES

1. R. Agrawal, T. Imielinski, and A. Swami, "Mining association rules between sets of items in large databases," in *Proceedings of 1993 ACM SIGMOD International Conference on Management of Data* (Washington, D.C.), pp. 207–216, May 1993.

2. R. Agrawal and R. Srikant, "Fast algorithms for mining association rules in large databases," in *Proceedings of 20th International Conference on Very Large Databases*, pp. 478–499, September 1994.

3. A. Savasere, E. Omiecinski, and S. Navathe, "An efficient algorithm for mining association rules in large databases," in *Proceedings of 1995 International Conference on Very Large Data Bases (VLDB '95)* (Zurich, Switzerland), pp. 432–443, September 1995.

4. J. S. Park, M. S. Chen, and P. S. Yu, "An effective hash-based algorithm for mining association rules," in *Proceedings of 1995 ACM-SIGMOD International Conference on Management of Data (SIGMOD '95)* (San Jose, CA), pp. 175–186, May 1995.

5. H. Toivonen, "Sampling large databases for association rules," in *Proceedings of 1996 International Conference on Very Large Data Bases (VLDB '96)* (Bombay, India), pp. 134–145, September 1996.

6. H. Mannila and H. Toivonen, "Levelwise search and borders of theories in knowledge discovery," *Data Mining and Knowledge Discovery*, vol. 1, pp. 241–258, 1997.

7. S. Brin, R. Motwani, J. D. Ullman, and S. Tsur, "Dynamic itemset counting and implication rules for market basket analysis," in *Proceedings of 1997 ACM-SIGMOD International Conference on Management of Data (SIGMOD '97)* (Tuscon, AZ), pp. 255–264, May 1997.

8. M. Zaki, S. Parthasarathy, M. Ogihara, and W. Li, "New algorithms for fast discovery of association rules," in *Proceedings of 3rd International*

Conference on Knowledge Discovery and Data Mining (KDD '97)) (California), pp. 283–296, 1997.

9. J. Han and M. Kamber, *Data Mining: Concepts and Techniques.* San Diego: Academic Press, 2001.

10. A. Silberschatz and A. Tuzhilin, "What makes patterns interesting in knowledge discovery systems," *IEEE Transactions on Knowledge and Data Engineering,* vol. 8, pp. 970–974, 1996.

11. C. C. Aggarwal and P. S. Yu, "A new approach to online generation of association rules," *IEEE Transactions on Knowledge and Data Engineering,* vol. 13, pp. 527–540, 2001.

12. R. Srikant and R. Agrawal, "Mining generalized association rules," in *Proceedings of 1995 International Conference on Very Large Data Bases (VLDB '95)* (Zurich, Switzerland), pp. 407–419, September 1995.

13. J. Han and Y. Fu, "Discovery of multiple-level association rules from large databases," in *Proceedings of 1995 International Conference on Very Large Data Bases (VLDB '95)* (Zurich, Switzerland), pp. 420–431, September 1995.

14. S. J. Yen and A. L. P. Chen, "A graph-based approach for discovering various types of association rules," *IEEE Transactions on Knowledge and Data Engineering,* vol. 13, pp. 839–845, 2001.

15. M. J. Zaki, "Scalable algorithms for association mining," *IEEE Transactions on Knowledge and Data Engineering,* vol. 12, pp. 372–390, 2000.

16. R. Srikant and R. Agrawal, "Mining quantitative association rules in large relational tables," in *Proceedings of 1996 ACM-SIGMOD International Conference on Management of Data (SIGMOD '96)* (Montreal, Canada), pp. 1–12, June 1996.

17. B. Oezden, S. Ramaswamy, and A. Silberschatz, "Cyclic association rules," in *Proceedings of 1998 International Conference on Data Engineering (ICDE '98)* (Orlando, FL), pp. 412–421, February 1998.

18. S. Ramaswamy, S. Mahajan, and A. Silberschatz, "On the discovery of interesting patterns in association rules," in *Proceedings of 1998 International Conference on Very Large Data Bases (VLDB '98)* (New York), pp. 368–379, August 1998.

19. C. C. Aggarwal, C. Procopiuc, and P. S. Yu, "Finding localized associations in market basket data," *IEEE Transactions on Knowledge and Data Engineering,* vol. 14, pp. 51–62, 2002.

20. R. Rastogi and K. Shim, "Mining optimized association rules with categorical and numeric attributes," *IEEE Transactions on Knowledge and Data Engineering*, vol. 14, pp. 29–50, 2002.

21. T. P. Hong, C. S. Kuo, and S. C. Chi, "Mining association rules from quantitative data," *Intelligent Data Analysis*, vol. 3, pp. 363–376, 1999.

22. A. Gyenesei and J. Teuhola, "Interestingness measures for fuzzy association rules," vol. 2168 of *Lecture Notes in Artificial Intelligence*, pp. 152–164, Heidelberg: Springer-Verlag, 2001.

23. Y. C. Hu, R. S. Chen, and G. H. Tzeng, "Finding fuzzy classification rules using data mining techniques," *Pattern Recognition Letters*, vol. 24, pp. 509–519, 2003.

24. G. Chen and Q. Wei, "Fuzzy association rules and the extended mining algorithms," *Information Sciences*, vol. 147, pp. 201–228, 2002.

25. J. A. Rushing, H. S. Ranganath, T. H. Hinke, and S. J. Graves, "Using association rules as texture features," *IEEE Transactions on Pattern Analysis and Machine Intelligence*, vol. 23, pp. 845–858, 2001.

8

Rule Mining with Soft Computing

8.1 INTRODUCTION

Rule generation refers to the extraction and/or refinement of rules. It can involve traditional rulebase generation by knowledge engineers, or incorporate some sort of automation. When applied from the perspective of large data, we term it as *rule mining*. As mentioned in Section 1.10, this includes association, classification and dependency rule mining. In this chapter we concentrate on the generation (or mining) of classification rules.

Rule generation from ANNs is gaining in popularity in recent times due to its capability of providing some insight to the user about the symbolic knowledge embedded within the network. Fuzzy sets are an aid in providing this information in a more human comprehensible or natural form, and can handle uncertainties at various levels. The neuro-fuzzy approach, symbiotically combining the merits of connectionist and fuzzy approaches, constitutes a key component of soft computing based rule generation [1].

Andrews et al. [2] have provided a classification scheme for connectionist rule extraction algorithms. They take into consideration the

- expressive power of the rules: (1) propositional or Boolean logic i.e., crisp or nonfuzzy, (2) nonconventional logic i.e., probabilistic or fuzzy;

- *translucency* of view taken in the algorithm about the underlying ANN units: (1) decompositional approach (more analytical), where each internal element of the *transparent* network is examined, (2) pedagogical or *blackbox* approach, where one observes only the input–output behavior of the *opaque* network;

293

- extent to which the underlying ANN incorporates specialized training regimes i.e., *portability*;

- quality of the rules: (1) accuracy i.e., generalization to test cases, (2) fidelity i.e., whether they can mimic the behavior of the ANN from which they were generated, (3) consistency i.e., whether they produce the same classification of test instances over different training instances, (4) comprehensibility, in terms of the size of the rule set and the number of antecedents per rule;

- algorithmic complexity of the technique.

Taha and Ghosh [3] have considered additional issues related to rule extraction. These include the granularity of explanation, modifiability, theory refinement capability (to handle incompleteness, inconsistency, and/or inaccuracy of initial domain knowledge), stability (robustness) to corruption in data or knowledge, and scalability for large datasets (or rulebases).

A recent trend in neural network design for large-scale problems is to split the original task into simpler subtasks and use a subnetwork module for each of the subtasks [4]. It has been shown that by combining the output of several subnetworks in an ensemble, one can improve the generalization ability over that of a single large network [5]. This type of *divide-and-conquer* strategy makes it possible to effectively mine large volumes of data while discovering information. Incorporation of high-level domain knowledge is also a useful feature of data mining. The use of knowledge-based networks is a step in this direction.

The present chapter provides a study on the modular approach to rule generation, with a focus on data mining. Section 8.2 provides a survey on existing connectionist rule generation methods, along with their hybridizations with other soft computing tools. Knowledge-based models are also discussed from this perspective. The concept of modular hybridization is elaborated upon in Section 8.3. Section 8.4 concludes the chapter.

8.2   CONNECTIONIST RULE GENERATION

The primary input to a connectionist rule generation algorithm is typically a representation of a trained feedforward ANN (of Section 2.2.3), in terms of its nodes and links, and sometimes the dataset. One interprets one or more hidden and output units into rules, which may later be combined and simplified to arrive at a more comprehensible rule set. These rules can also provide new insights into the application domain. The models are usually suitable in data-rich environments and seem to be capable of overcoming the problem of the *knowledge acquisition bottleneck* faced by knowledge engineers while designing the knowledge base of traditional expert systems. The trained link weights and node activation of the ANN are used to automatically generate the rules, either for later use in a traditional expert system or for refining the initial domain knowledge or for providing justification (explanation) in the case of an inferred decision.

In this section we provide a review on rule generation using neural (connectionist) models, along with their hybridizations involving other soft computing tools like fuzzy sets, genetic algorithms, and rough sets [1]. The use of knowledge-based networks, for this purpose, is also discussed in the soft computing framework.

8.2.1 Neural models

Let us first consider the layered connectionist model by Gallant [6] used for rule generation in the medical domain. The inputs and outputs consist of *crisp* variables in all cases. Generally, the symptoms are represented by the input nodes while the diseases and possible treatments correspond to the intermediate and/or output nodes. The model deals with *sacrophagal* problems, using a linear discriminant network (with no hidden nodes) that is trained by the simple *pocket algorithm*. The absence of the hidden nodes and nonlinearity limits the utility of the system in modeling complex decision surfaces. Dependency information regarding the variables, in the form of an adjacency matrix, is provided by the expert. Every input variable x is approximated by three Boolean variables x_1', x_2', x_3'. Cell activation is discrete, taking on values $+1$, -1, or 0, corresponding to logical values of *true, false,* or *unknown*. Each cell computes its new activation y_i' as a linear discriminant function of the x_j's.

Rules are generated by traversing the trained connection weights as follows:

1. List all inputs that are known and have contributed to the ultimate positivity of a discriminant.

2. Arrange the list by decreasing absolute value of the weights.

3. Generate clauses for an IF–THEN rule from this ordered list.

The user can also be queried to supplement incomplete input information. During question generation, the system selects that unknown output variable whose *confidence* is maximum. Then it backtracks along the connection weights to find an unknown input variable, whose value is queried from the user.

Ishikawa [7] demonstrates the training of a network using *structural learning with forgetting*. An examination of the resultant simplified and nonredundant network architecture leads to easy extraction of rules. The stationary (nonactive) positive weights get reduced and negative weights increased using a decay factor. A total of 8124 samples of mushrooms, with 22 attributes each, have been studied for the two-class (edible or poisonous) problem. The method selects two or four most relevant attributes. For the two-attribute case, *odor* and *spore–print–color* were found to be important. A sample extracted rule is as follows:

IF *(odor = almond* OR *anise* OR *none)* AND *(spore–print–color ≠ green)* THEN *mushroom = edible.*

Duch et al. [8] modified this algorithm by constraining the weights to $\{+1, -1, 0\}$. This is supposed to result in the extraction of rules with more logical interpretation. They have also used a generalization of RBF networks for interpreting node functions as rules.

Setiono [9] has used a pruned network for extracting compact, meaningful rules, in terms of hidden unit activation. The activation are clustered into discrete values, and a process of splitting of hidden units and creation of new subnetwork is repeated until each hidden unit has only a small number of inputs connected to it. A penalty term augments a cross-entropy error function that is minimized to encourage weight decay and remove redundant weights. The accuracy and number of rules generated are claimed to be better than those obtained by C4.5 [10]. Setiono has also reported [11] the extraction of M *of* N type rules (described in Section 8.2.3) from a trained feedforward network whose weights and inputs are restricted to values in $\{-1, 1\}$. The rules are claimed to possess desirable qualities like accuracy, simplicity and fidelity.

Setiono and Liu [12] have also developed oblique decision trees that partition the attribute space by hyperplanes (not necessarily axis-parallel) and can readily be translated into a set of rules. Since an oblique decision tree classifies patterns based on linear combinations of input attributes, the rules are more compact than that generated by an univariate tree over the same domain. Comparison is provided with other decision tree-based approaches, like C4.5 and CART [13]. The compactness of these oblique rules is said to result in better rule comprehensibility and consistency.

8.2.2 Neuro-fuzzy models

Nauck et al. [14, 15] have developed NEFCON, NEFCLASS, and NEFPROX, using generic fuzzy perceptron, to model Mamdani-type [16] neuro-fuzzy systems. Since fuzzy systems are designed to exploit the tolerance for imprecision, here they are not used to generate an *exact* solution. The learning procedure uses a fuzzy error, and can operate on both fuzzy sets and rules. The incremental rule learning algorithm can create a rulebase from scratch by adding rule after rule, or can also operate on prior knowledge. The knowledge base of the fuzzy system is implicitly embedded in the network structure. The system is claimed to be simple and highly interpretable, as well as suitable in providing support to users during decision-making involving classification and function approximation.

Rhee and Krishnapuram [17] generate rules from minimal approximate fuzzy aggregation networks, involving hybrid operators with compensatory behavior at the neuronal level. The linguistic labels and the corresponding triangular membership functions for the input features are estimated from the training data. The compensatory parameters are learned during gradient descent, to estimate the type of aggregation employed. Pruning of redundant features and/or hidden nodes helps in generating appropriate rules in terms of AND–OR operators that are represented by these hybrid functions. Zhang and Kandel [18] have also used compensatory fuzzy operators to effectively learn fuzzy IF–THEN rules from both well- and ill-defined data.

Mitra and Pal [19] have used a fuzzy logical MLP for inferencing and rule generation. The model consists of logical neurons employing conjugate pairs of *t-norms* T and *t-conorms* S, like *min–max* and *product–probabilistic sum*, in place of the *weighted sum* and *sigmoidal* functions of the conventional MLP. Various fuzzy implication operators are used to introduce different amounts of interaction during error backpropagation. The built-in AND–OR structure of the model helps it to generate appropriate rules, expressed as disjunction of conjunctive clauses.

8.2.3 Using knowledge-based networks

One of the major problems in connectionist or neuro-fuzzy design is the choice of the optimal network structure. This has an important bearing on any performance evaluation. Moreover, the models are generally very data-dependent, and the appropriate network size also depends on the available training data. Various methodologies developed for selecting the optimal network structure include growing and pruning of nodes and links, employing genetic search, and embedding initial knowledge in the network topology. The last approach – embedding initial knowledge – is usually followed in the case of knowledge-based networks. It is formally shown [20] that such knowledge-based networks require relatively smaller training set sizes for correct generalization. When the initial knowledge fails to explain many instances, additional hidden units and connections need to be added. The initial encoded crude domain knowledge may be refined with experience, by performing learning in the data environment. The resulting networks generally involve less redundancy in their topology. Embedding of prior knowledge, involving user interaction, is also a desirable feature of data mining.

8.2.3.1 Connectionist models   Towell and Shavlik [21] have designed a hybrid learning system KBANN and have applied it to problems of molecular biology. Disjunctive rules are rewritten as multiple conjunctive rules while mapping into the network structure. It is primarily a theory *refinement* system that is capable of pruning an inserted rule set, but not capable of adding new rules. It is largely topology-preserving and assumes that the initial domain theory is basically correct and nearly complete.

An expansion of the network guided by both the domain theory and training data has been reported in TopGen by Opitz and Shavlik [22]. Dynamic addition of hidden nodes are made at the best place by heuristically searching through the space of possible network topologies, in a manner analogous to the adding of rules and conjuncts to the symbolic rulebase. This approach uses a specialized ANN architecture with a specialized training algorithm. It generates sparser rule sets as compared to KBANN and overcomes the latter's limitation of not being able to extend a relatively weak initial domain theory. The additional computational expense is justified in terms of the human expert's willingness to wait for an extended period of time for better predictive accuracy.

A way of using the knowledge of the trained neural model to extract revised rules for the problem domain is described by Fu [23] (*Subset* algorithm) and Towell and Shavlik [24] (*M of N* algorithm). Knowledge, in the form of rules in disjunctive normal form, is encoded into the network. The other links represent low-weighted connections, allowing subsequent refinement. It is assumed that the neurons have binary inputs and hard-limiting activation functions. Even though the algorithms are exponential in complexity, their inherent simplicity makes them extremely useful.

The *Subset* algorithm [23] initially searches for any single weight (at the input of a neuron) exceeding its bias, and it rewrites all conditions so found as rules with single input variable. The breadth-first search for all the hidden and output nodes (over the input links) continues for increasing sizes of sets, until all such sets have been explored and possibly rewritten as rules in disjunctive normal form. The extracted rules are simple to understand and their size can be restricted by specifying the number of premises (antecedents) to be considered. Finally the algorithm removes subsumed and overly general rules. The main steps of the algorithm are outlined as follows:

For each hidden and output unit repeat steps 1 and 2.

1. Extract up to β_p subsets of the positively weighted incoming links, whose summed weight is greater than the bias of the unit.

2. **for** each subset $\mathcal{P}$ of β_p subsets found in step 1, **repeat** the following.

   (a) Extract up to β_n minimal subsets of negatively weighted links, whose summed weight is greater than the bias of the unit *minus* the sum of $\mathcal{P}$.

   (b) Let $\mathcal{Z}$ be a new predicate used nowhere else.

   (c) With each subset $\mathcal{N}$ of β_n subsets found in step 2(a), form the rule "IF $\mathcal{N}$ THEN $\mathcal{Z}$."

   (d) Form the rule "IF $\mathcal{P}$ and NOT $\mathcal{Z}$ THEN *name–of–unit.*"

However, some of the problems associated with this algorithm are as follows [3]. It requires lengthy, exhaustive searches of size $O(2^k)$ for a hidden or output node with fan-in of k. It extracts a large set of rules, up to $\beta_p * (1 + \beta_n)$, where β_p and β_n are the number of subsets of positively and negatively weighted links, respectively. Some of the generated rules may be repetitive, as permutations of rule antecedents are not taken care of automatically. Moreover, there is no guarantee that all useful knowledge embedded in the trained network will be extracted. To avoid the otherwise prohibitive combinatorics, all implementations of *Subset* algorithm typically use heuristics.

The *Subset* algorithm has been modified by Towell and Shavlik [24] to design the *M of N* algorithm for extracting meaningful rules. A general rule in this case is of the form: IF (*at least M* of the following *N* antecedents are true) THEN .... The rationale is to find a group of links that form an *equivalence class*, whose members have similar effect (weight values) and can be used interchangeably with one another.

The steps of this algorithm include

- *clustering* the weights of each (hidden and output) neuron into groups,

- *averaging* their values to create equivalence classes,

- *eliminating* low value weights if they have no significant effect on the sign of the total activation, and

- *optimizing*, by freezing the remaining weights and retraining the biases using the backpropagation algorithm.

This is followed by *rule extraction*. Arithmetic is performed such that one searches for all weighted antecedents, which, when summed up, exceed the threshold value of a given neuron. When possible, the rules are simplified to eliminate superfluous weights and thresholds.

This algorithm has good generalization (accuracy), but can have degraded comprehensibility [2]. Note that the algorithm considers groups of links as equivalence classes, thereby generating a bound on the number of rules rather than establishing a ceiling on the number of antecedents. The computational complexity is $\mathcal{O}(k^3 + (k^2.j))$, where j is the number of examples. Additionally, the rule extraction procedure involves a backpropagation step requiring significant computational overhead.

8.2.3.2 Incorporating fuzzy sets   A brief survey on the knowledge-based networks involving fuzziness at different stages is provided here. Knowledge extracted from experts in the form of membership functions and fuzzy rules (in AND-OR form) is used to build and preweight the neural net structure, which is then tuned using training data.

A major problem of using MLPs to refine rule-based knowledge [23, 24] is the preservation of symbolic knowledge (stability) under the weight tuning mechanism (plasticity) of the backpropagation algorithm. Another limitation is that unless the initial rulebase is roughly complete, the initial network architecture may not be sufficiently rich for handling the problem domain by incorporating new knowledge. The Adaptive Resonance Theory (ART) architecture [25] is designed to circumvent this *stability–plasticity* dilemma. Learning in ARTMAP [26] is match-based (not error-based); it does not wash away existing knowledge and the meanings of units do not shift. Use of fuzzy set theoretic concepts lead to the formulation of the fuzzy ARTMAP [27].

Tan [28] has used a generalization of fuzzy ARTMAP, called 'cascade ARTMAP', as a fuzzy knowledge-based network. It represents intermediate attributes and rule cascades of rule-based knowledge explicitly, and performs multistep inferencing. A rule insertion algorithm translates IF–THEN symbolic rules into cascade ARTMAP architecture. This knowledge can be refined and enhanced by the learning algorithm. During learning, new recognition categories (rules) can be created dynamically to cover the deficiency of the domain theory. The extracted rules involve discrete inputs and are of good quality. The algorithmic complexity is linear in the number of recognition categories. Results indicate that the performance is superior to that of the KBANN [21], ID3 and MLP. The extracted rules are claimed [28] to be simpler and more accurate than the M *of* N rules [24]. Besides, each extracted rule is associated with a confidence factor that indicates its importance or usefulness. This allows ranking and evaluation of the extracted knowledge.

Machado and Rocha [29] have used an interval-based representation for membership grades (MGI) to allow reasoning with different types of uncertainty, namely, vagueness, ignorance, and relevance. The model incorporates the facilities of incremental learning, inference, inquiry, censorship of input information, and explanation, as in expert systems. The utility-based inquiry process permits significant reduction of consultation cost or risk and gives the system the common sense property possessed by experts when selecting tests to be performed. The ability to criticize input data when they disrupt a trend of acceptance or rejection observed for a hypothesis mimics the behavior of experts, who are often able to detect suspicious input data and either reject them or ask for their confirmation. The explanation algorithm provides responses to queries such as *how* a particular conclusion was reached or *why* a particular question was formulated. The network forms a set of pathways that compete to send the largest evidential flow to the output neuron representing the hypothesis. The structure of the winning pathway represents a chain of fuzzy pseudo-production rules, which can be presented to the user either in a graphical format or as English text.

Application of this algorithm has been made to the deforestation monitoring of the Amazon region, using Landsat-V satellite images. The classes considered are forest, savanna, water, deforested area, cloud, and shadow. Eighty-two numerical features of spectral, textural, and geometric nature were measured on each image segment (of spectrally homogeneous regions, generated by region growing). Fuzzy classification allows the modeling of complex situations such as transition phenomena (as in the regeneration of forest in a previously burned area) or multiple classification (as in the case of forest overcast by clouds).

A model by Mitra et al. [30] has been developed for classification, inferencing, querying, and rule generation. It is capable of generating both *positive* (indicating the belongingness of a pattern to a class) and *negative* (indicating its degree of *not* belonging to a class) rules in linguistic form to justify any decision reached. This is found to be useful for inferencing in ambiguous cases. The knowledge encoding procedure, unlike many other methods [21, 23], involves a nonbinary weighting mechanism. The *a priori* class information and the distribution of pattern points in the feature space are taken into account while encoding the crude domain knowledge from the dataset among the connection weights, using fuzzy intervals and linguistic sets in the process. Each pattern class is modeled in terms of positive and negative hidden nodes. The trained knowledge-based network is used for rule generation in IF–THEN form. These rules describe the extent to which a test pattern belongs or does not belong to one of the classes, in terms of antecedent and consequent clauses provided in natural form. Backtracking along maximal weighted paths of the trained net, utilizing its input and output activation (with confidence factor), enables generation of these clauses.

8.2.3.3 Incorporating genetic algorithms   Opitz and Shavlik [31] use the domain theory of Towell and Shavlik [21, 24] to generate a knowledge-based network structure that is evolved using GAs. Random perturbation is applied to create an initial set of candidate networks or *population*. A node is perturbed by either deleting it or adding new nodes to it. Next, these networks are trained using backpropagation and placed back into the population. New networks are created by using crossover and mutation operators, specifically designed to function on these networks. The algorithm tries to minimize the destruction of the rule structure of the crossed-over networks, by keeping intact nodes belonging to the same syntactic rule (i.e., the nodes highly connected to each other). The mutation operator adds diversity to a population, while still maintaining a directed heuristic search technique for choosing where to add nodes. In this manner the algorithm searches the topology space, in order to find suitable networks which are then trained using backpropagation.

8.2.3.4 Incorporating rough sets   Concept of rough sets is integrated with fuzzy–neural network for designing a knowledge-based rough–fuzzy MLP [32, 33], where the theory of rough sets is utilized for extracting crude domain knowledge in the form of *IF-THEN* rules. These rules are encoded among the connection weights, with their number and syntax automatically determining the network topology in terms of hidden nodes and links. Methods are derived to model convex decision regions with single-object representatives, as well as arbitrary decision regions with multiple-object representatives. From the perspective of pattern recognition, this implies using a single prototype to model a (convex) decision region in the first case. In the second case, this means using multiple prototypes to serve as representatives of any arbitrary decision region. A three-layered fuzzy MLP is considered, where the feature space gives the condition attributes and where the output classes give the decision attributes, so as to result in a decision table. Rules are then generated from the table by computing relative reducts. The dependency factors of these rules are encoded as the initial weight values of the links.

8.3 MODULAR HYBRIDIZATION

It is believed that the use of Modular Neural Network enables a wider use of ANNs for large-scale systems. Embedding modularity (i.e., to perform local and encapsulated computation) into neural networks leads to many advantages as compared to the use of a single network. For instance, constraining the network connectivity increases its learning capacity and permits its application to large-scale problems [4] with relevance to data mining. It is easier to encode *a priori* knowledge in modular neural networks. In addition, the number of network parameters can be reduced by using modularity. This feature speeds computation and can improve the generalization capability of the system [34].

This section describes a way of integrating subnetworks of rough–fuzzy MLPs, using a modular evolutionary algorithm, for classification and rule generation [35, 36]. Rough set theory is applied for extracting dependency rules directly from real-valued attribute table consisting of fuzzy membership values. This helps in preserving all the class representative points in the dependency rules by adaptively applying a threshold that automatically takes care of the shape of membership functions.

An l-class classification problem is split into l two-class subproblems. Crude subnetwork modules are initially encoded, for each two-class sub-problem, from the dependency rules. These subnetworks are then combined and the final network is evolved using a GA with *restricted* mutation operator which utilizes the knowledge of the modular structure already generated, for faster convergence. The GA tunes the fuzzification parameters, and network weight and structure simultaneously, by optimizing a single fitness function. This methodology helps in imposing a structure on the weights, which results in a network more suitable for rule generation. Performance of the algorithm is compared with related techniques.

8.3.1 Rough fuzzy MLP

As pointed out in Section 5.6.3, an n-dimensional pattern $\mathbf{X_i}$ is represented in the form of Eq. (5.18), with $y_1^0, \ldots, y_{3n}^0$ being the activations of the $3n$ neurons in the input layer of the network. An l-class problem domain corresponds to l nodes in the output layer, such that the membership of the ith pattern in class k is defined by Eq. (5.23). The basics of rough sets have already been introduced in Section 2.2.6, for the benefit of the readers. Before going to the details of the modular hybrid system, we provide in this section an overview of the mathematical preliminaries using rough set theoretic concepts for the interested reader.

8.3.1.1 Rule generation Let $S = <U, A>$ be a decision table, with C and $D = \{d_1, ..., d_l\}$ its sets of condition and decision attributes, respectively. Divide the decision table $S = <U, A>$ into l tables $S_i = <U_i, A_i>$, $i = 1, ..., l$, corresponding to the l decision attributes $d_1, ..., d_l$, where
$$U = U_1 \cup ... \cup U_l \text{ and } A_i = C \cup \{d_i\}.$$
Let $\{x_{i1}, ..., x_{ip}\}$ be the set of those objects of U_i that occur in S_i, $i = 1, ..., l$.

Now for each d_i-reduct $B = \{b_1, ..., b_k\}$ (say), a discernibility matrix (denoted $\mathbf{M}_{d_i}(B)$) from the d_i-discernibility matrix is defined as follows [32].

$$c_{ij} = \{a \in B : a(x_i) \neq a(x_j)\}, \tag{8.1}$$

for $i, j = 1, ..., n$.

For each object $x_j \in x_{i_1}, \ldots, x_{i_p}$, the discernibility function $f_{d_i}^{x_j}$ is defined as

$$f_{d_i}^{x_j} = \bigwedge \{\bigvee(c_{ij}) : 1 \leq i, j \leq n, \ j < i, \ c_{ij} \neq \emptyset\}, \tag{8.2}$$

where $\bigvee(c_{ij})$ is the disjunction of all members of c_{ij}. Then $f_{d_i}^{x_j}$ is brought to its conjunctive normal form $(c.n.f)$. One thus obtains a dependency rule r_i, namely, $P_i \leftarrow d_i$, where P_i is the disjunctive normal form $(d.n.f.)$ of $f_{d_i}^{x_j}, j \in i_1, \ldots, i_p$.

The dependency factor df_i for r_i is given by

$$df_i = \frac{card(POS_i(d_i))}{card(U_i)}, \tag{8.3}$$

where $POS_i(d_i) = \bigcup_{X \in I_{d_i}} l_i(X)$, and $l_i(X)$ is the lower approximation of X with respect to I_i. In this case, $df_i = 1$ [32].

8.3.1.2 Knowledge encoding Consider the case of feature j for class C_k in the l-class problem domain. The inputs for the i-th representative sample $\mathbf{X}_i$ are mapped to the corresponding three-dimensional feature space of $\mu_{low(a_j)}(\mathbf{X}_i)$, $\mu_{medium(a_j)}(\mathbf{X}_i)$, and $\mu_{high(a_j)}(\mathbf{X}_i)$ by Eq. (5.18). Let these be represented by L_j, M_j, and H_j, respectively. As the method considers multiple objects in a class, a separate $n_k \times 3n$-dimensional attribute-value decision table is generated for each class C_k (where n_k indicates the number of objects in C_k).

The absolute distance between each pair of objects is computed along each attribute L_j, M_j, H_j for all j. We modify Eq. (8.1) to directly handle a real-valued attribute table consisting of fuzzy membership values. We define

$$c_{ij} = \{a \in B : \ |a(x_i) - a(x_j)| > Th\} \tag{8.4}$$

for $i, j = 1, \ldots, n_k$, where Th is an adaptive threshold. Note that the adaptivity of this threshold is in-built, depending on the inherent shape of the membership function.

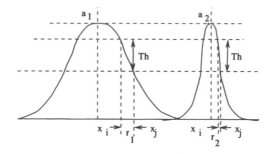

Fig. 8.1   Illustration of adaptive thresholding of membership functions.

Consider Fig. 8.1. Let a_1, a_2 correspond to two membership functions (attributes), with a_2 being steeper than a_1. It is observed that $r_1 > r_2$. This results in an implicit adaptivity of Th while computing c_{ij} in the discernibility matrix directly from the real-valued attributes. This is particularly useful in modeling multimodal class distributions.

The hidden layer nodes model the first-level (innermost) operator in the antecedent part of a rule, which can be either a conjunct or a disjunct. The output layer nodes model the outer-level operands, which can again be either a conjunct or a disjunct. For each inner-level operator, corresponding to one output class (one dependency rule), one hidden node is dedicated. Only those input attributes that appear in this conjunct or disjunct are connected to the appropriate hidden node, which in turn is connected to the corresponding output node. Each outer level operator is modeled at the output layer by joining the corresponding hidden nodes. Note that a single attribute (involving no inner level operators) is directly connected to the appropriate output node via a hidden node, to maintain uniformity in rule mapping.

Let the dependency factor for a particular dependency rule for class C_k be $df = \alpha = 1$ by Eq. (8.3). The weight w_{ki}^1 between a hidden node i and output node k is set at $\frac{\alpha}{fac} + \varepsilon$, where fac refers to the number of outer-level operands in the antecedent of the rule and ε is a small random number taken to destroy any symmetry among the weights. Note that $fac \geq 1$ and each hidden node is connected to only one output node. Let the initial weight so clamped at a hidden node be denoted as β. The weight $w_{ia_j}^0$ between an attribute a_j (where a corresponds to *low* (L), *medium* (M), or *high* (H)) and hidden node i is set to $\frac{\beta}{facd} + \varepsilon$, such that $facd$ is the number of attributes connected by the corresponding inner-level operator. Again $facd \geq 1$. Thus for an l-class problem domain there are at least l hidden nodes. All other possible connections in the resulting network are set as small random numbers. It is to be mentioned that the number of hidden nodes is automatically determined from the number of dependency rules, while their connectivity follows from the syntax of these rules.

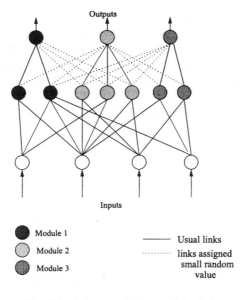

Outputs

Inputs

● Module 1	—————— Usual links
◐ Module 2	·········· links assigned
◉ Module 3	small random value

Fig. 8.2   Intra- and intermodule links.

8.3.2   Modular knowledge-based network

This involves two phases. First an l-class classification problem is split into l two-class problems. Rough set theoretic concepts are used to encode domain knowledge into each of the l subnetworks, using Eqs. (8.2)–(8.4). The number of hidden nodes and connectivity of the knowledge-based subnetworks is automatically determined. A two-class problem leads to the generation of one or more crude subnetworks, each encoding a particular decision rule. Let each of these constitute a pool. So we obtain $m \geq l$ pools of knowledge-based modules. Each pool k is perturbed to generate a total of n_k subnetworks, such that $n_1 = \ldots = n_k = \ldots = n_m$. These pools constitute the initial population of subnetworks, which are then evolved independently using genetic algorithms.

At the end of training, the modules (or subnetworks) corresponding to each two-class problem are concatenated to form an initial network for the second phase. The intermodule links are initialized to small random values as depicted in Fig. 8.2. A set of such concatenated networks forms the initial population of the GA. Note that the individual modules cooperate, rather than compete, with each other while evolving towards the final solution. The mutation probability for the intermodule links is now set to a high value, while that of intramodule links is set to a relatively lower value. This sort of *restricted* mutation helps preserve some of the localized rule structures, already extracted and evolved, as potential solutions. The initial population for the GA of the entire network is formed from all possible combinations of these individual network modules and random perturbations about them. This ensures that for complex multi-modal pattern distributions all the different representative points remain in the population. The algorithm then searches through the reduced space of possible network topologies. The steps are summarized below, followed by an example.

1. **for** each class, generate rough set dependency rules.

2. Map each of the dependency rules to a separate subnetwork module (fuzzy MLP).

3. Partially evolve each of the subnetworks using conventional GA.

4. Concatenate the subnetwork modules to obtain the complete network. For concatenation the intramodule links are left unchanged while the intermodule links are initialized to low random values. Note that each of the subnetworks solves a two-class classification problem, while the concatenated network solves the actual l-class problem. Every possible combination of subnetwork modules is generated to form a pool of networks.

5. The pool of networks is evolved using a *modified* GA with an adaptive or variable mutation operator. The mutation probability is set to a low value for the intramodule links and to a high value for the intermodule links.

8.3.2.1 Example Consider a problem of classifying a two dimensional data into two classes. The input fuzzifier maps the features into a six dimensional feature space. Let a sample set of rules obtained from rough set theory be

$$C_1 \leftarrow (L_1 \wedge M_2) \vee (H_2 \wedge M_1),\ C_2 \leftarrow M_2 \vee H_1,\ C_2 \leftarrow L_2 \vee L_1,$$

where L_j, M_j, H_j correspond to $\mu_{low(a_j)}$, $\mu_{medium(a_j)}$, $\mu_{high(a_j)}$, respectively. For the first phase of the GA three different pools are formed, using one crude subnetwork for class 1 and two crude subnetworks for class 2, respectively. Three partially trained subnetworks result from each of these pools. They are then concatenated to form $(1 \times 2) = 2$ networks. The population for the final phase of the GA is formed with these networks and perturbations about them. The steps followed in obtaining the final network is illustrated in Fig. 8.3. The corresponding impact of the different stages of network evolution on the decision regions, generated in the feature space, is depicted in Fig. 2.9.

8.3.2.2 Characteristics Use of this scheme for generating modular knowledge-based networks has several advantages.

- Sufficient reduction in training time is obtained, as the above approach parallelizes the GA to an extent. Because the search string of the GA for subnetworks is smaller, more than linear decrease in searching time is

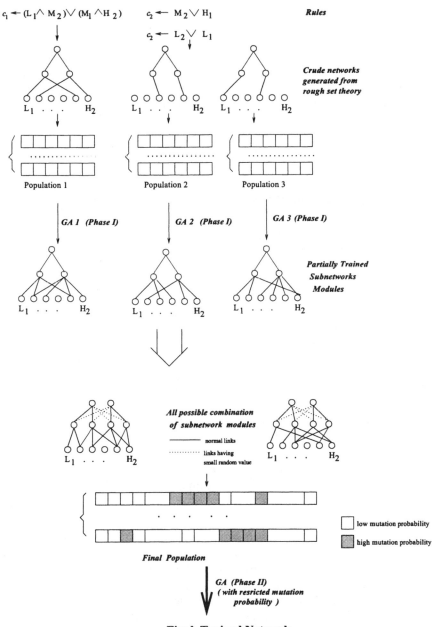

Fig. 8.3 Steps for designing a sample modular rough-fuzzy MLP.

obtained. Also very small number of training cycles are required in the refinement phase, as the network is already very close to the solution.

- The use of rough sets for knowledge encoding provides an established mathematical framework for network decomposition. The search space is reduced, leading to shorter training time. The initial network topology is also automatically determined and provides good *building blocks* for the GA.

- The algorithm indirectly constrains the solution in such a manner that a structure is imposed on the connection weights. This is helpful for subsequent rule extraction from the weights, as the resultant network has sparse but strong interconnection among the nodes.

8.3.3   Evolutionary design

Here we describe the use of GAs for evolving the weight values as well as the structure of the modular subnetworks. The input and output fuzzification parameters are also tuned. The initial population consists of all possible networks generated from rough set theoretic rules. As explained in Section 2.2.5, GAs involve three basic procedures, namely, (i) encoding of the problem parameters in the form of binary strings, (ii) application of genetic operators like crossover and mutation, and (iii) selection of individuals based on some objective function to create a new population. Each of these aspects is discussed below with relevance to this algorithm [36].

8.3.3.1 Chromosomal representation   The problem variables consist of the weight values and the input/output fuzzification parameters. Each of the weights is encoded into a binary word of 16-bit length, where [000...0] decodes to -128 and [111...1] decodes to 128. An additional bit is assigned to each weight to indicate the presence or absence of the corresponding link. If this bit is 0, then the remaining bits are unrepresented in the phenotype. The total number of bits in the string is therefore *dynamic*. Thus a total of 17 bits are assigned for each weight. The fuzzification parameters tuned are the centers (c) and radius (λ) for each of the linguistic attributes *low, medium,* and *high* of each feature, and output fuzzifier parameters f_d and f_e. These are also coded as 16-bit strings in the range $[0, 2]$. The chromosome is obtained by concatenating all the above strings. Sample values of the string length are around 2000 bits for reasonably sized networks.

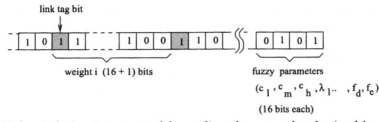

weight i (16 + 1) bits   fuzzy parameters

$$(c_1, c_m, c_h, \lambda_1 \cdots, f_d, f_e)$$

(16 bits each)

Initial population is generated by coding the networks obtained by rough set-based knowledge encoding and by random perturbations about them. A population size of 64 was considered.

8.3.3.2 Genetic operators Here we provide details on the implementation aspects of the different genetic operators, namely, crossover, mutation, selection, and fitness function used. These notions were introduced earlier in Section 2.2.5.

Crossover. It is obvious that due to the large string length, single-point crossover would have little effectiveness. Multiple-point crossover is adopted, with the distance between two crossover points being a random variable between 8 and 24 bits. The crossover probability is fixed at 0.7.

Mutation: Because the search string is very large, the influence of mutation is more on the search. Each of the bits in the string is chosen to have some mutation probability ($pmut$), but with a spatiotemporal variation. The mutation probabilities vary along the encoded string, with the bits corresponding to intermodule links being assigned a higher probability as compared to intramodule links. This is done to ensure least alterations in the structure of the individual modules already evolved, by incorporating the domain knowledge extracted through rough set theory.

Choice of fitness function: In GAs the fitness function is the final arbiter for string creation, and the nature of the solution obtained depends on the objective function. An objective function of the form described below is chosen.

$$F = \alpha_1 f_1 + \alpha_2 f_2 , \qquad (8.5)$$

where

$$f_1 = \frac{\text{No. of correctly classified samples in training set}}{\text{Total no. of samples in training set}}$$

$$f_2 = 1 - \frac{\text{No. of links present}}{\text{Total no. of links possible}} .$$

Here α_1 and α_2 determine the relative weightage of each of the factors. α_1 is taken to be 0.9 and α_2 is taken as 0.1, to give more importance to the classification score as compared to the network size in terms of number of links. Note that we optimize the network connectivity, weights, and input–output fuzzification parameters simultaneously.

Selection: This is done by the *roulette wheel* method. The probabilities are calculated on the basis of ranking of the individuals in terms of the objective function. *Elitism* is incorporated in the selection process by comparing the fitness of the best individual of a new generation to that of the current generation. If the latter has a higher value, then the corresponding individual replaces a randomly selected individual in the new population.

8.3.4   Rule extraction

A rule extraction algorithm [37], based on the hybrid model of Section 8.3.2, is presented here. The performance of the rules is evaluated quantitatively. A quantitative comparison of the rule extraction algorithm is made with some existing ones like *Subset* [23], *M of N* [24], and X2R [38]. The steps of the algorithm are provided below.

1. Compute the following quantities:
   $PMean$ = Mean of all positive weights, $PThres_1$ = Mean of all positive weights less than $PMean$, $PThres_2$ = Mean of all weights greater than $PMean$. Similarly, calculate $NMean$, $NThres_1$, and $NThres_2$ for negative weights.

2. **for** each hidden and output unit

   (a) **for** all weights greater than $PThres_2$, search for positive rules; and **for** all weights less than $NThres_2$, search for negative rules, only, by *Subset* method.

   (b) Search for combinations of positive weights above $Pthres_1$ and negative weights greater than $NThres_2$ that exceed the bias. Similarly, search for negative weights less than $NThres_1$ and positive weights below $PThres_2$.

3. Associate with each rule j a confidence factor cf_j, given by Eq. (2.36).

Since the learning algorithm imposes a structure on the network, resulting in a sparse network having few strong links, the $PThres$ and $NThres$ values are well separated. Hence the above rule extraction algorithm generates most of the embedded rules over a small number of computational steps.

The computational complexity of the algorithm is as follows. Let the network have i, h, o numbers of input, hidden, and output nodes, respectively. Let us make the assumption that $i = h = o = k$. Let the fraction of weights having value in $[0, PThres_1)$, $[PThres_1, PThres_2)$, $[PThres_2, \infty)$ be p_1, p_2, p_3, respectively. Similarly, let the corresponding fractions for negative weights be n_1, n_2, n_3. Then the computational complexity (C) becomes

$C = k.(\ 2^{(p_2+p_3)k+1} + 2^{(n_2+n_3)k+1} + 2^{(p_3+n_1)k+1} + 2^{(p_1+n_3)k+1} \ )$.

If n_1, n_2, p_1, $p_2 \ll p_3$, n_3,

$C \approx 4k(2^{p_3 k} + 2^{n_3 k}) = 4k(e^l n2.p_3 k + e^l n2.n_3 k)$.

Also if p_3, $n_3 \ll 1$,

$C \approx 4k(1 + \log 2(p_3 + n_3)k + 0.5(\log 2(p_3 + n_3))^2 k^2$, i.e., $C \approx \mathcal{O}(k^3)$.

An important consideration is the order of application of rules in a rule base. Since most of the real-life patterns are noisy and overlapping, rulebases obtained are often not totally consistent. Hence multiple rules may fire for a single example. Several existing approaches apply the rules sequentially [3], often leading to degraded performance. The confidence factors, associated with the extracted rules, help in circumventing this problem. The quantitative measures used to evaluate these generated rules have been described in Section 2.4.2.

8.3.5 Results

This genetic-rough-neuro-fuzzy algorithm has been implemented on both real-life (speech, medical) and artificially generated data [35, 36]. In this section we provide sample results on the *Vowel* data. Figure 5.10 depicts the six Telugu (it is a language in India) vowel classes in the F_1–F_2 plane. These overlapping classes will be denoted by $C_1, C_2, \ldots, C_6$. The rough set theoretic technique is applied on the data to extract some knowledge, which is initially encoded among the connection weights of the subnetworks. The data are first transformed into a nine-dimensional linguistic space.

The methodology described here is termed Model S. Other models compared include:
(i) Model O: An ordinary MLP trained using backpropagation (BP).
(ii) Model F: A fuzzy MLP trained using BP.
(iii) Model R: A rough–fuzzy MLP trained using BP.

8.3.5.1 Classification Recognition scores obtained by Model S are presented in Table 8.2. It also shows a comparison with other related MLP-based classification methods (Models O, F, R). In all cases, 10% of the samples are used as training set, and the remaining samples are used as test set. Ten such independent runs are performed, and the mean value and standard deviation of the classification accuracy, computed over them, are presented in Table 8.2. The dependency rules, as generated via rough set theory and used for encoding crude domain knowledge, are shown in Table 8.1. The values of input fuzzification parameters used are also presented.

The classification accuracies obtained by the models are analyzed for statistical significance. Tests of significance are performed for the inequality of means (of accuracies) obtained using the different algorithms. Since both mean pairs and the variance pairs are unknown and different, a generalized version of *t*-test is appropriate in this context [39]. The test confidence level considered was 95%. In Table 8.2, we present the mean and standard deviation (SD) of the accuracies. Based on these, the value of the test statistics is computed. If the value exceeds the corresponding tabled value, the means are unequal with statistical significance (algorithm having higher mean accuracy being significantly superior to the one having lower value).

Table 8.1 Rough set dependency rules for *Vowel* data and input fuzzification parameter values

$$
\begin{aligned}
C_1 &\leftarrow M_1 \vee L_3 \\
C_1 &\leftarrow M_1 \vee M_2 \\
C_2 &\leftarrow M_2 \vee M_3 \vee (H_1 \wedge M_2) \\
C_2 &\leftarrow M_2 \vee H_3 \\
C_3 &\leftarrow (L_1 \wedge H_2) \vee (M_1 \wedge H_2) \\
C_3 &\leftarrow (L_1 \wedge H_2) \vee (L_1 \wedge M_3) \\
C_4 &\leftarrow (L_1 \wedge L_2) \vee (L_1 \wedge L_3) \vee (L_2 \wedge M_3) \vee (L_1 \wedge M_3) \\
C_5 &\leftarrow (H_1 \wedge M_2) \vee (M_1 \wedge M_3) \vee (M_1 \wedge M_2) \vee (M_2 \wedge L_1) \\
C_5 &\leftarrow (H_1 \wedge M_2) \vee (M_1 \wedge M_2) \vee (H_1 \wedge H_3) \vee (H_2 \wedge L_1) \\
C_5 &\leftarrow (L_2 \wedge L_1) \vee (H_3 \wedge M_3) \vee M_1 \\
C_6 &\leftarrow L_1 \vee M_3 \vee L_2 \\
C_6 &\leftarrow M_1 \vee H_3 \\
C_6 &\leftarrow L_1 \vee H_3 \\
C_6 &\leftarrow M_1 \vee M_3 \vee L_2.
\end{aligned}
$$

Fuzzification parameters:

Feature 1: $c_L = 0.348$, $c_M = 0.463$, $c_H = 0.613$, $\lambda_L = 0.115$, $\lambda_M = 0.150$, $\lambda_H = 0.134$

Feature 2: $c_L = 0.219$, $c_M = 0.437$, $c_H = 0.725$, $\lambda_L = 0.218$, $\lambda_M = 0.253$, $\lambda_H = 0.288$

Feature 3: $c_L = 0.396$, $c_M = 0.542$, $c_H = 0.678$, $\lambda_L = 0.146$, $\lambda_M = 0.140$, $\lambda_H = 0.135$

It is observed from Table 8.2 that Model S performs the best with the least network size as well as least number of sweeps. For Model R, the classification performance on test set is marginally better than that of Model S, but with significantly higher number of links and training sweeps required. Comparing models F and R, we observe that the incorporation of domain knowledge in the latter through rough sets boosts its performance. The variation of the classification accuracy of the models with iteration is also studied. Model S converges after about 90 iterations of the GA, providing the highest accuracy compared to all the other models. The backpropagation-based models require about 2000–5000 iterations for convergence.

Table 8.2 Comparative performance of different models on *Vowel* data

Models	Model O		Model F		Model R		Model S	
	Train	Test	Train	Test	Train	Test	Train	Test
Accuracy(%)	65.4,	64.1,	84.1,	81.8,	86.7,	86.0,	87.1,	85.8,
(Mean, SD)	0.5	0.5	0.4	0.5	0.3	0.2	0.2	0.2
No. of links	131		210		152		84	
Sweeps	5600		5600		2000		90	

SD: Standard Deviation

It is observed that Model F results in a dense network with weak links, while the incorporation of rough sets, modular concepts, and GAs in Model S produces a sparse network with strong links. The latter is, therefore, more

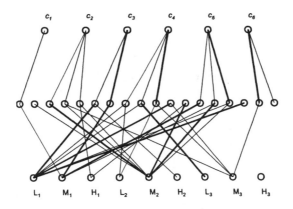

Fig. 8.4 Positive connectivity of the network obtained for *Vowel* data, using Model S. (Bold lines indicate weights greater than $PThres_2$, while others indicate values between $PThres_1$ and $PThres_2$).

suitable for rule extraction. The connectivity (positive weights) of the trained network is shown in Fig. 8.4.

8.3.5.2 Rule extraction We use the algorithm explained in Section 8.3.4 to extract refined rules from the trained network (Model S). These rules are compared to those obtained by the *Subset* method [23], *M of N* method [24], a pedagogical method X2R [38], and a decision tree-based method C4.5 [10] in terms of the quantitative performance measures (Section 2.4.2). The set of rules extracted from the network is presented in Table 8.3, along with their certainty (confidence) factors (*cf*). The values of the fuzzification parameters of the membership functions L, M, and H are also mentioned.

A comparison of the performance indices of the extracted rules is presented in Table 8.4. Since the network obtained using Model S contains fewer links, the generated rules are less in number and have high *certainty factor*. Accordingly, it possesses relatively higher percentage of uncovered region, though the accuracy does not suffer much. On the other hand, the *Subset* algorithm achieves the highest *accuracy* but requires the largest number of rules and computation time. In fact, while the accuracy (computation time) of *Subset* method is marginally better (or worse) than Model S, the size of the rule base of Model S is significantly lower.

The *accuracy, user's accuracy* and *kappa* achieved by Model S, are better than those of *M of N*, X2R, and C4.5. The X2R algorithm requires least computation time but achieves least accuracy with more rules. The *Conf* index is the minimum for rules extracted by Model S; it also has a high *fidelity* of 94.22%.

Table 8.3 Rules extracted from trained network for *Vowel* data and input fuzzification parameter values

$$
\begin{aligned}
C_1 &\leftarrow M_1 \vee L_3 \vee M_2 & cf &= 0.851 \\
C_1 &\leftarrow H_1 \vee M_2 & cf &= 0.755 \\
C_2 &\leftarrow M_2 \vee M_3 & cf &= 0.811 \\
C_2 &\leftarrow \overline{M}_1 \wedge \overline{H}_1 \wedge L_2 \wedge M_2 & cf &= 0.846 \\
C_3 &\leftarrow L_1 \vee H_2 & cf &= 0.778 \\
C_4 &\leftarrow L_1 \wedge L_2 \wedge \overline{L}_3 & cf &= 0.719 \\
C_5 &\leftarrow M_1 \wedge H_2 & cf &= 0.881 \\
C_5 &\leftarrow M_1 \wedge M_2 & cf &= 0.782 \\
C_5 &\leftarrow H_1 \wedge M_2 & cf &= 0.721 \\
C_6 &\leftarrow \overline{\overline{H}}_2 & cf &= 0.717.
\end{aligned}
$$

Fuzzification parameters :

Feature 1 : $c_L = 0.34,$ $c_M = 0.502,$ $c_H = 0.681,$
$\lambda_L = 0.122,$ $\lambda_M = 0.154,$ $\lambda_H = 0.177$

Feature 2 : $c_L = 0.217,$ $c_M = 0.431,$ $c_H = 0.725,$
$\lambda_L = 0.211,$ $\lambda_M = 0.250,$ $\lambda_H = 0.288$

Feature 3 : $c_L = 0.380,$ $c_M = 0.540,$ $c_H = 0.675,$
$\lambda_L = 0.244,$ $\lambda_M = 0.212,$ $\lambda_H = 0.224$

Table 8.4 Comparative performance of rules extracted by various methods for *Vowel* data

Algorithm	Accuracy (%)	User's accuracy (%)	Kappa (%)	Uncovered region (%)	No. of rules	CPU time (sec)	$Conf$
Model S	81.02	83.31	78.17	3.10	10	1.1	1.4
Subset	82.01	82.72	77.29	2.89	16	1.4	1.9
M of N	79.00	80.01	74.55	2.10	14	1.2	1.9
X2R	76.00	75.81	72.34	2.72	14	0.9	1.7
C4.5	79.00	79.17	77.21	3.10	16	1.0	1.5

8.4   CONCLUSIONS AND DISCUSSION

In this chapter we have provided an exhaustive survey of rule generation in the soft computing framework involving hybridization of its different tools like fuzzy sets, ANNs, rough sets, and GAs. Incorporation of domain knowledge involving user interaction generates knowledge-based networks. This is a useful feature in data mining. Rule generation from fuzzy and nonfuzzy knowledge-based networks are found to result in refined rules.

A divide-and-conquer strategy involving modular subnetworks is effective for mining large datasets. Such a methodology, incorporating the four soft computing tools (namely, ANNs, fuzzy sets, GAs, and rough sets), has been used for designing a knowledge-based network for pattern classification and rule generation. The algorithm involves synthesis of several fuzzy MLP modules, each encoding the rough set rules for a particular class. These knowledge-based modules are refined using a GA. The genetic operators are implemented in such a way that they help preserve the modular structure already evolved. It is found that this scheme results in superior performance in terms of classification score, training time, and network sparseness (thereby enabling easier extraction of rules).

The extracted rules are compared with some of the related rule extraction techniques on the basis of some quantitative performance indices. It is observed that these rules are less in number, yet accurate, and have high certainty factor and low confusion with less computation time. The investigation, besides having significance in soft computing research, has potential for application to large-scale problems involving knowledge discovery tasks [40].

REFERENCES

1. S. Mitra and Y. Hayashi, "Neuro-fuzzy rule generation: Survey in soft computing framework," *IEEE Transactions on Neural Networks*, vol. 11, pp. 748–768, 2000.

2. R. Andrews, J. Diederich, and A. B. Tickle, "A survey and critique of techniques for extracting rules from trained artificial neural networks," *Knowledge-Based Systems*, vol. 8, pp. 373–389, 1995.

3. I. A. Taha and J. Ghosh, "Symbolic interpretation of artificial neural networks," *IEEE Transactions on Knowledge and Data Engineering*, vol. 11, pp. 448–463, 1999.

4. B. M. Happel and J. J. Murre, "Design and evolution of modular neural network architectures," *Neural Networks*, vol. 7, pp. 985–1004, 1994.

5. L. Hansen and P. Salamon, "Neural network ensembles," *IEEE Transactions on Pattern Analysis and Machine Intelligence*, vol. 12, pp. 993–1001, 1990.

6. S. I. Gallant, "Connectionist expert systems," *Communications of the Association for Computing Machinery*, vol. 31, pp. 152–169, 1988.

7. M. Ishikawa, "Structural learning with forgetting," *Neural Networks*, vol. 9, pp. 509–521, 1996.

8. W. Duch, R. Adamczak, and K. Grabczewski, "Extraction of logical rules from neural networks," *Neural Processing Letters*, vol. 7, pp. 211–219, 1998.

9. R. Setiono, "Extracting rules from neural networks by pruning and hidden-unit splitting," *Neural Computation*, vol. 9, pp. 205–225, 1997.

10. J. R. Quinlan, *C4.5: Programs for Machine Learning*. San Mateo, CA: Morgan Kaufmann, 1993.

11. R. Setiono, "Extracting M of N rules from trained neural networks," *IEEE Transactions on Neural Networks*, vol. 11, pp. 512–519, 2000.

12. R. Setiono and H. Liu, "A connectionist approach to generating oblique decision trees," *IEEE Transactions on Systems, Man, and Cybernetics, Part B: Cybernetics*, vol. 29, pp. 440–444, 1999.

13. L. Breiman, J. H. Friedman, R. A. Olshen, and C. J. Stone, *Classification and Regression Trees*. Monterey, CA: Wadsworth and Brooks/Cole, 1984.

14. D. Nauck, F. Klawonn, and R. Kruse, *Foundations of Neuro-Fuzzy Systems*. Chichester, England: John Wiley & Sons, 1997.

15. D. Nauck and R. Kruse, "Neuro-fuzzy systems for function approximation," *Fuzzy Sets and Systems*, vol. 101, pp. 261–271, 1999.

16. E. H. Mamdani and S. Assilian, "An experiment in linguistic synthesis with a fuzzy logic controller," *International Journal of Man Machine Studies*, vol. 7, pp. 1–13, 1975.

17. F. C. H. Rhee and R. Krishnapuram, "Fuzzy rule generation methods for high-level computer vision," *Fuzzy Sets and Systems*, vol. 60, pp. 245–258, 1993.

18. Y. Q. Zhang and A. Kandel, "Compensatory neuro-fuzzy systems with fast learning algorithms," *IEEE Transactions on Neural Networks*, vol. 9, pp. 83–105, 1998.

19. S. Mitra and S. K. Pal, "Logical operation based fuzzy MLP for classification and rule generation," *Neural Networks*, vol. 7, pp. 353–373, 1994.

20. L. M. Fu, "Learning capacity and sample complexity on expert networks," *IEEE Transactions on Neural Networks*, vol. 7, pp. 1517–1520, 1996.

21. G. G. Towell and J. W. Shavlik, "Knowledge-based artificial neural networks," *Artificial Intelligence*, vol. 70, pp. 119–165, 1994.

22. D. W. Opitz and J. W. Shavlik, "Dynamically adding symbolically meaningful nodes to knowledge-based neural networks," *Knowledge-Based Systems*, vol. 8, pp. 310–311, 1995.

23. L. M. Fu, "Knowledge-based connectionism for revising domain theories," *IEEE Transactions on Systems, Man, and Cybernetics*, vol. 23, pp. 173–182, 1993.

24. G. G. Towell and J. W. Shavlik, "Extracting refined rules from knowledge-based neural networks," *Machine Learning*, vol. 13, pp. 71–101, 1993.

25. G. A. Carpenter and S. Grossberg, "A massively parallel architecture for a self-organising neural pattern recognition machine," *Computer Vision, Graphics and Image Processing*, vol. 37, pp. 54–115, 1987.

26. G. A. Carpenter, S. Grossberg, and J. H. Reynolds, "ARTMAP: Supervised real-time learning and classification of nonstationary data by a self-organizing neural network," *Neural Networks*, vol. 4, pp. 565–588, 1991.

27. G. A. Carpenter, S. Grossberg, N. Markuzon, J. H. Reynolds, and D. B. Rosen, "Fuzzy ARTMAP: a neural network architecture for incremental supervised learning of analog multidimensional maps," *IEEE Transactions on Neural Networks*, vol. 3, pp. 698–713, 1992.

28. A. H. Tan, "Cascade ARTMAP: Integrating neural computation and symbolic knowledge processing," *IEEE Transactions on Neural Networks*, vol. 8, pp. 237–250, 1997.

29. R. J. Machado and A. F. da Rocha, "Inference, inquiry, evidence censorship, and explanation in connectionist expert systems," *IEEE Transactions on Fuzzy Systems*, vol. 5, pp. 443–459, 1997.

30. S. Mitra, R. K. De, and S. K. Pal, "Knowledge-based fuzzy MLP for classification and rule generation," *IEEE Transactions on Neural Networks*, vol. 8, pp. 1338–1350, 1997.

31. D. W. Opitz and J. W. Shavlik, "Connectionist theory refinement: Genetically searching the space of network topologies," *Journal of Artificial Intelligence Research*, vol. 6, pp. 177–209, 1997.

32. M. Banerjee, S. Mitra, and S. K. Pal, "Rough fuzzy MLP: Knowledge encoding and classification," *IEEE Transactions on Neural Networks*, vol. 9, pp. 1203–1216, 1998.

33. S. Mitra, M. Banerjee, and S. K. Pal, "Rough knowledge-based network, fuzziness and classification," *Neural Computing and Applications*, vol. 7, pp. 17–25, 1998.

34. E. B. Baum and D. Haussler, "What size nets give valid generalizations?," *Neural Computations*, vol. 1, pp. 151–160, 1989.

35. P. Mitra, S. Mitra, and S. K. Pal, "Staging of cervical cancer with soft computing," *IEEE Transactions on Biomedical Engineering*, vol. 47, pp. 934–940, 2000.

36. S. Mitra, P. Mitra, and S. K. Pal, "Evolutionary modular design of rough knowledge-based network using fuzzy attributes," *Neurocomputing*, vol. 36, pp. 45–66, 2001.

37. S. K. Pal, S. Mitra, and P. Mitra, "Rough Fuzzy MLP: Modular evolution, rule generation and evaluation," *IEEE Transactions on Knowledge and Data Engineering*, vol. 15, pp. 14–25, 2003.

38. H. Liu and S. T. Tan, "X2R: A fast rule generator," in *Proceedings of the IEEE International Conference on Systems, Man, and Cybernetics* (Vancouver, Canada), pp. 215–220, 1995.

39. E. L. Lehmann, *Testing of Statistical Hypotheses*. New York: John Wiley & Sons, 1976.

40. S. Mitra, S. K. Pal, and P. Mitra, "Data mining in soft computing framework: A survey," *IEEE Transactions on Neural Networks*, vol. 13, pp. 3–14, 2002.

9

Multimedia Data Mining

9.1 INTRODUCTION

There has been a significant growth in information technology over the last decade because of the ever-growing power of the computing systems, advances in data storage management, and tremendous progress in communication technologies. A conventional information processing system has been mainly based on alphanumeric data with a very structured data representation, and the type of computation involved is mainly number crunching in nature. However, representation of digital information is no longer restricted in the form of numeric and alphanumeric data only.

Classically, databases were formed by tuples of numeric and alphanumeric contents. Today, information processing revolves around different datatypes in higher-order abstraction of data representation, such as text, document, image, video, graphics, speech, audio, hypertext, markup languages, etc. The growth in Internet technologies have added a new dimension to the interactive usage of these different datatypes as well. Interactive processing and management of these different datatypes is another important aspect of multimedia processing.

There has been tremendous demand in storage and management of multimedia data over the last decade. Progress in data compression research has been one of the enabling factors in this direction. A multimedia database management system stores and manages these large collection of multimedia datatypes, namely, text, digital image, digital video, graphics, voice, audio, etc. Popularity of multimedia database systems is increasing, with the growing use of interactive audio-visual systems, digital camera, scanner, CD-ROM, Internet, etc. Multimedia databases fall in the category of very large database management system. Today's *World Wide Web* can be considered to be a distributed multimedia database of the largest size ever used.

Multimedia data are usually semistructured and often very much unstructured, as compared to numeric and alphanumeric data structures that are usually dealt with in traditional database management systems. Most of the classical data mining algorithms and techniques were mainly developed for mining information from structured data, such as relational, transactional, and data warehouse data. They had been used typically in financial and business market analysis, forecast, etc. However, in reality not all datatypes are very structured, and a substantial amount of information is available as semistructured or unstructured multimedia data. As a result, retrieval of multimedia data is challenging [1].

Most of the information in government, business and other institutions are stored in the form of text databases. As a matter of fact, recent studies show that more than 80% of company information is stored in the form of textual documents. Visual information, available in the form of still imagery, video, and graphics, is a natural medium of communication by humans.

A tremendous amount of visual information is being processed and communicated everyday in this digital multimedia age. The medical community today relies upon the visual information conveyed by the digital medical images such as X-ray, MRI, CAT/SCAN, etc. Security and surveillance applications, based on online video and imaging applications, is becoming popular. Similarly, voice, audio, and speech data contain a huge amount of information in digital form as well. As a result, retrieval and mining of information from multimedia data will have significant impact in the current and future information age.

It is obvious that development of data mining techniques particularly useful for multimedia datatypes will continue to be challenging, and there needs to be focused efforts to influence this area of study. Development of sophistical data mining technologies for multimedia data could very well be the catalyst for the next-generation information technology revolution.

In this chapter we provide a study on the developments in multimedia data mining. Section 9.2 deals with different aspects of text mining. Section 9.3 presents issues in image mining, including color images and content-based image retrieval. Video mining, encompassing content-based video retrieval and MPEG standard, is described in Section 9.4. Section 9.5 provides an introduction to Web mining. Finally, Section 9.6 concludes the chapter.

9.2   TEXT MINING

Text data stored in most of the text databases are usually semistructured and possibly unstructured. There is a vast amount of information available in text or document databases, in the form of electronic publication of books, digital libraries, electronic mails, electronic media, technical and business documents, reports, research articles, Web pages in the Internet, hypertext, markup languages, etc. In order to aid mining of information from large collections of such text databases, special types of data mining methodologies have been developed recently. This domain of study is popularly known as '*text mining*' [2]–[4].

Text mining is an emerging area of study, currently under rapid development in scientific research. In addition to traditional data mining methodologies, text mining uses techniques from many multidisciplinary scientific fields in order to gain insight, understand and interpret, and automatically extract information from large quantities of text data available in text databases distributed everywhere. The functionalities of text mining methodologies have been mainly built on the results of *text analysis* techniques. Some of the other areas that have recently influenced text mining are string matching, text searching, artificial intelligence, machine learning, information retrieval, natural language processing, statistics, information theory, soft computing, etc. The *Internet search* engines, combined with various text analysis techniques, have paved the way for online text mining as well.

9.2.1   Keyword-based search and mining

The search of text databases is different from the search techniques applied in traditional relational database management systems. A crude way of mining text databases is to apply keyword based searching. In this simplistic approach the documents are considered to be strings, with a set of *keywords* being the signature of the text data and indexed accordingly. A keyword can be searched inside a text file using string matching techniques, which may involve exact match or approximate match as explained in Chapter 4. String-matched keywords or patterns, found inside the text, are then used to index the documents. After the documents have been identified by the keywords, traditional data mining techniques (such as classification, clustering, rule mining, etc.) can be applied with probably some degree of success depending upon the characteristics of the collection of the documents in the text database.

There are two major problems with such a simplistic approach that does not take the semantic meaning of the keywords into consideration. These two challenging problems are *synonymy* and *polysemy*, which have been a long standing problem in the area of *natural language processing*. A keyword provided by the user may not appear at all in the document, whereas the document may be very much related to the keyword because the same thing can often be described in different ways in a natural language.

For example, the keyword could be '*woman*', whereas the document may not exactly contain any instance of the word '*woman*' but contain the word '*lady*' frequently. This is known as the *synonymy* problem. This problem can be addressed to some extent by just filtering the document such that the words of similar meaning are replaced by a chosen canonical token word. For example, the words 'automobile', 'vehicle', and 'vehicular' can simply be replaced by the word 'car'. Similarly, the words 'is', 'are', 'am', 'were', 'was', 'been', 'being' can be replaced by the word 'be' when they appear in a document. However, this is not a very practical proposition, because it is not possible to maintain a universal list from the dictionary of English language to form the tokens of such types of words.

It is also possible that the same word may have different meanings in different contexts. For example, the word '*mining*' has different meaning in the context of '*data mining*' as compared to the aspect of '*coal mining*'. This is called the *polysemy* problem. Hence the success of the *natural language processing*, coupled with other artificial intelligence areas to solve these problems, will have great influence on text mining in the long run.

9.2.2 Text analysis and retrieval

Text analysis has been a field of study in natural language processing and information retrieval for quite a while. Since most of the Internet search techniques are text-based, text analysis also received prominence with the growth of the Internet.

Usually, text data are semistructured, and easy to read and interpret by humans. Text analysis techniques can be applied to extract relevant key features from a text, categorize the text documents based on its semantic contents, index the documents, extract the overview of large collection of text documents, organize large collections of documents in efficient ways, improve the effectiveness of automatic search process, detect duplicate documents in large text databases, etc.

In full-text retrieval systems, automatic indexing of the documents are often done based on statistical analysis of the common words and phrases that appear in the document. One such simple method for automated text document indexing can be defined by the following steps.

1. Find the unique words in each document in the document database.

2. Calculate the frequency of occurrence of each of these unique words for each document in the document database.

3. Compute the total frequency of occurrence of each word across all the documents in the database.

4. Sort the words in ascending order of their frequency of occurrence in the database.

5. Remove the words with very high frequency of occurrences from this sorted list.

6. Remove the words with low frequency of occurrences from this sorted list.

7. Use the remaining words as index for the text database.

9.2.3   Mathematical modeling of documents

The *text* data can be loosely considered as a composition of two basic units, namely, *document* and *term* [2, 5]. In the general sense, a *document* is a structured or semistructured segment of a text. For example, this book is a text *document* and it is structured in the form of a number of chapters, where each chapter is composed of sections, and each section may be composed of a number of subsections and paragraphs, etc. Similarly, an electronic mail can be considered a document because it contains a message header, title, and content of the message, in a defined structured fashion. There are many such documents that exist in practice. Some other examples are source codes, Web pages, spreadsheets, telephone directory, etc. A *term* is a word or group of words or a phrase that exists in a document. Terms are extracted from the documents using one of the string matching algorithms described in Chapter 4.

We can model a *text* document using this definition of *document* and *term* [2, 5]. Let us consider a set of N documents $D = (d_1, d_2, d_3, \cdots, d_N)$ and a set of M terms $T = (t_1, t_2, t_3, \cdots, t_M)$. We can model each document d_i as a vector $V_i = (v_{i,1}, v_{i,2}, \cdots, v_{i,M})$ in the M-dimensional space R^M. The entry $v_{i,j}$ represents a measure of association of the term t_j with the document d_i. The value of $v_{i,j}$ is 0 if the document d_i does not contain the term t_j and is nonzero otherwise. In simple boolean representation, $v_{i,j} = 1$ if the term t_j appears in document d_i. However, this measure is not found to be very robust in text retrieval. The more popular and practical measure of association $(v_{i,j})$ is the *term frequency*, which is simply defined as the number of occurrences of the term t_j in document d_i. Using this approach, the text is simply modeled as a *document-term frequency matrix* as depicted in Fig. 9.1.

In Fig. 9.1, we have shown a 5 × 4 array to represent the *document-term frequency matrix* for a set of five *documents* and four *terms*. Let us assume that the selected terms are

- t_1 = monkey,

- t_2 = bird,

- t_3 = flower,

- t_4 = sky.

The second row in the matrix is the vector (5, 9, 4, 3) representing the document d_2, in which the term monkey appears 5 times, bird appears 9 times, flower appears 4 times, and sky appears 3 times, respectively.

	t_1	t_2	t_3	t_4
d_1	10	8	1	0
d_2	5	9	4	3
d_3	0	15	10	1
d_4	23	0	0	7
d_5	52	19	2	8

Fig. 9.1 Document-term frequency matrix for five documents and four terms.

It is possible that some of the terms may appear more frequently in the documents set of many documents than the others. This may represent the fact that these terms are more important than others in determining the content of a document. For example, the term 'information' is definitely more important than the words 'is', 'the', 'are', 'am', 'of', etc. in any English text. The problem with document-term frequency matrix model is that it does not capture this phenomena. In order to increase the discrimination power for these terms, the corresponding term frequencies can be weighted by *inverse-document frequency (IDF)*. The *inverse-document frequency* of term t_j is defined by

$$IDF_j = 1 + \log \frac{n_j}{N}, \tag{9.1}$$

where N is the number of documents and n_j is the number of documents that contains the term t_j. The IDF favors the terms that appear in more documents than the others. The discriminating power can further be improved by updating each entry $v_{i,j}$ in the document-term frequency matrix as

$$\bar{v}_{i,j} = \frac{v_{i,j}}{\sum_{k=1}^{M} v_{i,k}} * IDF_j. \tag{9.2}$$

9.2.4   Similarity–based matching for documents and queries

When a document is modeled using the document-term frequency matrix representation or its variants, as explained above, the relative ordering of words in the text gets lost. Thereby the syntactic information of formation of the text, such as the grammar for the sentence structure in English text, also disappears. In spite of this, the term frequency modeling has been found to be very effective in a variety of text or document retrieval applications such as query processing, comparison of documents, document analysis, etc.

Once the document is represented in the matrix model, we can apply a distance measure to find the similarity of two documents. The simplest approach is to find the Euclidean distance between the two vectors, corresponding to the two documents. For example, if we want to search a query document d_q in the document database $D = (d_1, d_2, d_3, \cdots, d_N)$, we first form the frequency vector $v_q = (v_{q,1}, v_{q,2}, \cdots, v_{q,M})$ for the M terms of the term set $T = (t_1, t_2, t_3, \cdots, t_M)$. The Euclidean distance between the query document d_q and the document d_i in the document database D is

$$\delta(d_q, d_i) = \sqrt{\left[\sum_{j=1}^{M}(v_{q,j} - v_{i,j})^2\right]}. \tag{9.3}$$

We can also apply other well-defined statistical distance measures [6] (such as Mahalanobis distance, Manhattan distance, etc.) to find the similarity between two documents. However, the *cosine measure* of two vectors has been found to be very effective in the comparison of two documents. The *cosine measure* of two vectors v_i and v_j can be computed as

$$\cos(v_i, v_j) = \frac{\sum_{k=1}^{M}[v_{i,k} * v_{j,k}]}{\sqrt{\left[\sum_{k=1}^{M} v_{i,k}^2 \sum_{k=1}^{M} v_{j,k}^2\right]}}. \tag{9.4}$$

This is essentially the cosine of the angle between the two vectors. The cosine measure is nothing but the inner product of the two vectors, after both v_i and v_j have been normalized to have unity length. As a result, the cosine measure reflects the relative distribution of the terms in the vectors and this measure has been found to be very effective in document matching.

Using the numeric values of the above distance measures, we can find the similarity amongst the documents in a document collection. Similarity-based indices can be developed for these documents, followed by the application of traditional data mining techniques for clustering, classification and other operations on the documents based on these indices.

Queries can be expressed by the same term-based representation, considering the query itself as a document formed with a set of terms. As a result, we can also apply the above principles for query matching in a document. The query is expressed as a vector of weights corresponding to the terms that appear in the query, and the weight becomes implicitly zero for those terms not existent in the query. In its simplest form, the vector can contain weight one for the terms existing in the query and zero for others. The distance of the vector is then measured from the vectors corresponding to the documents in the document database.

The main discrepancy of the above document-term frequency matrix approach is that it loses the information regarding syntactic relationship amongst the words in the documents. The other problem with the document-term frequency matrix approach is that a query may contain terms with semantically same, but physically different terminology, as compared to the terms used to index a document. For example, the query may contain the term '*lad*' whereas the document may have been indexed by '*boy*'. Although these two words are semantically the same, from the similarity perspective they are quite different.

One way to solve this problem is to use a predefined dictionary or knowledge base (a thesaurus or ontology) linking semantically related terms together. However, such an approach is inherently very subjective regarding how the terms are related and how similar they are semantically with respect to the content of a particular database. Moreover, the thesaurus could be prohibitively large to contain all possible cases from English or any other human language.

In spite of reasonably good similarity measures, the computational requirements of the above approach is very high. In most of the practical text document databases, the number of terms in the term set could be more than 50,000 and the number of documents could also be very large in the document database. This makes the dimension of the document-term frequency matrix very high and prohibitively large for computational requirements. This high dimensionality also leads the matrix to be very sparse and can further enhance the difficulty in identifying the terms in the document.

9.2.5 Latent semantic analysis

In order to reduce the dimensionality of a matrix, an efficient technique has been developed to analyze text based on the popular *Singular Value Decomposition* used in *principal component analysis* [7, 8]. This technique is called *Latent Semantic Indexing*, and the text analysis using this method is called *Latent Semantic Analysis* (LSA) [2, 3]. As the name implies, this technique helps in extracting the hidden semantic structure from the text rather than just the usage of the term occurrences. LSA also provides a good metric of semantic similarities among documents, based on a term's context. The theory behind singular value decomposition of a matrix and generation of principal components has been discussed in detail in Section 3.7.

The dimensionality of the original document-term frequency matrix F is often prohibitively large. The *Latent Semantic Analysis* (LSA) approximates the original $M \times N$ document-term frequency matrix F to a much smaller matrix of size $N \times K$, using only K principal components generated by the singular value decomposition (SVD) method described in Section 3.7. In reality, the value of K can be much smaller than the original dimension N of the *term* set. Typical values of N could be 10,000 to 50,000 or more while K can be in the order of 100 or less, literally without significant loss of information. The SVD approach exploits the possible redundancy in the terms of the document.

Let us consider an example to better understand the significance of LSA. We can assume that the terms such as '*image*', '*picture*', '*pixel array*' can be expected to contain redundancy in the semantic sense in a document, because they are quite related and essentially mean the same thing. A text document discussing about multimedia or image processing aspects may contain all these terms, and they may appear in the document-term frequency matrix all together. The intuitive logic behind the principal component representation of the document-term frequency matrix is that the reduced matrix may capture semantic relationships among the original terms by creating new terms that compactly reflect the semantic content of the text document. As a result, the terms '*image*', '*picture*', '*pixel array*' are effectively mapped into a single principal component term, and this new term can be considered to indicate that the document is related to a multimedia or image processing topic. Hence this term can be used to create an index for the document. If a query contains the term '*picture*', the retrieval system based on this LSA approach will successfully identify a document related to '*image*' or *pixel array*. On the other hand, the simple document-term frequency-based approach will fail to properly identify this situation.

The LSA approach for text indexing employs the transformed document-term frequency matrix to compare the similarity between two documents by distance measures (of Section 9.2.4) or to extract a prioritized list of (say, N) matches for a query. The indices generated through text analysis can be used to classify the documents. Then association rule mining can be applied to the terms to discover sets of associated terms, which can be used to distinguish one class of documents from others.

The text mining process can be broadly separated in two phases, namely, *text refinement* and *knowledge extraction*. In the text refinement phase, the original unstructured or semistructured text document is transformed into a chosen intermediate form or model. In the second phase, the knowledge is then discovered from this intermediate model by extracting patterns and mining rules.

9.2.6 Soft computing approaches

Since the free-form text is usually unstructured or semistructured, the application of soft computing approaches can be promising to analyze the imprecise nature of the data and extraction of patterns for knowledge discovery. Recently, there have been some developments in this direction.

Inductive learning, using fuzzy decision tree (Section 5.6), has been developed for imprecise text mining [9]. A concept relation dictionary and a classification tree are generated from a random set of daily business reports database of text classes concerning retailing. In their experiments the authors use 10,000 evaluation examples, with a decision tree of maximum 90 nodes (37 intermediate and 53 terminal).

An approach in Ref. [10] uses fuzzy association thesaurus and query expansion for text retrieval. Fuzzy composition operations like *max-min*, *max-product* and *sum-product* are used for constructing the thesaurus. Interactive query expansion shows the user, upon initial query, a ranked list of documents suggested by the system based on the fuzzy relation composition. A measure of similarity helps select the correlated terms using queries with/without weight. The experiments use a collection of daily news in Chinese, with 981 homogeneous and 700 heterogeneous text documents.

An HTML document can be viewed as a structured entity, in which document subparts are identified by *tags* and each such subpart consists of text delimited by a distinct tag. A fuzzy representation of HTML documents is described in Ref. [11]. The HTML document is represented by a sum of fuzzy set terms

$$R(d) = \sum_{t \in T} \frac{\mu_d(t)}{t}, \tag{9.5}$$

where the importance of each term t in document d is given by the membership value

$$\mu_d(t) = \sum_{i=1}^{n} (\mu_{tag_i}(d, t) * w_i) * g(IDF_t),$$

w_i is the normalized importance weight associated with tag_i, n corresponds to the number of tags, $g(.)$ is a normalization function, and IDF_t is the inverse-document frequency. The significance of an index term is computed by weighting the occurrence of the term with the importance of the tag associated with it.

Recommending alternate queries during textual information retrieval is an important feature in a Web-based search engine, because users often do not know the exact terms to locate the information relevant to their interests. Fuzzy ontology is used for query refinement in a domain search engine named Personalizing Abstract Search Service (PASS) [12]. Fuzzy *narrower-* and *broader-than* term relations are defined using a fuzzy conjunction operator. Pruning of redundant relations is made by analyzing the sets of relations involving more than two terms. PASS is used to provide the abstracts of papers from the *IEEE Transactions on Neural Networks* journal.

A key issue in text mining is keyword extraction. This allows the automatic categorization and classification of text documents. Keyword extraction can be done using clustering methods. Relational Alternating Cluster Estimation (RACE), based on Levenshtein distance, was used to automatically extract the 20 most relevant keywords from Internet documents in Ref. [13]. Using these keywords, corresponding to the cluster centers, a classification rate of more than 80% could be achieved.

Self-organization of the Web (WEBSOM) [14, 15], based on Kohonen's SOM (Section 2.2.3.3), has been used for exploring document collections. A textual document collection is organized onto a graphical map display that provides an overview of the collection and facilitates interactive browsing. The browsing can be focused by locating some interesting documents on the map using content addressing. The excellent visualization capabilities of SOM are utilized for this purpose.

9.3   IMAGE MINING

Traditional data mining techniques have been developed mainly for structured datatypes. The image datatype does not belong to this structured category, suitable for interpretation by a machine, and hence the mining of image data is a challenging problem. Content of an image is visual in nature and the interpretation of the information conveyed by an image is mainly subjective, based on the human visual system.

Image data have been used for machine vision, based on extraction of desired features from an image and interpretation of these features for particular applications. This is a challenging area of study, and it has been extensively explored in pattern recognition and machine vision for quite some time. Although interpretation of the image content by the human visual system is a natural and apparently effortless procedure, it remains a mystery how the human brain processes this information. Hence modeling the process of human interpretation of the semantic content of images is still a research challenge. As a result, it is difficult to define a single set of algorithms or functionalities that can claim to comprise a complete set of image mining tools.

The research and development of mining image data is relatively new, and has become an emerging field of study today. Most of the activities in mining image data have been in the search and retrieval of images based on the analysis of similarity of a query image or its feature(s) with the entries in the image database. The image retrieval systems can be broadly categorized into two categories based on the type of searches, using either description of an image or its visual content.

In the first category, the images are described based on user-defined texts [16, 17]. The images are indexed and retrieved based on these rudimentary *descriptions*, such as their size, type, date and time of capture, identity of owner, keywords, or some text description of the image. As a result, this is often called *description based* or *text-based image retrieval* process. The image indices are predefined based on these descriptions, and they are searched on these indices when a query is posed as

"find the images from a image database which matches with the given set of descriptions, e.g. images captured on January 8 to January 12, 1999 and size bigger than 100 KByte."

The text-based descriptions of the images are usually typed manually for each image by human operators, because the automatic generation of keywords for the images is difficult without incorporation of visual information and feature extraction. As a result, this is a very labor-intensive process and is impractical in today's multimedia information age. Moreover, since the description of images are very much subjective, the automated process to generate a text-based description for indexing of the images could be very inaccurate and incomplete. In the second category, the query can be posed as

"find the images similar to a given query image."

This second category of similarity based image retrieval process is called *Content Based Image Retrieval* (CBIR) [18]–[22]. In CBIR systems, the images are searched and retrieved based on the visual content of the images. Based on these visual contents, desirable images features can be extracted and used as index or basis of search. *Content-based image retrieval* is highly desirable and has increasingly become a growing area of study towards the successful development of image mining techniques.

9.3.1   Content-Based Image Retrieval

There are, in general, three fundamental modules in a content-based image retrieval system. These are

1. Visual content or feature extraction,

2. Multidimensional indexing, and

3. Retrieval.

The images in an image database are indexed-based on extracted inherent visual contents (or features) such as color, texture, pattern, image topology, shape of objects and their layouts and locations within the image, etc. An image can be represented by a multidimensional vector of the extracted features from the image. The feature vector actually acts as the *signature* of the image. This feature vector can be assumed to be associated to a point in the

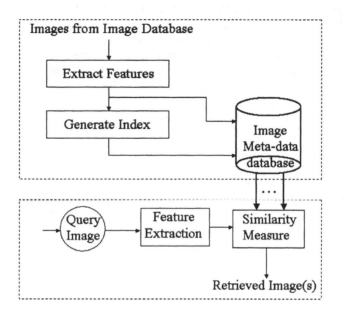

Fig. 9.2   Architecture of a Content Based Image Retrieval System.

multidimensional space. As an example, an image can be represented by an N-dimensional feature vector whose first n_1 components may represent *color*, the next n_2 components may represent *shape*, the following n_3 components may represent some image *topology*, and finally n_4 components may represent *texture* of the image, so that there are $N = n_1 + n_2 + n_3 + n_4$ components. As a result, an *example image* can simply be used as a query using visual content based indexing.

The query image can be analyzed to extract the visual features and can be compared to find matches with the indices of the images stored in the database. The extracted image features are stored as meta-data, and images are indexed based on these meta-data information. This meta-data information comprises some measures of the extracted image features. The feature vectors of similar images will then be clustered in the N-dimensional space. Retrieving *similar* images to a *query* image then boils down to finding the indices of those images in the N-dimensional search space whose feature vectors in the N-dimensional space are within some threshold of proximity to the point of the query image. This indexing structure is popularly known as *Multidimensional Access Structure* (MAS) [23].

The architecture for a possible content based image retrieval system is shown in Fig. 9.2. The CBIR systems architecture is essentially divided into two parts. In the first part, the images from the image database are processed off-line. The features from each image in the image database are extracted to form the meta-data information of the image, in order to describe the image using its visual content features. Next these features are used to index the image, and they are stored into the meta-data database along with the images. In the second part, the retrieval process is depicted. The query image is analyzed to extract the visual features, and these features are used to retrieve the similar images from the image database. Rather than directly comparing two images, similarity of the visual features of the query image is measured with the features of each image stored in the meta-data database as their signatures. Often the similarity of two images are measured by computing the distance between the feature vectors of the two images. The retrieval systems returns the first k images, whose distance from the query image is below some defined threshold.

Several image features have been used to index images for content-based image retrieval systems. Most popular amongst them are color, texture, shape, image topology, color layout, region of interest, etc. We discuss some of these features in greater detail in the following sections.

9.3.2 Color features

Color is one of the most widely used visual features in content based image retrieval [24]–[27]. While we can perceive only a limited number of gray levels, our eyes are able to distinguish thousands of colors and a computer can represent even millions of distinguishable colors in practice. Color has been successfully applied to retrieve images, because it has very strong correlations with the underlying objects in an image. Moreover, color feature is robust to background complications, scaling, orientation, perspective, and size of an image. A color pixel in a digital image is represented by three color channels (usually Red, Green and Blue). It is well known that any color can be produced by mixing these three primary colors.

Although we can use any color space for computation of a color histogram HSV (Hue, Saturation, and Value), HLS (Hue, Lightness, and Saturation), CIE color spaces (such as CIELAB, CIELUV) [28] were found to deliver better results as compared to the RGB space. Since these color spaces are visually (or perceptually) uniform compared to the RGB, they are found to be more effective to measure color similarities between images. We describe here the HSV color space, because that is widely used in the CBIR community. In the HSV color space,

- *Hue* of a color represents the relative color appearance; that is, 'redness', 'greenness,' and so on,

- *Value* indicates the darkness of the color (or the perceived illuminance), and

- *Saturation* represents the strength of the color.

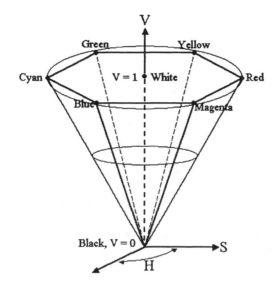

Fig. 9.3   Perceptual representation of HSV color space.

The perceptual representation of the HSV color space has a conical shape, as shown in Fig. 9.3. The 'Value' (V) varies along the vertical axis of the cone, the 'Hue' (H) varies along the periphery of the circle of the cone and is represented as an angle about the vertical axis, and the 'Saturation' (S) varies along the radial distance as shown in Fig. 9.3. We have shown the vertices a hexagon on the periphery of the circle in Fig. 9.3 to show six colors separated by 60° angles. Red is at 0° (coincides with 300°), Yellow at 60°, Green at 120°, Cyan at 180°, Blue at 240°, and Magenta at 300°. The complementary colors are 180° apart. For example, Blue and Yellow are the complementary colors. Apex of the cone ($V = 0$) represents 'Black'. Again, $V = 1$ and $S = 0$ represents 'White'. The colors have their maximum luminosity ($V = 1$) at the periphery of the circle. $V = 1$ and $S = 1$ represent the 'pure' hues for any color.

If the red, green, and blue component values of a color pixel in the RGB space are R, G, and B respectively, they can be linearly normalized to fractions r, g, and b in the range [0, 1] and these normalized values r, g, and b are used to transform into the HSV space. Transformation of RGB to HSV color space can be accomplished by the following set of equations [28]:

$$V = \max(r, g, b), \tag{9.6}$$

$$S = \begin{cases} 0 & \text{if } V = 0 \\ V - \frac{\min(r,g,b)}{V} & \text{if } V > 0, \end{cases} \tag{9.7}$$

$$H = \begin{cases} 0 & \text{if } S = 0 \\ \frac{60*(g-b)}{S*V} & \text{if } V = r \\ 60 * \left[2 + \frac{(b-r)}{S*V}\right] & \text{if } V = g \\ 60 * \left[4 + \frac{(r-g)}{S*V}\right] & \text{if } V = b, \end{cases} \tag{9.8}$$

$$H = H + 360 \quad \text{if } H < 0. \tag{9.9}$$

9.3.2.1 *Color histogram:* This is the most commonly used color feature in CBIR [24, 25]. Color histogram has been found to be very effective in characterizing the global distribution of colors in an image, and it can be used as an important feature for image characterization. To define color histograms, the color space is quantized into a finite number of discrete levels. Each of these levels becomes a bin in the histogram. The color histogram is then computed by counting the number of pixels in each of these discrete levels. There are many different approaches to quantize a color space to determine the number of such discrete levels [24]–[26].

Using the color histogram, we can find the images that have similar color distribution. One can think of the simplest measure of similarity by computing the distance between two histograms. Let us consider that $H^{(1)} = \{h_1^{(1)}, h_2^{(1)}, \cdots, h_K^{(1)}\}$ and $H^{(2)} = \{h_1^{(2)}, h_2^{(2)}, \cdots, h_K^{(2)}\}$ are two feature vectors generated from the color histograms of two images, where $h_j^{(1)}$ and $h_j^{(2)}$ are the count of pixels in the jth bin of the two histograms respectively, and K is the number of bins in each histogram. We can define a simple distance between two histograms as

$$d_1 = \sum_{j=1}^{K} |h_j^{(1)} - h_j^{(2)}|. \tag{9.10}$$

There is another popular distance measure between two histograms, popularly known as *histogram intersection*. The histogram intersection is the total number of pixels common to both the histograms. This can be computed as

$$I(H^{(1)}, H^{(2)}) = \sum_{j=1}^{K} \min(h_j^{(1)} - h_j^{(2)}). \tag{9.11}$$

The above equations can be normalized to maintain the value of the distance measure in the range [0, 1]. To normalize $I(H^{(1)}, H^{(2)})$, it is divided either

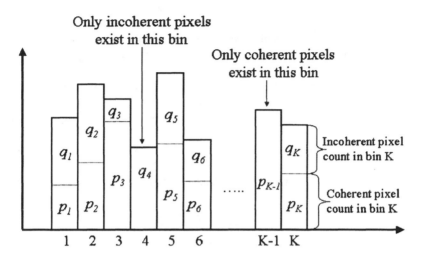

Fig. 9.4 Partitioning the color histogram with coherence and noncoherence pixel counts.

by the total number of pixels in one of the histograms or by the size of the image.

9.3.2.2 Color coherence vector: One problem with the above color histogram-based similarity measure approach is that the global color distribution doesn't reflect the spatial distribution of the color pixels locally in the image. This cannot distinguish whether a particular color is sparsely scattered all over the image or it appears in a single large region in the image.

The color coherence vector [27]-based approach was designed to accommodate the information of spatial color into the color histogram. Here we can classify each pixel in an image, based on whether it belongs to a large uniform region or not. For example, we can consider a region to be uniformly colored if it consists of the same color and the area of the region is above a certain threshold (say, 2%) of the whole image area. We refer to the pixels in these regions as *coherent* pixels.

In this approach, each histogram bin is divided into two parts. One contains the count of pixels belonging to a large uniformly colored region and the other contains the same colored pixels belonging to a sparse region. Let us consider that the ith bin of the histogram contains p_j coherent pixels and q_j incoherent pixels. Using this partition, the *color coherence vector* of an image can be expressed as $\{(p_1, q_1), (p_2, q_2), \cdots, (p_K, q_K)\}$. We have shown this in Fig. 9.4. It should be noted that $\{p_1 + q_1, p_2 + q_2, \cdots, p_K + q_K\}$ is the original color histogram without this distinguishing power. The color coherence vectors provide superior retrieval results with this additional distinguishing capability, as compared to the global color histogram method [27].

9.3.2.3 Color moment: This is a compact representation of the color feature to characterize a color image [25]. It has been shown that most of the color distribution information is captured by the three low-order moments. The first-order moment (μ) captures the mean color, the second-order moment (σ) captures the standard deviation, and the third-order moment captures the skewness (θ) of color. These three low-order moments (μ_c, σ_c, θ_c) are extracted for each of the three color planes, using the following mathematical formulation.

$$\mu_c = \frac{1}{MN} \sum_{i=1}^{M} \sum_{j=1}^{N} p_{ij}^c, \tag{9.12}$$

$$\sigma_c = \left[\frac{1}{MN} \sum_{i=1}^{M} \sum_{j=1}^{N} (p_{ij}^c - \mu_c)^2 \right]^{\frac{1}{2}}, \tag{9.13}$$

$$\theta_c = \left[\frac{1}{MN} \sum_{i=1}^{M} \sum_{j=1}^{N} (p_{ij}^c - \mu_c)^3 \right]^{\frac{1}{3}}, \tag{9.14}$$

where p_{ij}^c is value of the cth color component of the color pixel in the ith row and jth column of the image. As a result, we need to extract only nine parameters (three moments for each of the three color planes) to characterize the color image. Weighted Euclidean distance between the color moments of two images has been found to be effective to calculate color similarity [25].

9.3.2.4 Linguistic color tag: The global color distribution using color histogram does not take advantage of the fact that the adjacent histogram bins might actually represent roughly the same color, because of the limited ability of the human perceptual system. Moreover, only a limited number of color shades are sufficient for visual discrimination between two images. To take advantage of this, a color matching technique based on *linguistic tags*, to identify a color with a name, has been proposed recently [29]. The concept behind this technique is to construct *equivalence classes* of colors, which are identified by *linguistic tags* (or color name such as pink, maroon, etc.) that perceptually appear the same to the human eye but are distinctly different from that of neighboring subspaces. Using this approach, the dimensionality of color features are significantly reduced. This also helps to reduce computations for color similarity measures. A color palette of 15 colors corresponding to

15 equivalent classes were developed by Iqbal and Aggarwal, using this technique, and was applied effectively in color similarity measure to distinguish color images [29].

9.3.3 Texture features

Texture is a very interesting image feature that has been used for characterization of images, with application in content-based image retrieval. There is no single formal definition of *texture* in the literature. However, a major characteristic of texture is the *repetition of a pattern or patterns over a region* in an image. The elements of patterns are sometimes called *textons*. The size, shape, color, and orientation of the textons can vary over the region. The difference between two textures can be in the degree of variation of the textons. It can also be due to spatial statistical distribution of the textons in the image. Texture is an innate property of virtually all surfaces, such as bricks, fabrics, woods, papers, carpets, clouds, trees, lands, skin, etc. It contains important information regarding underlying structural arrangement of the surfaces in an image. When a small area in an image has wide variation of discrete tonal features, the dominant property of that area is *texture.* On the other hand, the *gray tone* is a dominant property when a small area in the image has very small variation of discrete tonal features. Texture analysis has been an active area of research in pattern recognition since the 1970s [30, 31].

A variety of techniques have been used for measuring textural similarity. In 1973, Haralick et al. proposed co-occurrence matrix representation of texture feature to mathematically represent gray level spatial dependence of texture in an image [30]. In this method the co-occurrence matrix is constructed based on the orientation and distance between image pixels. Meaningful statistics are extracted from this co-occurrence matrix, as the representation of texture. Since basic texture patterns are governed by periodic occurrence of certain gray levels, co-occurrence of gray levels at predefined relative positions can be a reasonable measure of the presence of texture and periodicity of the patterns.

Several texture features such as *entropy, energy, contrast,* and *homogeneity,* can be extracted from the co-occurrence matrix of gray levels of an image [32]. The gray level co-occurrence matrix $C(i\,j)$ is defined by first specifying a displacement vector $d_{x,y} = (\delta x,\ \delta y)$ and then counting all pairs of pixels separated by displacement $d_{x,y}$ and having gray levels i and j. The matrix $C(i\,j)$ is normalized by dividing each element in the matrix by the total number of pixel pairs. Using this co-occurrence matrix, the texture features metrics are computed as follows [32].

$$Entropy = -\sum_i \sum_j C(i,j) \log C(i,j), \qquad (9.15)$$

$$Energy = \sum_i \sum_j C^2(i,j), \tag{9.16}$$

$$Contrast = \sum_i \sum_j (i-j)^2 C(i,j), \tag{9.17}$$

$$Homogeneity = \sum_i \sum_j \frac{C(i,j)}{1+|i-j|}. \tag{9.18}$$

Practically, the co-occurrence matrix $C(i,j)$ is computed for several values of displacement $d_{x,y}$, and the one which maximizes a statistical measure is used.

Tamura et al. proposed computational approximations to the texture features, based on the psychological studies in visual perception of textures [31]. The texture properties they found visually meaningful for texture analysis are *coarseness, contrast, directionality, linelikeness, regularity*, and *roughness*. These texture features have been used in many content based image retrieval systems [18, 19]. Popular signal processing techniques have also been used in texture analysis and extraction of visual texture features. Wavelet transforms (Section 2.2.7) have been applied in texture analysis and classification of images, based on multiresolution decomposition of the images and representing textures in different scales [33]–[36]. Amongst the different wavelet filters, Gabor filters were found to be very effective in texture analysis.

9.3.4   Shape features

Shape is another image feature applied in CBIR. Shape can roughly be defined as the description of an object minus its position, orientation and size. Therefore, shape features should be invariant to *translation, rotation*, and *scale*, for an effective CBIR, when the arrangement of the objects in the image are not known in advance. To use *shape* as an image feature, it is essential to segment the image to detect object or region boundaries; and this is a challenge. Techniques for shape characterization can be divided into two categories.

The first category is *boundary-based*, using the outer contour of the shape of an object. The second category is *region-based*, using the whole shape region of the object. The most prominent representatives of these two categories are *Fourier Descriptors* [37] and *Moment Invariants* [38]. The main idea behind the *Fourier Descriptors* is to use the Fourier-transformed boundaries of the objects as the shape features, whereas the idea behind *Moment Invariants* is to use region-based geometric moments that are invariant to translation and rotation. Hu identified seven normalized central moments as shape features, which are also scale invariant. We provide expressions for these seven invariants below.

9.3.4.1 Moment invariants   Let $F(x, y)$ denote an image in the two-dimensional spatial domain. *Geometric Moment* [39]–[41] of order $p + q$ is denoted as

$$m_{p,q} = \sum_x \sum_y x^p y^q F(x, y), \tag{9.19}$$

for $p, q = 0, 1, 2, \dots$. The central moments are expressed as

$$\mu_{pq} = \sum_x \sum_y (x - x_c)^p (y - y_c)^q F(x, y), \tag{9.20}$$

where $x_c = \frac{m_{1,0}}{m_{0,0}}$, $y_c = \frac{m_{0,1}}{m_{0,0}}$, and (x_c, y_c) is called the center of the region or object. Hence the *Central Moments*, of order up to 3, can be computed as

$$\left. \begin{aligned}
\mu_{0,0} &= m_{0,0} \\
\mu_{1,0} &= 0 \\
\mu_{0,1} &= 0 \\
\mu_{2,0} &= m_{2,0} - x_c m_{1,0} \\
\mu_{0,2} &= m_{0,2} - y_c m_{0,1} \\
\mu_{1,1} &= m_{1,1} - y_c m_{1,0} \\
\mu_{3,0} &= m_{3,0} - 3x_c m_{2,0} + 2m_{1,0} x_c^2 \\
\mu_{1,2} &= m_{1,2} - 2y_c m_{1,1} - x_c m_{0,2} + 2y_c^2 m_{1,0} \\
\mu_{2,1} &= m_{2,1} - 2x_c m_{1,1} - y_c m_{2,0} + 2x_c^2 m_{0,1} \\
\mu_{0,3} &= m_{0,3} - 3y_c m_{0,2} + 2y_c^2 m_{0,1}.
\end{aligned} \right\} \tag{9.21}$$

The *normalized central moments*, denoted $\eta_{p,q}$, are defined as

$$\eta_{p,q} = \frac{\mu_{p,q}}{\mu_{0,0}^{\gamma}}, \tag{9.22}$$

where

$$\gamma = \frac{p + q + 2}{2} \tag{9.23}$$

for $p + q = 2, 3, \dots$. A set of seven *transformation invariant moments* can be derived from the second- and third-order moments as follows.

$$\left. \begin{aligned}
\phi_1 &= (\eta_{2,0} + \eta_{0,2}) \\
\phi_2 &= (\eta_{2,0} - \eta_{0,2})^2 + 4\eta_{1,1}^2 \\
\phi_3 &= (\eta_{3,0} - 3\eta_{1,2})^2 + (3\eta_{2,1} - \eta_{0,3})^2 \\
\phi_4 &= (\eta_{3,0} + \eta_{1,2})^2 + (\eta_{2,1} + \eta_{0,3})^2 \\
\phi_5 &= (\eta_{3,0} - 3\eta_{1,2})(\eta_{3,0} + \eta_{1,2})[(\eta_{3,0} + \eta_{1,2})^2 - 3(\eta_{2,1} + \eta_{0,3})^2] \\
&\quad + (3\eta_{2,1} - \eta_{0,3})(\eta_{2,1} + \eta_{0,3})[3(\eta_{3,0} + \eta_{1,2})^2 - (\eta_{2,1} + \eta_{0,3})^2] \\
\phi_6 &= (\eta_{2,0} - \eta_{0,2})[(\eta_{3,0} + \eta_{1,2})^2 - (\eta_{2,1} + \eta_{0,3})^2] \\
&\quad + 4\eta_{1,1}(\eta_{3,0} + \eta_{1,2})(\eta_{21} + \eta_{03}) \\
\phi_7 &= (3\eta_{2,1} - \eta_{0,3})(\eta_{3,0} + \eta_{1,2})[(\eta_{3,0} + \eta_{1,2})^2 - 3(\eta_{2,1} + \eta_{0,3})^2] \\
&\quad + (3\eta_{1,2} - \eta_{3,0})(\eta_{2,1} + \eta_{0,3})[3(\eta_{3,0} + \eta_{1,2})^2 - (\eta_{2,1} + \eta_{0,3})^2].
\end{aligned} \right\} \tag{9.24}$$

This set of normalized central moments is invariant to translation, rotation, and scale changes in an image.

In addition to the geometric moments, the circularity, aspect ratio, symmetricity, and concavity are also used for segmentation and shape detection in images [42]. We exclude detailed discussions on these features here.

The problem with shape-based CBIR system development is that the shape features need very accurate segmentation of images to detect the object or region boundaries. Image segmentation is an active area of research and most of the segmentation algorithms are still computationally very expensive for on-line image segmentation. Robust and accurate segmentation of images still remains a challenge in computer vision. As a result, shape feature based image retrieval has been mainly limited to image databases where objects or regions are readily available.

9.3.5   Topology

A digital image can be represented by one or more topological properties [40], which typically represent the geometric shape of an image. The interesting characteristic of topological properties is that when changes are made to the image itself, such as stretching, deformation, rotation, scaling, translation, or other rubber-sheet transformations, these properties of the image do not change. As a result, topological properties can be quite useful in characterization of images and can be used as a signature of an image content to use in content based image retrieval.

One topological property of a digital image is known as *Euler number* [40]. The *Euler number* is usually computed in a binary image. However, it can be extended to characterize gray-tone images as well by defining a vector of Euler numbers of the binary planes of the gray-tone image. This has been called the *Euler Vector* [43]. The *Euler number* is defined as the difference between number of *connected components* and number of *holes* in a binary image. Hence if an image has C connected components and H number of holes, the *Euler number* E of the image can be defined as

$$E = C - H. \tag{9.25}$$

The *Euler number* of the binary image in Fig. 9.5(a) is 0 because the image has one connected component and one hole, whereas the Euler number of Fig. 9.5(b) is 2 because it has seven connected components and five holes. The binary image of letter **B** will have Euler number -1 because it has one connected component and two holes.

The Euler number remains invariant despite the transformation of the image due to translation, rotation, stretching, scaling, etc. For some classes of digital images, Euler numbers have strong discriminatory power. In other words, once the Euler number for a particular digital image is known, the digital image may readily be distinguished from other digital images in its class.

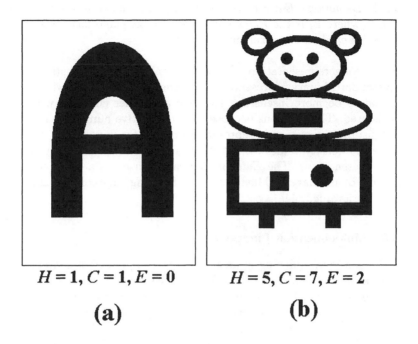

$H = 1, C = 1, E = 0$ $\qquad\qquad$ $H = 5, C = 7, E = 2$

(a) $\qquad\qquad\qquad$ **(b)**

Fig. 9.5 Sample binary images with (a) Euler number 0 and (b) Euler number 2.

This implies that the Euler number may be used for more efficient searching or matching of digital images. For example, the Euler number may be used in medical diagnosis such as the detection of malaria infected cells. As the Euler number of an infected cell is often different from that of a normal cell, the malaria infected cells may be identified by calculating the Euler number of each cell image. The *Euler number* may also be used for image searching, such as in a database of logo images.

9.3.5.1 Euler Vector Bishnu et al. [43] extended the above usage of Euler number to gray-tone images, by defining a vector of Euler numbers. This vector is called the *Euler Vector*. Intensity value of each pixel in an 8-bit gray-tone image can be represented by an 8-bit binary vector b_i, $i = 0, 1, \cdots, 7$, that is, $(b_7, b_6, b_5, b_4, b_3, b_2, b_1, b_0)$, where $b_i \in \{0, 1\}$. The ith bit plane is formed with b_i's from all the pixels in the gray-tone image. To define Euler vector, we retain the first four most significant bit planes corresponding to (b_7, b_6, b_5, b_4), because they contain most of the information of the image. This 4-bit binary vector is converted to its corresponding reflected gray code (g_7, g_6, g_5, g_4), where $g_7 = b_7$, $g_6 = b_7 \otimes b_6$, $g_5 = b_6 \otimes b_5$, $g_4 = b_5 \otimes b_4$, and $\otimes$ denotes the binary XOR (modulo-2) operation.

9.3.5.2 Definition   Euler vector of a gray-tone image is a 4-tuple (E_7, E_6, E_5, E_4), where E_i is the *Euler number* of the bit-plane formed with reflected gray codes g_i of all the pixels in the image.

Gray code representation of intensity values offers a distinct advantage over standard binary representation in this particular context. *Euler vector* is found to be more insensitive to noise and other changes, when the gray code is used. This happens because two consecutive numbers have unit Hamming distance in gray-code representation and, for most of the cases, a small change in intensity values cannot affect all the 4 bit planes simultaneously in gray representation. The *Euler vector* can be used as a quick combinatorial signature of an image and has been used for image matching in content-based image retrieval [43, 44].

9.3.6 Multidimensional indexing

Multidimensional indexing is an important component of content-based image retrieval. Development of indexing techniques has been an active area in database management, computational geometry, and pattern recognition. However, the notion of indexing has subtle difference in different communities. The notion of indexing in multimedia data mining and content-based image retrieval is different than its notion in the traditional database management systems. In traditional database management system (particularly for relational database), the indexing refers to the access structure of the database files in terms organization of the records. Indexes are specified based on one or more attributes of the records in order to process queries based on those attributes. These record and file structures are well organized and supported by an access structure such as hashing, B-tree, etc. In the information retrieval community, the indexing mechanism is concerned with the process to assign terms (or phrases or keywords or descriptors) to a document so that the document can be retrieved based on these terms. The indexing in content-based image retrieval or mining multimedia data is similar to the notion adopted in the information retrieval. The primary concern of indexing is to assign a suitable description to the data in order to detect the information content of the data. As we explained in the previous sections, the descriptors of the multimedia data are extracted based on certain features or feature vector of the data. These content descriptors are then organized into a suitable access structure for retrieval.

The key issues in indexing for content-based image retrieval are (i) reduction of high dimensionality of the feature vectors, (ii) finding an efficient data structure for indexing, and (iii) finding suitable similarity measures.

In CBIR, the dimensionality of features vectors is normally very high. Today the dimensionality is typically of the order of 10^2. With the exploration of multimedia content, this order may grow in future. Before indexing, it is very important to reduce the dimensionality of the feature vectors. The most popular approach to reduce high dimensionality is application of the principal component analysis, based on singular decomposition of the feature matrices. The theory behind singular value decomposition of a matrix and generation of principal components for reduction of high dimensionality has been discussed in detail in Section 3.7. The technique has also been elaborated in Section 9.2.5 with regard to text mining. This can be applied to both text and image datatypes in order to reduce the high dimensionality of the feature vectors and hence simply the access structure for indexing the multimedia data.

After dimensionality reduction, it is very essential to select an appropriate multidimensional indexing data structure and algorithm to index the feature vectors. There are a number of approaches proposed in the literature. The popular amongst them are multidimensional binary search trees [45], R-Tree [46], variants of R-Tree such as R^*-Tree [47], SR-tree [48], SS-tree [49], Kd-tree [50], etc. All these indexing methods provide reasonable performance for dimensions up to around 20, and the performance deteriorates after that. Moreover, most of these tree-based indexing techniques have been designed for traditional database queries such as point queries and range queries, but not for similarity queries for multimedia data retrieval. There have been some limited efforts in this direction. Multimedia database indexing particularly suitable for data mining applications remain a challenge. So exploration of new efficient indexing schemes and their data structure will continue to be a challenge for the future.

After indexing of images in the image database, it is important to use a proper similarity measure for their retrieval from the database. Similarity measures based on statistical analysis have been dominant in CBIR. Distance measures such as Euclidean distance, Mahalanobis distance, Manhattan distance [6], and similar techniques have been used for similarity measures. Distance of histograms and histogram intersection methods have also been used for this purpose, particularly with color features.

Another aspect of indexing and searching is to have minimum disk latency while retrieving similar objects. Chang et al. proposed a clustering technique to cluster similar data on disk to achieve this goal, and they applied a hashing technique to index the clusters [51]. In spite of lots of development in this area, finding new and improved similarity measures still remains a topic of interest in computer science, statistics, and applied mathematics.

9.3.7 Results of a simple CBIR system

Saha et al. proposed a simple image matching scheme for an experimental content-based image retrieval system that uses moment, shape, and texture features extracted from the images [42]. The shape features have been extracted using moment computation (feature set A) of the regions, combined with circularity, aspect ratio, concavity, and symmetricity metrics (feature set B). The texture of the images have been generated using the energy,

Table 9.1   CBIR match performance (%)

Image group	A	B	A+B	A+B+C
AEROPLANE	71.3	69.68	73.39	73.23
CAR	78.90	74.11	78.30	82.56
FLOWER	51.22	38.64	43.64	43.48
ANIMAL	25.44	48.45	48.89	49.56
Overall	62.70	38.90	64.80	66.55

A: Moment invariants only.
B: Circularity, symmetricity, aspect ratio and concavity.
C: Energy, entropy, contrast and homogeneity.

entropy, contrast, and homogeneity measure as image features (set C). We present here results of this system using around 290 samples taken from an image database containing several classes of images, including animals, cars, flowers, etc. Distance of the query image from the database images have been computed simply as $\sum_i | f_i - f_i' |$, where f_i and f_i' are the values of the ith feature of the database image and query image respectively. The top ten closest images have been taken as the query result, excluding the query image itself if it is present in the database.

Table 9.2   CBIR weighted match performance (%)

Image group	All features (No weight)	All features (With weight)
AEROPLANE	73.23	69.84
CAR	82.56	86.75
FLOWER	43.48	77.03
ANIMAL	49.56	72.44
Overall	66.55	77.79

Tables 9.1 and 9.2 provide the results, where each database image is used as a query image to find the top ten from the database. From Table 9.1, we observe that the overall performance can be improved by mixing the different feature sets for image query.

Further improvement can be achieved by assigning weights to each feature as follows:

$$\sum_i W_{gi} | f_i - f_i' |,$$

where W_{gi} is the weight of the ith feature for image group g and the database image belongs to image group g. Here W_{gi} is computed as $\frac{1}{1 + \sigma_{gi}}$, where σ_{gi} is the standard deviation of the ith feature value of the images in group g. Table 9.2 indicates that this improves the matching performance.

The summary of the results is presented in Fig. 9.6 for eight query images. In each row the first column indicates the query image. For all rows the five best matches are shown, with the query image (as all of them are present in the database) naturally coming first as the best match.

9.4 VIDEO MINING

Currently text-based search engines are commercially available, and they are predominant in the *World Wide Web* for search and retrieval of information. However, demand for search and mining multimedia data based on its content description is growing. Search and retrieval of contents is no longer restricted to traditional database retrieval applications. As an example, it is often required to find a video clip of a certain event in a television studio. In the future the content customers will demand to search and retrieve video clips based on content description in different forms. It is not difficult to imagine that one may want to mine and download the images or video clips containing the presence of Mother Teresa from the Internet or search and retrieve them from a video archival system. It is even possible to demand for retrieval of a video which contains a tune of a particular song.

In order to meet the demands for retrieval of audio–visual contents, there is a need of efficient solution to search, identify and filter various types of audio-visual content of interest to the user using non-text based technologies. Recognizing this demand, the MPEG (Moving Picture Expert Group) standard committee, under the auspices of the International Standard Organization, is engaged in a work item to define a standard for multimedia audio-visual content description interface [52]. JPEG2000 is the new standard for still picture compression and has been developed in such a way that metadata information can be stored in the file header for access and retrieval by users as well [53, 54]. There is a mode in JPEG2000 standard which particularly focuses on compressing moving pictures or video and its content description.

All these developments will influence effective mining of video data in the near future. Video mining is yet to take off as a mainstream active area of research and development by the data mining community. The development has so far been restricted to retrieval of video content only. However, there are ample opportunities that data mining principles can offer in conjunction with the video retrieval techniques, towards the successful development of video data mining. In order to influence the readers towards this direction, we present here a brief description of the MPEG-7 standard for multimedia con-

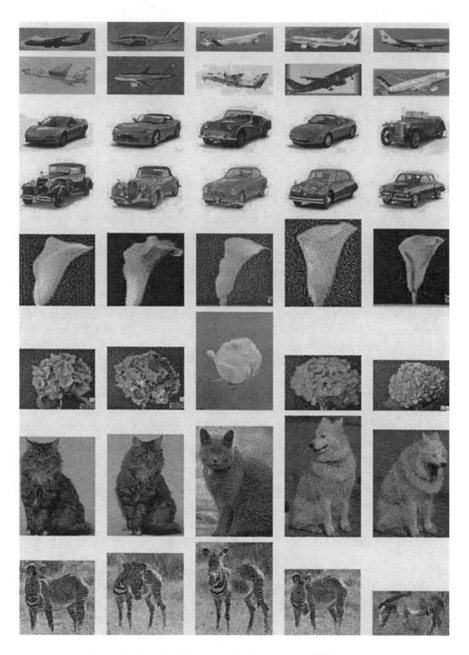

Fig. 9.6 Results of image matching in the CBIR system.

tent description interface and a general discussion on a possible video retrieval system. Application of data mining techniques on top of this development is left to the readers for their imagination.

9.4.1 MPEG-7: Multimedia content description interface

There is a wrong notion amongst many of us that MPEG-7 is another video compression standard. However, adoption of data compression principles are essential to define this standard for compact description of the multimedia contents. The goal of the MPEG-7 activity is not to define another video compression standard. The purpose of this standardization activity is to specify a standard set of descriptors that can be used to identify content and permit search for a particular multimedia content in a multimedia information system.

The goal of MPEG-7 is to define a standard set of descriptors that can be used to describe various types of multimedia information, as well as the relationship between the various descriptors and their structures. In principle these descriptors will not depend on the way the content is available, either on the form of storage or on their format. For example, video information can be encoded with any compression scheme (MPEG-1, MPEG-2, MPEG-4, JPEG, JPEG2000, or any other proprietary algorithm) or it can be uncompressed in its raw format without any encoding. It is even possible to generate a description of an analog video, or a picture drawn on paper. The audio–visual data description in MPEG-7 may include still pictures, video, graphics, audio, speech, three-dimensional models, and information about how these data elements are combined in the multimedia presentation.

The top level scope of the MPEG-7 standard is shown in Fig. 9.7. The block diagram emphasizes that only the audio–visual description of multimedia data is meant to be standardized. The standard neither defines nor deals with the mechanism for extraction of features from the multimedia data, nor is it connected with its encoding or search and retrieval mechanism. Accordingly, the MPEG committee was chartered to standardize the following elements as described in the requirement document for MPEG-7 work item [55]:

1. A set of *descriptors* - A *descriptor* is a representation of a feature, such as color, shape, texture, image topology, motion, or title, to name a few. The descriptor defines the syntax and semantics of representation of the feature.

2. A set of *description schemes* - A *description scheme* specifies the structure and semantics of the relationships between its components, which may be both *descriptors* and *description schemes* as well.

3. A set of *coding schemes* for the descriptors.

4. A *Description Definition Language* (DDL) to specify the description schemes and descriptors.

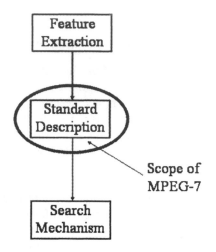

Fig. 9.7   Scope of the MPEG-7 standard.

The goal of MPEG-7 work item is a tall order. The final output of the standard is yet to be seen.

9.4.2   Content-based video retrieval system

Content-based image retrieval techniques can be extended, in principle, to video retrieval systems. However, this is not very straightforward because of the temporal relationship of video frames and their inherent structure. A video is not only a sequence of pictures, it represents the actions and events in a chronological order to convey a story and represent a moving visual information. In other words, one may argue that each video clip can be considered as a sequence of individual still pictures and each individual frame can then be indexed and stored using the traditional content-based image retrieval techniques. Again, this is not very practical given the number of frames in a good quality video clip of even a few minutes. This also does not capture the story structure, which is a collection of actions and events in time.

A generic video retrieval system, which can fit in MPEG-7 model, is shown in Fig. 9.8. As shown in this figure, a video clip is first temporarily segmented into video *shots*. A *shot* is a piece of a video clip (i.e., a group of frames or pictures), where the video content from one frame to the adjacent frames

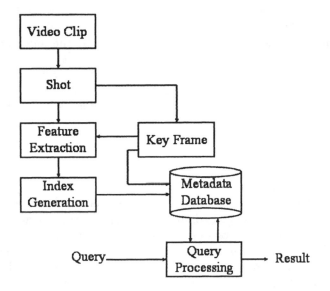

Fig. 9.8   Video retrieval systems architecture.

does not change abruptly. One of these frames in a shot is considered to be a *key frame*. This key frame is considered to be a representative for the picture content in that shot. Sequence of key frames can define the sequence of events happening in the video clip. This is very useful to identify the type and content of the video. Detection of shots and extraction of the key frames from video clips is a research challenge [56, 57].

As an individual still picture, each key frame can be segmented into a number of objects with desired meaningful image features such as shape, texture, color, topology, and many others as defined in Section 9.3 for content-based image retrieval. The semantic relationship between these individual features or feature vectors defines an object of interest to the user. We can apply similar feature extraction techniques and generate index structures for the key frames using the feature vectors, as described for content-based image retrieval. These indexed feature data and the corresponding key frames are stored in the *metadata* database. Collection of these metadata information describes the content of the video clip.

In a video retrieval system, the *query processing* depends upon the applications. It can be similar to content-based image retrieval, as described in Section 9.3, or it can be more complex depending upon the type of query processing. In its simplest form, a picture can be supplied to the video retrieval system as a *query* image. This query image is then matched with each and every key frame stored in the metadata database. The matching technique is repeated, based on the extraction of different features from the query image, followed by the matching of these features with the stored features of the key frames in the database. Once a match of the query picture with a key frame is found, the piece of video can be identified by the index of the key frame along with the actual shot and the video clip.

Success of the MPEG-7 standardization process will have a significant impact in multimedia and video content retrieval and will influence the future development of multimedia data mining on a standardized platform based on its definition.

9.5   WEB MINING

World Wide Web is the largest database that ever existed. It serves as a widely distributed data or information repository system to warehouse different datatypes. Extraction of information and knowledge discovery from World Wide Web is an important area of study. The problem for knowledge extraction from World Wide Web is even more challenging because the data stored in the Web is very dynamic in nature, and constantly changing due to continuous update of the existing data or Web pages and addition of new information every moment. The complexity of Web pages is greater than that of traditional text document databases. Web data is often composed of different multimedia datatypes, mixed and sometimes interspersed together. As a result, Web mining will remain to be a challenge in the coming years.

Web mining [58] uses data mining techniques to automatically retrieve, extract, and evaluate information for knowledge discovery from the Web. Almost 99% of the data in the Web is useless for a particular user, and often it does not represent any relevant information that the user is looking for. Taking into account the huge amount of data storage and manipulation needed for (say) a simple query, the processing essentially requires adequate tools suitable for extracting only the relevant, sometimes hidden, knowledge as the final result of the problem under consideration.

The subtle difference between data mining and Web mining suggests the use of new or modified tools and algorithms for appropriate handling of the Internet. Web mining typically addresses semistructured or unstructured data, like Web and log files with mixed knowledge involving multimedia, flow data, etc., often represented by imprecise or incomplete information.

Web mining can be broadly categorized as

1. Web Content Mining of multimedia documents, involving text, hypertext, image, audio, and video. This deals with the extraction of concept hierarchies or relations from the Web, along with their automatic categorization.

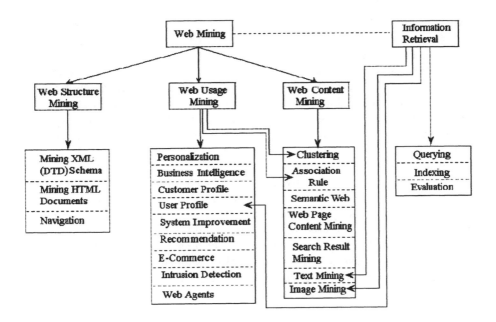

Fig. 9.9 A Web mining taxonomy.

2. Web Structure Mining of interdocument links, provided as a graph of links in a site or between sites. For example, in Google a page is important if important pages point to it.

3. Web Usage Mining of the data generated by the users' interactions with the Web, typically represented as Web server access logs, user profiles, user queries, and mouse-clicks. This includes trend analysis (of the Web dynamics information) and Web access association or sequential pattern analysis.

Fig. 9.9 provides a taxonomy for Web mining [59]. The different functions falling under the three major categories are highlighted. Web mining typically encompasses ways of improving search or customization by (i) learning about the users interests based on access patterns, (ii) providing users with pages, sites, and advertisements of interest, and (iii) using XML to improve search and information discovery on the Web.

9.5.1 Search engines

Web search engines are programs written to query and retrieve information stored in databases (fully structured), HTML pages (semistructured) and free text (unstructured) on the Web. The most popular indices have been created by Web robots such as AltaVista and WebCrawler, which scan millions of

Web documents and store an index of the words in the documents. There are over a dozen different indices currently in active use, each with a unique interface and a database covering a different fraction of the Web. Some of these indices have been discussed, with respect to text mining, in Section 9.2.

MetaCrawler presents the next level of the information food chain, by providing a single unified interface for Web document searching [60]. It submits the query to nine indices in parallel, and then it collates the results and prunes them. Thus instead of tackling the Web directly, MetaCrawler mines robot-created searchable indices.

Future resource discovery systems will make use of automatic text categorization technology to classify Web documents into categories. This technology could facilitate the automatic construction of Web directories, such as Yahoo, by discovering documents that fit Yahoo categories. Alternatively, the technology could be used to filter the results of queries to searchable indices. For example, in response to a query such as "find me product reviews of Encarta," a discovery system could take documents containing the word "Encarta" found by querying searchable indices and then identify the subset that corresponds to product reviews.

It often happens that, upon matching the user's query with locally cached documents or those in remote Web sites, the search engine comes up with too many poorly matched documents. Some Web search algorithms, such as Hyperlink Induced Topic Search (HITS) and PageRank, rank these matched documents according to some content criteria like structural information of hyperlinks. Thereby, the best fits of the ranked matches can be presented to the user.

There are two important types of Web pages, namely,

- *authorities*, providing the best source of information about a given topic, and

- *hubs*, providing a collection of links to authorities.

The hyperlink structure connects the different pages of the Web. A good hub is a page that points to several good authorities, while a corresponding good authority is a page that is pointed to by many good hubs. HITS works on this mutually reinforcing relationship by searching for good hubs and good authorities.

The HITS algorithm proceeds by

1. *sampling*, where it generates a focused collection of Web pages that are likely to be rich in relevant information, and

2. *weight propagation*, where an iterative procedure is pursued to determine an estimate of the hubs and authorities in order to obtain the most relevant hubs and authorities.

The Web is considered as a directed graph of pages. HITS initially constructs a subgraph based on the query terms, using a root set of pages generated by some index-based search engine. The goal is to generate a subgraph rich in relevant and authoritative pages. The root set is expanded to a base set by including all pages that are linked to from here, but limited by a prespecified cutoff size.

Let each page p belonging to the base set V be associated with positive weights a_p and h_p, corresponding to its authority and hub weights. The objective of weight propagation (updating) is to extract good hubs and authorities from this base set V. The weights are normalized, so that their total sum remains bounded. Initially, all a and h values are set to uniform constants. If a page p is pointed to by many good hubs, its authority weight is increased by updating

$$a_p = \sum h_q, \tag{9.26}$$

$\forall q$, such that $q \to p$, that ia, for all pages q that link to p. Similarly, if a page p points to many good authorities, its hub weight is increased as

$$h_p = \sum a_q, \tag{9.27}$$

$\forall q$, where $p \to q$. Note an interesting analogy with the weight updating in STIRR, as explained in Section 6.6. Typically, pages with large weights represent a dense pattern of linkages. HITS finally outputs a short list of pages with the largest hub weights and largest authority weights, corresponding to the given search topic.

While HITS basically works on the static information concerning a Web site structure, LOGSOM uses dynamic information about user behavior using the SOM (described in Section 2.2.3.3). LOGSOM can be used by, say, a company to analyze the navigation patterns of its Web pages by its potential customers, in order to make improved decisions.

Here the users' navigation patterns are mapped onto a two-dimensional map. It utilizes the excellent clustering and visualization abilities of the SOM. The system starts with a Web log file, consisting of the date, time, and address of the requested Web pages, along with the IP address of the user's machine. Clustering using c-means (Section 6.3.1.1) may initially be applied for reduction of the huge volume of Web data. LOGSOM causes the mapping of each Web page (URL) onto a SOM unit, based on its similarity with other URLs in terms of user navigation patterns. The similarity is measured in terms of the distance on the map.

9.5.2 Soft computing approaches

The huge amount of multivariate information offered by the Web has opened up new possibilities for many areas of research. Due to the involvement of human interaction in Web information (like text, image, sound, and linkages between them), new tools and methodologies need to be extended in order to deal with the incomplete or imprecise information. Soft computing promises to open up new avenues in this direction.

Considering the Web as a large distributed multimedia database, an extension of methodologies to deal with them and their mining algorithms can be considered under image mining. The huge volumes of compressed and uncompressed information stored in images, and their subjective evaluation by humans in interaction with the Web, is another focus of current data mining research requiring soft computing-based treatment [59].

There is a growing awareness that, in practice, it is easy to discover a huge amount of information from the Web, where most of these patterns are actually obvious, redundant, and useless or uninteresting to the user. To prevent the user from being overwhelmed by a large number of uninteresting patterns, soft computing techniques are needed to identify only the useful or interesting patterns and present them to the user. Different interestingness measures (of Sections 7.4 and 7.10) can be used for this purpose.

According to Zadeh [61], fuzzy logic may serve as the backbone of the semantic Web, an extension of the current Web in which information is given well-defined meaning. This enables computers and people to work in greater cooperation. The role of fuzzy sets in Web mining [62] holds promise in

- handling of fuzzy queries involving natural language and/or linguistic quantifiers like *almost, about,*

- evaluation of the matching of documents as a fuzzy similarity relation,

- deduction and summarization,

- document and user clustering, and

- information fusion in multimedia data.

User feedback is a process where the user expresses an opinion about the documents that the system has retrieved as an answer to a certain query. This user evaluation or opinion can be (a) used for training the classification system and (b) reflected in the corresponding user profile. Fuzzy linguistic modeling is useful in handling such preference relations. This information can also be utilized by (say) marketing experts to analyze user interests.

Ordinary end-users often face difficulties in formulating a precise representation of their information needs in a Boolean query. This affects the efficiency of the information retrieval process. Hence Web search engines require the use of fuzzy aggregation operators. These are especially suitable in flexible query answering and information retrieval. Fuzzy statistics may be used to emphasize the significance of the occurrence of a term in certain portions of a document, like URL, title, abstract, etc.

9.5.2.1 Clustering The importance of clustering to Web mining, specifically in the domains of Web Content and Web Usage mining, make Web clustering an interesting topic of research. This includes clustering of Web documents, snippets, and access logs. Usually the Web involves overlapping clusters. So a crisp usage of metrics is better replaced by fuzzy sets that can reflect, in a more natural manner, the degree of belongingness (or membership) to a cluster.

The fuzzy *c*-medoids (of Section 6.5.1) is used to cluster relational data from Web documents and snippets in Ref. [63]. The algorithms are applied to a collection of 1042 abstracts from the Cambridge Scientific Abstract Web site, corresponding to ten topics. A preprocessing stage is used to filter and remove irrelevant words, in order to generate the input feature vector that is computed using the *inverse-document frequency* method. This 500-dimensional feature vector (keywords) is reduced using principal component analysis, resulting in a selection of 10 eigenvector values. The algorithms are also tested on a collection of snippets, corresponding to 200 Web documents collected by a search engine in response to a query. The results are extended in Ref. [64] using robust estimators, providing a computational complexity $O(n \log n)$ instead of $O(n^2)$. This is suitable for clustering noisy data that are characteristic of Web documents.

Relational alternating cluster estimation (RACE) [65] is used to handle non-numerical patterns in relational datasets. The authors consider two types of patterns related to the Web, namely, (i) document contents such as text parts of Web pages (Web content mining) and (ii) sequences of Web pages visited by users, such as Web logs (Web usage mining).

9.5.2.2 *Association rule mining*
Association rules, in the context of Web mining, refer to the determination of (say) those URLs that tend to be requested together. This can be categorized under Web Usage and Web Content mining.

Web mining of inference amplification is made in Ref. [66], using inference logic from fuzzy cognitive maps in three phases. The first stage mines association rules with the *A priori* algorithm (Section 7.2.1), from a Web-log database. A corresponding fuzzy knowledge map involving causality (the cognitive map uses values between -1 and $+1$) is built in the second stage, incorporating both positive and negative rules. In the final stage, the system applies inference amplification in order to enrich the resulting Web mining association rules. Experiments are made using a Web-log file from a real online shop, specializing in computers and peripherals. The causal knowledge is represented as an adjacency matrix, including the connectivity $W^T = \{w_{ij}|w_{ij} \in \{-1, +1\}\}$. Here w_{ij} indicates the causal value (weight) of the arc from vertex/node C_i to C_j.

9.5.2.3 *Web navigation*
Navigation is categorized as Web Structure mining. An optimization of the path for surfing the Web, given a target, is described in Ref. [67]. The connected Web sites are represented by a directed graph with source and destination nodes, and in addition to a links set along the path. The frequency of accessing various links (access rate) and the time taken to retrieve target pages (retrieval rate) are considered as the decisive factors. These are affected by criteria like the availability of channels, server capability,

and access time. The expected access rate and the required retrieval rate are expressed as fuzzy sets. Link weights are associated with appropriate linguistic values. A fuzzy opinion matrix expresses subjective estimation of users during their surfing of specified links on the path. The general evaluation of the link, with respect to interest rate of users, is provided as the intersection among the estimation made by the different users. The optimal path is computed as the minimum fuzzy distance estimated between a fuzzy *Hurwicz opinion set* (derived in terms of optimism–pessimism index) and the actual requirement set.

9.5.2.4 Web personalization

The increasing popularity of the Internet and the exponential increase in the number of its users has led to the creation of new paradigms of knowledge discovery, like Web personalization, mining bookmarks, mining e-mail correspondences, recommendation systems, and so on. These are grouped as Web Usage mining.

Mining typical user profiles and URL associations from the vast amount of access logs is an important component of Web personalization, which deals with tailoring a user's interaction with the Web information space based on information about her/him. Nasraoui et al. [68] have defined a *user session* as a temporally compact sequence of Web accesses by a user and used a dissimilarity measure between two Web sessions to capture the organization of a Web site. Automatic discovery of user session profile is made using fuzzy Competitive Agglomeration for Relational Data (CARD) algorithm. Complex, non-Euclidean distance/similarity measures can be handled in this framework. Log files are collected from a real site in order to mine the user profiles. The experimental results "capture" the pattern for users in profiles like outside visitor, prospective student, those that attend lessons by the same professor, an so on. To discover user profiles from real log files, various fuzzy clustering methods have been applied.

9.5.2.5 Information retrieval

Typically, four main constituents can be identified in the process of information retrieval from the Internet.

- Indexing: generation of document representation

- Querying: expression of user preferences through natural language or terms connected by logical operators

- Evaluation: performance of matching between user query and document representation

- User profile construction: storage of terms representing user preferences, especially to enhance the system retrieval in future accesses by the user

Due to the presence of *multimedia* information repositories consisting of mixed media data, the information retrieved can be text as well as image document or a mixture of both.

Fuzzy genes are used as intelligent agents for information retrieval from the Web [69]. User profiles are built from the user preferences, represented by chromosomes made up of a vector of fuzzy genes. Each chromosome is associated with a fitness corresponding to the system's belief in the hypothesis that the chromosome, as a query, represents the user's information needs. Every gene represents, by a fuzzy set, the number of occurrences that characterizes the documents considered relevant by the user. The fitness of the chromosome is adjusted based on the comparison between the user's evaluation of the retrieved documents and the score computed by the system. GAs are used to track the user's preferences and adapt the profile by incorporating her/his relevance feedback, while fuzzy sets handle the imprecision in the user's preferences and evaluation of the retrieved documents.

9.6 CONCLUSIONS AND DISCUSSION

In this chapter, we discussed how the data mining techniques can be applied in multimedia data. Multimedia data consist of a mixture of text, image, video, graphics, audio, speech, hypertext, markup languages, etc. Multimedia databases are large databases, and mining multimedia data is challenging because of the inherently unstructured characteristics of these data. Keeping this in view, we have presented here different aspects of multimedia data mining principles and applications.

Textual documents were considered in the framework of text mining. We have discussed how the semistructured text can be modeled and feature vectors can be generated from this model, so that they can be indexed and used for query and mining operations. We have presented issues and principles behind image mining, particularly in the light of content-based image retrieval. The underlying principles of content-based image retrieval, based on several image features such as color, shape, texture, etc., have been provided. We have introduced the purpose and target of MPEG-7 standard for Multimedia Content Description Interface. Video retrieval system was described, in the light of MPEG-7 as well as content-based image retrieval. Finally we discussed Web mining, and the role of soft computing in mining Web data.

REFERENCES

1. M. T. Maybury, ed., *Intelligent Multimedia Information Retrieval.* Menlo Park, CA: AAAI Press, 1997.

2. D. Hand, H. Mannila and P. Smyth, *Principles of Data Mining.* Cambridge, MA: The MIT Press, 2001.

3. M. Kantardzic, *Data Mining: Concepts, Models, Methods, and Algorithms.* Hoboken, NJ: John Wiley & Sons, 2002.

4. J. Han and M. Kamber, *Data Mining: Concepts and Techniques.* San Francisco, CA: Morgan Kaufmann Publishers, 2001.

5. G. Salton and C. Buckley, "Term-weighting approaches in automatic text retrieval," *Information Processing and Management,* vol. 24, pp. 513-523, 1988.

6. P. A. Devijver and J. Kittler, eds., *Pattern Recognition Theory and Applications.* Berlin: Springer-Verlag, 1987.

7. I. T. Jolliffe, *Principal Component Analysis.* New York: Springer-Verlag, 1986.

8. A. N. Netravali and B. Haskell, *Digital Pictures.* New York: Plenum Press, 1988.

9. S. Sakurai, Y. Ichimura, A. Suyama, and R. Orihara, "Inductive learning of a knowledge dictionary for a text mining system," in *Proceedings of 14th International Conference on Industrial and Engineering Applications of Artificial Intelligence and Expert Systems (IEA/AIE 2001)* (L. Monostori, J. Vancza, and M. Ali, eds.), vol. LNAI 2070, Berlin: Springer–Verlag, 2001, pp. 247–252.

10. H. M. Lee, S. K. Lin, and C. W. Huang, "Interactive query expansion based on fuzzy association thesaurus for web information retrieval," in *Proceedings of the 10th IEEE International Conference on Fuzzy Systems,* pp. 2:724–2:727, 2001.

11. A. Molinari and G. Pasi, "A fuzzy representation of HTML documents for information retrieval systems," in *Proceedings of the Fifth IEEE International Conference on Fuzzy Systems,* pp. 1:107–1:112, 1996.

12. D. H. Widyantoro and J. Yen, "Using fuzzy ontology for query refinement in a personalized abstract search engine," in *Proceedings of Joint 9th IFSA World Congress and 20th NAFIPS International Conference* (Vancouver, Canada), pp. 1:610–1:615, July 2001.

13. T. A. Runkler and J. C. Bezdek, "Relational clustering for the analysis of Internet newsgroups," in *Exploratory Data Analysis in Empirical Research, Proceedings of the 25th Annual Conference of the German Classification Society* (O. Opitz and M. Schwaiger, eds.), Studies in Classification, Data Analysis, and Knowledge Organization, Berlin: Springer–Verlag, 2002, pp. 291–299.

14. T. Kohonen, S. Kaski, K. Lagus, J. Salojarvi, J. Honkela, V. Paatero, and A. Saarela, "Self organization of a massive document collection," *IEEE Transactions on Neural Networks,* vol. 11, pp. 574–585, 2000.

15. S. Kaski, T. Honkela, K. Lagus, and T. Kohonen, "WEBSOM – Self-organizing maps of document collections," *Neurocomputing*, vol. 21, pp. 101–117, 1998.

16. H. Tamura and N. Yokoya, "Image database systems: A survey," *Pattern Recognition*, vol. 17, pp. 29–43, 1984.

17. S.-K. Chang and A. Hsu, "Image information systems: Where do we go from here?," *IEEE Transactions on Knowledge and Data Engineering*, vol. 4, pp. 431–442, 1992.

18. M. Flickner, H. Sawhney, W. Niblack, J. Ashley, Q. Huang, B. Dom, M. Gorkani, J. Hafine, D. Lee, D. Petkovic, D. Steele, and P. Yanker, "Query by image and video content: The QBIC system," *IEEE Computer Magazine*, vol. 28, pp. 23–32, 1995.

19. A. Pentland, R. Picard, and S. Sclaroff, "Photobook: Content-based manipulation of image databases," *International Journal of Computer Vision*, vol. 18, pp. 233–254, 1996.

20. A. Gupta and R. Jain, "Visual information retrieval," *Communications of the ACM*, vol. 40, pp. 71–79, 1997.

21. J. R. Smith and S.-F. Chang, "Visually searching the web for content," *IEEE Multimedia Magazine*, vol. 4, pp. 12–20, 1997.

22. W.-Y. Ma and B. S. Manjunath, "Netra: A toolbox for navigating large image databases," *Multimedia Systems*, vol. 7, pp. 184–198, 1999.

23. H. Samet, *Application of Spatial Data Structures: Computer Graphics, Image Processing and GIS*. Reading, MA: Addison-Wesley, 1990.

24. M. Swain and D. Ballard, "Color indexing," *International Journal of Computer Vision*, vol. 7, pp. 11–32, 1991.

25. M. Stricker and M. Orengo, "Similarity of color images," in *Proceedings of SPIE Storage and Retrieval for Image and Video Databases III*, vol. 2185 (San Jose, CA), pp. 381–392, February 1995.

26. H. J. Zhang and D. Shong, "A scheme for visual feature-based image indexing," in *Proceedings of SPIE Conference on Storage and Retrieval for Image and Video Databases III*, vol. 2185 (San Jose, CA), pp. 36–46, February 1995.

27. G. Pass and R. Zabith, "Histogram refinement for content-based image retrieval," in *Proceedings of of IEEE Workshop and Applications of Computer Vision*, pp. 96–102, 1996.

28. H. R. Kang, *Color technology for electronic imaging devices*. Bellingham, Washington, USA: SPIE Optical Engineering Press, 1997.

29. Q. Iqbal and J. K. Aggarwal, "Combining structure, color and texture for image retrieval: A performance evaluation," in *Proceedings of International Conference on Pattern Recognition* (Quebec City, Canada), 2002.

30. R. M. Haralick, J. Shanmugam, and I. Dinstein, "Texture feature for image classification," *IEEE Transactions on Systems, Man, and Cybernetics*, vol. 3, pp. 610–621, 1973.

31. H. Tamura, S. Mori, and T. Yamawaki, "Texture features corresponding to visual perception," *IEEE Transactions on Systems, Man, and Cybernetics*, vol. 8, pp. 460–473, 1978.

32. R. Jain, R. Kastuni, and B. G. Schunck, *Machine Vision*. New York: McGraw-Hill, 1995.

33. T. Chang and C. J. Kuo, "Texture analysis and classification with tree-structured wavelet transform," *IEEE Transactions on Image Processing*, vol. 2, pp. 429–441, 1993.

34. A. Laine and J. Fan, "Texture classification by wavelet packet signatures," *IEEE Transactions on Pattern Recognitions and Machine Intelligence*, vol. 15, pp. 1186–1191, 1993.

35. W.-Y. Ma and B. S. Manjunath, "A comparison of wavelet features for texture annotation," in *Proceedings of IEEE Int. Conf. on Image Processing II* (Washington, D.C.), pp. 256–259, 1995.

36. B. S. Manjunath and W.-Y. Ma, "Texture features for browsing and retrieval of image data," *IEEE Transactions on Pattern Analysis and Machine Intelligence*, vol. 18, pp. 837–842, 1996.

37. E. Persoon and K. Fu, "Shape discrimination using Fourier descriptors," *IEEE Transactions on Systems, Man and Cybernetics*, vol. 7, pp. 170–179, 1977.

38. M. K. Hu, "Visual pattern recognition by moment invariants," in *Computer Methods in Image Analysis* (J. K. Aggarwal, R. O. Duda, and A. Rosenfeld, eds.), Los Angeles: IEEE Computer Society, 1977.

39. W. K. Pratt, *Digital Image Processing*. New York: Wiley-Interscience, 1991.

40. R. C. Gonzalez and R. E. Woods, *Digital Image Processing*. Reading, MA: Addison-Wesley, 1993.

41. D. Luo, *Pattern Recognition and Image Processing*. New York:Horwood Publishing, 1998.

42. S. K. Saha, A. K. Das, and B. Chanda, "Content-based image retrieval: An experiment with shape and texture features," *Technical Report No.*

BEC09-04-2002, Department of Computer Science and Technology, Bengal Engineering College (Deemed University), India, May 2003.

43. A. Bishnu, B. B. Bhattacharya, M. K. Kundu, C. A. Murthy, and T. Acharya, "Euler vector: A combinatorial signature of gray-tone images," in *Proceedings of the IEEE Int. Conf. on Information Technology: Coding & Computing* (Las Vegas), pp. 121–126, April, 2002.

44. A. Bishnu, P. Bhunre, B. B. Bhattacharya, M. K. Kundu, C. A. Murthy, and T. Acharya, "Content based image retrieval: Related issues with Euler Vector," in *Proceedings of the IEEE Int. Conf. on Image Processing* (Rochester, NY), pp. II:585–II:588, September, 2002.

45. J. L. Bentley, "Multidimensional binary search trees used for associative searching," *Communications of the ACM*, vol. 18, pp. 509–517, 1975.

46. A. Guttman, "R-trees: A dynamic index structure for spatial searching," in *Proceedings of ACM SIGMOD* (Boston), pp. 47–57, June, 1984.

47. N. Beckmann, H.-P. Kriegel, R. Schneider, and B. Seeger, "The R^*-tree: An efficient and robust access method for points and rectangles," in *Proc. of ACM SIGMOD*, May, 1990.

48. N. Katamaya and S. Satoh, "The SR-tree: An index structure for higher-dimensional nearest neighbor queries," in *Proc. of the Int. Conf. on Management of Data, ACM SIGMOD*, pp. 13-15, May, 1997.

49. A. W. David and J. Ramesh, "Similarity indexing with SS-tree," in *Proc. of the 12th Int. Conf. on Data Engineering* (New Orleans), pp. 516–523, February, 2002.

50. M. Overmars, M. D. Berg, M. V. Kreveld, and O. Schwarzkopf, *Computational Geometry: Algorithms and Applications.* New York: Springer–Verlag, 1997.

51. E. Chang, C. Li, J. Z. Wang, P. Mork, and G. Wiederhold, "Searching near-replicas of images via clustering," in *Proc. of the SPIE Symposium of Voice, Video, and Data Communications* (Boston), pp. 281–292, September, 1999.

52. MPEG-7: ISO/IEC JTC1/SC29/WG211, N2207, Context and objectives, March, 1998.

53. "Information technology – JPEG2000 Image Coding System," Final Committee Draft Version 1.0 ISO/IEC JTC 1/SC 29/WG 1 N1646R, March 2000.

54. D. S. Taubman and M. W. Marcellin, *JPEG2000: Image Compression Fundamentals, Standards and Practice.* Boston: Kluwer Academic Publishers, 2002.

55. MPEG-7: ISO/IEC JTC1/SC29/WG211, N2727, MPEG-7 requirements, MPEG Seoul Meeting, 1999.

56. B. C. O'Connor, "Selecting key frames of moving image documents: A digital environment for analysis and navigation," *Microcomputers for Information Management*, vol. 8, pp. 119–133, 1991.

57. A. Nagasaka and Y. Tanaka, "Automatic video indexing and full-search for video appearances," in *Visual Database Systems* (E. Knuth and I. M. Wegener, eds.), Elsevier Science Publishers, Vol. II, Amsterdam, pp. 113–127, 1992.

58. R. Kohavi, B. Masand, M. Spilipoulou, and J. Srivastava, "Web mining," *Data Mining and Knowledge Discovery*, vol. 6, pp. 5–8, 2002.

59. D. Arotaritei and S. Mitra, "Web mining: A survey in the fuzzy framework," *Fuzzy Sets and Systems*, 2003 (accepted).

60. O. Etzioni and M. Perkowitz, "Adaptive Web sites: An AI challenge," in *Proceedings of 15th National Conference on Artificial Intelligence* (Madison, WI), July 1998.

61. L. A. Zadeh, "A new direction in AI: Towards a computational theory of perceptions," *AI Magazine*, vol. 22, pp. 73–84, 2001.

62. F. Crestani and G. Pasi, eds., *Soft Computing in Information Retrieval: Techniques and Application*, vol. 50. Heidelberg: Physica-Verlag, 2000.

63. R. Krishnapuram, A. Joshi, and L. Yi, "A fuzzy relative of the k-medoids algorithm with application to document and snippet clustering," in *Proceedings of IEEE International Conference on Fuzzy Systems* (Korea), pp. 3:1281–3:1286, August, 1999.

64. R. Krishnapuram, A. Joshi, O. Nasraoui, and L. Yi, "Low complexity fuzzy relational clustering algorithms for Web mining," *IEEE Transactions on Fuzzy Systems*, vol. 9, pp. 595–607, 2001.

65. T. A. Runkler and J. Bezdek, "Web mining with relational clustering," *International Journal of Approximate Reasoning*, vol. 32, pp. 217–236, 2003.

66. K. C. Lee, J. S. Kim, N. H. Chung, and S. J. Kwon, "Fuzzy cognitive map approach to Web mining inference amplification," *Expert Systems with Applications*, vol. 22, pp. 197–211, 2002.

67. C. W. Chong, V. Ramachandran, and C. Eswaran, "Path optimization using fuzzy distance approach," in *Proceedings of 1999 IEEE International Fuzzy Systems Conference (FUZZ-IEEE 99)* (Seoul, Korea), pp. III:1771–III:1774, August 1999.

68. O. Nasraoui, H. Frigui, R. Krishnapuram, and A. Joshi, "Extracting web user profiles using relational competitive fuzzy clustering," *International Journal on Artificial Intelligence Tools*, vol. 9, 2000.

69. M. J. Martin-Bautista, H. L. Larsen, and M. A. Vila, "A fuzzy genetic algorithm approach to an adaptive information retrieval agent," *Journal of the American Society for Information Science*, vol. 50, pp. 760–771, 1999.

10

Bioinformatics: An
Application

10.1 INTRODUCTION

Computational Molecular Biology [1] is an interdisciplinary subject involving fields as diverse as biology, computer science, information technology, mathematics, physics, statistics, and chemistry. Bioinformatics [2]–[4] concentrates on the information science related aspect of this. Since the inception of the Human Genome Project, Bioinformatics has drawn a lot of attention. Upon completion of this project, one needs to analyze and interpret the vast amount of data that are now available. This involves the decoding of 50,000–100,000 human genes. Data mining holds promise in this direction. High-dimensional clustering is a potential for grouping genes and proteins with many attributes. In addition to the combinatorial approach for solutions, there also exists scope for soft computing, especially for generating low-cost, low-precision good solutions.

Bioinformatics [2]–[4] can be defined as the application of computer technology to the management of biological information. It encompasses a study of the inherent genetic information, underlying molecular structure, resulting biochemical function, and the exhibited phenotypic symptoms. Here computers are used to gather, store, analyze, and integrate biological and genetic information, which can then be applied to gene-based drug discovery and development. Current research involves the design and implementation of programs and systems for the storage, management, and analysis of the vast amounts of DNA and protein sequence data. *Biological data mining* is an emerging field of research and development for further progress in this direction [4].

The high-volume, data-driven nature of modern experimental biology has led to the creation of many databases that contain genomes, protein sequences, gene expression data, and other datatypes. Researchers often retrieve information from these databases based on one characteristic, such as amino acid sequence, gene annotation, or protein name. Answering queries involves some form of data analysis, such as statistical significance, clustering, or sequence homology search. The Basic Alignment Search Tool (BLAST) [5] is typically the first Bioinformatics tool a biologist uses when examining a new DNA or protein sequence. BLAST compares the new sequence to all sequences in the database to find the most similar known sequences. Advances related to recognizing protein interactions, improving homology search, and identifying cellular location, in the context of data mining, are discussed in Ref. [6]. Techniques from string matching with examples demonstrating how they can be applied in DNA search were presented earlier in Section 4.3 in Chapter 4.

Unlike a genome, which provides only static sequence information, microarray experiments produce gene expression patterns that provide dynamic information about cell function. This information is useful while investigating complex interactions within the cell. For example, data mining methods can ascertain and summarize the set of genes responding to a certain level of stress in an organism [3]. Microarray technologies have been utilized to evaluate the level of expression of thousands of genes in colon, breast and blood cancer treatment [4]. The sheer volume of the data makes it impossible to view a large microarray clustering result on a 2D/3D display. Efficient interactive visualization tools are needed to facilitate pattern extraction from microarray datasets. Gene expression data being typically high-dimensional, it requires appropriate data mining strategies like clustering and string matching for further analysis.

Recent years have seen (a) an explosion in the availability of structural information pertaining to drug targets and (b) the growth of computational chemistry and Bioinformatics methods to exploit these. Simultaneously, combinatorial chemistry and screening technologies have greatly advanced, analyzing large amounts of structure-based design inputs in order to discover small molecule leads and then optimizing their potency and *pharmacokinetic* properties to produce useful drugs.

Proteins constitute an important ingredient of living beings and are made up of a sequence of amino acids. There can be a large number of 3D states for a protein. The determination of an optimal conformation constitutes protein folding. This promises to provide enormous information on the presence of active sites and possible drug interaction. Incomplete folds can cause disabling diseases like Alzheimer's and "mad cow" syndrome. Misfolding also causes respiration and locomotion failures, as attempted in *biowarfare*, because protein functions cannot be fully carried out in that environment.

The folding of a protein is a highly complex process. There are nearly 100,000 proteins encoded in the human genome, and there are thought to be more than a thousand fundamentally distinct structural architectures into which folded proteins can be classified. To establish how a newly formed *polypeptide* sequence of amino acids finds its way to its correct fold, rather than the countless alternatives, is one of the greatest challenges in modern structural biology. To respond to this challenge requires interdisciplinary research involving the most advanced techniques available to the chemists and structural biologists. A good survey on molecular modeling of proteins and prediction of their structures is provided in Ref. [7].

Soft computing tools like neural networks and genetic algorithms have been used for analyzing the different protein structures and folds [8]–[11]. Since the work entails processing huge amounts of incomplete or ambiguous data, the learning ability of neural networks, uncertainty handling capacity of fuzzy sets, and the searching potential of genetic algorithms are utilized in this direction.

In this chapter we focus on the Information Science-related aspects of Bioinformatics, particularly microarray data, gene expression profiles, protein structure prediction and folding, including soft computing-based methods. Section 10.2 provides an introduction to the basics of protein structure and microarray data. The Information Science-related aspects of Bioinformatics are described in Section 10.3, with appropriate emphasis on data mining. High-dimensional clustering of microarray data to analyze gene expressions is discussed in Section 10.4. Mining of association rules in Bioinformatics is described in Section 10.5. The role of soft computing is highlighted in Section 10.6. Finally, Section 10.7 concludes the chapter.

10.2 PRELIMINARIES FROM BIOLOGY

Proteins are built up by polypeptide chains of amino acids, which consist of the deoxyribonucleic acid (DNA) as the building block. In this section we provide a basic understanding of the protein structure and DNA microarray data.

10.2.1 Deoxyribonucleic acid

The nucleus of a cell contains chromosomes that are made up of the double helical DNA molecules. The DNA consists of two strands of phosphate and deoxyribose sugar molecules, joined by covalent bonds. To each sugar molecule is attached one of the four nitrogenous bases, namely, adenine (A), cytosine (C), guanine (G), thymine (T). Note that uracil (U) exists in place of T in ribose sugar. Bases between the strand pairs are attached by hydrogen bonds, such that either AT or GC comes together. The *monomeric* units of nucleic acids, within the DNA, are called nucleotides. A nucleotide is a combination of a phosphate, a sugar, and a purine or a pyrimidine base, where a purine (or pyrimidine) consists of A, G (or C, T).

There are approximately 3 billion base pairs in our body. The DNA is a string of A, C, G, T, and the whole stretch of DNA is called the genome of the organism. Genes are coded in fragments of DNA (either strand) that are dispersed in the genome. Each gene contains information to produce a single protein. The DNA codes for protein (unbranched organic polymers), and the enzymes and hormones are also proteins. Understanding what parts of the genome encodes which genes is the topic of the Human Genome project.

DNA in the human genome is arranged into 24 distinct chromosomes, that are physically separate molecules ranging in length from about 50 million to 250 million base pairs. Each chromosome contains many genes, the basic physical and functional units of heredity. However, genes comprise only about 2% of the human genome; the remainder consists of noncoding regions, whose functions may include providing chromosomal structural integrity and regulating where, when, and in what quantity proteins are made.

The DNA is *transcribed* to produce messenger (m)-RNA, which is then *translated* to produce protein. The m-RNA is single-stranded and has a ribose sugar molecule. There exist '*Promoter*' and '*Termination*' sites in a gene, responsible for the initiation and termination of transcription. Translation consists of mapping from triplets (codons) of four bases to the 20 amino acids building block of proteins.

10.2.2   Amino acids

An amino acid is an organic molecule consisting of an amine (NH) and a carboxylic (CO) acid group (backbone), together with a side chain (hydrogen atom and residue R) that differentiates between them. More than one triplet of DNA can map to the same amino acid, but the same triplet cannot map to two different amino acids. A sequence of amino acids, held together by peptide bonds forming a polypeptide chain, endow a protein with its 3D structure. In humans a gene consists of exons that get translated into an amino acid sequence, separated by introns (that are not translated). The carboxyl and amino groups of a pair of amino acids react through hydrolysis (removal of water molecule) to link and form a peptide bond. Similar reactions occur along the chain to form a protein molecule.

Proteins are polypeptides, formed within cells as a linear chain of amino acids. The length of a protein can vary from 10s to 1000s of amino acid monomers. Each monomer or amino acid, itself, consists of 10 or more atoms, making the macromolecule extremely large and complex. It is therefore not surprising that the many interactions cause the chain to fold and twist. Proteins in the living world reach a stable, unique, 3D structure, and this is responsible for a biological function.

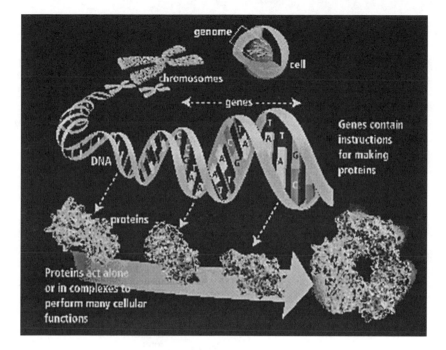

Fig. 10.1   Molecular biology

10.2.3 Proteins

Although genes get a lot of attention, the proteins are the ones that perform most life functions and even make up the majority of cellular structures in our body. Proteins are large, complex molecules made up of smaller subunits called amino acids. Chemical properties that distinguish the 20 different amino acids cause the protein chains to fold up into specific three-dimensional structures that define their particular functions in the cell. Figure 10.1 depicts the whole system.

The constellation of all proteins in a cell is called its *proteome*. Unlike the relatively unchanging genome, the dynamic proteome changes from minute to minute in response to tens of thousands of intra- and extracellular environmental signals. A protein's chemistry and behavior are specified by the gene sequence and by the number and identities of other proteins made in the same cell at the same time and with which it associates and reacts. Studies to explore protein structure and activities, known as proteomics, will be the focus of much research for decades to come and will help elucidate the molecular basis of health and diseases. Proteins are the primary carriers of signals in an organism. Figure 10.2 summarizes how information gets transferred to proteins.

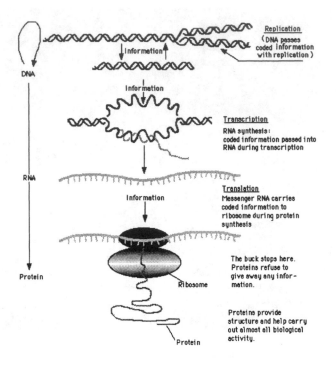

Fig. 10.2 Central dogma of molecular biology.

Proteins are involved in virtually every biological process in a living system. They are synthesized on ribosomes as linear chains of, typically, several hundred amino acids in a specific order from information encoded within the cellular DNA. In order to function, these chains must fold into the unique native three-dimensional structures that are characteristic of the individual proteins. In a cell, this takes place in a complex highly crowded molecular environment. There are several families of cellular proteins whose job is to catalyze the folding process of the other proteins that are required by the living organism.

In a cellular environment, molecular *chaperones* help to protect the incompletely folded polypeptide chains from aggregating. Even after the folding process is complete, however, a protein can subsequently experience conditions under which it unfolds, at least partially, and then again becomes prone to aggregation. It is becoming clear that the failure of proteins to fold correctly or to remain folded under all appropriate physiological conditions can give rise to a wide range of pathological conditions. Diseases associated with misfolding now include genetic, sporadic, and even infectious ailments.

10.2.4   Microarray and gene expression

DNA microarrays (gene arrays or gene chips) [3] usually consist of thin glass or nylon substrates containing specific DNA gene samples spotted in an array by a robotic printing device. Researchers spread fluorescently labeled m-RNA from an experimental condition onto the DNA gene samples in the array. This m-RNA binds (hybridizes) strongly with some DNA gene samples and weakly with others, depending on the inherent double helical characteristics. A laser scans the array and sensors to detect the fluorescence levels (using red and green dyes), indicating the strength with which the sample expresses each gene. The logarithmic ratio between the two intensities of each dye is used as the gene expression data. The relative abundance of the spotted DNA sequences in a pair of DNA or RNA samples is assessed by evaluating the differential hybridization of the two samples to the sequences on the array.

Gene expression levels can be determined for samples taken (i) at multiple time instants of a biological process (different phases of cell division) or (ii) under various conditions (tumor samples with different histopathological diagnosis). Each gene corresponds to a high-dimensional row vector of its expression profile.

10.3   INFORMATION SCIENCE ASPECTS

Bioinformatics requires handling large volumes of data, involving natural interaction with information science. One needs to consider the problems of data storage, analysis, and retrieval, along with the computational modeling and simulation. Data mining, image processing, and visualization are the other important constituents required to help the user with a visual environment that facilitates high-dimensional data dependent on many parameters. Information theory based lossless data compression techniques can play a vital role in management of this high volume of data.

Genomes cannot be sequenced all at once. This involves around 40K–100K base pairs, broken into 400–2000 small fragments of about 1000 base pairs. It is an NP-hard combinatorial problem, involving factors such as (i) unknown relative position and orientation of fragments within original DNA sequence and (ii) noisy and partial information about sequence of each fragment. The different aspects currently handled by information scientists include

- Protein folding problem

- Genomic sequence analysis

- Homology search and multiple alignment

- Searching biological databases.

In this section we concentrate on some of these problems in detail. The data mining aspects are appropriately highlighted.

10.3.1   Protein folding

Given the *primary* structure of a protein, in terms of a linear sequence of amino acids, the aim is to predict its 3D structure. The 3D structure is related to the functionality, say the diversity or specificity involved. It is useful in designing efficient drugs to cure diseases. However, considering all interactions governed by the laws of physics and chemistry to predict 3D positions of different atoms in the protein molecule, a reasonably fast computer would need one day to simulate 1 ns of folding. This gives an idea about the complexity of the problem under consideration.

Protein folding is a thermodynamically determined problem. It is also a reaction involving other interacting amino acids and water molecules. The *secondary* structure can involve an α helix (with the CO group of the ith residue hydrogen (H)-bonded to the NH group of the $(i + 4)$th one) or a β sheet (corrugated or hairpin structure) formed by the H-bonds between the amino acids. The parts of the protein that are not characterized by any regular H-bonding patterns are called random coils. Neural nets (MLP) have been used to predict the secondary structure of proteins [8][10]. These are described in further detail in Section 10.6.

The *tertiary* structure refers to the 3D conformation of the protein. Since the search space is large, there can exist many possible 3D structural conformations for a short primary sequence. The objective is to determine the minimum energy state for a polypeptide chain folding. GAs have been used for the prediction of tertiary structures [11]. This is discussed in Section 10.6. There also exists a *quaternary* structure pertaining to certain proteins that contain more than one polypeptide chain.

The process of protein folding involves minimization of an energy function, that is expressed in terms of several variables like bond lengths, bond angles and torsional angles. The major factors affecting folding include (i) hydrogen bonding, (ii) hydrophobic effect, (iii) electrostatic interactions, (iv) Van der Waals forces, and (v) conformational entropy.

10.3.1.1 Hydrogen bonding   Polypeptides contain numerous proton donors and acceptors, both in their backbone and in the R-groups of the amino acids. The environment in which proteins are found also contains ample H-bond donors and acceptors of the water molecule. H-bonding, therefore, occurs not only within and between polypeptide chains but also with the surrounding aqueous medium.

10.3.1.2 Hydrophobic forces   Proteins are composed of amino acids that contain either hydrophilic or hydrophobic R-groups. It is the nature of the interaction of the different R-groups with the aqueous environment that plays a major role in shaping protein structure. The spontaneous folded state of globular proteins is a reflection of a balance between (a) the opposing energetics of H-bonding between hydrophilic R-groups and the aqueous environment and (b) the repulsion from the aqueous environment by the hydrophobic R-groups. The hydrophobicity of certain amino acid R-groups tends to drive them away from the exterior of proteins into the interior. This driving force restricts the available conformations into which a protein may fold.

10.3.1.3 Electrostatic forces Electrostatic forces are mainly of three types, namely, charge–charge, charge–dipole and dipole–dipole. Typical charge-charge interactions, which favor protein folding, are those between oppositely charged R-groups. A substantial component of the energy involved in protein folding is from charge–dipole interactions. This refers to the interaction of ionized R-groups of amino acids with the dipole of the water molecule. The slight dipole moment that exists in the polar R-groups of amino acid also influences their interaction with water. It is, therefore, understandable that the majority of the amino acids found on the exterior surfaces of globular proteins contain charged or polar R-groups.

10.3.1.4 Van der Waals forces There are both attractive and repulsive Van der Waals forces that control protein folding. Attractive Van der Waals forces involve the interactions among induced dipoles, which arise from fluctuations in the charge densities occurring between adjacent uncharged nonbonded atoms. Repulsive Van der Waals forces involve the interactions that occur when uncharged nonbonded atoms come very close together but do not induce dipoles. The repulsion is the result of the electron-electron interaction that occurs as two clouds of electrons begin to overlap. Although Van der Waals forces are extremely weak, relative to other forces governing a stable conformation, it is the huge number of such interactions that occur in large protein molecules that makes them significant to the folding of proteins.

10.3.2 Protein structure modeling

There are three broad approaches to predicting the structure of an unknown protein, based on its similarity to known protein structures. These are

- Comparative or homology modeling: Predicts protein structure based on the strength of a protein sequence similarity to known structures. This is also termed template detection, and it is generally undertaken in case of greater than 30% similarity with an available template structure.

- Protein threading: Given a sequence of proteins with unknown structure and a database of known folds, it finds the most plausible fold after evaluating the quality or stability of the arrangement. This approach is typically undertaken in case of around 20–30% similarity.

- Ab initio: Calculates coordinates of protein sequences without reference to existing protein structures. This technique is followed when the similarity is even lower, and hence the former two approaches cannot be applied.

Detecting repeatedly occurring 3D structures in molecules can help biologists to understand their functions. This is particularly useful in modeling the tertiary structures of proteins. Wang et al. [12] have approached the problem by finding *patterns* in 3D graphs. Each node in the graph is an undecomposable or atomic unit and has a label, with edges linking them. Patterns are defined as *rigid substructures* that may occur in a graph after allowing for an arbitrary number of whole-structure rotations and translations, as well as a small number of user-specified edit operations (namely, relabeling, deleting, inserting) either in the patterns or in the graph. A geometric hashing technique is used to hash node-triplets of the graphs into a 3D table and compress their label-triplets. The algorithm proceeds by finding candidate patterns from the graphs and calculating their occurrence numbers to determine which of them satisfy the user-specified requirements. Applications are made in scientific data mining by (i) locating frequently occurring *motifs* in two families of proteins and applying the discovered patterns to classify large 3D protein structures and (ii) clustering chemical compounds based on the 3D patterns occurring in them. The performance of the algorithm is good in terms of high recall and precision rates, both for classification and clustering.

10.3.3 Genomic sequence analysis

Gene hunting is a complex task. This is because coding regions account for only 3% of the human genome; and of the 694,000 sequences available in public databases, only around 2000 unique protein structures have been found. Experimental structure elucidation by X-ray crystallography and/or NMR is very slow. Data mining can be usefully applied to deal with such large volumes of data. Correctly predicting the position of genes in the DNA and knowing their encoded 3D protein structure will be helpful in drug and vaccine design and individual characteristics determination. GENSCAN [13] has been designed for this purpose using the Hidden Markov Model.

10.3.4 Homology search

Proteins in different organisms are related to one another by evolution from a common ancestor. Those proteins related with respect to the common ancestor are called *homologues*. This relationship can be recognized by multiple sequence comparisons. A similar primary structure leads to a similar 3D structure, resulting in a similar functionality of the proteins. It is even more challenging to find similarity between two distant homologues. The problem of finding closely related homologues has been solved to some extent by adopting the techniques in string matching for string alignment and similarity matching algorithms. As a matter of fact, string matching techniques have been widely used DNA sequencing and homology search in Bioinformatics. We have described the foundation of string matching algorithms and some of the classical algorithms for string matching including k-approximate matching of strings in Chapter 4. The principles behind the k approximate string matching, edit distance between two strings, and pattern search with k-mismatches can be adopted in the development of homology search as well as biological database search.

The dynamic programming approach has been adopted to find DNA sequence alignment. The principle is similar to the one described in Section 4.4. However, the traditional dynamic programming method for local alignment is too slow. Fast Alignment (FASTA) [14] and Basic Local Alignment Search Tool (BLAST) [5] are often found to be more efficient.

10.3.4.1 Dynamic programming for sequence alignment

Dynamic programming is a very powerful mathematical and algorithmic tool and has been used in many real-life problems. We have shown how this tool has been used in approximate string matching in Chapter 4. Here we use the dynamic programming approach for solving sequence alignment of two DNA strings.

As we know, a string is defined as a sequence of characters or symbols from an alphabet. Let us consider two strings $S_1 = S_1[1 \cdots m]$ and $S_2 = S_2[1 \cdots n]$ of length m and n respectively. We further assume that these strings do not have any blank character to begin with. Let us denote the blank character as '_'. A string S can be transformed to a string $\bar{S}$ by inserting one or more blank characters in any position in the string S. For example, string $S =$ '*twobooks*' of length 8 can be transformed to $\bar{S} =$ '*two_book_s*' of length 10.

An alignment of S_1 and S_2 is the choice of inserting blank characters in S_1 or S_2 or both, so that there is no k for which both $\bar{S}_1[k]$ and $\bar{S}_2[k]$ are blanks. For example, alignment of $S_1 =$ '*mood*' and $S_2 =$ '*igloo*' may be $\bar{S}_1 =$ '*_m_ood*' and $\bar{S}_2 =$ '*igloo_*'.

We can assign a scoring factor for the above alignment [15]. Although there are a number of ways to assign scoring factor, the most common scoring factor used by many algorithms is the linear additive scoring scheme. The score $\omega(a, b)$ maps two characters or symbols a and b from an alphabet (including a blank) to real numbers, and $\omega(a, b) = \omega(b, a)$. The score Ω of the alignment of two strings is calculated by accumulating some matching points in each character location. Let us assume that for each match one gets 2 points, 0 points for each mismatch, and -1 for each blank. Then the score of alignment of the above example will be

$$\begin{aligned} \Omega(\bar{S}_1, \bar{S}_2) &= \omega(\_, i) + \omega(m, g) + \omega(\_, l) + \omega(o, o) + \omega(o, o) + \omega(d, \_) \\ &= (-1) + 0 + (-1) + 2 + 2 + (-1) = 1. \end{aligned}$$

A high score obviously reflects a good alignment between two strings, and hence intuitively may detect the organisms with close evolutionary relationships. Based on this assumption, we can now formulate the dynamic programming problem as follows.

Given two strings S_1 and S_2 and a scoring scheme, an alignment of S_1 and S_2 is optimal if there is no other alignment with a higher score. The highest possible score is called the similarity of S_1 and S_2, denoted by $Sim(S_1, S_2)$. Let

$$f(i,j) = sim(S_1[1 \cdots i],\ S_2[1 \cdots j]),$$

where $i = 1$ to $|S_1|$ and $j = 1$ to $|S_2|$, and then

$$sim(S_1,\ S_2) = f(|S_1|,\ |S_2|).$$

The key idea behind the solution is that for $i, j > 1$, if we know the values of $f(i-1, j)$, $f(i, j-1)$, and $f(i-1, j-1)$, then we can easily compute, by a recursive step [16],

$$f(i, j) \quad = \max\{ \quad \begin{aligned} &f(i-1,\ j-1) + \omega(S_1[i],\ S_2[j]), \\ &f(i-1,\ j) + \omega(S_1[i],\ \_), \\ &f(i,\ j-1) + \omega(\_,\ S_2[j]) \quad \} \end{aligned} \qquad (10.1)$$

The first element of the maximum occurs when $S_1[i]$ and $S_2[j]$ are both non-blanks, the second element occurs when $S_1[i]$ is non-blank but the character following $S_2[j]$ is blank, and the third element in the maximum occurs when the character following $S_1[i]$ is a blank and $S_2[j]$ is a non-blank. This two-dimensional recursion for $f(i,\ j)$ can be computed in a tabular fashion, similar to that shown in Section 4.4 for k-approximate string matching, with the two strings to be aligned written along the row and column of the table [15]. We avoid the details here.

When the alignments are computed over the whole of strings S_1 and the whole string S_2, the problem is called a global alignment problem. The local alignments of S_1 and S_2 deals with alignments of a substring of S_1 and a substring of S_2. Using linear scoring schemes, $Sim(S_1,\ S_2)$ can be computed in time $O(|S_1| * |S_2|)$ by the method of dynamic programming. However, it is still slow for local alignment. 'Fast Alignment' (FASTA) [14] and 'Basic Local Alignment Search Tool' (BLAST) [5] are often more efficient. We describe below the BLAST algorithm.

10.3.4.2 *The BLAST algorithm*   BLAST is a heuristic method to find the highest locally optimal alignments between a query sequence and a database [5]. It does not allow the presence of gaps in between. BLAST improves the overall speed of search while retaining good sensitivity (important as the databases continue to grow), by breaking the query and database sequences into fragments (words) and initially seeking matches between these fragments. The idea behind the BLAST algorithm can be best illustrated by an example. If the query is '*MOONLIGHT*', the search is performed using a small stretch of say 4 letters. For example '*MOON*' closely matches with other words of same length like '*SOON*', '*MOOD*', '*GOON*', etc. These words are then extended to locate '*MOONLIGHT*' in the database. The three main steps of

the algorithm are as follows.

Step (1)(a): For a query of length L, find all overlapping words of length W, where $W = 3$ for proteins and $W = 3$ for DNA. For example, for the query $ABCDEFGH$ with $W = 3$ and $L = 8$, there will be $L - W + 1 = 6$ overlapping words of length 3, namely, ABC, BCD, CDE, DEF, EFG, FGH.

Step (1)(b): For each of these 6 words from the query, we find a list of (close relatives) words that will score at least a threshold T when using a suitable substitution matrix (e.g., PAM or BLOSUM matrices that determine the similarity between amino acids). For example, ADC has close words ADD, AEC, EDC, which score above T. The threshold T is chosen by the user. A similar decomposition is done for the database once and for all. In the database all the sequences can be thought of as being combined into one big sequence, which is then divided into words of length W.

Step (2): The word list generated from the query is compared with the database list to identify the exact matches. This comparison can be accelerated by using a hash table.

Step (3): Word hits are extended in either direction to generate an alignment with a score exceeding the threshold S (High-score Segment Pair, HSP). In the example above, $MOONLIGHT$ is an HSP.

After the alignment is done, the match must be statistically checked to see if it occurred purely by chance or if there is indeed some homology between the sequences. Here T dictates the speed and sensitivity of the search. A low value of T reduces the possibility of missing HSPs with the required S score. However, lower T values also increase the size of the hit list generated, and hence the execution time and memory required. BLAST is unlikely to be as sensitive for all protein searches as a full dynamic programming algorithm. Nevertheless, the underlying statistics provide a direct estimate of the significance of any match found.

Some of the efficient extensions to BLAST include

- Gapped BLAST [17]: Allows insertions and deletions to be introduced into alignments.

- Position-specific iterative BLAST (Psi-BLAST) [17]: Includes gaps, as well as searches for distant homologies by building a profile (general characteristics).

- Pattern Hit Initiated BLAST (Phi-BLAST) [18]: Amino acid pattern present in a query is defined and searched.

With the availability of nucleic acid sequence information from viruses and bacteria, efforts have been directed towards generation of highly specific pathogen signatures [19], including foot-and-mouth and human immunodeficiency viruses. BLAST was used to compare the entire genome of the target pathogen with all the microbial genomes in Genbank. Several gigabytes of raw BLAST output were parsed, and all exact match regions of the pathogen genome were *masked out* after comparison. The remaining part of the genome was considered to be *potentially unique* to the target pathogen.

10.4 CLUSTERING OF MICROARRAY DATA

Microarrays provide a powerful basis to monitor the expression of thousands of genes, in order to identify mechanisms that govern the activation of genes in an organism. Short DNA patterns (or binding sites) near the genes serve as switches that control gene expression. Therefore, similar patterns of expression correspond to similar binding site patterns. A major cause of coexpression of genes is their sharing of the regulation mechanism (coregulation) at the sequence level. Control (or promoter) regions in the neighborhood of the genes contain specific short sequence patterns, called *binding sites.* The detection of such "statistically overrepresented patterns in DNA or amino acid sequences" is called *"motif" finding.* Clustering of coexpressed genes, into biologically meaningful groups, have been integrated with the discovery of binding motifs in order to discover regulatory motifs from microarray data [20]. Clustering also helps in inferring the biological role of an unknown gene that is coexpressed with a known gene(s).

Motifs are found in two broad ways. Word counting methods from string matching are based on counting the number of occurrences of each DNA word (or oligonucleotide) and comparing this number with the expected number of occurrences based on some statistical model. Probabilistic sequence models build a likelihood function for the sequences based on the motif occurrences and a model of the background sequence. Optimization methods like expectation maximization (EM) and Gibbs sampling are used to search for good motif configurations.

Clustering of gene expression profiles often require preprocessing along the following lines.

1. Normalizing the hybridization intensities within a single array experiment.

2. Transforming the data using a nonlinear function, like the logarithm in case of expression ratios.

3. Estimating and replacing missing values in expressions, or adapting existing algorithms to handle missing values.

4. Filtering gene expression profiles, to eliminate those that do not satisfy some simple criteria.

5. Standardizing or rescaling the profiles, say, to generate vectors of length one.

Cluster validation is essential, from both the biological and statistical perspectives, in order to biologically validate and objectively compare the results generated by different clustering algorithms. Statistical cluster validation is done by evaluating cluster coherence, predictive accuracy, and robustness to noise. Based on biological intuition, a cluster result can be termed reliable if the within-cluster distance is small (i.e., all genes within a cluster are tightly coexpressed) and the maximal inter-cluster distance is large (or, the cluster has an average profile well delineated from the remaining dataset). Quantitative statistics like Dunn's validity index [21] and Figure of Merit [22] have been used to compare different clustering algorithms.

A categorization of clustering algorithms (dedicated to microarray data) is provided by Moreau et al. [20], grouping some of the later methods designed specifically to handle gene expression profiles to be in the second generation.

10.4.1   First-generation algorithms

First-generation clustering algorithms, used on gene expression profiles, include c-means [23], self-organizing maps (SOMs) [24], and hierarchical clustering [25]–[27]. The SOM neural net has been applied to the exploratory data analysis of gene expression data from a yeast DNA microarray [28]. Hierarchical clustering is the most widely used method, given its good visualization properties. Clusters are generated by cutting the dendogram at a certain level. However, it is arbitrary to predict the level that would correspond to the best *biological results*. Moreover, the quadratic complexity of the method is a source of inconvenience for mining the large volumes of data. In case of c-means algorithm, the center corresponds to the average expression vector. But the prediction of the number of clusters in advance is often arbitrary from the context of biology. SOMs require a selected node in the gene expression space (along with its neighbors) to be rotated in the direction of a selected gene expression profile (pattern). Again, the predefinition of a two-dimensional topology of nodes can be a problem considering *biological relevance*.

An inherent problem with all these algorithms is that they force every data point into a cluster. In case of microarray data, a considerable number of genes do not contribute to the biological process being studied and hence lack coexpression with other genes. Inclusion of such *noisy* genes in any cluster causes contamination, making it less suitable for further analysis. Besides, the computational and memory complexities of these methods often limit the number of expression profiles that can be handled.

10.4.2   Second-generation algorithms

These include the self-organizing tree algorithm (SOTA) [29], model-based clustering [30, 31], and quality-based clustering [32, 33].

The SOTA [29] is a dynamic binary tree that combines the characteristics of SOMs and divisive hierarchical clustering. As in SOMs, the gene expression profiles are sequentially and iteratively presented at the terminal nodes, and the mapping of the node that is closest (along with its neighboring nodes) is appropriately updated. Upon convergence, the node containing the most variable (measured in terms of distance) population of expression profiles is split into sister nodes, causing a growth of the binary tree. Unlike conventional hierarchical clustering, SOTA is linear in complexity to the number of profiles. The number of clusters need not be known in advance, as in c-means algorithm. A statistical procedure is followed for terminating the growing of the tree, thereby eliminating the need for an arbitrary choice of cutting level as in hierarchical models. However, no validation is provided to establish its biological relevance.

Model-based clustering [30, 31] typically assumes multivariate probability (normal) distributions to represent clusters. The covariance matrix for each cluster is expressed by its eigenvalue decomposition, which controls the orientation, shape, and volume parameters. Initially the model parameters are estimated by the EM algorithm using fixed cluster number and covariance structure. Then the best from this group of models is selected, based on an information theoretic criterion.

Quality-based clustering (QT_Clust) [32] generates clusters with a quality guarantee (user-defined threshold), ensuring that each member of a cluster is coexpressed with all other members. It is a greedy procedure, generating clusters satisfying the quality guarantee with a maximum number of expression profiles. The algorithm terminates when the number of points in the largest remaining cluster falls below a specified threshold. However, the user-defined quality guarantee is often difficult for biologists to handle and often leads to extensive parameter fine-tuning. The computational complexity is quadratic in the number of expression profiles.

Adaptive quality-based clustering [33] uses an estimate of the quality of the cluster, so that the initial center is located in a region of locally dense gene expression profiles. In an adaptive step, the quality of the cluster is re-estimated to determine significant coexpression of genes in terms of a *significance level*. The process is repeated until the relative difference between the initial and re-estimated quality is sufficiently small. The computational complexity of the algorithm is linear in the number of expression profiles and has been biologically validated. However, the approach is heuristic and not proven to converge in every situation.

10.5 ASSOCIATION RULES

Rule mining in Bioinformatics analyzes large collections of molecules to discover some regularity among molecules of a specific class. For example, in drug discovery a biologist tries to find new drug candidates based on experimental evidence of activity against a certain disease by screening the data. In chemical synthesis success prediction, on the other hand, the aim is to detect molecular features that inhibit the desired reaction.

Linear fragments or chains of atoms have been mined [34] using a technique similar to the *A priori* algorithm of Section 7.2.1. However, this restriction to linear fragments eliminates consideration of ring-like substructures that are common to most real-world applications involving molecular representations.

Association rules have been mined for molecular fragments, which help discriminate between different classes of activity on the National Cancer Institute's HIV-screening dataset [35]. Here a restricted depth-first search algorithm, similar to the *Eclat* association rule mining strategy [36], is used to determine connected substructures. It maintains parallel embeddings of a fragment in all molecules throughout the growth process of the search tree, while exploiting the local order of the atoms and bonds (single, double, triple, or aromatic) in the fragment to prune the tree.

Association rules can reveal biologically relevant associations between different genes, which are highly expressed or repressed in diseased and/or healthy cells. They can also be used to express associations between cellular environmental effects and gene expression, to diagnose (say) a profiled tumor sample or a drug treatment given to cells in the sample before profiling. Efficient mining of association rules from 300 gene expression profiles of yeast, demonstrating diverse mutations and chemical treatments, has been reported in Ref. [37] using the *A priori* algorithm. A gene expression profile is considered to be a single transaction, with each transcript or protein being an item in it. The measured value of the gene expression data is put in bins and is marked as being up (highly expressed), down (highly repressed), or neither up nor down.

10.6 ROLE OF SOFT COMPUTING

In this section we attempt to highlight the role of soft computing in Bioinformatics. The learning ability of neural networks has been utilized to predict the secondary structure of proteins [8]–[10]. The searching potential of GAs has been applied for prediction of the tertiary structure of proteins [11]. The uncertainty handling capacity of fuzzy sets is used in Ref. [38].

10.6.1   Predicting protein secondary structure

Prediction of protein structure from the primary amino acid sequence is a challenging task. The problem has been approached from several angles. A step on the way to a prediction of the full 3D structure of protein is predicting the local conformation of the polypeptide chain, called the secondary structure.

The whole framework was pioneered by Chou and Fasmann [39]. They used a statistical method, with the likelihood of each amino acid being one of the three (alpha, beta, coil) secondary structures being estimated from known proteins. Around 1988 the first attempts were made by Qian and Sejnowski [8], to use multilayer perceptrons to predict protein secondary structure. The performance of this method was improved by Rost and Sander [9], by using multiple-sequence alignment.

This has been further developed by Riis and Krogh [10], with ensembles of combining networks, for greater accuracy in prediction. The *Softmax* method is used to provide simultaneous classification of an input pattern into multiple classes. A normalizing function at the output layer ensures that the three outputs always sum to one. A logarithmic likelihood cost function is minimized, instead of the usual squared error. A window is selected from all the single structure networks in the ensemble. The output is determined for the central residue, with the prediction being chosen as the largest of the three outputs normalized by Softmax. Figure 10.3 provides the overall network structure.

10.6.2   Predicting protein tertiary structure

Protein binding sites exhibit highly selective recognition of small organic molecules, utilizing features like complex three-dimensional *lock* (active sites) into which only specific *keys* (drug molecules) will fit. This has been exploited by medicinal chemists in the design of molecules to selectively augment or retard biochemical pathways and thereby exhibit desired clinical effects. X-ray crystallography has been used to reveal the structure of many of these binding sites. Given the active site geometry of a protein molecule, it is now possible to obtain computer-aided design of therapeutic molecules in order to predict and explain the binding mode of novel chemical entities. This, in essence, is the *docking problem* that is of paramount importance in drug design.

Any solution to the docking problem requires a powerful search technique to explore the conformation space available to the protein and *ligand*, along with a good understanding of the process of molecular recognition to devise scoring functions for reliably predicting binding modes. A ligand can be a drug molecule, or even an enzyme. Genetic Optimization for Ligand Docking (GOLD) [40] is an automated ligand docking program that uses a GA to explore the full range of ligand conformational flexibility with partial flexibility of the protein, while satisfying the requirement that the ligand must displace loosely bound water molecules upon binding. A simple scoring function is

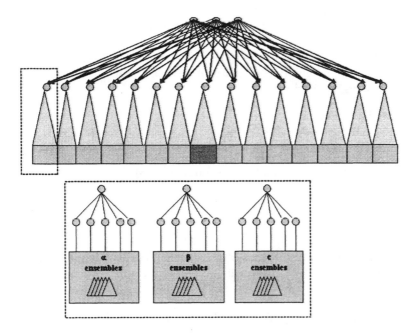

Fig. 10.3   The ensemble of combining and filtering network.

used to rank the generated binding modes. This comprises terms attributed to hydrogen bonding, pairwise dispersion potential to account for hydrophobic energy of binding, and molecular mechanics-based internal energy of the ligand.

Inspection of the X-ray crystallographic structures of proteins with associated high-affinity ligands reveals that the ligands appear to conform closely to the shape of the binding cavity, by maximizing their hydrophobic contribution and interacting at a number of hydrogen bonding sites. Additionally, dispersive interactions between protein and ligand atoms are involved along with an entropic contribution from the displacement of water molecules from the active site into the solvent. Sufficiently accurate simulation of many of these interactions may be enough to predict the binding mode of the majority of high-affinity ligands.

Tertiary protein structure prediction, using GAs, has also been reported in Ref. [11]. The objective is to generate a set of *native-like* conformations of a protein based on a force field. Proteins can be represented in terms of (a) three-dimensional Cartesian coordinates of its atoms and (b) the torsional angle Rotamers.

The Cartesian coordinates representation has the advantage of being easily converted to and from the 3D conformation of a protein. Bond lengths, b, are specified in these terms. However, it has the disadvantage that a mutation operator would in most instances create invalid protein conformations, where some atoms lie too far apart or collide. Therefore a filter is needed to eliminate invalid individuals.

In the torsional angles representation, the protein is described by a set of angles under the assumption of constant standard binding geometries. The different angles involved are the

1. Bond angle θ,

2. Torsional angle ϕ, between N (amine group) and C_α,

3. angle ψ, between C_α and C' (carboxyl group),

4. Peptide bond angle ω, between C' and N, and

5. Dihedral angle.

The potential energy $U(r_1, \ldots, r_N)$ between N atoms is minimized. It is expressed in terms of the different factors mentioned in Section 10.3.1, and is computed as

$$
\begin{aligned}
U(r_1, \ldots, r_N) = \ & \textstyle\sum_i K_b(b_i - b_0^i)^2 + \sum_i K_\theta(\theta_i - \theta_0^i)^2 \\
& + \textstyle\sum_i K_\phi[1 - \cos(n\phi_i - \delta)] + \sum_{i,j} \frac{q_i q_j}{4\pi\varepsilon_0\varepsilon_r r_{ij}} \\
& + \textstyle\sum_{i,j} \varepsilon\left[\left(\frac{\sigma_{ij}}{r_{ij}}\right)^{12} - 2\left(\frac{\sigma_{ij}}{r_{ij}}\right)^6\right],
\end{aligned}
\tag{10.2}
$$

where the first three harmonic terms on the right-hand side involve the bond length, bond angle, and torsional angle of covalent connectivity, with b_0^i and θ_0^i indicating the down-state (low energy) bond length and bond angle, respectively for the ith atom. The effects of hydrogen bonding and that of solvents (for nonbonded atom pairs i, j, separated by at least four atoms) is taken care of by the electrostatic Coulomb interaction and Van der Waals' interaction, modeled by the last two terms of the expression. Here K_b, K_θ, K_ϕ, and δ are constants, q_i and q_j are the charges of atoms i and j, separated by distance r_{ij}, and ε indicates the dielectric constant.

A protein acquires a folded conformation favorable to the solvent present. The calculation of the entropy difference between a folded and unfolded state is based on the interactions between a protein and solvent pair. The term E_{pe}, for a conformation, is a function of its actual diameter. Here the diameter is defined to be the largest distance between a pair of carbon atoms in a conformation. We have

$$
E_{pe} = 4^{(actual\_diameter - expected\_diameter)} \ kcal/mol.
\tag{10.3}
$$

This is the conformational entropy constituent of potential energy, in addition to the factors involved in Eq. (10.2). It implies that extended conformations have larger energy values and are therefore less fit for reproduction than *glob-ular* conformations.

An active site structure determines the functionality of a protein. A ligand (enzyme or drug) docks into an active site of a protein. GOLD [40] evaluates nonmatching bonds while minimizing the potential energy (fitness function), defined in terms of the Van der Waals' internal and external (or ligand-site) energy, torsional (or dihedral) energy, and hydrogen bonds. The output is the ligand and protein conformations, associated with the fittest chromosome in the population, when the GA terminates. The files handled are the Cambridge Crystallographic Database (by Cambridge University-Glaxo collaboration), Brookhaven Protein Database (PDB), and the Rotamer library.

10.6.3 Determining binding sites

The DEZYMER algorithm [41] is used to identify potential new ligand bind-ing sites in proteins of known 3D structure. It alters only the sequence and side chain structure, leaving the protein backbone fold intact. The algorithm searches for a constellation of backbone positions arranged such that if ap-propriate side chains were placed there, they would bind the ligand according to a predefined geometry of interaction. It avoids bad *steric* contact between atom pairs. Atomic close packing is preserved to fill the available space to the fullest extent, while satisfying potential hydrogen-bond-forming groups.

The protein database (PDB) contains known 3D atomic coordinates of the target protein. The Rotamer libraries for the different side chains provide a collection of allowed conformations of side chains obtained from the crys-tal structures of proteins. A predefined ligand binding geometry is provided considering bond lengths, bond angles, dihedral angles and nonbonded (Van der Waals) contacts. The algorithm measures the quality of fit between the desired geometry and the one found in a particular test configuration, and it arrives at or near a global minimum in the dihedral space for a given se-quence in a predicted design. A test configuration is generated by evaluating an objective function. Fuzzy set theoretic concepts have been applied in the DEZYMER algorithm [38], to handle existing uncertainties in the modeling.

10.6.4 Classifying gene expression data

Classification of acute leukemia, having highly similar appearance in gene expression data, has been made by combining a pair of classifiers trained with mutually exclusive features [42]. Gene expression profiles were constructed from 72 patients having acute lymphoblastic leukemia (ALL) or acute myeloid leukemia (AML), each constituting one sample of the DNA microarray. Each pattern consists of 7129 gene expressions. Feature selection was employed to generate 25 top-ranked genes for the experiment.

A neural network combines the outputs of the multiple classifiers. Feature selection with nonoverlapping correlation (such as Pearson and Spearman correlation coefficients) encourages the classifier ensemble to learn different aspects of the training data in a wide solution space. The recognition accuracy and generalization capacity are higher than those involving support vector machines [43, 44], SOM, decision tree, and k-NN classifier.

10.7   CONCLUSIONS AND DISCUSSION

Bioinformatics is a new area of science where the combination of statistics, molecular biology, and computational methods is used for analyzing and processing biological information like gene, DNA, RNA, and proteins. Proteins play a very important role in Bioinformatics. Improper folding of protein structure is responsible for causing many diseases. Therefore, accurate structure prediction of proteins is one of the main goals for proteomics.

The principles and results of string matching have been used to solve many problems in Bioinformatics, especially for DNA sequencing, alignment, homologue search, etc. We have discussed these issues in this chapter. We have also shown how string matching techniques can be used to search patterns in DNA sequence in Chapter 4.

Soft computing tools like neural networks and genetic algorithms have been used for analyzing the different protein structures and folds. Since the work entails processing huge amounts of incomplete or ambiguous data, the learning ability of neural networks, uncertainty handling capacity of fuzzy sets, and the searching potential of GAs are utilized in this direction. Artificial neural networks have been used for the determination of secondary structures of proteins. GAs are used for the prediction tertiary structure, by minimizing a potential energy function.

Microarray Bioinformatics has aided in a massive parallelization of experimental biology [3]. Hierarchical clustering has been shown to be effective in microarray data analysis for identifying genes with similar profiles and, possibly, similar functions. Recent decision tree packages let users manipulate incoming data and the rules generated, then examine the results with color- and size-coded visualizations. This capacity to interact and explore lets domain experts apply their knowledge by quickly testing hypotheses and performing exploratory data analysis. Microarrays, sequenced genomes, and the explosion of Bioinformatics research have led to astonishing progress in our understanding of molecular biology. Hybrid approaches, combining powerful algorithms and interactive visualization tools with the strengths of fast processors, hold promise for enhanced performance in the near future.

Interactive clustering with good visualization is being applied in the Bioinformatics domain [45]. Users are often willing to accept models with nonoptimal generalization performance, provided that they can explore the underlying decision process and possibly influence the construction of the model interactively using domain knowledge. The neighborhood of each cluster, expressed in termed of a representative sample, is analyzed to select the optimal cluster representative. Visual clustering results are provided for AIDS Antiviral Screen dataset [45].

Bioinformatics, with its huge volume of high-dimensional data, holds ample promise for the emergent field of biological data mining. Development of lossless data compression holds promise to compress and manage such huge volume of data. Some of the techniques used in very large database management systems and data mining area to reduce high-dimensionality of data need to be utilized in biological data also, for efficient storage, retrieval, and data management.

Some of the implications of the just completed Human Genome project have thrown up the following possibilities.

- Cure of genetic diseases like sickle cell anemia, etc., caused by a certain mutation, could become a reality.

- Cure for cancer could be contemplated.

- Sequencing genomes of bacteria could be useful in energy production, environmental remediation, waste management, and biotechnology industry.

- Tackling the docking problem for drug design.

- Interference with the laws of Nature by humans.

However, the field being still in a nascent state, we tried to compile in this chapter a concise treatise on the varied aspects of Bioinformatics currently available in literature. We attempted to bring in flavors from applications involving string matching, classification, clustering, and rule mining, which pertain to the scope of this book. We look forward to a successful marriage between biological data and mining tools, in the near future, for the betterment of the human race.

REFERENCES

1. S. L. Salzberg, D. B. Searls, and S. Kasif, eds., *Computational Methods in Molecular Biology.* Amsterdam: Elsevier Sciences B. V., 1998.

2. P. Baldi and S. Brunak, *Bioinformatics: The Machine Learning Approach.* Adaptive Computation and Machine Learning, Cambridge, MA: The MIT Press, 2001.

3. "Special Issue on Bioinformatics," *IEEE Computer*, vol. 35, July 2002.

4. "Special Issue on Bioinformatics, Part I: Advances and Challenges," *Proceedings of the IEEE*, vol. 90, November 2002.

5. S. F. Altschul, W. Gish, W. Miller, E. W. Myers, and D. J. Lipman, "Basic Local Alignment Search Tool," *Journal of Molecular Biology*, vol. 215, pp. 403–410, 1990.

6. L. Hirschman, J. C. Park, J. Tsujii, L. Wong, and C. H. Wu, "Accomplishments and challenges in literature data mining for biology," *Bioinformatics*, vol. 18, pp. 1553–1561, 2002.

7. A. Neumaier, "Molecular modeling of proteins and mathematical prediction of protein structure," *SIAM Reviews*, vol. 39, pp. 407–460, 1997.

8. N. Qian and T. Sejnowski, "Predicting the secondary structure of globular proteins using neural network models," *Journal of Molecular Biology*, vol. 202, pp. 865–884, 1988.

9. B. Rost and C. Sander, "Prediction of protein secondary structure at better than 70 accuracy," *Journal of Molecular Biology*, vol. 232, pp. 584–599, 1993.

10. S. K. Riis and A. Krogh, "Improving prediction of protein secondary structure using structured neural networks and multiple sequence alignments," *Journal of Computational Biology*, vol. 3, pp. 163–183, 1996.

11. S. Schulze-Kremer, "Genetic algorithms for protein tertiary structure prediction," in *Parallel Problem Solving from Nature II* (R. Männer and B. Manderick, eds.). Amsterdam: Elsevier Sciences B. V., 1992.

12. X. Wang, J. T. L. Wang, D. Shasha, B. A. Shapiro, I. Rigoutsos, and K. Zhang, "Finding patterns in three-dimensional graphs: Algorithms and applications to scientific data mining," *IEEE Transactions on Knowledge and Data Engineering*, vol. 14, pp. 731–749, 2002.

13. C. Burge and S. Karlin, "Prediction of complete gene structures in human genomic DNA," *Journal of Molecular Biology*, vol. 268, pp. 78–94, 1997.

14. W. R. Pearson, and D. J. Lipman, "Improved tools for biological sequence comparison", *Proceedings of the National Academy of Sciences*, vol. 85, pp. 2444–2448, 1988.

15. J. Setubal and J. Meidanis. *Introduction to Computational Molecular Biology*. PWS Publishing Company, 1997.

16. R. M. Karp, "Mapping in genome: Some combinatorial problems arising in molecular biology," in *Proceedings of the Twenty-Fifth Annual ACM Symposium on the Theory of Computing* (San Diego, CA), pp. 278-285, 1993.

17. S. F. Altschul, T. L. Madden, A. A. Schaffer, J. Zhang, Z. Zhang, W. Miller, and D. J. Lipman, "Gapped BLAST and PSI-BLAST: A new generation of protein database search programs," *Nucleic Acids Research*, vol. 25, pp. 3389–3402, 1997.

18. Z. Zhang, A. A. Schaffer, W. Miller, T. L. Madden, D. J. Lipman, E. V. Koonin, and S. F. Altschul, "Protein sequence similarity searches using patterns as seeds," *Nucleic Acids Research*, vol. 26, pp. 3986–3990, 1998.

19. J. P. Fitch, S. N. Gardner, T. A. Kuczmarski, S. Kurtz, R. Myers, L. L. Ott, T. R. Slezak, E. A. Vitalis, A. T. Zemla, and P. M. McCready, "Rapid development of nucleic acid diagnostics," *Proceedings of the IEEE*, vol. 90, pp. 1708–1721, 2002.

20. Y. Moreau, "Functional Bioinformatics of microarray data: From expression to regulation," *Proceedings of the IEEE*, vol. 90, pp. 1722–1743, 2002.

21. F. Azuaje, "A cluster validity framework for genome expression data," *Bioinformatics*, vol. 18, pp. 319–320, 2002.

22. K. Y. Yeung, D. R. Haynor, and W. L. Ruzzo, "Validating clustering for gene expression data," *Bioinformatics*, vol. 17, pp. 309–318, 2001.

23. S. Tavazoie, J. D. Hughes, M. J. Campbell, R. J. Cho, and G. M. Church, "Systematic determination of genetic network architecture," *Nature Genetics*, vol. 22, pp. 281–285, 1999.

24. P. Tamayo, D. Slonim, J. Mesirov, Q. Zhu, S. Kitareewan, E. Smitrovsky, E. S. Lander, and T. R. Golub, "Interpreting patterns of gene expression with self-organizing maps: Methods and applications to hematopoietic differentiation," *Proceedings of National Academy of Sciences USA*, vol. 96, pp. 2907–2912, 1999.

25. M. B. Eisen, P. T. Spellman, P. O. Brown, and D. Botstein, "Cluster analysis and display of genome-wide expression patterns," *Proceedings of National Academy of Sciences USA*, vol. 95, pp. 14863–14868, 1998.

26. J. Quackenbush, "Computational analysis of microarray data," *Nat. Rev. Genetics*, vol. 2, pp. 418–427, 2001.

27. G. Sherlock, "Analysis of large-scale gene-expression data," *Current Opinion in Immunology*, vol. 12, pp. 201–205, 2000.

28. K. Torkkola, R. M. Gardner, T. Kaysser-Kranich, and C. Ma, "Self-organizing maps in mining gene expression data," *Information Sciences*, vol. 139, pp. 79–96, 2001.

29. J. Herrero, A. Valencia, and J. Dopazo, "A hierarchical unsupervised growing neural network for clustering gene expression patterns," *Bioinformatics*, vol. 17, pp. 126–136, 2001.

30. D. Ghosh and A. M. Chinnaiyan, "Mixture modeling of gene expression data from microarray experiments," *Bioinformatics*, vol. 18, pp. 275–286, 2002.

31. K. Y. Yeung, C. Fraley, A. Murua, A. E. Raftery, and W. L. Ruzzo, "Model-based clustering and data transformations for gene expression data," *Bioinformatics*, vol. 17, pp. 977–987, 2001.

32. L. J. Heyer, S. Kruglyak, and S. Yooseph, "Exploring expression data: Identification and analysis of coexpressed genes," *Genome Research*, vol. 9, pp. 1106–1115, 1999.

33. F. De Smet, J. Mathys, K. Marchal, G. Thijs, B. De Moor, and Y. Moreau, "Adaptive quality-based clustering of gene expression profiles," *Bioinformatics*, vol. 18, pp. 735–746, 2002.

34. S. Kramer, L. de Raedt, and C. Helma, "Molecular feature mining in HIV data," in *Proceedings of 7th International Conference on Knowledge Discovery and Data Mining (KDD-2001)* (San Francisco, CA), pp. 136–143, 2001.

35. C. Borgelt and M. R. Berthold, "Mining molecular fragments: Finding relevant substructures of molecules," in *Proceedings of IEEE International Conference on Data Mining* (Maebashi, Japan), December 2002.

36. M. Zaki, S. Parthasarathy, M. Ogihara, and W. Li, "New algorithms for fast discovery of association rules," in *Proceedings of 3rd International Conference on Knowledge Discovery and Data Mining (KDD 97)* (California), pp. 283–296, 1997.

37. C. Creighton and S. Hanash, "Mining gene expression databases for association rules," *Bioinformatics*, vol. 19, pp. 79–86, 2003.

38. J. S. Fetrow and J. Skolnick, "Method for prediction of protein function from sequence using the sequence-to-structure-to-function paradigm with application to Glutaredoxins/Thioredoxins and t_1 Ribonucleases," *Journal of Molecular Biology*, vol. 281, pp. 949–968, 1998.

39. P. Chou and G. Fasmann, "Prediction of the secondary structure of proteins from their amino acid sequence," *Advances in Enzymology*, vol. 47, pp. 45–148, 1978.

40. G. Jones, P. Willett, R. C. Glen, A. R. Leach, and R. Taylor, "Development and validation of a genetic algorithm for flexible docking," *Journal of Molecular Biology*, vol. 267, pp. 727–748, 1997.

41. H. W. Hellinga and F. M. Richards, "Construction of new ligand binding sites in proteins of known structure," *Journal of Molecular Biology*, vol. 222, pp. 763–785, 1991.

42. S. B. Cho and J. Ryu, "Classifying gene expression data of cancer using classifier ensemble with mutually exclusive features," *Proceedings of the IEEE*, vol. 90, pp. 1744–1753, 2002.

43. T. S. Furey, N. Cristianini, N. Duffy, D. W. Bednarski, M. Schummer, and D. Haussler, "Support vector machine classification and validation of cancer tissue samples using microarray expression data," *Bioinformatics*, vol. 16, pp. 906–914, 2000.

44. A. Ben-Dor, L. Bruhn, N. Friedman, I. Nachman, M. Schummer, and N. Yakhini, "Tissue classification with gene expression profiles," *Journal of Computational Biology*, vol. 7, pp. 559–584, 2000.

45. M. R. Berthold, B. Wiswedel, and D. E. Patterson, "Neighborgram clustering: Interactive exploration of cluster neighborhoods," in *Proceedings of IEEE International Conference on Data Mining* (Maebashi, Japan), December 2002.

Index

About the Authors

Sushmita Mitra is an *Associate Professor* at the Machine Intelligence Unit, Indian Statistical Institute, Kolkata. She obtained her B.Sc. (Honors) in Physics and B.Tech and M.Tech in Computer Science from the University of Calcutta, India in 1984, 1987, and 1989, respectively. She was awarded a Ph.D. in Computer Science by the Indian Statistical Institute, Calcutta in 1995. Since 1989, she has been employed at the Indian Statistical Institute.

From 1992 to 1994 she was in the European Laboratory for Intelligent Techniques Engineering (RWTH), Aachen, as a *German Academic Exchange Service (DAAD)* Fellow. She was a *Visiting Professor* in the Computer Science Departments of the Meiji University, Japan in 1999, and Aalborg University Esbjerg, Denmark in 2002.

Dr. Mitra received the *National Talent Search Scholarship* (1978-1983) from the National Council for Educational Research and Training, India, the *IEEE TNN Outstanding Paper Award* in 1994 for her pioneering work in neuro-fuzzy computing, and the *CIMPA-INRIA-UNESCO Fellowship* in 1996. She is an author of the book *Neuro-Fuzzy Pattern Recognition: Methods in Soft Computing* (New York: Wiley, 1999) and has more than 50 research publications in referred international journals. According to the Science Citation Index (SCI), two of her papers have been ranked 3rd and 15th in the list of *Top-cited papers in Engineering Science* from India during 1992–2001. Currently, she is guest editing a special issue of the *Fuzzy Sets and Systems* on "Web Mining Using Soft Computing."

She served in the programme committees of many International conferences. Dr. Mitra is a Senior Member of IEEE. Her current research interests include data mining, pattern recognition, soft computing, and Bioinformatics.

Tinku Acharya is a Senior Executive Vice President and a Chief Science Officer of Avisere Inc., Tucson, Arizona. He is also an Adjunct Professor in the Department of Electrical Engineering, Arizona State University, Tempe, Arizona. He received his B.Sc. (Honors) in Physics and his B.Tech and M.Tech in Computer Science from University of Calcutta, India in 1984, 1987, and 1989, respectively. He received his Ph.D. in Computer Science from the University of Central Florida, Orlando, Florida in 1994.

Dr. Acharya served in Intel Corporation from June 1996 to June 2002, where he led several R&D teams in numerous projects towards development of algorithms and architectures in image and video processing, multimedia computing, PC-based digital camera, high-performance reprographics architecture for color photo-copers, biometrics, Multimedia architecture for 3G Cellular Mobile Telephony, analysis of next generation microprocessor architecture, etc. During his tenure in Intel Corporation, he served as a "Principal Engineer" for a number of years. Before joining Intel Corporation in 1996, he was a consulting Engineer in AT&T Bell Laboratories (1995–1996) in New Jersey, a research faculty member at the Institute of Systems Research, University of Maryland at College Park (1994–1995), and held visiting faculty positions at Indian Institute of Technology (IIT), Kharagpur (in several occasions during 1998–2001). He also served as a Systems Analyst in National Informatics Center, Planning Commission, Government of India (1988–1990) prior to his doctoral studies in the United States. He collaborated in research and development with Palo Alto Research Center (PARC) of Xerox Corporation, Kodak Corporation, and many other academic institutions and research laboratories worldwide.

Dr. Acharya is the inventor of 44 awarded patents, and more than 85 patents are currently pending in the US Patent Office. His pioneering works got him international acclamation. He has been awarded the *Most Prolific Inventor* in Intel Corporation Worldwide in 1999 and *Most Prolific Inventor* in Intel Corporation Arizona site for five consecutive years (1997–2001). His contribution in intellectual properties has been specially mentioned in a leading business journal in Phoenix, Arizona in its January 2002 issue. Dr. Acharya received many awards including a "Divisional Recognition Award" by the Connected Product Division from Intel Corporation in 2000 for development of key intellectual properties in digital camera and image processing architectures.

He contributed in over 60 referred technical papers published in International Journals, conferences, and book chapters. He is also co-author of the book *Information Technology: Principles and Applications*, scheduled to be published by Prentice-Hall, New Delhi, India.

Dr. Acharya is a Senior Member of IEEE, SPIE Optical Society. He served in the US National Body of JPEG2000 Standard committee (1998–2002) and represented Intel Corporation in this committee as its primary member. He served in programme committees of several international conferences and many other professional bodies in academia and industry.

His current research interests are in computer vision for enterprize applications, multimedia computing, biometrics, multimedia data mining, VLSI architectures, and algorithms.